The International Financial Crisis

Have the Rules of Finance Changed?

World Scientific Studies in International Economics

(ISSN: 1793-3641)

---

*Published**

Vol. 8 Challenges of Economic Development in the Middle East and North Africa Region
by Julia C Devlin (University of Virginia, USA)

Vol. 9 Globalization and International Trade Policies
by Robert M Stern (University of Michigan, USA)

Vol. 10 The First Credit Market Turnoil of the 21st Century: Implications for Public Policy
edited by Doughlas D Evanoff (Federal Reserve Bank of Chicago, USA, Philipp Hartmann (European Central Bank, Germany) & George G Kaufman (Loyola University, USA)

Vol. 11 Free Trade Agreements in the Asia Pacific
edited by Christopher Findlay (University of Adelaide, Australia) & Shujiro Urata (Waseda University, Japan)

Vol. 12 The Japanese Economy in Retrospect, Volume I and Volume II
Selected Papers by Gary R. Saxonhouse
by Robert M Stern (University of Michigan, USA), Gavin Wright (Stanford University, USA) & Hugh Patrick (Columbia University, USA)

Vol. 13 Light the Lamp
Papers on World Trade and Investment in Memory of Bijit Bora
edited by Christopher Findlay (University of Adelaide, Australia), David Parsons (KADIN Indonesia) & Mari Pangestu (Trade Minister of Indonesia)

Vol. 14 The International Financial Crisis: Have the Rules of Finance Changed?
edited by Asli Demirgüç-Kunt (The World Bank, USA), Douglas D Evanoff (Federal Reserve Bank of Chicago, USA) & George G Kaufman (Loyola University of Chicago, USA)

Vol. 15 Systemic Implications of Transatlantic Regulatory Cooperation and Competition
edited by Simon J Evenett (University of St Gallen, Switzerland) & Robert M Stern (University of Michigan, USA)

*The complete list of the published volumes in the series, can also be found at
http://www.worldscibooks.com/series/wssie_series.shtml

14
World Scientific
Studies in
International
Economics

The International Financial Crisis

Have the Rules of Finance Changed?

edited by

Asli Demirgüç-Kunt
The World Bank, USA

Douglas D Evanoff
Federal Reserve Bank of Chicago, USA

George G Kaufman
Loyola University Chicago, USA

World Scientific

NEW JERSEY • LONDON • SINGAPORE • BEIJING • SHANGHAI • HONG KONG • TAIPEI • CHENNAI

Published by

World Scientific Publishing Co. Pte. Ltd.
5 Toh Tuck Link, Singapore 596224
USA office: 27 Warren Street, Suite 401-402, Hackensack, NJ 07601
UK office: 57 Shelton Street, Covent Garden, London WC2H 9HE

British Library Cataloguing-in-Publication Data
A catalogue record for this book is available from the British Library.

World Scientific Studies in International Economics — Vol. 14
THE INTERNATIONAL FINANCIAL CRISIS
Have the Rules of Finance Changed?

ISBN-13 978-981-4322-08-9
ISBN-10 981-4322-08-3

Typeset by Stallion Press
Email: enquiries@stallionpress.com

Printed in Singapore.

Preface

The great financial meltdown of 2007–2009 appeared to have run its course and morphed into the Great Recession by the time the 12th annual Federal Reserve Bank of Chicago International Banking Conference, co-sponsored by the World Bank, was held in Chicago on September 24–25, 2009. Thus, the papers presented and discussions at the conference addressed both the background to the crisis and its early aftermath. Participants analyzed the causes of the turmoil, the damage that ensued, the role of bank regulators and other policymakers in failing to prevent the crisis and their role in combating it, and what should be done to prevent future crises. Because of the severity of the meltdown, many questioned whether the old rules of finance still apply or whether we need to search for new ones.

The conference was attended by some 150 participants from over 30 countries and international organizations. The participants represented both private and public sectors and included bankers, other financial practitioners, bank regulators, financial policymakers, trade association representatives, academics, and researchers. This volume contains the papers presented at the conference, the comments of the panelists and commentators, and the keynote addresses.

The publication of these papers and discussions is intended to disseminate the ideas, analyses, and conclusions from the conference to a broader audience. We seek to enhance the readers' understanding of the causes of the turmoil, the damage done, and the potential need to search for new rules of finance in order to facilitate the development of public and private policies that can mitigate, if not prevent, future financial crises.

Douglas D. Evanoff
Federal Reserve Bank of Chicago

Asli Demirgüç-Kunt
World Bank

George G. Kaufman
Loyola University Chicago
and Federal Reserve Bank of Chicago

Acknowledgments

The conference and this volume represent a joint effort of the Federal Reserve Bank of Chicago and the World Bank. Various people at each institution contributed to the effort. The three editors served as the principal organizers of the conference program and would like to thank all those who contributed their time and energy to the effort. At the risk of omitting someone, we would like to thank Julia Baker, Han Choi, John Dixon, Ella Dukes, Hala Leddy, Rita Molloy, Kathryn Moran, Loretta Novak, Elizabeth Taylor, and Barbara Van Brussell. Special mention must be accorded Helen O'D. Koshy and Sheila Mangler, who had primary responsibility for preparing the manuscripts for this book, as well as Sandy Schneider and Blanca Sepulveda, who expertly managed the administrative duties.

Contents

I. SPECIAL ADDRESSES

The International Financial Crisis: Asset Price Exuberance and Macroprudential Regulation

Charles L. Evans*
Federal Reserve Bank of Chicago

Thank you, Justin. I am Charlie Evans, President and CEO of the Federal Reserve Bank of Chicago. On behalf of the World Bank and everyone here at the Chicago Fed, it is my pleasure to welcome you to the 12th annual International Banking Conference. Over the years, this conference has served as a valuable forum for the discussion of current issues affecting global financial markets, such as international regulatory structures, the globalization of financial markets, systemic risk, and the problems involved with the resolution of large, globally active banks. Also, we have been fortunate to have leading academics, regulators, and industry executives participate in the various venues, providing valuable perspectives and enriching the discussions on these issues.

This year's theme is the international financial crisis. If you look back at the past conferences, you will see that the most common theme over the years deals with various aspects of financial crises. After looking over this year's program, I want to compliment the organizers from both the World Bank and the Chicago Fed for putting together a very impressive group of experts in the current debate on how best to reduce the probability of another financial crisis and, if one should occur, how to respond. I look forward to the next two days and believe you will find the discussion cutting edge and useful for deciding how we, as a global financial community, should move forward. Again, on behalf of the World Bank and the Federal Reserve Bank of Chicago, enjoy the 12th annual International Banking Conference.

---

* Charles L. Evans is President and Chief Executive Officer of the Federal Reserve Bank of Chicago. The views presented here are his own, and not necessarily those of the Federal Open Market Committee or the Federal Reserve System.

Before I turn the podium over to Doug, I would like to offer a few remarks on the theme of this year's conference — financial crisis — with an emphasis on the oversight of financial markets. I should note that my remarks reflect my own views and are not those of the Federal Open Market Committee or the Federal Reserve System.

When thinking about the events of the past couple of years, what comes to mind most often, or the big "take away" from all of this, is that we do not *ever* want to find ourselves in this situation again. If we are committed to that outcome, we should ask ourselves, first, how can policies be changed so that in the future it will be much less likely that systemically important financial institutions will find themselves in crisis situations? And, second, if such crises do occur, how can we best contain them, preventing them from having a major impact on the rest of the economy as in the recent crisis? Surely, prevention should form our first and strongest line of defense, and remedial or containment policies should form the second.

I recently gave a speech to the European Economics and Financial Centre on the issues associated with "too big to fail". I argued that in the current regulatory environment it is unrealistic to expect that regulators would allow the uncontrolled failure of a large, complicated, and interconnected financial institution — certainly not if they had the ability to avoid it and if there were systemic ramifications to the failure. If you accept this premise, and I believe the failure of Lehman Brothers is the counterexample that proves it, then it becomes imperative to construct an environment that prevents our economic and financial system from again reaching the crisis state we have seen over this past year.

In my earlier speech, I stressed the need for policy reforms, such as the introduction of an orderly and efficient failure resolution process that would create a credible regulatory environment in which firms and their creditors would not expect rescues or bailouts. This would reduce the moral hazard issues associated with the "too big to fail" perception. It would also better align the incentives of the stakeholders of financial firms with those of society at large. In addition, it would allow a larger role for financial markets to oversee and regulate firm behavior. However, even though I think we can significantly strengthen the role of market discipline, regulation will continue to play a very important role in ensuring financial stability.

The kinds of events that have led to our recent interventions inevitably occur during periods of financial exuberance. One way or another, asset prices rise beyond conservative fundamental valuations and risk premiums fall well below appropriate compensation levels. We typically use the loose term "asset price bubble" to describe such situations. Although I will continue that tradition, we should keep in mind that not all increases in asset prices represent departures from fundamentals, and not all asset bubbles need be disruptive.[1] Definitions aside, it seems clear that we need to find a way to deal with potential exuberance in financial markets if we want to ensure financial stability.

Some seven years ago, at an earlier International Banking Conference, which was also co-sponsored by the World Bank, we discussed the implications of asset bubbles (see Hunter *et al.*, 2003). The typical view expressed at the conference, which aligned well with much of the research literature at the time, was that central banks should not use monetary policy tools to "manage" or lean against the inflated prices associated with asset bubbles. In the event of a sudden collapse in asset prices, central banks were expected to respond with their standard policy tools to address any adverse impact on real economic activity. In other words, monetary policy should be prepared to "clean up" *ex post* rather than try to prevent *ex ante* a run-up in asset prices (see Bernanke and Gertler, 2001; Bernanke *et al.*, 1999).[2] However, given the enormous costs of the recent financial crisis, as well as new research suggesting an increase in the frequency and amplitude of asset price cycles,[3] many commentators are reassessing the proper role of the central bank in monitoring and trying to deflate rising asset prices.

In re-evaluating the effectiveness of monetary policy for this purpose, two approaches are typically considered. One is for the central bank to take an activist role and directly incorporate asset price fluctuations into its monetary policy deliberations — that is, explicitly putting asset prices

---

[1] Evidence of the disagreement concerning what constitutes an asset bubble can be found in Garber (2000) and McGrattan and Prescott (2003).

[2] A quick aside, it should be emphasized that policymakers do currently take asset bubbles into account to the extent that they affect the real sector of the economy. Thus, it is not a question of whether policymakers address bubbles. At issue is whether they should or can address asset price increases *ex ante* to avoid a resulting sudden decline in prices that more adversely affects the real economy than would have occurred without the bubble.

[3] For example, see Kroszner (2003) and Borio and Lowe (2003).

into the policy response function and "leaning against the wind". As an alternative, policymakers could incorporate asset prices into the price indexes used in determining the future direction of monetary policy.

While recent events have indeed imposed significant costs on society, I fear that monetary policy tools may be too blunt for such a fine-tuning policy.[4] Central bankers have imperfect information and, for many asset classes, sudden price declines may have a minimal impact on the real economy.[5] So, my concern is that using monetary policy to "lean against bubbles" could end up causing more harm than good to the economy.

To elaborate a bit, taking an activist role would likely mean having a policy aimed at explicitly hitting some target range for asset prices or risk premiums. So, we would first have to determine those target ranges. I do not know of any economic theory or empirical evidence we currently have in hand that would give us adequate guidance here. In addition, there is the "bluntness" of monetary policy. Using wide-reaching monetary policy to slow the growth of certain asset prices could have significant adverse effects on other sectors of the economy. In normal times, we use our policy instrument, the short-term federal funds rate, to try to achieve our dual mandate goals of maximum sustainable employment and price stability. Adding a third target — asset prices — would likely mean that we could not do as well on the other two.

The desirability of incorporating asset prices into the inflation measures targeted by central banks is also not obvious. Some claim that standard consumer price indexes do not adequately incorporate inflationary expectations; rather, they only account for past price adjustments. Certain asset prices, for example, those of equities or real estate, may better incorporate such expectations. Thus, some argue that, to the extent these asset prices are predictors of future price changes, including them in the target price indexes provides a reasonable operating procedure that leans against rising asset prices and adds an automatic stabilizer to monetary policy.

---

[4] There is broad literature on this issue. See Friedman (2003), Goodfriend (2003), Meltzer (2003), Mishkin and White (2003), Mussa (2003), Trichet (2003), Kroszner (2003), Bernanke *et al.* (1999), Bernanke and Gertler (2001), Mishkin (2008), and Yellen (2009).

[5] Mishkin (2008) makes the argument that not all bubbles have the same impact on the real economy. In particular, he argues that bubbles associated with credit booms are more dangerous because they put the financial system at risk and may result in negative spillover effects for the real economy. Thus, these bubbles may deserve a more activist approach.

One potential issue with this argument is whether real estate or equity market prices accurately forecast future inflation rates. A bigger question, however, is how to operationalize such an index. What weights should be assigned to asset prices in the aggregate indexes? Index number theory provides the conceptual linkage between utility maximization and the expenditure weights used to construct consumer price indexes. I have not yet seen the theoretical work that says how to include asset prices in an aggregate index. I am open-minded to new research making the case for using monetary policy to address asset inflation. But as of now, I am skeptical.[6]

Fortunately, monetary policy is not the only tool that central banks have to deal with asset price swings and their potentially disruptive consequences. In my view, redesigning regulations and improving market infrastructure offer more promising paths to increased financial stability. This is the "prevention" that forms the first line of defense in our efforts to never be in this position again. Regulation may or may not be sufficient to avoid *all* of the market events that help to create excessive exuberance, but it should play a very large role in controlling the existence, size, and consequences of any bubble. For example, research suggests that a crisis caused by sudden declines in asset prices is less disruptive to markets when financial systems and individual bank balance sheets are in sound condition before the crisis (see Mishkin and White, 2003). Better supervision and a sound regulatory infrastructure can increase the resiliency of markets and institutions, enabling them to better withstand adverse shocks.

How do we promote such increased resiliency? First, we can make more effective use of our existing regulatory structure, tools, and authority. Second, a number of reforms of our current infrastructure — both market and regulatory — may help us to better address the type of problems we saw emerge during the recent crisis.

Within the existing structure, regulators have the ability to promote better, more resilient financial markets, either through making rules or by serving as a coordinator of private initiatives.[7] They can also encourage more and better disclosure of information — a key element of effective risk management.

---

[6] For an alternative discussion of potential problems, see Trichet (2003).

[7] An example here would be the central bank serving a coordinative role, encouraging banks to address operational risks associated with back-office operations in credit default swap contracts.

Regulators and supervisors are also often in a position to foresee emerging problems before they grow into crises. Along these lines, supervisors can do more "horizontal supervision", similar to the Supervisory Capital Assessment Program (SCAP) that was designed for the 19 largest U.S. banks. Using procedures similar to those in the SCAP, the likely performance of banks can be evaluated on a consistent basis under alternative stress scenarios. In addition to evaluating resiliency to future conditions, this type of "stress test" also enables supervisors to identify best practices in risk management and to push banks with weak risk management to improve.[8]

When emerging issues or practices that could lead to disruptions are identified, regulators can more effectively use tools such as memorandums of understanding or supervisory directives to dampen the adverse impact of a variety of financial shocks.[9] Indeed, we probably should have been more aggressive in utilizing this supervisory power during the period leading up to the recent crisis. It can be an effective and powerful tool.

Although I believe we can use existing regulatory tools more effectively, we may also need to address the shortcomings of current regulations. Already, policymakers in the U.S. and elsewhere are exploring a variety of reforms (see U.S. Department of the Treasury, 2009).[10]

Introducing a systemic regulator who can identify, monitor, and collate information on industry practices across various institutions tops most of the reform agendas. While plans for systemic regulation vary in the structures they propose — for example, a single regulator versus a committee of regulators — they all envision macroprudential supervision and regulation as the key mandate of the new regulator. This would be a major component of what I called our first line of defense.

Reform proposals also typically include ways in which we can make capital requirements more dynamic and tailor them to the type of risks an institution poses for the financial system. Varying capital requirements and loan loss provisions over the business cycle are examples of these proposals. History shows that during boom times, when financial institu-

---

[8] For a further discussion of the SCAP, see Tarullo (2009).

[9] For example, memorandums could have addressed the rising role of commercial real estate in bank portfolios, or they could have addressed practices in mortgage lending that may have contributed to poor underwriting.

[10] I have previously discussed these policy issues in somewhat more detail (Evans, 2009); see also Squam Lake Group (2010).

tions are perhaps in an exuberant state, they may not price risks fully in their underwriting and risk-management decisions. During downturns, faced with eroding capital cushions, increased uncertainty, and binding capital constraints, some institutions may become overcautious and excessively tighten lending standards. Both behaviors tend to amplify the business cycle. Allowing the required capital ratio to vary over the cycle could serve to offset some of this volatility and partially offset the boom–bust trends we have seen in the past. Alternatively, varying loan loss provisions over the business cycle is a complementary way to better cushion firms against sudden declines in asset prices.

Capital requirements could also be adjusted by extending risk-based weighting schemes to account for institutions' contributions to systemic risk. This could involve higher risk weights based on factors such as institution size and the extent of off-balance-sheet activities. It might also include some assessment of the degree to which the institution is interconnected with others. Such adjustments to capital requirements would make the decisions of financial institutions more closely reflect their impact on society. The information needed to account for the new risk factors — for example, the degree of interconnectedness — fits well within the framework of information that would be required by a new systemic regulator, and is now being considered in regulatory reform proposals in the U.S.

So, in order to fortify our first line of defense, we must make more effective use of the existing regulatory structure and tools, introduce a systemic risk regulator, and reform capital requirements to make them more dynamic and tailored to systemic risks. However, adjustments to the current regulations and infrastructure alone are probably not enough. We also need to fortify our second line of defense: containing the disruptive spillovers that result from the failure of systemically important institutions, without resorting to bailouts or ad hoc rescues. A necessary element of this is having a mechanism for resolving the failure of a systemically important institution. This is something we currently lack in many cases, though there are now proposals under discussion that would provide this resolution power (see U.S. Department of the Treasury, 2009).

Another reform proposal that I think can play an important role in the resolution process of systemically important institutions is what is typically referred to as a "shelf bankruptcy" plan. Under this proposal, systemically important institutions would be required to provide the information necessary to determine how their failures could be handled in a relatively short period of time, as well as design a plan to efficiently implement such a resolution (see Rajan, 2009; Squam Lake Group, 2010). I see a number of ways these plans can fortify both our first and second lines of defense.

Requiring systemically important institutions to identify and think through their organizational structure and interactions with various parties can improve the risk-management practices of their institutions. By developing plans to address systemic problem areas *ex ante*, the need for an *ex post* "too big to fail" action could be reduced. In addition, should the first line of defense fail, these plans could provide an initial blueprint for the resolution of large interconnected institutions and, in so doing, improve our second line of defense. Currently, individual institutions may not have an incentive to make such plans; after all, they would bear the costs of the planning and see little of the benefits.[11] But, society as a whole would benefit from such contingency planning.

Another way to cushion financial firms against sudden asset price declines would be to require them to hold contingent capital (see Flannery, 2005; Squam Lake Group, 2010). Under this proposal, systemically important banks would be required to issue "contingent capital certificates". These would be issued as debt securities, which would be converted into equity shares if some predetermined threshold was breached.[12] It would provide firms with an additional equity injection at the very time that equity would be difficult to issue, thus enabling firms to better withstand sudden shocks and potential spillover effects.

These new policy options, while not easy to implement, would enhance the ability of banks and other financial intermediaries to survive shocks — whether from a sudden fall in asset prices or from some other source. I am fully aware that the challenges in reforming regulatory structures and practices are not insignificant. But, given the magnitude of the cost incurred

---

[11] Not only would banks not see the benefits of disclosing this information; they could actually benefit from keeping this information from the supervisors. The more opaque the operations and risk of institutions, the more likely they could be considered "too big to fail" if they encounter difficulties. Thus, the "shelf plan" could force these issues to be on the table for discussion.

[12] This would be somewhat similar to previous proposals requiring banks to hold subordinated debt to better discipline bank behavior and to be able to absorb losses when difficulties are encountered (see Evanoff and Wall, 2000). However, the convertibility of the new instrument would most likely occur when the bank is better capitalized, thus augmenting equity capital and providing an earlier cushion against losses. The trigger to convert the debt would most likely also be supervisory instead of market-induced.

in the wake of the recent crisis and the possible benefits that would arise from making our economy more resilient to such events, it is imperative that we take on these challenges.

Therefore, I think we need to strengthen our existing regulatory infrastructure and give strong consideration to making the adjustments that could reduce the likelihood of a crisis similar in magnitude to the one we have seen over the past two years. We also need to devise mechanisms to dampen the adverse effects of any disruption that might occur.

This year, as in others, this conference invites us to examine and discuss financial crises and asks whether the rules of finance have changed. I have argued that, in order to avoid a situation like the one we have faced in the past two years, we need to fortify our regulatory lines of defense. We need to have the rules of regulation change not necessarily through more regulation, but through better regulation that is more efficient and effective in its design and implementation. I hope this conference serves as a platform to inform your thinking and to stimulate good debate about the issues I have laid out.

Thank you.

References

Bernanke, B. and M. Gertler (2001). Should central banks respond to movements in asset prices? *American Economic Review*, 91(2), May, 253–257.

Bernanke, B., M. Gertler, and S. Gilchrist (1999). The financial accelerator in a quantitative business cycle framework. In Taylor, J. and M. Woodford (eds.), *Handbook of Macroeconomics*, Vol. 1C, New York: Elsevier Science-North Holland, 1341–1393.

Borio, C. and P. Lowe (2003). Imbalances or bubbles? Implications for monetary and financial stability. In Hunter, W. C., G. G. Kaufman, and M. Pomerleano (eds.), *Asset Price Bubbles: The Implications for Monetary, Regulatory, and International Policies*, Cambridge, MA: MIT Press, 247–263.

Evanoff, D. and L. Wall (2000). Subordinated debt as bank capital: a proposal for regulatory reform. *Economic Perspectives — Federal Reserve Bank of Chicago*, 24(2), 40–53.

Evans, C. (2009). Too-big-to-fail: a problem too big to ignore. Speech to the European Economics and Financial Centre, London, July 1.

Flannery, M. (2005). No pain, no gain? Effecting market discipline via reverse convertible debentures. In Scott, H. S. (ed.), *Capital Adequacy Beyond Basel: Banking, Securities, and Insurance*, Oxford: Oxford University Press, Chapter 5.

Friedman, B. M. (2003). Comments on implications of bubbles for monetary policy. In Hunter, W. C., G. G. Kaufman, and M. Pomerleano (eds.), *Asset Price Bubbles: The Implications for Monetary, Regulatory, and International Policies*, Cambridge, MA: MIT Press.

Garber, P. M. (2000). *Famous First Bubbles: The Fundamentals of Early Manias*. Cambridge, MA: MIT Press.

Goodfriend, M. (2003). Interest rate policy should not react directly to asset prices. In Hunter, W. C., G. G. Kaufman, and M. Pomerleano (eds.), *Asset Price Bubbles: The Implications for Monetary, Regulatory, and International Policies*, Cambridge, MA: MIT Press.

Hunter, W. C., G. G. Kaufman, and M. Pomerleano (eds.) (2003). *Asset Price Bubbles: The Implications for Monetary, Regulatory, and International Policies*. Cambridge, MA: MIT Press.

Kroszner, R. (2003). Asset price bubbles, information, and public policy. In Hunter, W. C., G. G. Kaufman, and M. Pomerleano (eds.), *Asset Price Bubbles: The Implications for Monetary, Regulatory, and International Policies*, Cambridge, MA: MIT Press, 3–12.

McGrattan, E. and E. Prescott (2003). Testing for stock market overvaluation/undervaluation. In Hunter, W. C., G. G. Kaufman, and M. Pomerleano (eds.), *Asset Price Bubbles: The Implications for Monetary, Regulatory, and International Policies*, Cambridge, MA: MIT Press.

Meltzer, A. H. (2003). Rational and nonrational bubbles. In Hunter, W. C., G. G. Kaufman, and M. Pomerleano (eds.), *Asset Price Bubbles: The Implications for Monetary, Regulatory, and International Policies*, Cambridge, MA: MIT Press.

Mishkin, F. S. (2008). How should we respond to asset price bubbles? Speech to the Wharton Financial Institutions Center and Oliver Wyman Institute's Annual Financial Risk Roundtable, Wharton School, University of Pennsylvania.

Mishkin, F. S. and E. N. White (2003). U.S. stock market crashes and their aftermath: implications for monetary policy. In Hunter, W. C., G. G. Kaufman, and M. Pomerleano (eds.), *Asset Price Bubbles: The Implications for Monetary, Regulatory, and International Policies*, Cambridge, MA: MIT Press, 53–76.

Mussa, M. (2003). Asset prices and monetary policy. In Hunter, W. C., G. G. Kaufman, and M. Pomerleano (eds.), *Asset Price Bubbles: The Implications for Monetary, Regulatory, and International Policies*, Cambridge, MA: MIT Press.

Rajan, R. (2009). Too systemic to fail: consequences and potential remedies. Presented at the Conference on Bank Structure and Competition, Federal Reserve Bank of Chicago, May.

Squam Lake Group (2010). Squam Lake Working Group proposals. Available at http://www.squamlakegroup.org/.

Tarullo, D. K. (2009). Bank supervision. Testimony before the U.S. Senate Committee on Banking, Housing, and Urban Affairs, Washington, D.C., August 4.

Trichet, J.-C. (2003). Asset price bubbles and their implications for monetary policy and financial stability. In Hunter, W. C., G. G. Kaufman, and M. Pomerleano (eds.), *Asset Price Bubbles: The Implications for Monetary, Regulatory, and International Policies*, Cambridge, MA: MIT Press.

U.S. Department of the Treasury (2009). Financial regulatory reform — a new foundation: rebuilding financial supervision and regulation. Proposal, Washington, D.C., June 17. Available at http://www.financialstability.gov/docs/regs/FinalReport_web.pdf/.

Yellen, J. L. (2009). A Minsky meltdown: lessons for central bankers. Speech at the 18th Annual Hyman P. Minsky Conference on the State of the U.S. and World Economies — "Meeting the Challenges of the Financial Crisis", Bard College, New York City, April 16.

Back from the Brink

Christina D. Romer*
Council of Economic Advisers

The anniversary of the collapse of Lehman Brothers has spurred countless speeches, newspaper articles, and conferences such as this one. I think many have rightly felt a need to reflect on the national economic nightmare that began last September. I am certainly no exception. But, I find myself looking at the past year from two very different perspectives. One is as a policymaker focused on current economic challenges and charged with helping to shape the policy response. The other is as an economic historian with a special interest in the Great Depression.

In my talk today, I hope to blend those two perspectives. I want to reflect on what we have been through, particularly how it compares with the experience of the 1930s. I want to discuss how the shocks we have faced have been similar in the two episodes, but the policy responses have been vastly different. As a result, the economy this time did not go over the edge as it did in the 1930s. At the same time, and perhaps most importantly, I want to discuss where we go from here and the challenges that lie ahead. Eighty years later, are there still lessons to be learned from the Great Depression?

1. The Initial Shocks

I feel strongly that the shocks that hit the U.S. economy last fall were at least as large as those in 1929. In both cases, the economy had been in a gentle decline before the crisis: the recession that became the Great Depression began in August 1929, while the current recession had been going on for nine months before the Lehman Brothers collapse. And in both cases, a financial crisis greatly accelerated and strengthened the decline.

* Christina D. Romer chairs the U.S. President's Council of Economic Advisers. Keynote address delivered on September 24, 2009.

A key precipitating shock in both episodes was a decline in household wealth. The Great Crash of the stock market reduced stock prices by 33% from September to December 1929.[1] However, the Crash followed a run-up in stock prices of 27% from June to August 1929; over the whole year, the market declined by a more modest 14%. Since house prices declined only slightly, the fall in household wealth was just 3% between December 1928 and December 1929.[2] In 2008, the collapse in wealth was far more dramatic. Stock prices fell by 24% in September and October alone, and house prices fell by 9% over the year.[3] All told, household wealth fell by 17% between December 2007 and December 2008, more than five times the decline in 1929.[4]

Economic theory suggests that such declines in wealth can have important contractionary effects on consumption and investment. Volatility in asset prices can also have important impacts. In a paper I wrote many years ago, I argued that stock price volatility caused income uncertainty in 1929 and was an important factor in depressing consumer spending in the first year of the Depression (Romer, 1990). In an even older paper, Bernanke (1983) showed that uncertainty could depress investment. More recent research suggests an important role for uncertainty in macroeconomic fluctuations (Bloom, 2009; Bloom *et al.*, 2009).

Asset price volatility, which was very high in late 1929, was even greater in the fall and winter of 2008. We can measure the volatility of stock prices using the variance of daily returns. Using the S&P index, this measure was more than one-third larger in the current episode than in the final four months of 1929.[5]

---

[1] Data for 1929 are for the S&P 90; data for 2008 are for the S&P 500. The data are from Global Financial Data (https://www.globalfinancialdata.com), series SPXD.

[2] See Kopczuk and Saez (2004). Estimates of nominal end-of-year household net worth were provided by the authors via email.

[3] House price data are from the Federal Housing Finance Agency. The calculation uses the seasonally adjusted purchase-only house price index (http://www.fhfa.gov/webfiles/14980/MonthlyHPI92209.pdf).

[4] Board of Governors of the Federal Reserve System, Flow of Funds Accounts of the United States, Table B.100 (http://www.federalreserve.gov/datadownload). The Flow of Funds estimate includes wealth of both households and nonprofit organizations. The Kopczuk and Saez (2004) estimate of household net worth overlaps with the Flow of Funds estimate for the years 1952–2002; over this period, the correlation between the two series of annual percent change in real net worth is 0.99.

[5] Data for 1929 are for the S&P 90, a daily index with 50 industrial stocks, 20 railroad stocks, and 20 utilities. Data for 2008 are for the S&P 500. Variances

If a decline in asset prices was the precipitating factor in both 1929 and 2008, the defining feature in both cases was a full-fledged financial panic. In 1929, the financial system actually weathered the stock market crash fairly well, in part because of a timely injection of liquidity by the Federal Reserve (Friedman and Schwartz, 1963, pp. 334–339). It was not until late 1930 that the economy suffered what Friedman and Schwartz (1963, pp. 308–313) describe as the first wave of banking panics, highlighted by the failure of the official-sounding Bank of the United States in December.[6]

In 2008, the U.S. financial system had similarly survived the initial declines in house and stock prices, again in considerable part because of a vigilant Federal Reserve. But the outright failure of Lehman Brothers proved too much for the system. As has been described by many others, the breakdown in funding relationships in the week following Lehman Brothers' collapse was almost unfathomable. The financial system truly froze and liabilities once assumed to be completely safe, such as money market mutual funds, threatened to trade at a discount.[7]

Whether the collapses of the Bank of the United States in 1930 and of Lehman Brothers in 2008 were bad luck, the almost inevitable consequence of declining asset values and a weakening economy, the result of poor behavior, or a policy failure is still a matter of hot debate. All four points of view surely have a claim to at least an element of truth. Whatever one's perspective, what is unquestionably true is that, once the panic began, it was a severe shock to the U.S. financial system.

One frequently cited indicator of the depth of the panic in September 2008 is the skyrocketing of credit spreads. The TED spread, which is a measure of the risk in the banking system, rose by nearly 400 basis points and interest rates on U.S. government debt fell dramatically as world investors sought safety.[8] One spread for which we have data back to the

---

are calculated over the daily percent return for September through December of each year. The variance was 16.3 for September through December 2008, and 12.0 for September through December 1929. The variance was 2.4 for all of 1930, and 3.3 for September through December 1930.

[6] Though dwarfed by the later waves of panics, 608 banks failed in the last two months of 1930.

[7] See Gullapalli and Anand (2008), for example.

[8] Board of Governors of the Federal Reserve System, 3-Month Treasury Bills, and 3-Month LIBOR. Downloaded from Bloomberg, September 14, 2009.

1920s is that between Moody's AAA and BAA grade bonds. That spread rose by 156 basis points between August and November 2008, peaking at 338 basis points in December 2008. In the fall of 1929, this spread increased by less than 10 basis points, consistent with the stock market crash having only a modest impact on perceptions of risk. After the September 1930 banking panic, it rose to 219 basis points in December 1930, but this is still far less than we experienced in 2008.[9]

This discussion suggests that the shocks affecting the U.S. financial system in the fall of 2008 — whether measured by their impact on wealth, volatility, or risk spreads — were at least as great as, and probably greater than, those at the start of the Great Depression. Consistent with this, the U.S. economy went into free fall shortly following Lehman Brothers' collapse. From where we sit now, it is hard to believe that last fall there was still debate about whether Wall Street and Main Street were connected. The experience of the past year is dramatic proof that credit market disturbances affect production and employment. Following Lehman Brothers' collapse, job loss accelerated from less than 200,000 in August 2008 to almost 600,000 in November 2008.[10] Real GDP, which rose in the second quarter of 2008, fell at an annual rate of 2.7% in the third quarter and 5.4% in the fourth quarter.[11] Moreover, these declines showed every sign of continuing: employment fell by 741,000 in January 2009 and real GDP declined at an even faster annual rate of 6.4% in the first quarter of 2009.

2. The Policy Response

This comparison between the initial months of the 1929 and 2008 crises makes real the frequent claim that the U.S. economy following the collapse of Lehman Brothers did come to the edge of a cliff. That we did not

---

[9] Board of Governors of the Federal Reserve System, Selected Interest Rates (http://www.federalreserve.gov/datadownload). AAA rates through December 6, 2001 are an average of AAA utility bonds and AAA industrial bonds. AAA rates from December 7, 2001 onwards are an average of AAA industrial bonds only.

[10] Employment data are from the Bureau of Labor Statistics (http://www.bls.gov/data/#employment), series CES0000000001.

[11] Real GDP data are from the Bureau of Economic Analysis (http://www.bea.gov/national/nipaweb/Index.asp), Table 1.1.1.

go over is a tribute to vast differences in economic policy. In 1930 and after, the initial shocks were compounded by even more shocking policy mistakes. In 2008 and 2009, in contrast, policy has counteracted rather than exacerbated the effects of the initial shocks.

Although the Federal Reserve had responded appropriately to the 1929 stock market crash by increasing liquidity, that was the full extent of the early policy response. Nothing substantive was done over the next 12 months as output plummeted and unemployment rose dramatically. When the first banking panic hit, the Federal Reserve was largely passive, failing to act as a lender of last resort, much less engage in a truly expansionary monetary policy, Over 1931, the Fed stood on the sidelines through two further waves of panics and a decline in the money supply of more than 10%. In October 1931, it raised the discount rate by 200 basis points to defend the gold standard.[12] In 1932, the federal government passed the largest peacetime tax increase up to that point, raising revenues at a given level of income by nearly 2% of GDP.[13]

The consequence of these and other policy errors was a contraction of aggregate demand unmatched before or since. This contraction resulted in a collapse of output and employment that was similarly unprecedented. Only after three and a half years of depression and after the unemployment rate had reached 25% was a genuinely expansionary policy instituted.[14]

The policy response in the current episode, in contrast, has been swift and bold. The Federal Reserve's creative and aggressive actions last fall to maintain lending will go down as a high point in central bank history. As credit market after credit market froze or evaporated, the Federal Reserve created many new programs to fill the gap and maintain the flow of credit.

Congress's approval of the not-always-popular Troubled Asset Relief Program (TARP) legislation was another bold move. Creating a fund that

---

[12] See Friedman and Schwartz (1963, Chapter 7). The data on the money stock refer to the sum of currency and demand deposits, and are from Table A-1, column 7.

[13] The U.S. Department of the Treasury (1932, p. 21) estimated that the bill would increase revenue in fiscal 1933 by US$1.1185 billion. The 1932 and 1933 nominal GDP figures (from the Bureau of Economic Analysis (http://www.bea.gov/national/nipaweb/Index.asp), Table 1.1.5) are averaged to estimate nominal GDP in fiscal 1933.

[14] The unemployment data are from the U.S. Bureau of the Census (1975, Part 1, p. 135, series D86).

could be used to shore up the capital position of banks and take troubled assets off banks' balance sheets has proven both necessary and valuable. I firmly believe that the capital infusions last fall, many of which are now being paid back with interest, were a key part of the thin green line between stability and continued crisis.

Congress's willingness to release the second tranche of TARP funds at President-Elect Obama's request last January was a vote of confidence in the President and his designated Secretary of the Treasury. It gave the new administration the tools it needed to further contain the damage and start repairing the financial system. The stress test, conducted early last spring to give a read on the health of the 19 largest banks, was only possible because we could credibly commit to filling any identified capital needs with public capital if necessary. As it turned out, the scrubbing of the books of our major financial institutions, and the public release of that information, calmed fears and led to a much-needed and very valuable wave of private capital raising. In many ways, the impact of the stress test on confidence and stock prices mimicked the effects of President Roosevelt's "Bank Holiday" in 1933. In both cases, lessening uncertainty calmed financial markets and set the stage for recovery.

The American Recovery and Reinvestment Act of 2009 (ARRA) was the Obama administration's signature rescue measure. Providing US$787 billion of tax cuts and spending increases, it is the boldest countercyclical fiscal expansion in American history. To put its size in perspective, the ARRA provides a fiscal stimulus of roughly 2% of GDP in 2009 and 2.5% of GDP in 2010.[15] During the New Deal, the largest swing in the budget deficit was a rise of 1.5% of GDP in 1936, which was followed by a counteracting swing in the opposite direction in the very next year that was even larger.[16]

In a report to Congress issued two weeks ago, the Council of Economic Advisers (2009a) reported that approximately US$63 billion of

---

[15] The US$787 billion figure is from the Congressional Budget Office (2009). Adding their estimate of the stimulus in fiscal year 2009 and one-quarter of the estimate for fiscal 2010 yields US$285 billion in calendar year 2009, or about 2% of GDP. A similar procedure yields US$333 billion in 2010, or about 2.5% of GDP.

[16] The deficit figures are from the U.S. Bureau of the Census (1975, Part 2, p. 1104, series Y337). Nominal GDP data are from the Bureau of Economic Analysis (http://www.bea.gov/national/nipaweb/Index.asp), Table 1.1.5. Calendar-year nominal GDP figures are averaged to estimate fiscal-year values.

tax cuts and US$89 billion of government spending had occurred as of the end of August 2009. In addition, another US$128 billion of government spending had been obligated, meaning that funds were available as expenses were incurred and projects completed. Using two very different estimation methods, the Council of Economic Advisers found that the fiscal stimulus has raised real GDP growth by roughly 2 to 3 percentage points in both the second and third quarters of 2009. We estimated that, as of August 2009, it had raised employment relative to what otherwise would have occurred by approximately one million. We also showed that our estimates were very much in line with those of a broad range of private forecasters and the Congressional Budget Office. There is a widespread consensus (except perhaps on the op-ed page of *The Wall Street Journal*) that this aspect of the policy response has been highly effective in alleviating the real decline and counteracting the effects of the financial crisis.

Noticeably missing from my discussion so far has been any mention of the international dimension of the downturn. Though centered in the United States, the financial crisis and the real economic collapse quickly enveloped the rest of the world. In this regard as well, the current crisis mimics that of 1929. But, as with the domestic policy response, the international response in 2009 has been dramatically better than it was in the late 1920s and early 1930s.

One striking feature of the international policy response has been the widespread use of fiscal expansion. The report by the Council of Economic Advisers (2009a) details the degree to which both advanced and emerging economies have supplemented monetary easing with fiscal stimulus.[17] Our analysis also shows that countries that have used fiscal stimulus more aggressively experienced better outcomes in the second quarter of 2009, relative to forecasts from last fall, than countries following less expansionary policies. This analysis both confirms the notion that fiscal stimulus is effective and highlights the role of policy in stemming the crisis.

3. Other Stabilizing Forces

Another source of the better outcomes this time can be found in policy and institutional developments between the 1930s and today. One important

[17] A more detailed analysis of the international evidence is presented in the Council of Economic Advisers (2009b).

development is the rise of automatic stabilizers. Since the Great Depression, the government budget has become substantially more cyclically sensitive. We have a larger tax system and a social safety net that automatically leads to higher government spending in a recession. The result is a budget deficit that naturally swells in a severe downturn. This process is helpful in counteracting the decline in aggregate demand and has been working strongly in the current episode.

The problem the Obama administration has faced is that the natural and desirable swelling of the budget deficit in a downturn has come on top of a large and growing structural budget deficit. Policymakers in the past have been far too willing to give away temporary improvements in the budget, rather than pocket them as they should have against temporary deteriorations. And, policymakers of both parties have failed to insist that permanent expenditure increases or tax cuts be paid for. As a result, in the midst of macroeconomic shocks as great as any in our history, the country has been limited in its fiscal response by deficit and funding concerns.

Another policy development that has made this episode different has been the anchoring of inflationary expectations. In late 1929 and early 1930, the financial crisis and drops in output almost immediately gave rise to deflation. The Consumer Price Index (CPI) fell by 4.0% between September 1929 and September 1930, increasing the real value of outstanding debts and lowering the value of collateral.[18] And, though a point of some debate, studies by Nelson (1991) and Cecchetti (1992) suggest that expectations of deflation also developed in 1930, leading to substantial rises in real interest rates. Both of these developments served to further restrict desired spending and spur continued financial distress.

In the current episode, in contrast, inflationary expectations have been remarkably well anchored. While overall price indexes like the CPI and Producer Price Index (PPI) have fallen, in large part because of oil price declines, core CPI inflation has shown only mild moderation. The change in the core CPI from 12 months before was 2.5% in August 2008 and 1.4% in August 2009.[19] Even more telling is the fact that inflationary

[18] CPI data are from the Bureau of Labor Statistics (http://www.bls.gov/data/#prices), series CUUR0000SA0.

[19] CPI data are from the Bureau of Labor Statistics (http://www.bls.gov/data/#prices), series CUUR0000SA0.

expectations measured by forecasting models, surveys, and the rates on inflation-indexed bonds have remained at roughly 1% to 2%.[20]

The source of this stability in inflationary expectations is almost surely the history of the past 25 years of monetary policy. Since Paul Volcker's pioneering crusade to bring down inflation in the early 1980s, the Federal Reserve has proven itself a reliable steward of price stability. Both ordinary citizens and sophisticated bond traders are confident — with good reason — that the Federal Reserve will take actions to keep inflation from either falling much below 2% or rising much above. In the current episode, this confidence has prevented the development of expectations of deflation that would have exacerbated the other shocks affecting the economy. It has also allowed the Federal Reserve to engage in a rapid expansion of its balance sheet with no rise in inflationary expectations.

A third past policy development that has served us extremely well in the current crisis has been the existence of deposit insurance. Despite the uproar in financial markets last fall, one striking fact is that ordinary Americans never lost faith in the security of their bank deposits. It is a credit to the quiet efficiency and stellar reputation of the Federal Deposit Insurance Corporation (FDIC) that over 100 banks have failed since last fall with barely a ripple felt by depositors.[21] This well-functioning system short-circuited a channel through which the financial crisis could have mushroomed. The FDIC's ability and willingness to insure the issuance of debt by larger banks was also a key factor containing the crisis.

---

[20] The forecasting firm Macroeconomic Advisers predicts an average core CPI inflation rate of 1% (at an annual rate) from 2009Q3 to 2011Q4 as of September 21, 2009. Differences between yields on Treasury Inflation-Protected Securities (TIPS) and yields on nominal Treasury notes imply measures of break-even inflation rates that are the rate of inflation that would give an investor the same return at maturity on a nominal security and on a TIPS. These break-even inflation rates reflect investors' inflation expectations as well as liquidity premia and inflation risk premia. At the end of August 2009, the implied break-even inflation rate over 5 years from 5-year TIPS was 1.3%, and the implied break-even inflation rate over 10 years from 10-year TIPS was 1.8%. The TIPS and nominal rates were reported by the Board of Governors of the Federal Reserve System, and the calculations were done by Haver Analytics. The Federal Reserve Bank of Philadelphia (2009) reports expected CPI inflation based on surveys of 1.7% for 2009–2010; their long-term (10-year) CPI expectation is 2.36%.

[21] The list of failed banks is available on the FDIC website (http://www.fdic.gov/bank/individual/failed/banklist.html).

4. The Outlook for Recovery

This cataloging of the shocks we have endured and the policy response and other stabilizing forces is important. The accomplishment of walking the American economy back from the edge of a second Great Depression is real and deserves to be celebrated. But it deserves to be celebrated only in the same way that victory in one battle in the midst of a necessary war deserves to be celebrated. It is just one step on the road to a far more important accomplishment. Also, we can never lose sight of the fact that there have been many casualties along the way.

Although conditions could have been far worse given the shocks we have endured, it is still the case that the economy is in severe distress. The unemployment rate reached 9.7% in August 2009, and we anticipate further rises before it finally begins to decline. Real GDP has fallen by 4% since its peak in the second quarter of 2008, and its level is now more than 7% below most estimates of trend production.[22] Employment has declined by 6.9 million since the business cycle peak in December 2007, and will surely decline further before growing again.[23] To put it bluntly, in the year following the collapse of Lehman Brothers, the American economy and American workers in particular have been through hell.

But, just as we saw in the aftermath of the Great Depression, effective policy as well as the resilience of the American economy and American workers are helping us turn the corner on this recession. Data on industrial production and surveys of manufacturers show that American factories are starting to produce again.[24] Building permits and orders for durable goods suggest that investment is starting to pick up.[25] Even the

---

[22] Real GDP data are from the Bureau of Economic Analysis (http://www.bea.gov/national/nipaweb/Index.asp), Table 1.1.6. Assuming that real GDP was equal to its trend level in 2007Q4 and that trend GDP has been growing at an annual rate of 2.6% implies that real GDP in 2009Q2 was 7.4% below trend.

[23] Employment data are from the Bureau of Labor Statistics (http://www.bls.gov/data/#employment), series CES0000000001.

[24] The industrial production data are from the Board of Governors of the Federal Reserve System, Industrial Production and Capacity Utilization (http://www.federalreserve.gov/datadownload). The manufacturing data are from the Institute for Supply Management, Manufacturing Report on Business (http://www.ism.ws/ISMReport/content.cfm?ItemNumber=10752&navItemNumber=12961).

[25] The building permit data are from the U.S. Bureau of the Census (http://www.census.gov/const/www/permitsindex.html#estimates). The data on advanced durable goods orders, shipments, and inventories are from the U.S. Bureau of the Census (http://www.census.gov/indicator/www/m3).

reluctant consumer is starting to spend again, though an important part of this in July and August 2009 was due to the very popular "Cash for Clunkers" program.[26] Because of these positive signs, virtually every forecaster from industry, the government, and the financial sector expects positive GDP growth starting in the current quarter.

The key question is whether growth will be strong enough to generate material improvement in the labor market. For the last several months, productivity growth has been exceedingly high. As a result, the improvement in the trajectory of GDP has only partly translated into an improving trajectory for employment. For the unemployment rate to fall, we need not just that GDP growth be positive, but likely that it be greater than the normal growth rate of about 2.5%. The more GDP growth exceeds its normal growth, the more likely it is that firms will begin to hire again in substantial numbers and that the unemployment rate will fall significantly.

The importance of rapid growth to the recovery of employment means that policymakers will need to be very careful in managing the winding down of the extraordinary policy response. In this regard, we have another chance to learn from the mistakes of the 1930s. A common misperception is that the recovery from the Great Depression was anemic. In fact, real GDP growth averaged nearly 10% per year between 1933 and 1937, and the unemployment rate fell by more than 11 percentage points over that period.[27] The reason that we tend to think of the recovery as slow is that it was interrupted by a second severe recession from mid-1937 to mid-1938.

The source of this second recession was an unfortunate combination of monetary and fiscal contraction. The Federal Reserve, fearing that it might not be able to tighten when it needed to, tried to legislate away banks' vast holdings of excess reserves by raising reserve requirements — only to discover that nervous banks wanted excess reserves and so contracted loans to replace them (Friedman and Schwartz, 1963, Chapter 9). On the fiscal side, Social Security taxes were collected for the first time

---

[26] Retail sales data are from the U.S. Bureau of the Census (http://www.census.gov/retail/marts/www/retail.html). For an analysis of the effects of the "Cash for Clunkers" program, see Council of Economic Advisers (2009c).

[27] GDP data are from the Bureau of Economic Analysis (http://www.bea.gov/national/nipaweb/Index.asp), Table 1.1.1. Unemployment data are from the U.S. Bureau of the Census (1975, Part 1, p. 135, series D86).

in 1937, and government spending declined substantially following the one-time veterans' bonus of 1936.[28]

The economic historian in me cringes every time I hear mention of "exit" from fiscal stimulus and rescue operations in the current situation. "Exit strategy" is one thing; of course, we should be planning for the time when private demand has recovered and government-stimulated demand can be withdrawn. But to talk seriously about stopping policy support at a time when the unemployment rate is nearing 10% and still rising is to risk nipping the nascent recovery in the bud.

5. The Challenges Ahead

So far, I have emphasized how, despite the enormity of the shocks we have endured, the U.S. economy has avoided a more calamitous decline because of the policy actions that have been taken. However, there is an area where modern policymakers risk being less forward-looking than our predecessors in the 1930s: financial regulatory reform.

In response to the pain of the Great Depression, President Roosevelt and the Congress put in place a regulatory and policy structure that helped prevent severe financial crises for the next 75 years. The Banking Act of 1933 created the FDIC. The Securities Exchange Act of 1934 created the Securities and Exchange Commission, which put in place requirements for disclosure and fair dealing in stock markets. The Banking Act of 1935 created the Federal Open Market Committee, replacing a system in which it was not clear where ultimate responsibility for monetary policy lay and in which a single regional Federal Reserve Bank could create major barriers to policy actions. The Investment Company Act of 1940 brought regulation and disclosure to mutual funds, and the Investment Advisers Act of 1940 did the same for financial advisers.[29] Finally, the Employment Act of 1946 explicitly charged the government with responsibility for macroeconomic stabilization — and, I cannot help but mention, created the Council of Economic Advisers. These major legislative accomplishments

[28] For the veterans' bonus, see Telser (2003–2004). For Social Security taxes, see http://www.ssa.gov/history/hfaq.html/. The data on expenditures are from the U.S. Bureau of the Census (1975, Part 2, p. 1104, series Y336).

[29] For a description of these and other financial regulatory reforms, see Chandler (1970, Chapter 9).

created a structure to provide sensible protection for investors, rules of the road for financial institutions, and a framework for monetary and fiscal policy.

What the current crisis has shown us is that this 1930s structure has not kept up with the evolution of financial markets. We now see that there are crucial gaps and weaknesses in our regulatory structure. The most glaring gap is that the current structure is designed to evaluate individual institutions and no regulator has a mandate to evaluate risk to the entire system. A related gap is that some institutions that potentially pose systemic risk are either not regulated at all or are inadequately regulated because of regulatory arbitrage. A third gap is that the government does not have a resolution mechanism for major non-bank financial institutions. The government currently faces the unacceptable choice between disorganized, catastrophic failure and a taxpayer-funded bailout. Finally, regulation of consumer lending is spread across many agencies, and no agency has consumer financial protection as its central mandate. The proposal for financial regulatory reform that the administration has laid out seeks to close these and other important gaps in our regulatory framework.

A central part of the administration's reform proposal is to give the Federal Reserve regulatory responsibility for all financial institutions whose failure could threaten financial stability. Regardless of whether they call themselves banks, hedge funds, investment banks, or insurance companies, if they are large enough and interconnected enough that their failure could threaten the system, the Federal Reserve should regulate them. In our view, a key part of that regulation will involve setting capital standards high enough so that institutions have the necessary incentives to be prudent. Placing the regulation of systemically important institutions in the hands of the Federal Reserve makes sense because it has the knowledge, infrastructure, and reputation for independence necessary to do the job. Concentrating responsibility in one place guarantees the American people that accountability will be centered in one place as well.

A second part of the proposal for regulatory reform is the creation of a council of regulators. This council would serve a number of purposes. Together with the Federal Reserve, it will evaluate systemic risk and identify emerging financial innovations. It will be part of the early-warning system needed to stop problems before they threaten the stability of the financial system. A coordinated council of regulators will also ensure that institutions do not fall through the cracks. Regulators will speak with one voice and apply uniform standards.

A third part of the proposal is resolution authority. One of the miracles of the current system is the way the FDIC is able to close a bank on Friday afternoon, send in a team to figure out the books over the weekend, and reopen the bank on Monday morning under new management. The FDIC can do this because it has the authority to impose settlements and force action. Regulators need that same power for large, systemically important non-bank financial institutions.

Finally, the administration has proposed concentrating authority for consumer financial regulation in a new Consumer Financial Protection Agency. Consumers will be served best by a single agency charged only with looking out for their interests. This new agency will not seek to limit innovation or thwart the provision of credit. Its job will be to ensure that consumers are well informed, that they always have the choice of a standard and easy-to-understand credit option, and that they are protected from unfair and predatory practices.

6. Conclusion

There is no question that the economic crisis that began in earnest last fall has been unlike any since the Great Depression. As I have described today, the key reason that we begin this fall with a sense of hope rather than dread of a second Great Depression is because the policy response in 2008 and 2009 has been fast, bold, and effective.

But, now is not the time for a victory lap. To turn that sense of hope into reality for the millions of Americans without a job will require continued vigilance and the courage to stick with programs that are working until their work is truly done. And, to turn the pain of the last year into more than just a bad memory, we have to use it to spur fundamental improvements in our regulatory structure. Only by building a new regulatory framework for the 21st century can we help ensure that our children and grandchildren will not have to walk their economies back from the brink, as we have had to do this past frightful year.

References

Bernanke, B. S. (1983). Irreversibility, uncertainty, and cyclical investment. *Quarterly Journal of Economics*, 98, February, 85–106.

Bloom, N. (2009). The impact of uncertainty shocks. *Econometrica*, 77, May, 623–685.

Bloom, N., M. Floetotto, and N. Jaimovich (2009). Really uncertain business cycles. Unpublished paper, July.

Cecchetti, S. G. (1992). Prices during the Great Depression: was the deflation of 1930–32 really unanticipated? *American Economic Review*, 82, March, 141–156.

Chandler, L. V. (1970). *America's Greatest Depression, 1929–1941*. New York: Harper & Row.

Congressional Budget Office (2009). Cost estimate for the conference agreement for H.R. 1. February 13. Available at http://www.cbo.gov/ftpdocs/99xx/doc9989/hr1conference.pdf/.

Council of Economic Advisers (2009a). The economic impact of the American Recovery and Reinvestment Act of 2009: first quarterly report. September 10. Available at http://www.whitehouse.gov/assets/documents/CEA_ARRA_Report_Final.pdf/.

Council of Economic Advisers (2009b). The effects of fiscal stimulus: a cross-country perspective. September 10. Available at http://www.whitehouse.gov/administration/eop/cea/EffectsofFiscalStimulus/.

Council of Economic Advisers (2009c). Economic analysis of the Car Allowance Rebate System. September. Available at http://www.whitehouse.gov/assets/documents/CEA_Cash_for_Clunkers_Report_FINAL.pdf/.

Federal Reserve Bank of Philadelphia (2009). *The Livingston Survey*. June. Available at http://www.phil.frb.org/research-and-data/real-time-center/livingston-survey/.

Friedman, M. and A. J. Schwartz (1963). *A Monetary History of the United States: 1867–1960*. Princeton: Princeton University Press for NBER.

Gullapalli, D. and S. Anand (2008). Bailout of money funds seems to stanch outflow. *The Wall Street Journal*, September 20.

Kopczuk, W. and E. Saez (2004). Top wealth shares in the United States, 1916–2000. *National Tax Journal*, 57, June, 445–487.

Nelson, D. B. (1991). Was the deflation of 1929–30 anticipated? The monetary regime as viewed by the business press. *Research in Economic History*, 13, 1–65.

Romer, C. D. (1990). The Great Crash and the onset of the Great Depression. *Quarterly Journal of Economics*, 105, August, 597–624.

Telser, L. G. (2003–2004). The veterans' bonus of 1936. *Journal of Post-Keynesian Economics*, 26, Winter, 227–243.

U.S. Bureau of the Census (1975). *Historical Statistics of the United States: Colonial Times to 1970*. Washington, D.C.: U.S. Government Printing Office.

U.S. Department of the Treasury (1932). *The Annual Report of the Secretary of the Treasury on the State of Finances, 1932*. Washington, D.C.: U.S. Government Printing Office.

Getting the New Regulatory Framework Just Right: Six Questions for Policymakers

José Viñals*
International Monetary Fund

Thank you for that kind introduction and good evening, ladies and gentlemen. Today I would like to take the opportunity to discuss with you the direction that I think global financial regulation is heading in, as well as some of the questions and challenges that confront us as academics, practitioners, and policymakers.

Obviously, we are all hoping to achieve a delicate balance and get the reforms to the financial structure "just right", so that the financial system is strengthened and the sort of crisis that we have lived through in the past two years is not repeated. But, we have to avoid two risks in this process:

- The risk that our reforms overburden the financial system with excessive regulation and unintended consequences; and
- At the other extreme, the risk that the reform agenda is too timid or is stalled, as the financial sector and the real economy begin to normalize and the momentum for reform loses steam.

Let me discuss the future regulatory landscape in two main dimensions. First, I will describe what I think are necessary improvements to microprudential regulation. These result from the failures in the oversight of individual financial institutions that have been brought to light by the crisis. Then, I will turn to the area now termed macroprudential regulation, which attempts to address systemic (as opposed to individual institution) risks. This focus results from the realization that the goal of maintaining

* José Viñals is the Financial Counselor and Director of the Monetary and Capital Markets Department of the International Monetary Fund.

"safe and sound" institutions individually does not guarantee overall financial stability.

I am afraid that I do not have all of the answers to the questions I will raise, but hopefully I can suggest some of the right questions for us all to consider in the course of this conference.

1. Microprudential Regulatory Reforms

Let me begin with microprudential regulation. We have seen from the crisis that our existing rules and their implementation proved inadequate to the task of keeping the financial system safe and sound. It is clear that we need better rules to govern the financial sector. I would suggest the following priorities:

- First and foremost is more higher-quality capital and less leverage. Overall, financial institutions, not just banks, will need to have stronger capital buffers and capital that has more loss-absorbing ability. What this means will be different for different institutions, but for banks this means larger capital buffers and higher quality of capital (i.e., capital with more equity-like characteristics). It also means a financial system that is less leveraged. To preclude the build-up in leverage that was present even with risk-weighted capital requirements, an overall leverage ratio — one that is simple and difficult to circumvent — will be helpful.
- The second priority under better rules is better liquidity. The defining characteristic of this crisis is probably the extent to which institutions with funding liquidity mismatches had grown dependent on continuous access to capital markets. This exacerbated the crisis.

The recent announcement from Basel by the Group of Central Bank Governors and Heads of Supervision, outlining their comprehensive response to the crisis, shows the broad agreement in the international official community for this reform agenda. The financial industry (and particularly banks) is faced with a future that is less leveraged and less profitable, but hopefully less risky.

This leads me to my first question: *how soon should these new and more conservative rules apply, and how high should new capital requirements be?*

Clearly, financial institutions want sufficient lead time to adjust their business models and balance sheets to meet these new requirements. At the same time, regulators and their political masters want to show that concrete actions are being taken. However, time is needed to do proper impact studies and calibrate the detailed supervisory requirements to minimize unintended consequences. We also need to avoid exacerbating the ongoing de-leveraging process. Thus, the timing and size of the adjustment to capital levels is a difficult trade-off with no easy answers. I would hope that the discussions that you have been having today, and will continue with tomorrow, can shed some light on how to get the levels and the timing right under the present circumstances.

In addition to better rules, we need better application of rules. Even the most well-designed rules and supervisory policies will have no effect unless they are consistently enforced across institutions and countries. The crisis has shown that supervisors and regulators often did not have the necessary resources, tools, or incentives to adequately monitor and assess the rapid innovations occurring in the institutions under their watch. For example, off-balance-sheet vehicles were at the periphery of the radar screen of many regulators, and consolidated supervision was not enforced vigorously enough. The oversight of underwriting standards by some bank managers and their supervisors also became lax as the good times continued and the complexity of transactions grew. Lessons learned in previous crises concerning the risks of 100% loan-to-value ratios and low-documentation loans were clearly forgotten. This prompts my second question: *how do we design better regulatory and supervisory structures to avoid capture and complacency?* This is a key question that we as policymakers and academics can usefully turn our minds to in the coming months and years.

The final topic I would like to mention in the microprudential dimension of reforms is better risk management by financial institutions. While it is true that inadequate regulation allowed imprudent behavior on the part of financial institutions, it was the decisions taken by the private sector that led to the crisis. Time and time again, managers of banks were caught off-guard by the size of their exposure to subprime mortgages and other risky products. True, many firms are now altering their risk management models to avoid the use of short time periods and to rely on underlying data that are "through the cycle". But beyond just tinkering with the models is a more fundamental need to improve the governance structures in individual institutions, to enhance the accountability and oversight of risks taken. Here, compensation schemes play an important role. The Financial Stability Board's (2009) *FSB Principles for Sound Compensation Practices* provides a good start at codifying how to approach this topic. This raises a third question that we will need to consider: *how do we align compensation and incentive schemes with complex risk management challenges in a way that is conducive for financial stability?*

2. Macroprudential Regulatory Reforms

Turning now to macroprudential regulation, what has become clear from the crisis is that the total risk of the system is greater than the sum of its parts, and that this requires a paradigm shift in our approach to supervision and regulation. We must take a macroprudential approach to financial policy. But what exactly does this entail?

Certainly, a first step is to observe that institutions are connected in ways that are unanticipated. The failure of Lehman Brothers revealed that greater attention needs to be paid to interconnectedness, rather than just size, as an element of what makes an institution systemically important. We also better understand that market infrastructures have an implication for system risks. The over-the-counter credit default swap market, where counterparty uncertainty was allowed to breed, is a case in point. We need to be able to identify systemically important institutions, markets, and instruments. The International Monetary Fund (IMF), alongside the Bank for International Settlements (BIS) and the Financial Stability Board (FSB), is developing a framework to help identify systemically important institutions and markets using a broad set of criteria. This notion of identifying systemically important financial institutions, regardless of their legal set-up or their role in the financial sector, will take some time and experimentation to perfect. It also raises a set of thorny questions for us to consider:

- *How should we define the regulatory perimeter around systemically important institutions, so that regulators have adequate information and tools at their disposal to oversee the most important players in the financial system and to prevent regulatory arbitrage?*

- *How do we avoid designating a class of institutions as too important to fail, and creating a host of moral hazard problems?*
- *How do we discourage unfettered increases in the size of institutions, including funeral and automatic de-leveraging plans?*

Systemic liquidity management is another dimension of the macro-prudential approach that we need to consider. This area is less well developed, but the notion is that central bank policies need to change, perhaps permanently, to accommodate the externalities caused by private underprovision of liquidity during times of stress. Again, we need to do so in a fashion that does not relieve institutions from the need to manage their own liquidity risk effectively.

The macroprudential dimension to policy making should also adopt policies to help mitigate procyclicality — the element that makes the amplitude of cycles larger. While most of the discussion revolves around countercyclical capital requirements and provisioning rules, we should not forget accounting rules and regulations and, as I mentioned earlier, private-sector risk management and compensation schemes.

We also need to bear in mind the combined impact of all these proposed changes to regulations, by adopting a general equilibrium approach to the necessary impact studies. This will help to ensure that the overall impact on the financial system is properly taken into account as we design and implement new regulations.

Another point that has been driven home in this crisis is the need to improve cooperation and coordination across national borders by supervisors, regulators, and central banks. As a starting point, having a separate insolvency code for financial institutions that facilitates orderly resolutions would help. The latest upgrade of supervisory colleges, involving the supervisors of the key countries in which a global institution operates, will also improve coordination. However, the crisis has demonstrated the need to adopt a global cooperative view on how to act in periods of stress, crisis management arrangements, and how to deal with cross-border entities' insolvency. The impediments to cross-border resolutions remain large, but discussions are ongoing about contingency planning that may include a template for firms to "de-risk" or wind down in an orderly manner should they be faced with failure.

3. Getting Things Just Right

Having considered both the microprudential and macroprudential approaches to regulatory reform, I would like to turn to my final question: *what will be the growth impact of all the regulatory changes we are proposing, when properly considered in a general equilibrium context?*

What are the risks that our reformist zeal will stifle activity in the financial sector? In moving to a new, and hopefully safer, environment, the benefits to a less risky system are clear: fewer crises and financial institution failures, more stable financial markets, and, most likely, more sustainable and less volatile economic growth. But there may be a cost: the long-term growth path of the economy could be lower. However, this is not a necessary outcome. The financial sector may have gotten too big, with some of its activity providing little value to the real economy; if so, reallocating the valuable human resources and capital to other sectors of the economy may ultimately promote higher growth in other sectors that offsets lower growth from the financial sector.

At the other extreme, there is the risk that our reform efforts are stalled, as the financial sector and the real economy begin to normalize and the support for reform is lost until the next crisis. At the moment, this is my greatest fear — that improvements in the health of institutions, lower volatility, declining spreads, and the increased euphoria we are seeing will sap our energy for the difficult financial reforms required. We must not fall into complacency once the financial sector appears to be stronger. Regulators and supervisors will need to be strong in their convictions and their actions in getting reforms passed and implemented. For this, they will need the support of their politicians and, ultimately, the public at large.

In closing, let me say that we face many difficult and challenging questions as a result of the crisis. It is certainly an exciting time to be an economist and a policymaker as we grapple with these complex issues. As a colleague of mine has noted, it took Milton Friedman and Anna Schwartz (1963) 30 years to provide a definitive analysis of the Great Depression, but for this crisis we are being asked for solutions in real time. Hopefully, we can get some of the answers right and remember the lessons from history as we confront this once-in-a-lifetime challenge.

Thank you.

References

Financial Stability Board (2009). *FSB Principles for Sound Compensation Practices*. September 25. Available at http://www.financialstabilityboard.org/publications/r_090925c.pdf/.

Friedman, M. and A. J. Schwartz (1963). *A Monetary History of the United States, 1867–1960*. Princeton: Princeton University Press (for the National Bureau of Economic Research).

Longer Days, Fewer Weekends

Kevin M. Warsh*
Board of Governors of the Federal Reserve System

Recent media stories and more substantial works chronicle in great detail the events of the past couple of years. A pair of conclusions might be fairly drawn from these early drafts of history. First, the financial market turmoil of the past year has proved to be of significant consequence to the economy. Second, the Federal Reserve has distinguished itself from historical analogues by taking extraordinary actions to address risks to the economy. The commentary, however, tends to part ways as to whether the extraordinary actions undertaken are to the good or the detriment of the U.S. economy in the long run.

As my fellow members of the Federal Open Market Committee (FOMC) and I stated earlier this week, economic activity has picked up, conditions in financial markets have improved further, and longer-term inflation expectations are stable. Nonetheless, the second anniversary of the onset of the financial crisis — and about a year from the darkest days of the Panic of 2008 — is no time to declare victory, scarcely the moment to hand out medals.[1] I cannot help but think of the strong but weary athlete who, after a morning swim, embarks upon a grueling cycling contest to a rising din of cheers and a smattering of boos, only to be reminded that he is participating in a triathlon and that he has a long run still before him.

In my view, it is unwise to prejudge the Fed's policy strategy — or to declare the victor or the vanquished — by the split time, however notable

---

* Kevin M. Warsh serves as a governor on the Board of Governors of the Federal Reserve System. The views expressed herein are his own and do not necessarily reflect the views of other members of the Board of Governors of the Federal Reserve System or of the Federal Open Market Committee. The author is grateful for the valuable assistance of Daniel Covitz, Eric Engstrom, Nellie Liang, and David Reifschneider of the Board staff, who contributed to these remarks.

[1] See Warsh (2009a).

it might be. We are at a critical transition period, of still unknown duration, and we must prepare diligently for an uneven road race ahead. If policy is not implemented with skill and force and with some sense of proportionality, the success of the overall endeavor could suffer.

Judgments made by policymakers in the current period are likely to be as consequential as any made in the depths of the panic. This means that policymakers should continue to communicate as clearly as possible the guideposts, conditions, and means by which extraordinary monetary accommodation will be unwound, including the removal of excess bank reserves.[2] It also means that policymakers should acknowledge the heightened costs of policy error. The stakes are high, in part, because the policy accommodation that requires timely removal as the economy rebounds is substantial. Our policy judgments will ultimately prove worthy of the accolades, and tender the ultimate rejoinder to their critics, if we rise to meet this heightened responsibility. I am confident we will.

The final recounting of economic history, I submit, will judge that winning the battle against the Panic of 2008 was a necessary but insufficient condition to achieve peace and ensure a strong foundation for economic prosperity. Such an outcome will require that policymakers have equal parts capability, clairvoyance, and courage, the most important of which is perhaps courage.

For those of us at the Federal Reserve, the task ahead involves longer days and, in all likelihood, fewer weekends. While the undertaking is as challenging as any we have faced in the preceding period, it is exceptionally well suited to the Federal Reserve's comparative advantages of deliberation, dispassion, and a determination to make judgments based on the long-term interests of the U.S. economy.

1. The Task Ahead

Economic histories in the United States and elsewhere are packed with examples in which the monetary authorities, with the overwhelming benefit of hindsight, may have misjudged the communication, timing, or force of their exit strategies. In some cases, policymakers may have waited too long to remove easy-money policies. In other cases, policymakers may

---

[2] See Bernanke (2009a, 2009b).

have acted too abruptly, normalizing policy before the economy was capable of self-sustaining growth.

Errors of each sort are neither uncommon nor unexpected in the normal conduct of monetary policy. During normal turns in the business cycle, the consequences of policy error to the broad economy tend to be meaningful: forgone output, higher unemployment, or threats to price stability. None of these are — or should be — acceptable to the Federal Reserve or to the broader body politic. However, the current environment is anything but normal. There are uncertainties regarding the trajectory of the economy recovering from a major financial crisis and a deep recession. Equally, there are uncertainties about the performance of the monetary transmission mechanism and the operation of the Federal Reserve's unconventional policy tools. A nimble, even-handed approach toward our risk-management challenges will prove necessary.

Monetary policy rules have for some time served as an alluring guide for policymakers, particularly at transition points when guidance is especially useful. In particular, the Taylor rule has proven to be informative in describing, if not prescribing, how a central bank might adjust its interest rate policy instrument in response to developments in inflation and macroeconomic activity (Taylor, 1993). But, to make the outputs operational, we need reasonable conviction in the reliability of our estimates of current resource utilization and inflation or, for some alternative rules that have been proposed, forecasts of these model inputs (Orphanides, 2007). It is these kinds of estimates that appear especially uncertain during this period of economic history, emblematic of the challenging task ahead. Policy rules and models alike tend to presume average historical responses, incorporating typical transmission effects and normal market functioning, which may not fairly capture the current state of play.

Nonetheless, policymakers strive to answer the following questions. How is the economy currently performing relative to its long-run potential, and is this likely to change in the next few months? Where is inflation now relative to its desired level, and what are the prospects for an acceleration or deceleration in prices in the near term? Will changes in the federal funds rate interact with financial conditions and affect future real activity and inflation consistent with past practice? Or have these interactions changed, with implications for both the outlook and the conduct of policy?

It may be, for example, that potential output has fallen by virtue of the panic and its aftermath. If the resulting economy proves less adaptive, the natural rate of unemployment may well threaten to move upward, implying tighter labor markets at higher unemployment rates and lower potential output. These estimates are especially difficult to ascertain, given the uncertain contour of the financial architecture and the greater-than-usual reallocation (and risk of misallocation) of labor and capital across sectors.

Of course, countervailing risks could cause a markup in economic potential that cannot be dismissed. Productivity gains may turn out to be larger and more enduring than we expect, and the remarkable resiliency of the U.S. economy could defy skeptics as it has done repeatedly in the post-World War II era. Indeed, data in the past couple of months show continued improvement in real economic performance. In combination with the repair in financial markets, the outlook for gross domestic product (GDP) in the next few quarters appears better, improving the odds of a more enduring positive feedback loop arising from market developments and real activity.

However, the medium-term risks to the outlook are still disquieting. Policies, broadly defined, that purport to bring stability to the macroeconomy could risk lowering output potential over the horizon.[3] The uncertainty of the capital and labor reallocation process, a global trade environment in transition, and a shifting regulatory environment represent downside risks. The possibility that we could fail to accurately gauge the resulting changes in economic and inflation prospects — by virtue of the remarkable, iterative changes in private sector practices and public policy prescriptions — is a foremost risk for policymakers. In this environment, we should maintain considerable humility about optimal policy.

2. Preliminary, Provisional, Subject-to-Revision, Condition-Dependent Forecast

I have just sought to describe the challenges in conducting monetary policy in this environment. That should caution us to steer clear of iron-clad policy prescriptions. Nevertheless, I would hazard the view that prudent risk management suggests that policy will likely need to begin normalization before it is obvious that it is necessary, possibly with greater force

[3] See Warsh (2009b).

than is customary, and taking proper account of the policies being instituted by other authorities. Allow me to elaborate on each of these three items.

2.1 *First, when will the Fed's extraordinary policy accommodation demand removal?*

The central banker's standard reply, to which I would associate myself here, fits the bill: when conditions warrant. The FOMC stated on Wednesday that "economic conditions are likely to warrant exceptionally low levels of the federal funds rate for an extended period." Although it just might be a central banker's rationalized excuse for not knowing, I genuinely believe that more precise timing is unknowable.

In my view, if policymakers insist on waiting until the level of real activity has plainly and substantially returned to normal, and the economy has returned to self-sustaining trend growth, they will almost certainly have waited too long. A complication is the large volume of banking system reserves created by the non-traditional policy responses. There is a risk, of much debated magnitude, that the unusually high level of reserves, along with substantial liquid assets of the banking system, could fuel an unanticipated, excessive surge in lending. Predicting the conversion of excess reserves into credit is more difficult to judge due to the changes in the credit channel.[4]

Financial market developments bear especially careful watching. They may impart a more forward-looking sign of growth and inflation prospects than arithmetic readings of stimulus-induced GDP or lagged composite readings of inflation.

The rapid, global revaluation of asset prices — in both directions — has served as a hallmark of the past two years. Monitoring this trend, and gauging its durability, will demand keen judgment. If asset prices find a new and enduring equilibrium, market participants and policymakers alike may well gain additional comfort that the real economy is poised for sustainable recovery. However, if asset prices retrace their recent gains, the real economy would be adversely affected.

Understanding risk premiums embedded in asset prices will be critical to this task. In general, risk premiums across asset classes have

---

[4] See Warsh (2008).

fallen significantly in the past six months but remain elevated, roughly consistent with prior recession periods. Some portion of the decline in premiums and the concomitant run-up in equity prices, for example, can be fairly ascribed to the abatement of tail risk that became apparent during the panic. Option prices across broad equity market indexes show a substantial markdown in the likelihood of a substantial market correction. But, the broad and continued ascent in equities appears increasingly to reflect a new judgment about the modal outcome for economic growth and corporate earnings. If it turns out that equity risk premiums continue their recent trajectory, real economic performance would be bolstered further by sturdier household, business, and financial firm balance sheets.

It is not just the trend or level of asset prices that should inform policymakers. Correlations of asset prices across markets also provide important insights. In times of panic, historical correlations break down and commonality predominates. Those firms and individuals with purportedly "well-diversified portfolios" going into the panic bore painful witness to this truth. During extreme conditions, sharp swings in investor sentiment often dominate changes in relative valuations and, for a time, limit the degree to which financial markets effectively allocate credit.

This breakdown in historical correlations is not unique to the onset of panics. It may even predominate when panic conditions are in retreat. For instance, in the past couple of months, U.S. stock market indexes and corporate bond prices have both moved meaningfully higher, while Treasury yields and the foreign exchange value of the dollar have fallen. These movements are difficult to reconcile with historical experience or by ascribing them to changes in the modal growth path for the economy. Rather, this odd constellation of movements in asset prices may indicate changes in investor preferences and in the distribution of outlook for inflation and growth. It would be more reassuring to growth and inflation prospects in the coming months if asset prices were to signal a clearer, more reliable message.

2.2 *Second, how might the policy response evolve?*

Many of the programs created during the panic were designed to atrophy, due to their changing relative attractiveness in price and other terms, as market conditions improved. This natural unwinding has proven largely successful. As a result, the Federal Reserve's balance sheet composition has changed in recent months, even while the overall balance sheet size has remained relatively constant.

Several of the Fed's non-traditional programs to provide monetary stimulus were established under Section 13(3) of the Federal Reserve Act, the Fed's governing statute. The Congress authorized the Federal Reserve to lend to non-depository institutions, as the programs do, only under "unusual and exigent circumstances." The judgment that the 13(3) standard is no longer satisfied would cause an unwinding of non-traditional policy tools by the Fed, and presage a normalization of policy.[5]

Ultimately, when the decision is made to remove policy accommodation further, prudent risk management may prescribe that it be accomplished with greater swiftness than is customary by modern central banks. The Federal Reserve acted preemptively in providing monetary stimulus, especially in early 2008 when the economy appeared on an uneven, uncertain trajectory. If the economy were to turn up smartly and durably, policy might need to be unwound with a resolve equal to that in the accommodation phase. That is, the speed and force of the action ahead may bear some corresponding symmetry to the path that preceded it. Of course, if the economy remains mired in weak economic conditions, and inflation and inflation expectation measures are firmly anchored, then policy could remain highly accommodative.

"Whatever it takes" is said by some to be the maxim that marked the battle of the last year. But it cannot be an asymmetric mantra, trotted out only during times of deep economic and financial distress and discarded when the cycle turns. If "whatever it takes" was appropriate to arrest the panic, the refrain might turn out to be equally necessary at a stage during the recovery to ensure the Fed's institutional credibility. The asymmetric application of policy could ultimately cause the innovative policy approaches introduced in the past couple of years to lose their standing as valuable additions in the arsenal of central bankers.

---

[5] This standard represents a prudent framework from which responsibility is delegated to the central bank. The grant of authority from the Congress is standards-based with clear limits and bounds. It might serve as a useful model worthy of broader application in the ongoing debate about regulatory reform.

2.3 *Third, how might U.S. monetary policy be affected by other macroeconomic policies?*

Monetary policy is not conducted in a vacuum. The Federal Reserve, and other monetary policymakers, will be keen observers to the judgments made by the fiscal authorities around the world. Central bankers will necessarily take account of these judgments.

Financial markets' affection for de-coupling — that is, the disassociation of U.S. economic prospects from the rest of the world — tends to wax and wane. My own views on the subject are less ephemeral. Our prospects for economic growth are highly correlated with the prospects of our large trading partners. If fiscal, regulatory, and trade policies diverge or deteriorate, economic prospects globally could suffer. However, if the better path prevails — that borne of the past couple of generations of economic dynamism, positive-sum trade flows, fiscal sustainability, and regulatory best practices — we will emerge from this crisis with a stronger, more integrated global economy and more resilient financial markets.

Monetary policy convergence has proven remarkable, and remarkably constructive, throughout the crisis. When the removal of accommodation begins in earnest, we should be alert to see if this trend continues.

References

Bernanke, B. S. (2009a). Semiannual Monetary Policy Report to the Congress. Statement before the Committee on Financial Services, U.S. House of Representatives, July 21.

Bernanke, B. S. (2009b). The Fed's exit strategy. *The Wall Street Journal*, July 21.

Orphanides, A. (2007). Taylor rules. Finance and Economics Discussion Series Working Paper 2007-18, Board of Governors of the Federal Reserve System, Washington, January.

Taylor, J. B. (1993). Discretion versus policy rules in practice. *Carnegie-Rochester Conference Series on Public Policy*, 39, December, 195–214.

Warsh, K. (2008). The promise and peril of the new financial architecture. Speech delivered at the Money Marketeers of New York University, New York, November 6.

Warsh, K. (2009a). The Panic of 2008. Speech delivered at the Council of Institutional Investors 2009 Spring Meeting, Washington, April 6.

Warsh, K. (2009b). Defining deviancy. Speech delivered at the Institute of International Bankers Annual Meeting, New York, June 16.

Banking Regulation: Changing the Rules of the Game

Philipp M. Hildebrand*
Swiss National Bank

1. Introduction

I want to thank the Federal Reserve Bank of Chicago for the kind invitation and the opportunity to speak to you this evening. It is a privilege to be here.

A year ago, we were in the midst of a perfect financial storm. Following the bankruptcy of Lehman Brothers in mid-September 2008, the imminent collapse of the global financial system became a distinct possibility. To avert such an outcome, a bold and unprecedented international policy response was needed and promptly initiated. In the U.S. as well as in Europe, several of the world's largest financial institutions required public capital injections, and their non-deposit liabilities had to be guaranteed. A number of countries were forced to expand their deposit insurance programs. In some cases, governments or central banks purchased or guaranteed bank assets.[1]

In spite of the rapid policy response aimed at stabilizing the global financial system, the broader economy was heavily hit. Trade and industrial production literally fell off a cliff. In the fourth quarter of 2008 and the first quarter of 2009, global economic activity recorded its weakest performance in decades.

---

* Philipp M. Hildebrand is Chairman of the Swiss National Bank's Governing Board. He would like to thank Jürg Blum, Rita Kobel, and Signe Krogstrup for their valuable support in drafting this speech. He also wants to thank Bertrand Rime for helpful comments and discussions.

[1] Ben S. Bernanke (2009) gave a thorough overview of the various measures taken worldwide.

Today, the situation has improved very significantly. The unprecedented global policy response has had its intended effect. The financial system is showing clear signs of stabilization. Incoming economic data over the last couple of weeks suggest that global economic activity is improving. The economic rebound in the coming months may even exceed expectations. At the same time, looking beyond the near-term horizon, our economies and the financial system continue to face considerable uncertainties and challenges, yet certain parts of the financial industry appear tempted to go back to business as usual. Industry statements and comments made by some banks on regulatory reforms reflect this trend.

Ladies and gentlemen, I am deeply convinced that it is our common responsibility and duty not to let this happen. Let me begin by laying out three hopefully compelling reasons why we must secure fundamental regulatory reform of the financial sector.

The first reason is that too much of the risk taken in the financial sector ultimately resides with taxpayers. The rescue of significant parts of the global financial system from near-certain collapse by public authorities came at very substantial risk and costs to taxpayers. According to data collected by the Bank for International Settlements, here in the United States, for example, the total potential costs of various support measures taken — capital injections, asset purchases, and guarantees of bank debt — amount to about 40% of GDP. For some European countries, these numbers are even higher. While in some cases governments and central banks have been able to reduce their exposure, sometimes even with a profit, the involvement of the public sector remains important. The ultimate outcome of this involvement is uncertain. Moreover, the consequences of the crisis in terms of job and wealth losses, huge increases in discretionary and non-discretionary public spending, and dramatic declines in public revenue are bound to be enormous. In some countries, public debt is set to rise at a pace never seen before during peacetime. In the end, the citizens of our respective countries will have to foot the bill, one way or another.

The second reason is that the crisis has also generated important intangible costs which are often overlooked. Confidence in the financial sector and those running it has been severely damaged. Furthermore, because a small number of individuals have dogmatically equated markets with the unbounded pursuit of short-term profits, faith in the benefits of a market-based economic system has been undermined. Finally, the extraordinary public policy response to the crisis has potentially prepared the grounds for even more moral hazard in the future.

The third reason is that this financial crisis will not be the last one. Between 1973 and 1997 alone, there were 139 documented financial crises in various parts of the world (Eichengreen and Bordo, 2002). Some suggest that we should redesign the global financial system in such a way that there will never be a financial crisis again; this is neither desirable nor realistic. As long as we want a financial system that performs a meaningful and useful function for the real economy, we will have to live with financial cycles. Moreover, the current crisis has clearly demonstrated the limitations of complex regulations and models. Even the most complex models will never be infallible. What we can and should do is to limit the likelihood of and the fallout from future crises.

It would be an inexcusable mistake to miss this opportunity to see through fundamental regulatory reform. We have to address the vulnerabilities that were at the root of this crisis and are likely to be at the root of those in the future. For this purpose, we need simple, effective measures that can be implemented rapidly once the crisis is over.

There are intensive efforts under way to increase the resilience of the financial system. With the support of the G-20 leaders, the Financial Stability Board (FSB) has initiated an impressive number of reform projects.[2] Good progress has been made on many measures. In some important areas, however, decisions have yet to be taken. In line with proposals by the FSB, I believe we need to pursue a dual-track approach to reforming the global financial system, combining preventive measures with measures facilitating the orderly resolution of large international banks in the event of a future crisis.

2. An Ounce of Prevention

We have all been told that an ounce of prevention is worth a pound of cure. Considering the enormous costs associated with the cure of the current crisis, this holds especially true when it comes to financial stability. Most importantly, we need to strengthen the shock absorbers of the financial system. In the context of banks, this means that they have to hold more capital and more liquidity.

[2] See the recommendations and principles to strengthen financial systems by the Financial Stability Forum (2008, 2009).

Strengthened shock absorbers in the form of higher capital and liquidity buffers have several beneficial effects. Bigger buffers enable banks to absorb larger negative shocks without triggering an idiosyncratic, let alone a systemic, crisis. Furthermore, bigger buffers ensure that banks themselves bear a larger share of their downside risks. Not only does this reduce the potential burden for taxpayers, but it also creates stronger incentives for the banks themselves to operate prudently. If shareholders know that they have to absorb potential future losses rather than passing them on to taxpayers, they will likely become less willing to let management engage in excessively risky activities. Ultimately, this incentive effect can help make future crises less likely.

2.1 *Strengthening capital requirements*

The crisis has nakedly exposed the dangers of excessive leverage. It has also revealed a number of fundamental weaknesses of existing capital requirements. While model-driven risk-weighted capital requirements are sensible and should be maintained, they are not perfect and very likely will never be. Most of us have had to learn the hard way that the modeling of risk involves substantial risks itself. Despite risk-weighted capital ratios which in most cases exceeded the regulatory minimum, leverage was a key source of vulnerability going into the crisis. Excessive leverage not only intensified the impact of mistakes on the financial situation of individual banks; it also amplified the crisis, as ongoing de-leveraging in the industry inevitably put downward pressure on financial markets and on the real economy. In addition, it is now also clear that banks were undercapitalized at the start of the crisis. Mounting losses quickly depleted their capital base, and, with a few notable exceptions, the banks found themselves in desperate need of massive support measures by the public sector.

To address these weaknesses, a considerable amount of work has been done and is still under way by the FSB and by a number of working groups of the Basel Committee on Banking Supervision. In line with and in full support of these efforts, I am convinced that a more robust capital framework needs to be built around the following features:

- The amount and the quality of capital have to be increased very substantially. Capital buffers need to be high and robust enough for banks to survive a crisis on their own and thus to foster confidence in the system as a whole. In the medium term, this will be feasible without causing drastic adjustments at banks that might be harmful to the real economy. Looking at the banks that received public support, many of them paid out more in dividends and share buybacks during the years preceding the crisis than they subsequently faced in losses.

- As a supplement to the risk-based capital requirements, a simple and commonly defined leverage ratio restriction needs to be introduced. A leverage ratio prevents the build-up of excessive leverage and serves as a backstop to the complex, but fallible, risk-based capital requirements.
- To address procyclicality, banks will have to build up capital buffers above the minimum requirements in good times. During difficult times, banks will be allowed to fall significantly below the target levels defined for good times. Allowing banks to draw down capital without violating any minimum requirements helps to mitigate the harmful effects of de-leveraging.

Overall, regulators must no longer allow banks, especially systemically important ones, to operate at such worryingly low capital levels as was observed in the build-up to the current crisis. At the beginning of this month, the G-20 Finance Ministers and Central Bank Governors (2009) were very explicit on this.

2.2 *More robust liquidity requirements*

The crisis has also provided a number of important lessons regarding liquidity. In short, banks' liquidity holdings were insufficient. This holds true for the quantity as well as the quality of liquidity. One of the explanations for these insufficient holdings of liquidity was that the stress scenarios considered by banks were far too optimistic. While secured funding remained the most stable source of refinancing, it was much less stable than what banks and regulators had assumed. Moreover, it quickly became apparent that liquidity problems at single banks imposed considerable stress on the entire international system.

As in the area of capital, the FSB and the Basel Committee are working at full throttle towards an internationally coordinated liquidity standard for banks. In my view, this internationally harmonized standard needs to have the following basic features to be effective:

- The standard should reflect a very adverse scenario, including a massive loss of confidence from depositors, a disruption of secured funding, and a loss of liquidity in major segments of the securities markets. The new standard will only be able to promote stability if the underlying scenario is severe enough. A moderate scenario is not sufficient to bolster confidence in situations of turmoil.
- The standard should require banks to hold a buffer consisting of assets whose liquidity and value are robust to massive disruptions in the financial markets. The presumption should be that government securities form the bulk of the buffer.

Overall, the new liquidity standard should substantially strengthen banks' liquidity base. Banks must be in a much better situation to weather liquidity shocks without having to resort to public support.

As a consequence of these higher capital and liquidity buffers, the relevant banks may seem more boring. Their rate of return on equity will be lower. However, their earnings are bound to be less volatile and they will likely be more beneficial for the economy as a whole. With such changes must come a change in banks' compensation policies and practices. Compensation cannot be a one-way street, and must become risk-aligned and long-term-oriented.

3. Facilitating the Orderly Resolution of Banking Problems

Prevention is key, but it is not foolproof. Even with these better shock absorbers in place, large and systemically important banks will again experience severe financial stress at some point in the future. Here, we must accept that we still have not dealt with the fundamental reason why systemically important banks cannot be allowed to fail. The truth is that, if tomorrow morning a systemic institution were to be on the brink of failure, we would again face the terrible choice of coming to its rescue or risking the stability of the financial system.

The fact that financial institutions which are too big or too interconnected to fail exist is a flagrant contradiction of one of the key principles and beliefs on which any market-based economy is built: competition should ensure that the most efficient — and not the largest and most risk-loving — survive in the marketplace. It is evident that a change of rules is required. The financial system of the future should expose financial institutions of all sizes and structures to the test of the marketplace. In the event that some of them fail, we need a system that allows for the orderly resolution of large and complex financial institutions. In other words, we require a system that permits us to let systemically relevant institutions fail safely.

One of the principal hurdles to achieving this objective is that it requires international coordination. Many of you will argue that the notion that we could agree on an international framework for the orderly resolution of cross-border financial institutions is utopian. Your skepticism is understandable. After all, much work has gone into trying to address this problem for at least 30 years, arguably with little concrete success. The many technical and legal problems have impeded any meaningful progress.

Despite this unfortunate track record, I would argue that the real problem has not simply been a lack of technical answers to admittedly very difficult problems. After all, "where there's a will, there's a way." What we urgently need now is the political will to address the technical difficulties and to cooperate internationally in pursuit of a solution. In 1961, President Kennedy announced to the world that the United States would go to the moon before the end of the decade. At that point, the NASA engineers clearly had not solved all of the technical problems associated with landing a man on the moon. It seems to me that the key to solving these problems was a clearly stated political objective. Much like John F. Kennedy's commitment nearly 50 years ago, we now need a bold and international political commitment to put in place a framework for the orderly resolution of cross-border financial institutions. Provided we have such an unequivocal commitment, solutions will eventually emerge.

A new framework needs to ensure that a failing bank can continue to fulfill the functions that are critical for the functioning of the economy. It needs to provide regulatory tools that will help reduce the size and complexity of systemic institutions. This will require a close dialogue and meaningful cooperation between the public authorities and the banks. The framework should also prevent destabilizing effects of a failure on the rest of the financial sector, for example, by building and improving financial market infrastructures that reduce counterparty credit risk. Ultimately, however, it must not exclude the possibility that a large and complex cross-border financial institution can and should be subject to insolvency proceedings where reorganization is not possible.

Of course, we must accept the reality that different national resolution regimes will continue to coexist. To make it perfectly clear, I am not proposing to create a global resolution regime to replace national regimes. Such an endeavor strikes me as the equivalent of a journey not to the moon, but to outer space. But, that should be no excuse for not improving the framework for cooperation across the relevant countries.

4. Concluding Remarks

The worst of the crisis is behind us, and there are intensive efforts under way to increase the resilience of the financial system. Banks are again generating profits (in some cases, very substantial profits), not least because of the costly public support measures, many of which remain in place. As the situation improves, complacency can easily become the rule of the game. We may forget the severity of the crisis and fall prey to renewed lobbying of a powerful and recovering industry. We must not let this happen. Strong and bold entrepreneurial and political leadership is now required to see the necessary changes for the financial system through, as demonstrated today by the G-20 leaders in Pittsburgh. Clearly, there are many areas in financial regulation that can and, in many cases, should be improved. Given what is at stake, there is clearly a need to prioritize. I have briefly laid out to you this evening where I see those priorities.

Thank you for your hospitality and patience.

References

Bernanke, B. S. (2009). Reflections on a year of crisis. Speech given at the Federal Reserve Bank of Kansas City's Annual Economic Symposium, Jackson Hole, August 21.

Eichengreen, B. and M. D. Bordo (2002). Crises now and then: what lessons from the last era of financial globalization? NBER Working Paper No. 8715, January.

Financial Stability Forum (2008). *Report of the Financial Stability Forum on Enhancing Market and Institutional Resilience*. April 7. Available at http://www.financialstabilityboard.org/publications/r_0804.pdf/.

Financial Stability Forum (2009). *FSF Principles for Sound Compensation Practices*. April 2. Available at http://www.financialstabilityboard.org/publications/r_0904b.pdf/.

G-20 Finance Ministers and Central Bank Governors (2009). Declaration on further steps to strengthen the financial system. Statement made at the Meeting of G-20 Finance Ministers and Central Bank Governors, London, September 4–5.

II. WHAT BROKE? THE ROOT CAUSES OF THE CRISIS

The Causes of the Financial Crisis and the Impact of Raising Capital Requirements

Martin Neil Baily*
Brookings Institution

Douglas J. Elliott
Brookings Institution

1. Introduction[1]

The financial crisis that is wreaking havoc in financial markets in the U.S. and across the world has its origins in an asset price bubble that interacted with new kinds of financial innovations which masked risk, with companies which failed to follow their own risk management procedures, and with regulators and supervisors who failed to restrain excessive taking. We start by giving the factors that we judge contributed to the bubble in home prices and its interaction with financial markets.[2] We then turn our attention to the issue of increases in capital requirements for financial institutions. Lack of capital, or excess leverage, was only one of the culprits in the disaster; however, raising capital requirements is an important step towards a more stable financial sector.

---

* Martin Neil Baily is a senior fellow and the Bernard L. Schwartz Chair at the Brookings Institution. Douglas J. Elliott is a fellow at the Brookings Institution and a member of the Initiative on Business and Public Policy.

[1] This paper is based on a much longer version that was given at the conference. The longer version can be found on the Brookings Institution website.

[2] There exists much literature that also seeks to explain the events leading up to the crisis; see Ashcraft and Schuermann (2008), Calomiris (2009), Foote *et al.* (2008), Gorton (2008), and Demyanyk and Van Hemert (2008), among many others.

2. The Causes of the Crisis

2.1 *Home prices were expected to keep rising*

Nominal or dollar prices for residential housing had, on average, followed an almost unbroken upward path over the decades leading up to the financial crisis. Housing price declines had hit specific geographic regions, but these were local or regional events and did not overcome the rising certainty in the minds of many people that there was little or no risk of sustained price declines in a well-diversified portfolio of assets underwritten by the value of residential housing.

2.2 *Long and short interest rates were low*

The combination of low interest rates sustained by the Federal Reserve after the 2001 recession and the availability of large public and private pools of funds in the global capital market ensured that mortgage interest rates would be low, increasing the demand for housing. Low interest rates also fueled a desire for yield among investors, encouraging them to take on greater risks.

2.3 *Housing demand built on itself to create a bubble in prices*

Declining interest rates and the greater availability of mortgages were key drivers of the growth in housing demand, but demand can also build on itself. As people witness price increases year after year, and witness those around them investing in homes, a "contagion" of expectations of future price increases can (and did) form and perpetuate price increases. Buying a house, buying a bigger house, or adding on to an existing house not only provided people with more (tax-advantaged) consumption, i.e., the benefit of having more space or amenities; it also provided an investment with a great expected return. In the late 1990s, investing in stocks, especially technology stocks, became the rage and there was a bubble in equities. Once the technology bubble burst in 2000, however, the alternative investment of buying a home or a second home became even more attractive.

2.4 *Shifting types of lending and the erosion of standards*

As the economy recovered from the 2001 recession, the expansion of lending was in conformable and other prime mortgages; but as the boom proceeded, a larger fraction of the lending was for subprime, Alt-A, and home equity lending. In 2001, there was US$2.2 trillion worth of mortgage originations, with 65% of these in the form of conventional conforming loans as well as Federal Housing Administration (FHA) and Department of Veterans Affairs (VA) loans. An additional 20% were prime jumbo mortgages, issued to those with good credit buying houses that were too expensive to be conforming, meaning that 85% of originated loans in 2001 were of prime quality. There was a huge expansion of mortgage lending over the next couple of years, and in 2003 nearly US$4 trillion worth of loans was issued, but the share of prime mortgages remained steady at 85% as the volume of conformable mortgages soared.

The total volume of mortgage lending dropped after 2003, to around US$3 trillion a year in 2004–2006, but the share of subprime and home equity lending expanded greatly. Prime mortgages dropped to 64% of the total in 2004, 56% in 2005, and 52% in 2006, meaning that nearly half of the mortgage originations in 2006 were subprime, Alt-A, or home equity loans. It is clear that there was a significant change in lending patterns apparent in the composition of loans going back to 2004. In addition, there was an expansion of loans to lower-income, higher-credit-risk families, including from the government-sponsored enterprises (GSEs), Fannie Mae and Freddie Mac, as they sought to expand home ownership for the benefits it brings in terms of sustaining neighborhoods.

Lending standards deteriorated around 2004 or 2005. Families that lacked the income and down payment to buy a house under the terms of a conforming mortgage were encouraged to take out a mortgage that had a very high loan-to-value ratio, perhaps as high as 100% (often using second or even third mortgages). This meant that they started with no initial equity, and thus no true financial stake, in the house.

As it became easier to borrow using a home as collateral and as home prices continued to rise, families started using their homes as an ATM, refinancing and taking out any equity that had built up. Americans were tapping into the rising wealth they had in their homes in order to finance consumption. Greenspan and Kennedy (2007) estimate that homeowners extracted US$743.7 billion in net equity from their homes at the peak of the housing boom in 2005, up from US$229.6 billion in 2000 and US$74.2 billion in 1991. The increase in house prices allowed a borrowing spree.

2.5 *Economic incentives in the housing and mortgage origination markets*

In many U.S. states, it is possible to repay a mortgage early without penalty. This option meant that households were encouraged to take out mortgages with terms that looked good in the short run, but were unfavorable in future years. They expected to refinance later on better terms, and without incurring a prepayment penalty.

The most perverse incentive in the mortgage origination market, though, was the ability of originators to immediately sell a completed loan off their books to another financial institution. Most mortgage loans were originated by specialists and brokers who did not provide the funding directly. One institution provided the initial funding of the mortgage but then quickly sold it off to another financial institution, where it was either held on a balance sheet or packaged with other mortgages to be securitized (see below).[3] The key issue here is that the institution which originated the loan had little or no financial incentive to make sure the loan was a good one. Most brokers and specialists are paid based on the volume of loans they process; therefore, they had an incentive to keep the pace of borrowing rolling along, even if that meant making riskier and riskier loans.

2.6 *Securitization and the funding of the housing boom*

Securitization was seen as a solution to the problems with the old savings and loan (S&L) model, as it freed mortgage lenders from the liquidity constraint of their balance sheets. Under the old system, lenders could only make a limited number of loans based on the size of their balance sheet.

[3] Mortgage sales contracts often allowed the buyer to "put" back the mortgage to the seller for a limited period (e.g., a year or two). But in an era of rising housing prices and thus low delinquencies, originators did not view these "puts" as a serious risk.

The new system allowed lenders to sell off loans to a third party, take it off their books, and use that money to make even more loans. The GSEs, notably Fannie Mae and Freddie Mac, were created by the federal government in 1938 and 1970, respectively, to perform precisely this function: the GSEs bought mortgage loans that met certain conditions (called "conforming loans") from banks in order to facilitate mortgage lending and (theoretically) lower mortgage interest rates.[4]

The GSEs could then either sell the mortgage-backed securities (MBS) on the open market, or they could issue their own bonds, use the revenue to buy the MBS, and hold them on their own books. They earned a profit because they earned a higher interest return on the mortgage assets than they paid on the bonds that they had issued. This has some similarity to the S&L model, except that Fannie Mae and Freddie Mac could hold much larger pools of mortgages that were geographically dispersed. In addition, the GSEs were seen as implicitly guaranteed by the federal government (a guarantee that has since become explicit), so they paid only a few basis points above Treasury yields on their bond issuance. This implicit government backing lowered their cost of borrowing and allowed them to inflate their balance sheets enormously. The GSEs became major participants in the mortgage market; and by 2008, Fannie Mae and Freddie Mac held or guaranteed US$5.4 trillion in mortgage debt.

The GSEs were allowed to operate with very little capital, which made them very vulnerable to an increase in defaults. In addition, their problems also came from their efforts to meet the affordable housing goals set by Congress. Congress pushed them to provide more loans to low-income borrowers to justify the capital advantage they had because of the implicit federal guarantee. They did not buy subprime whole loans directly, but they bought large amounts of subprime MBS from private issuers that they then kept on their books. Indeed, the two GSEs bought between US$340 and US$660 billion in private-label subprime and Alt-A MBS from 2002 to 2007.[5]

[4] There are different estimates of the extent to which the GSEs provided lower interest rates for borrowers. Most suggest that the impact on mortgage rates was fairly small; see Passmore *et al.* (2005), for example. Presumably without the GSEs, other financial institutions would have had a bigger role.

[5] See OFHEO (2008). The wide range is because data for Freddie Mac's purchases of subprime and Alt-A MBS only go back to 2006, so its purchases are estimated from 2002 to 2005.

Many have pointed to the combination of the GSEs and Congressional pressures to make loans to low-income borrowers as one of the main culprits in the financial crisis (see, for example, the comments by Peter Wallison at this conference). Moreover, some critics of the GSEs argue that these institutions were not telling the truth about the extent of their purchases of bad loans. Offsetting this view, however, is data reported by the Federal Reserve that indicate that the foreclosure rates on the Fannie Mae and Freddie Mac mortgage portfolios are lower than the foreclosure rates on mortgage portfolios held by private sector banks. Getting to the bottom of this issue fully is a project that goes beyond the scope of this paper.

Securitization played an increasingly important role in financing the housing boom, especially as it created assets that could be sold to overseas buyers. The real boom in securitization since 2001 came from subprime and Alt-A loans (Alt-A mortgage loans are made to borrowers with pretty good credit ratings but who do not provide full income and asset documentation), as the share of these loans that were securitized jumped 75% after 2001. By 2006, securitization was funding most of the mortgage loans in the lower-rated categories — the loans that are now in trouble.

2.7 *More securitization and more leverage — CDOs*

Over time, the financing of mortgage-backed debt grew more complex and opaque. Not only did the market become riskier and less transparent, but it shifted into areas that were unregulated or weakly regulated. Banks, brokers, hedge funds, and other institutions utilized financial innovations to increase their holdings of these products; and large amounts were sold overseas, particularly to European financial institutions. Securitization has been an extremely positive innovation for credit markets; but as the securitized assets were sliced and diced and placed in off-balance-sheet entities, the increases in risk were being obscured by the complexity of the instruments.[6]

As the securitization of mortgages increasingly became an affair of the private financial sector, it spurred further innovation in products that in good times generated large profits but have also been the source of some of the biggest losses since the crisis unfolded in 2007. Collateralized debt obligations (CDOs) represented a further step into the new world of securitization

[6] For a more technical explanation of structured finance projects, see Ashcraft and Schuermann (2008) or Gorton (2008).

that exploded after 2000. A CDO is an instrument that redistributes the underlying risks from a mortgage or other assets lying beneath it. CDO issuers purchased different tranches of MBS and pooled them together with other asset-backed securities (ABS). In fact, it became possible to build a highly rated CDO from a pool of assets, each one of which alone was quite risky. By giving first claim to the senior tranche and "overcollateralizing" the pool (so that a portion could default before any tranche was affected), the issuers were able to create AAA CDOs even when they were starting out with pools of risky assets. The issuers worked directly with rating agencies to structure the CDO tranches, so that they could optimize the size of highly rated tranches in order to lower the funding costs of the CDOs.

There is a general perception that there was "grade inflation" by the rating agencies who worked with the issuers, a perception we agree with. There were also conflicts of interest by the rating agencies who were advising the issuers and being paid for that advice, even as they were deciding what rating to give. There may also have been some collusion on the part of the groups buying the CDOs to raise the rating. Some financial managers are restricted by law to holding only investment-grade securities, and that means highly rated tranches. The fund managers were paid at the end of the year on the basis of the returns achieved in their funds, and the AAA CDOs carried attractive rates of return and made them look good — until the crash.

2.8 *Structured investment vehicles and off-balance-sheet entities*

One of the constraints on banks and some other institutions is that they must meet capital requirements, that is to say, they must fund a given percentage of their assets with shareholders' capital rather than with some form of debt. Capital requirements for banks are mandated jointly by the Federal Deposit Insurance Corporation (FDIC), the Office of the Comptroller of the Currency (OCC), and the Federal Reserve. Capital requirements lower the profitability of banks, since they limit the extent to which banks can leverage any initial shareholder investment (plus accumulated retained earnings). Naturally, therefore, banks looked for ways to circumvent the requirements. The favored means of getting around these mandated capital requirements became what were known as structured investment vehicles (SIVs), an off-balance-sheet special purpose vehicle (SPV) set up by banks to hold MBS, CDOs, and other long-term institutional debt as their assets.[7] By dodging capital requirements, SIVs allowed banks to leverage their holdings of these assets more than they could on their balance sheets. SIV assets reached US$400 billion in July 2007, according to Moody's Investors Service (2008).

2.9 *Leverage and the push to short-term borrowing*

The increase in leverage over the course of the subprime bubble was widespread, spanning across many financial institutions and across many forms of instruments. Adrian and Shin (2007) illustrate the perhaps counterintuitive, but extremely important, empirical insight that when financial institutions are forced to mark to market, meaning they must assign a value to an asset based on its current market valuation, rising asset prices immediately show up on banks' balance sheets, which increases the banks' net worth and directly reduces their leverage ratio.

Investment banks were not supervised like deposit-taking commercial banks and did not have the same capital requirements; thus, they were able to increase leverage to a greater extent. Investment banks were also not subject to the regulatory restrictions that accompany the capital requirements. Institutions such as Bear Stearns and Lehman Brothers borrowed at very short term and held risky longer-term assets, with low levels of capital or reserves to cover changing market conditions. Greenlaw *et al.* (2008) calculate that, while commercial banks are on average leveraged at 9.8:1, brokers/dealers and hedge funds are leveraged at nearly 32:1 (the GSEs were leveraged at 24:1 even though they were regulated).

One of the favorite instruments of short-term borrowing for investment banks became the overnight repurchase agreement or "repo loan".[8] Overnight repos are a form of collateralized borrowing, whereby a bank pledges its assets as collateral in an overnight loan with another bank.

2.10 *Credit insurance and the growth in credit default swaps*

The process of securitization was further aided by the growth of credit insurers and derivatives called credit default swaps (CDS), which in

---

[7] IMF (2008) cites Standard & Poor's to estimate that close to 30% of SIV assets were MBS as of October 2007, with 8.3% in subprime MBS; 15.4% were CDOs.

[8] See Morris and Shin (2008) for an insightful discussion.

principle allowed the default risk to be taken out of MBS and CDOs before they were marketed to general investors. The first forms of credit insurance were developed by so-called monoline insurers. Having developed this line of business, the monoline companies — along with banks, hedge funds, and financial guarantors such as AIG — expanded their business model into structured products related to the housing market, selling CDS to insure holders of MBS, CDOs, and other assets against mortgage default risk. However, many of these transactions were not overseen by any regulatory body. They were done in over-the-counter (OTC) markets, so that no one other than the two parties involved knew the terms of the contract.

AIG became the biggest player in the CDS market, and its operations were carried out through an AIG subsidiary in London. After 2000, the business of insuring mortgage-related assets, along with corporate bonds and other assets, grew exponentially. The size of outstanding CDS reached US$60 trillion in 2007. As of September 2008, AIG, a financial guarantor, had itself sold nearly US$500 billion worth of CDS with little capital in place to protect against widespread losses.

2.11 *The failure of company risk management practices*

Many financial companies have lost huge amounts of money in the aftermath of the crisis, and many CEOs have lost their jobs. The crisis reflects poor internal corporate governance, poor infrastructure in and oversight of opaque financial markets, and, most of all, mistakes made by decision makers in the private sector.

There have been two important assessments made of the failures (and successes) of risk management practices at financial institutions in the wake of the crisis. On March 6, 2008, the Senior Supervisors Group (2008) issued a report based on a survey of 11 of the largest banking and securities firms (plus a roundtable meeting that included five additional firms). The report identifies risk management practices that helped some of these institutions avoid the worst of the losses as well as practices that led to failures. The failure of financial institutions to follow sound risk management practices was a major cause of the crisis. The second assessment was the report to shareholders prepared by the Swiss bank UBS (2008) at the request of regulators that described in great detail the risk management failures that took place at the bank prior to the crisis.

2.12 *Regulation and supervision*

Despite a general move towards deregulation in the United States, there was still an extensive regulatory apparatus in place in financial markets leading up to the crisis. As described by a senior executive at one of the large U.S. banks, there were "roomfuls of regulators" going over the books. The failure of regulators to force financial institutions to follow sound risk management practices was also one of the most important reasons for the financial crisis. The widespread belief developed over the past 20 years or so that markets can regulate themselves may have contributed to the regulatory laxity, which in turn contributed heavily to the crisis. An additional reason for regulatory failure was a significant share of subprime mortgages — those that are at the root of the current financial crisis — which were originated by independent mortgage companies, or non-depository companies unaffiliated with any bank. These independent companies were not covered by the FDIC, the Federal Reserve, or federal regulation, but rather only by state regulation.

This concludes our discussion of the causes of the crisis. We now turn to summarize the impact of raising capital requirements, which might have prevented or at least eased the crisis.

3. What Is the Impact of Increasing Capital Requirements?[9]

One of the regulatory reforms with the strongest support among policy analysts and regulators is to significantly increase the capital requirements for banks. All else equal, this should make the banks safer by providing a greater cushion to survive the mistakes and accidents from which they inevitably suffer. Higher capital requirements should also discourage transactions of lower economic value by creating a higher hurdle rate, since the extra units of capital need to be paid for by additional expected return. Some of the regrettable transactions that seemed attractive during the bubble might not have been undertaken at a higher hurdle rate.

Unfortunately, higher capital requirements are not free. At the margin, the increased hurdle rates are likely to make it harder for businesses and individuals to obtain loans, raise the cost of loans, lower the interest

[9] The authors would like to gratefully acknowledge the support of the Financial Reform Project of The Pew Charitable Trusts for Mr. Elliott's work related to this section of the paper.

rates offered to depositors and other suppliers of funds, and reduce the market value of the common stock of existing banks. One of the keys to determining the exact right size for an increase in minimum capital levels is to quantify these effects.

We take a pragmatic approach to answering a more specific question: what are the likely effects on loan pricing and availability of an increase in minimum capital requirements for U.S. banks over the next few years? The specificity allows us to focus on the key variables and relationships as they exist here today. Thus far, the debate and analysis surrounding bank capital increases have been heavily qualitative. There is a need to supplement these important considerations with numbers. Given space requirements, we cannot present our analysis of the numbers, but we will summarize the conclusions. It should be noted that this section of the paper is excerpted from a far more detailed analysis and, therefore, a great deal of the commentary has been left out in the interest of space. For the full-length version, please visit the Brookings Institution website.

Our analysis strongly suggested that the U.S. banking industry could adjust to higher capital requirements on loans through a combination of actions that would not wreak havoc on the system. Not surprisingly, the adjustments would need to come from a range of actions, since the rebalancing appears tough to achieve with the adjustment of any single factor. Fortunately, the banks do have a variety of levers to pull, which should allow them to make the transition. These findings imply that there would likely be relatively small changes in loan volumes by U.S. banks as a result of higher capital requirements on loans retained on the banks' balance sheets. The various actions required to restore an acceptable return on common equity appear unlikely to be large enough, even in the aggregate, to significantly discourage customers from borrowing or move them to other credit suppliers in a major way.

These findings may seem counterintuitive, given the large percentage increase in required common equity devoted to lending considered here and the strong focus of bank managers on rationing that common equity. Three points may help clarify the results. First, banks are highly levered institutions: a great bulk of the funding for a loan comes from deposits and debt. Even though common equity is expensive, it accounts for less than a fifth of the cost of a typical loan. Second, higher equity levels reduce the risk of a bank and therefore lower the returns demanded by debt and equity investors, reducing the cost of each dollar of debt or equity supporting the loans. Third, as shown in detail below, reasonable actions by the banks can restore returns on equity to levels that are attractive to investors. Thus, there should be the ability for banks over time to raise new equity sufficient to maintain their loan volumes. It is true that large amounts of capital would need to be raised, but this appears quite feasible given a reasonable phase-in of the new rules. A four-percentage-point increase in the level of common equity as a percentage of the roughly US$7.5 trillion of loans in the U.S. banking system would require about US$300 billion of new equity. This would represent an approximately 20% increase in the existing US$1.4 trillion of equity.[10] Put another way, this could be obtained by retaining roughly two years' worth of the system's earnings, assuming even a 10% return on equity for the banks as a whole. In practice, a mixture of capital raising and earnings retention would likely provide the needed capital.

We side with the large majority of policy analysts who favor higher capital requirements for banks as a key step in providing greater stability to the financial system. So, we are heartened by these initial findings, which strongly suggest that a significant increase in bank capital requirements would have substantially smaller effects on lending than some have argued.

4. Conclusions

Some people have argued that the cause of the crisis was greedy banks. Others have argued that government policies, notably towards the GSEs, caused the crisis. Yet another argument is that government regulators failed to stop bad behavior by greedy banks and other institutions. Our view is that all of the above factors contributed to the crisis, and we would further add that excessive borrowing by consumers was also a factor.

It is proposed that higher capital standards would help avoid another crisis. We agree and argue that reasonable increases in capital standards would not undermine the ability of banks to provide financial intermediation.

---

[10] The banking system in the U.S. has approximately US$1.4 trillion of common equity, according to the FDIC, of which roughly US$1.0 trillion is tangible common equity. For reference, a 10% return on common equity would therefore be about a 14% return on tangible common equity.

References

Adrian, T. and H. S. Shin (2007). Liquidity and leverage. Unpublished paper, Federal Reserve Bank of New York and Princeton University, September.

Ashcraft, A. B. and T. Schuermann (2008). *Understanding the Securitization of Subprime Mortgage Credit*. Federal Reserve Bank of New York Staff Report No. 318, March.

Calomiris, C. (2009). The subprime turmoil: what's old, what's new, and what's next. *Journal of Structured Finance*, 15, Spring, 6–52.

Demyanyk, Y. and O. Van Hemert (2008). Understanding the subprime mortgage crisis. Unpublished paper, Federal Reserve Bank of St. Louis and New York University, February.

Foote, C., K. Gerardi, L. Goette, and P. Willen (2008). Just the facts: an initial analysis of subprime's role in the housing crisis. *Journal of Housing Economics*, 17, 291–305.

Gorton, G. B. (2008). The subprime panic. National Bureau of Economic Research Working Paper No. 14398.

Greenlaw, D., J. Hatzius, A. K. Kashyap, and H. S. Shin (2008). Leveraged losses: lessons from the mortgage market meltdown. Paper prepared for the U.S. Monetary Policy Forum, University of Chicago and the Rosenberg Institute of Global Finance at Brandeis University, February.

Greenspan, A. and J. Kennedy (2007). Sources and uses of equity extracted from homes. Finance and Economics Discussion Paper No. 2007-20, Board of Governors of the Federal Reserve System, March.

International Monetary Fund (IMF) (2008). *Global Financial Stability Report: Containing Systemic Risks and Restoring Financial Soundness*. Washington, D.C., April.

Moody's Investors Service (2008). *Moody's Update on Structured Investment Vehicles*. International Structured Finance Special Report, January.

Morris, S. and H. S. Shin (2008). Financial regulation in system context. *Brookings Papers on Economic Activity*, Fall, 229–274.

Office of Federal Housing Enterprise Oversight (OFHEO) (2008). *Report to Congress*.

Passmore, W., S. M. Sherlund, and G. Burgess (2005). The effect of housing government-sponsored enterprises on mortgage rates. *Real Estate Economics*, 33, Fall, 427–463.

Senior Supervisors Group (2008). *Observations on Risk Management Practices During the Recent Market Turbulence*. March 6.

UBS (2008). *Shareholder Report on UBS's Write-Downs*. April 18. Available at http://www.ubs.com/.

Origins of the Subprime Crisis

Charles W. Calomiris*
Columbia Business School and National Bureau of Economic Research

1. Introduction

Financial crises not only impose short-term economic costs, but also create enormous regulatory risks. The financial crisis that has been gripping the global economy for the past two years is already inspiring voluminous proposals for regulatory reform coming from all quarters. Previous financial crises — most obviously the Great Depression — usually have brought significant financial regulatory changes in their wake.

Some crises breed sensible reforms. For example, in Great Britain, policy reforms in the 1850s and 1860s that changed the rules governing Bank of England assistance to distressed banks (effectively ending bailouts of banks during crises) had enormous consequences for incentives toward risk taking, which stabilized the financial system dramatically. Britain had experienced severe banking panics in 1825, 1836, 1847, 1857, and 1866, but (with the exception of the upheaval in 1914 as the world prepared for World War I) none for more than a century afterward (Calomiris, 2009a).

The Great Depression, in contrast, gave rise to a raft of changes in bank regulations, most of which were subsequently discredited by economists and economic historians as counterproductive and destabilizing (Calomiris, 2000). Since the 1980s, the U.S. has been removing many of the regulatory missteps that arose out of the financial collapse of the Great Depression by allowing banks to pay market interest rates on deposits, operate across state lines, and offer a wide range of financial

* Charles W. Calomiris is the Henry Kaufman Professor of Financial Institutions at Columbia Business School and a research associate at the National Bureau of Economic Research.

services and products to their customers (which has diversified banks' sources of income and improved the efficiency of bank services to clients). It is worth remembering how long it took for unwise regulatory actions taken in the wake of the Depression to be reversed. Indeed, some regulatory policies introduced during the Depression — most notably, deposit insurance — will likely never be reversed, despite the fact that financial economists and economic historians regard the adverse incentive consequences of deposit insurance (and other safety-net policies) as the primary source of the unprecedented financial instability that has arisen worldwide over the past 30 years (Barth *et al.*, 2006; Demirgüç-Kunt *et al.*, 2009).

A major lesson of the regulatory response to the Great Depression (and many other post-crisis policy reactions), therefore, is that unwise policy reactions to crises can have very long lives and very large social costs. Unwise reactions to crises have two sources: bad thinking about the sources of crises, and ulterior (politically captured) motives of "reformers" (which, to some extent, thrive because of a lack of general understanding of the true causes of crises). It is thus important, in the interest of shaping desirable reform, to get our story straight about what happened to cause the recent crisis.

In my discussion, I will focus on the United States for the simple reason that the U.S. was the place where the earliest, largest, and most persistent shocks originated, namely the problems in the intermediation of subprime mortgage risk. That is not to say that the U.S. was unique in its high-risk, high-leverage binge from 2002 to 2007; many other countries (including, for example, the U.K., Iceland, Spain, Ireland, and Hungary) have also suffered from their overexposure to risk during that period. However, I would argue that, without the U.S.'s uniquely large subprime shock, the global financial crisis and its severe macroeconomic consequences for the world would have been mild and short.

Why the focus on subprime shocks? After all, U.S. and global banks are ultimately facing losses on virtually all kinds of loans. While that is true, the losses on other categories of assets were smaller and came later in the cycle (because they reflect the endogenous economic consequences of the shocks that originated in subprime loans, such as the losses in credit card lending). In other words, it was not just a worldwide asset price bubble or a U.S. asset price bubble; it was first and foremost (although not exclusively) a U.S. subprime credit-driven housing bubble. This particularity requires an explanation.

Furthermore, everyone was not equally exposed to subprime losses (or to losses more generally), and any attempt to come to grips with the causes of the subprime crisis that does not explain this cross-sectional variation is incomplete. JPMorgan Chase, Bank of America, Deutsche Bank, Goldman Sachs, Morgan Stanley, Barclays, and Credit Suisse had relatively little exposure to subprime lending; indeed, some of these institutions benefited in some ways from the crisis, either because they were able to buy competitors at low cost (e.g., JPMorgan's acquisition of Bear Stearns) or because their competitors disappeared. In contrast, for those financial firms with large subprime exposure — Fannie Mae, Freddie Mac, Bear Stearns, Lehman Brothers, AIG, Merrill Lynch, Citibank, and UBS — the crisis was an utter disaster that forced them either (1) to be placed in bankruptcy or conservatorship (Fannie, Freddie, and Lehman), (2) to be acquired by private firms (Bear and Merrill), or (3) to receive heavy assistance from governments to survive as independent firms (AIG, Citibank, and UBS).

The stories about the origins of the subprime shock that are being told are not all the same, and some popular stories do not withstand scrutiny. For example, some critics point to allegedly obvious incentive problems inherent in the "originate and distribute" model that led to the failure of securitization as an intermediation technology. The problem, we are told, is that securitization permits sponsors to have too little skin in the game. However, two facts belie this view. First, sponsors actually retained large amounts of the subprime debts that they issued (and have the losses to show it). Second, securitization *per se* did not fail. Credit card securitization, an alternative product to subprime mortgage-backed securities (MBS) for consumer finance-based securitized debts, has operated reasonably well for three decades. It maintained a fairly normal deal flow until September 2008, when all financial transactions shrank dramatically, but it has recovered along with other financial flows in recent months.

Others point to rating agencies as the culprits for the crisis. But here again, there was not uniformity in behavior. Research for over a decade has noted that ratings of securitized debts tend to be inflated relative to corporate debts, so there is evidence of a general inflation of ratings for securitized products. However, during the financial crisis, the severe errors in rating methodology that produced grossly overstated ratings were specific to subprime-related securities.

When searching for explanations for these and other facts about the origins of the U.S. subprime crisis, something else should be kept in mind.

This was a *banking* crisis, not just a financial crisis broadly defined. The history of banking crises — that is, financial collapses in which banks are severely exposed to loss — provides helpful guidance of where to look for explanations. Macroeconomic factors, including monetary policy laxity, are generally associated with financial booms and busts, but they do not explain banking crises; when one looks specifically at banking crises, these macroeconomic circumstances are not sufficient conditions to produce a banking crisis. Banking crises typically result from severe *microeconomic* distortions, often relating to government subsidization of risk (Calomiris, 2009a).

In summary, when coming to grips with the origins of the current global financial crisis, one should (1) place this banking crisis in the broader context of the history of banking crises, which suggests an emphasis on microeconomic distortions in incentives toward risk; (2) explain the particular origins of subprime-related risk taking in the U.S. and its timing; (3) explain why some, but not all, large financial firms had taken on large subprime risks; and (4) explain the breakdown in the rating process for subprime-related securitized debts, but not other debts.

2. Government Policy and the Origins of the Subprime Crisis

The default risk on subprime mortgages was substantially underestimated in the market during the subprime boom of 2003–2007 (Calomiris, 2009b). One starting point for explaining the origins of the subprime crisis is to ask whether the large losses and huge underestimation of risk that occurred in the pricing of subprime-related securities were the result of identifiable and predictable errors or, alternatively, just bad luck.

Recent academic studies describe in detail the faulty assumptions that underlay the massive securitization of subprime mortgages and related collateralized debt obligations (CDOs).[1] It can be difficult to establish the *ex ante* unreasonableness of any assumption; but in the case of subprime securitizations, it was not so difficult. Some facts known to everyone in advance of the subprime collapse were simply put aside in the modeling of risk. In retrospect, the two most important errors of subprime risk modeling were (1) the assumption that house prices would not fall

[1] See Mason and Rosner (2007a, 2007b), International Monetary Fund (2008), Ellis (2008), Keys *et al.* (2010), Rajan *et al.* (2008), and Calomiris (2009b).

(an especially important assumption, given that subprime MBS were much more sensitive to house price assumptions than normal MBS, as discussed further below); and (2) the assumption that ignoring "soft" information and allowing lending through "no-doc" or "low-doc" mortgages based entirely on Fair Isaac Corporation (FICO) credit scores would not result in significant adverse selection in the pool of no-doc and low-doc mortgages. In other words, the models wrongly assumed that a mortgage with a 600 FICO score and with proper documentation of employment was roughly as good as a mortgage with a 600 FICO score with no documentation. According to recent research by Rajan *et al.* (2008), each of these two modeling errors was of roughly equal importance in producing the massive shortfalls of performance in subprime mortgage portfolios. Without these assumptions, there would have been no subprime debt crisis; yet these assumptions were obviously unreasonable on an *ex ante*, not just *ex post*, basis during the subprime boom, as they contradicted both logic and experience.

What was the basis for assuming that house prices would never fall? Subprime lending was a relatively new product that grew from humble beginnings in the early 1990s and remained small even as recently as 2003, after which it took off, roughly tripling in 2004 and peaking in 2006 and early 2007. Subprime risk models based their stress tests, including their house price stress tests, on a short "look-back" period. For some variables in the models (say, interest rates), that may have been a reasonable practice given the short track record of the product, but it was not reasonable to base projections of the possible paths of housing prices on a 10-year retrospective history of house price change. Doing so meant that modelers relied on the experience of housing prices during the 2001 recession to gauge the potential downside for the housing market, as this was the only recession in their limited sample. It was also a unique recession from the standpoint of the housing cycle in that it was the only recession in U.S. history in which housing price growth was sharply positive; other prior recessions show a very different pattern. Wouldn't it have been more reasonable to assume in 2003–2007 that the next recession might see a flattening or a decline in housing prices, which was the rule rather than the exception?

Indeed, some risk managers worried that the U.S. was overdue for a housing price decline, partly because of the extremely positive performance of the 1990s and early 2000s. David Andrukonis, a risk manager at Freddie Mac, recognized in his April 5, 2004 letter to a superior that the reliance of underwriters on house price appreciation to bail out subprime lenders was based on a false extrapolation of the past into the future: "We are less likely to get the house price appreciation we've had in the past 10 years to bail this program out if there's a hole in it" (quoted in Calomiris, 2008).

By "this program", David Andrukonis was referring to the proposed entry of Freddie Mac into no-doc lending on a large scale. The assumption that no-doc mortgages would have the same risk as well-documented mortgages with similar FICO scores defied economic logic and the experience of the mortgage market with no-doc products in the 1980s, and Mr. Andrukonis weighed in to discourage his superiors from entering this product area in 2004. He reminded them that "in 1990 we called this product 'dangerous' and eliminated it from the marketplace." Unfortunately, no one listened. The growth in subprime originations from 2004 to 2007 was meteoric, and was accompanied by a significant deterioration in borrower quality due to the growth in no-doc and low-doc mortgages. The heavy weight of no-doc mortgages in subprime portfolios after 2004 largely reflected the decisions of Fannie Mae and Freddie Mac (the "800-pound gorillas" in the mortgage market) to enter massively into purchases of no-doc subprime MBS in mid-2004, over the strong objections of their risk managers, who pointed to large adverse-selection consequences from doing so and whose objections were specifically based on the experience they had with no-doc mortgages in the 1980s. Not only did lenders know better from their own experience, but, using simple economic theory, the consequences of no-doc lending were predictable. If a mortgage lender hangs out a shingle saying that he will ask no questions but the FICO score, then he will attract (or adversely select) people who know that their FICO scores are about to deteriorate. The three primary reasons for consumer defaults are the loss of a job, a severe health problem, and divorce. All of these three events are known to the borrowers long before their consequences show up in the FICO score; only by doing proper due diligence can a lender detect these problems before they show up in the FICO score. Banks that do not perform such due diligence will predictably adversely select lower-quality borrowers.

Even more remarkably, subprime and Alt-A originations for late 2006 and early 2007 continued at peak levels, despite mounting evidence beginning in mid-2006 that housing prices were flattening (which had predictably disastrous consequences for subprime portfolios) and that unprecedented performance problems were beginning to occur in existing portfolios (which were discussed openly by the rating agencies). Josef Ackerman, the CEO of Deutsche Bank, in a speech given at the European Central Bank in December 2008, said that Deutsche Bank fled the subprime market in mid-2006 in reaction to these obvious signals of problems. Professor Gary Gorton of Yale University, in his oral comments at the August 2008 Federal Reserve Bank of Kansas City's Jackson Hole Conference, described the continuing high volume of originations in 2006 and 2007 by Merrill Lynch, UBS, and Citibank as "shocking", in light of the obvious problems brewing in the housing market. As Gorton (2008) emphasizes, the core assumption on which subprime lending had been based was the permanent appreciation of home prices. By the middle of 2006, that assumption was being disproven, yet no one — least of all the rating agencies — seemed to care.

The rating agencies did *notice* the problem; they just did not *react* to it. According to Fitch Ratings' (2006) extremely negative discussion of subprime prospects in December 2006, the environment became increasingly negative after the first quarter of 2006, as reflected in the fact that "the number of sub-prime downgrades in the period between July and October 2006 was the greatest of any four-month period in Fitch's history for that sector" (up to that point). Fitch Ratings (2006) correctly predicted that:

> [T]he sensitivity of sub-prime performance to the rate of HPA [home price appreciation] and the large number of borrowers facing scheduled payment increases in 2007 should continue to put negative pressure on the sector. Fitch expects delinquencies to rise by at least an additional 50% from current levels throughout the next year and for the general ratings environment to be negative, as the number of downgrades is expected to outnumber the number of upgrades.

Nonetheless, in the midst of all this negative news, the originations continued at a feverish pace, and not until the middle of 2007 did these serious problems become reflected in any significant (albeit still inadequate) changes in modeling assumptions by the rating agencies.

The predictable risk-taking mistakes of financial managers were not the result of random mass insanity; rather, they reflected a policy environment that strongly encouraged financial managers to underestimate risk in the subprime mortgage market. Risk taking was driven by government policies. Four categories of government error were instrumental in producing the crisis.

2.1 *Monetary policy and global imbalances*

First, lax Fed monetary policy, especially from 2002 through 2005, promoted easy credit and kept interest rates very low for a protracted period. As I have already noted, the history of banking crises teaches us that, while monetary policy laxity by itself is not a sufficient condition for generating a banking crisis, it is frequently a contributor to aggravating bad decision making by empowering bad decision makers with easy credit (Bordo, 2009; Calomiris, 2009b). As Figure 1 shows, the history of postwar monetary policy has seen only two episodes in which the real federal funds rate remained negative for several consecutive years: the high-inflation episode of 1975–1978 (which was reversed by the anti-inflation rate hikes of 1979–1982), and the accommodative policy environment of 2002–2005. As Figure 2 shows, the Federal Reserve deviated sharply from its "Taylor rule" approach to setting interest rates during the 2002–2005 period; the federal funds rate remained substantially and persistently below the levels that would have been consistent with the Taylor rule.

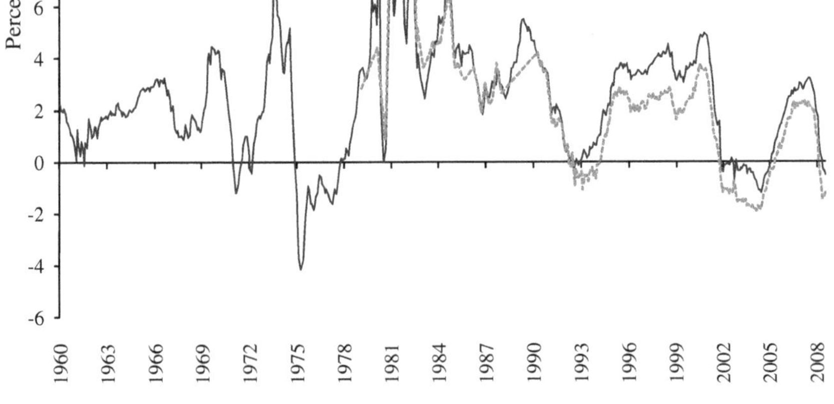

Figure 1. The real federal funds rate in the postwar era.

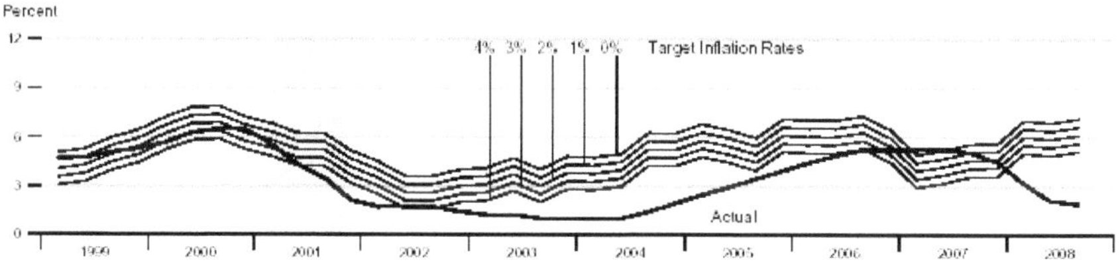

Figure 2. The federal funds rate and inflation targets.

Not only were short-term real rates held at persistent historical lows; but because of peculiarities in the bond market related to global imbalances and Asian demand for medium- and long-term U.S. Treasuries, the Treasury yield curve was virtually flat during the 2002–2005 period, implying extremely low interest rates across the yield curve. Hence, accommodative monetary policy and a flat yield curve meant that credit was excessively available to support expansion in the housing market at abnormally low interest rates, which encouraged the overpricing of houses.

2.2 *Subsidization of mortgage risk*

Second, numerous government policies specifically promoted or subsidized subprime mortgage-related risk taking by financial institutions (Calomiris, 2009b, 2009c). These policies included (1) political pressures from Congress on the government-sponsored enterprises (GSEs), Fannie Mae and Freddie Mac, to promote "affordable housing" by investing in high-risk subprime mortgages; (2) lending subsidies via the Federal Home Loan Bank System to its member institutions that promoted high mortgage leverage and risk; (3) Federal Housing Administration (FHA) subsidization of high mortgage leverage (nearly zero down payments) and high borrower default risk; (4) government and GSE mortgage foreclosure mitigation protocols that were developed in the late 1990s and early 2000s to reduce the costs to borrowers of failing to meet debt service requirements on mortgages, which encouraged risky mortgage borrowing by forcing originators to renegotiate delinquencies rather than foreclose (these new protocols were associated with a substantial reduction from the mid-1990s to the early 2000s in the probability of foreclosure occurring, conditional on 90-day delinquency); and — almost unbelievably — (5) 2006 legislation that prohibited so-called "notching", which encouraged rating agencies to relax their standards for measuring risk in subprime securitizations.

All of these government policies contributed to encouraging the underestimation of subprime risk, but the politicization of Fannie Mae and Freddie Mac as well as the actions of members of Congress to encourage reckless lending by the GSEs in the name of affordable housing were arguably the most damaging microeconomic policy actions leading up to the crisis. In order for Fannie and Freddie to maintain their implicit (now explicit) government guarantees on their debts, which contributed substantially to their profitability, they believed (with good cause) that they had to cater to the political agendas of their supporters in Congress. In the context of recent times, this meant making a huge amount of risky subprime loans (Wallison and Calomiris, 2009). Fannie and Freddie ended up holding US$1.6 trillion in exposure to these toxic mortgages, which constitutes half of the total non-FHA outstanding amount of toxic mortgages (Pinto, 2008). Calomiris (2008) argues that it is likely that, absent the involvement of Fannie and Freddie in aggressive subprime buying beginning in 2004, the total magnitude of toxic mortgages originated would have been less than half its actual amount, since Fannie and Freddie crowded in market participation more than they crowded it out. Their entry into no-doc mortgages in an aggressive manner in 2004 was associated with a tripling of subprime originations in that year. In mid-2006, when housing price weakness led others like Goldman Sachs and Deutsche Bank to pull back, Fannie and Freddie continued to make markets in subprime securities which produced a disastrous prolongation of peak-level deal flow well into 2007.

2.3 *Prudential regulatory failure*

Third, prudential regulation of commercial banks by the government has proven to be ineffective. This failure reflects (1) fundamental problems in measuring bank risk resulting from regulation's ill-considered reliance on credit rating agencies' assessments and internal bank models to measure risk; and (2) the "too big to fail" problem (Stern and Feldman, 2004), which makes it difficult to credibly enforce effective discipline on large, complex financial institutions (like Citibank, Bear Stearns, AIG, and

Lehman Brothers), even if regulators detect that those institutions have suffered large losses and have accumulated imprudently large risks.

The risk measurement problem has been the primary failure of banking regulation and a subject of constant academic regulatory criticism for decades. Bank regulators utilize various means to assess risk, depending on the size of the bank. Under the simplest version of regulatory measurement of bank risk, subprime mortgages have a low asset risk weight (50% of that of commercial loans), even though they are much riskier than most bank loans. A more complex measurement of subprime risk (applicable to larger U.S. banks) relies on the opinions of rating agencies or the internal assessments of banks; unsurprisingly, neither of these assessments is independent of bank management.

2.3.1 *Subprime ratings inflation and the regulatory reliance on ratings*

Rating agencies are supposed to cater to buy-side market participants (i.e., banks, pensions, mutual funds, and insurance companies that maintained subprime-related asset exposure). However, when their ratings are used for regulatory purposes, buy-side participants reward rating agencies for underestimating risk, since that helps the buy-side clients avoid regulation. Many observers wrongly believe that the problem with rating agency grade inflation of securitized debts is that sellers of these debts (sponsors of securitizations) are the ones who pay for ratings; on the contrary, the problem is that the *buyers* of the debts want inflated ratings because of the regulatory benefits they receive from those inflated ratings.

Rating agencies had no incentive to construct realistic models or respond realistically to bad news relating to subprime instruments for a simple reason: their buy-side clients did not want them to. Institutional investors managing the portfolios of pensions, mutual funds, insurance companies, and banks continued to buy subprime-related securitization debt instruments well into 2007. Even the banks who sponsored these instruments (and who presumably had the clearest understanding of their toxic content) continued to retain large amounts of the risk associated with the subprime MBS and CDO securitizations they packaged through purchases of their own subprime-related debts and credit enhancements for subprime conduits. Were the bankers who created these securitizations and retained large exposure for the banks related to them, along with other sophisticated institutional investors who bought subprime-related securities, aware of the flawed assumptions regarding housing prices and no-doc mortgages that underlay the financial engineering of subprime MBS by rating agencies? These assumptions were widely publicized as part of the process of selling the securities. Did they object? Apparently not.

Why did these bank investors create these risks for themselves and other institutions, and why did sophisticated institutional investors buy these overpriced securities? The obvious answer is that asset managers were placing someone else's money at risk, and earning huge salaries, bonuses, and management fees for being willing to pretend that these were reasonable investments. Rating agencies gave legitimacy to this pretense, and were paid to do so. Investors may have reasoned that other competing banks and asset managers were behaving similarly, and that they would be able to blame the collapse (when it inevitably came) on a surprising shock. The script would be clear and would give plausible deniability to all involved: "Who knew? We all thought that the model gave the right loss assumption! That was what the rating agencies used." Plausible deniability was a coordinating device for allowing asset managers to participate in the feeding frenzy at little risk of losing customers (precisely because so many participated). Because asset managers could point to market-based data and ratings at the time as confirming the prudence of their actions on a forward-looking basis, they were likely to bear little cost from investor losses.

In short, the regulatory reliance on ratings magnified a pre-existing agency problem on the buy side of the securitized debt market. Asset managers willingly invested too much in risky assets because of an incentive conflict or agency problem; while rating agencies, and the regulators who relied on their ratings, were their willing (fee-receiving) accomplices. If asset managers had informed their clients of the truth — that the supply of good investments in risky assets had been outstripped by the flood of financial savings, and that consequently the risk-reward trade-off did not warrant further investment in risky assets — then asset managers would have been required to return money to clients rather than invest in risky assets. Presumably, the money would then have ended up in bank deposit accounts or other low-risk (and low-fee-generating) investments. Returning the money to investors under these circumstances would have made investors better off (given the poor return to bearing risk), but it would have made asset managers worse off because their compensation depends primarily on the size of the funds they manage (management fees earned grow in proportion to the amount of funds invested in risky assets).

To what extent is it plausible to argue against this view by pointing to the novelty of securitization products (subprime MBS, CDOs, etc.), which may have made investors and rating agencies unable to gauge risk properly in advance of the crisis? As I have already noted, data and logic available prior to the crisis showed that key assumptions regarding the possible path of home prices and the adverse-selection consequences of no-doc mortgages were unrealistic. Furthermore, the novelty of a securitization product, in and of itself, should be an indicator of the need to adjust estimates of risk *upward*. Experience suggests that rating agencies have frequently underestimated the risks of new products and have only adapted their behavior after major credit or fraud events occurred, which shows that their risk measures and controls for new products tend to be inadequate. Experience prior to the subprime collapse (in credit card securitization, delinquent consumer account receivable securitization, and other areas) has shown that the learning curve related to underestimation of risk can be steep. Decades of experience with steep learning curves in new securitization products indicate yet another reason that properly incentivized institutional investors should have been cautious about the new, fast-growing markets in subprime mortgages and CDOs.

Indeed, it is particularly revealing to contrast the measurement of subprime risk with the measurement of risk in the much older credit card securitization business. In credit card securitization, even during the subprime crisis, market participants paid close attention to the identities of originators, to their performance in the past, to the composition of portfolios, and to how compositions changed over time; originators were thus rewarded with greater leverage tolerance for "seasoned" receivables with good track records. In contrast, until the middle of 2007, the ratings of subprime portfolios (based largely on the unrealistic expected loss assumptions) seem to have been extremely insensitive to changes in borrower quality, product type (which is correlated with unobservable aspects of borrower quality), or the state of the housing market. There was also a dramatic new entry into subprime origination in 2004–2006 by fly-by-night originators, yet these new entrants offering new, riskier products to new customers seem to have been able to raise funds under more or less the same low-loss assumptions as old originators who offered older, lower-risk products. The principles learned over 20 years in the credit card securitization business were thrown out the window when rating subprime-related securitizations.

This account does not place the primary blame for the mispricing of risk on securitization sponsors (the sell side) or on rating agencies. After all, sponsors were only supplying what asset managers of their own institutions or outside buyers were demanding. The rating agencies were also doing what the investors wanted: going through the mechanical process of engineering conduit debt structures, and rating them, based on transparently rosy assumptions. Rating agencies were not deceiving sophisticated institutional investors about the risks of the products they were rating; rather, they were transparently understating risk and inflating the grading scale of their debt ratings for securitized products, so that institutional investors — who are constrained by various regulations to invest in debts rated highly by Nationally Recognized Statistical Rating Organizations (NRSROs) — would be able to invest as they liked without being bound by the constraints of regulation or the best interests of their clients.[2]

Many observers wrongly attribute rating agencies' behavior to the fact that sponsors, rather than investors, paid for the ratings. However, this fact is not relevant. Sponsors and investors alike knew what was going on; and if the investors had not wanted the models to be misspecified and the ratings to be inflated, then the rating agencies would not have built such faulty models and would not have generated such inflated ratings. Ratings inflation and model misspecification of subprime-related securitized debts were demand-driven, and thus would have occurred even if the buy side had paid for ratings.

2.3.2 *Too big to fail*

The "too big to fail" problem relates to the lack of credibility of regulatory discipline for large, complex banks. For large, complex banks, the

[2] Calomiris (2009e) shows that ratings shopping — the practice whereby originators of subprime-related securitizations get a preview of rating agencies' views before choosing which ones to permit to rate their debts — produced a "race to the bottom" among agencies. It is important to recognize that, in order for ratings shopping to result in a "race to the bottom" in ratings, that "race to the bottom" must be welcomed by the buy side of the market; ratings shopping will not benefit the sell side without the buy side's cooperation. If institutional investors punish the absence of good rating agencies in an offering (by refusing to buy, or by paying a lower price, when a reputable rating agency is excluded from rating a securitization), then would-be ratings shoppers would have no incentive to exclude reputable rating agencies. Thus, the fact that ratings shopping tends to exclude relatively reputable rating agencies and leads to low-quality, inflated ratings implies that the buy side favors a ratings shopping process that results in low-quality, inflated ratings.

prospect of failure is considered so potentially disruptive to the financial system that regulators have an incentive to avoid intervention. The incentives that favor forbearance and/or explicit government assistance *ex post* can make it hard for regulators to ensure compliance *ex ante*. The "too big to fail" problem magnifies the so-called "moral hazard" problem of the government safety net: banks which expect to be protected by deposit insurance, Fed lending, and Treasury–Fed bailouts, and which believe that they are beyond discipline, will tend to take on excessive risk, since the taxpayers share the costs of that excessive risk on the downside.

The moral hazard of the "too big to fail" problem was clearly visible in the behavior of the large investment banks in 2008. After Bear Stearns was rescued by a Treasury–Fed bailout in March 2008, Lehman Brothers, Merrill Lynch, Morgan Stanley, and Goldman Sachs sat on their hands for six months awaiting further developments (i.e., either an improvement in the market environment or a handout from Uncle Sam). In particular, Lehman did little to raise capital or shore up its position. However, when conditions deteriorated and the anticipated bailout failed to materialize for Lehman in September 2008 — showing that there were limits to Treasury–Fed generosity — the other major investment banks immediately either became acquired or transformed themselves into commercial bank holding companies to increase their access to government support.

2.4 *Corporate governance problems in large banks*

Fourth, government regulations limiting who can buy stock in banks have made effective corporate governance within large banks virtually impossible, which contributed to the buy-side agency problems within banks who took large subprime risks. Hedge funds and private equity funds have traditionally been barred from controlling bank holding companies. Pension funds, mutual funds, and insurance companies are limited by regulations to only own a small stake in any public firm, including banks. Given the importance of the incentives that come from ownership concentration in enforcing effective corporate governance, these regulations make the managers of large banks virtually immune to effective challenges from sophisticated shareholders.

Lax corporate governance allowed bank management to pursue investments that were unprofitable for stockholders in the long run, but that were very profitable to management in the short run, given the short time horizons of asset managers' compensation systems. When stockholder discipline is absent, managers are able to set up the management of risk within the firms they manage so as to benefit themselves at the expense of stockholders. An asset bubble (like the subprime bubble of 2003–2007) offers an ideal opportunity: if senior managers establish compensation systems that reward subordinates based on total assets managed or total revenues collected, without regard to risk or future potential loss, then subordinates are incentivized to expand portfolios rapidly during the bubble without regard to risk. Poor asset risk management on the buy side, which reflected poor corporate governance and compensation practices at some firms, was thus a key contributor to underestimation of risk, and helps to explain why some firms fared worse than others.

This review of the four areas in which government policy contributed to the financial crisis has made no mention of deregulation. During the 2008 presidential election, many candidates (including Barack Obama) frequently made vague claims that deregulation had caused the crisis. However, this claim made no sense: involvement by banks and investment banks in subprime mortgages and mortgage securitization was in no way affected by the deregulation of the last two decades. In fact, deregulation cushioned the financial system's adjustment to the subprime shock by making banks more diversified and by allowing troubled investment banks to become stabilized by becoming, or being acquired by, commercial banks (Calomiris, 2009b). Since the election, President Obama and other erstwhile critics of deregulation have changed their emphasis, and now properly focus on failures of regulation, rather than deregulation, as causes of the crisis.

2.5 *The size of the shock vs. the size of the crisis*

The severity of the crisis may seem paradoxical given the limited size of the subprime market. Roughly US$3 trillion in non-FHA subprime mortgages were outstanding at the time of the crisis, and ultimate losses on those securities will likely be roughly $600 billion.[3] Why did this limited

[3] Because of creative accounting practices by Fannie Mae and Freddie Mac, which disguised the true size of their subprime mortgage exposure, it was not widely known until roughly September 2008 that Fannie Mae and Freddie Mac held half of the total subprime exposure, or that the total amount of subprime exposure was so high (Pinto, 2008; Wallison and Calomiris, 2009). Thus, prior to mid-2008, the general perceptions of total exposure and expected loss were even lower.

loss cause such widespread havoc throughout global financial markets? The answer to this question revolves around liquidity risk. The shocks of financial loss are magnified when the distribution of loss is hard to ascertain. This "asymmetric information" problem produces a widespread scramble for liquidity throughout the financial system, which causes suppliers of credit to refuse to roll over debts and causes interest rates on risky securities and loans to rise dramatically, reflecting not only the fundamental credit risk in the system but also the illiquidity of the markets. This scramble magnifies losses and the risk of financial failure far beyond what they would have been if it were easy to identify exactly who suffered from the fundamental exogenous shocks giving rise to the crisis.

As Gorton (2008) shows, the complexity of subprime-related securitizations contributed greatly to the inability of markets to identify the distribution of loss in the system once the crisis began. This inability reflected the complex design of the distribution of cash flows in the various securitizations, the multiple layers of securitization, and the sensitivity of securitization portfolios to uncertain changes in housing prices. The sensitivity of subprime mortgage valuation to housing prices was particularly problematic because subprime securities payouts had been based on scenarios that only envisioned rising housing prices, which made it especially difficult to project payouts in a declining housing price environment.

Schwarz (2009) devises an innovative means of distinguishing between the exogenous effects of fundamental loss expectations and the endogenous effects of the scramble for liquidity in explaining the widening of credit spreads during the crisis. Liquidity risk is captured by market factors unrelated to default risk (e.g., spreads on sovereign bonds of different liquidity), while credit risk is captured by differences between banks in the rates they paid in the interbank market (abstracting from changes in the average interest rate and, therefore, from the common effect of liquidity risk). She found that roughly two-thirds of the widening of credit spreads was attributable to liquidity risk.

3. Conclusion

Loose monetary policy and global imbalances explain the timing of the subprime crisis; but like other severe banking crises historically, microeconomic government policies that distorted the risk-taking decisions of financial institutions were crucial, necessary conditions for causing the crisis. The microeconomic policy errors enumerated above that caused the subprime crisis relate to the fundamental design of the financial system — housing finance policy, prudential regulatory policy, and corporate ownership rules relating to large banks — all of which had already been the subjects of substantial academic research prior to the financial crisis. It is no surprise, therefore, that credible solutions to these problems have been identified by financial economists who write about public policy, and those proposals are reviewed elsewhere (Calomiris, 2009b, 2009c, 2009d, 2009e). Successful reform must begin with the recognition that major flaws in policy and regulation have existed for decades, and that these flaws must be addressed if we hope to avoid a repeat of the recent crisis.

References

Barth, J. R., G. Caprio, Jr., and R. Levine (2006). *Rethinking Bank Regulation: Till Angels Govern.* Cambridge: Cambridge University Press.

Bordo, M. D. (2009). The crisis of 2007: the same old story, only the players have changed. Working paper, Rutgers University.

Calomiris, C. W. (2000). *U.S. Bank Deregulation in Historical Perspective.* Cambridge: Cambridge University Press.

Calomiris, C. W. (2008). Statement before the Committee on Oversight and Government Reform, United States House of Representatives. December 9.

Calomiris, C. W. (2009a). Banking crises and the rules of the game. NBER Working Paper No. 15403, October.

Calomiris, C. W. (2009b). The subprime turmoil: what's old, what's new, and what's next. *Journal of Structured Finance*, Spring, 6–52.

Calomiris, C. W. (2009c). Financial innovation, regulation, and reform. *Cato Journal*, Winter, 65–92.

Calomiris, C. W. (2009d). Prudential bank regulation: what's broke and how to fix it. In Anderson, T. L. and R. Sousa (eds.), *Reacting to the Spending Spree: Policy Changes We Can Afford*, Stanford, CA: Hoover Institution Press, 17–34.

Calomiris, C. W. (2009e). The debasement of ratings: what's wrong and how we can fix it. Working paper, Columbia Business School.

Demirgüç-Kunt, A., E. Kane, and L. Laeven (eds.) (2009). *Deposit Insurance Around the World.* Cambridge, MA: MIT Press.

Ellis, L. (2008). The housing meltdown: why did it happen in the United States? Working Paper No. 259, Bank for International Settlements.

Fitch Ratings (2006). *2007 Global Structured Finance Outlook: Economic and Sector-by-Sector Analysis*. December.

Gorton, G. (2008). The Panic of 2007. In *Maintaining Stability in a Changing Financial System: A Symposium Sponsored by the Federal Reserve Bank of Kansas City*, 131–262.

International Monetary Fund (2008). *Global Financial Stability Report*. Washington, D.C.: IMF.

Keys, B. J., T. K. Mukherjee, A. Seru, and V. Vig (2010). Did securitization lead to lax screening? Evidence from subprime loans. *Quarterly Journal of Economics*, February, 263–305.

Mason, J. R. and J. Rosner (2007a). How resilient are mortgage backed securities to collateralized debt obligation market disruptions? Working paper, Louisiana State University.

Mason, J. R. and J. Rosner (2007b). Where did the risk go? How misapplied bond ratings cause mortgage backed securities and collateralized debt obligation market disruptions. Working paper, Louisiana State University.

Pinto, E. J. (2008). Statement before the Committee on Oversight and Government Reform, United States House of Representatives. December 9.

Rajan, U., A. Seru, and V. Vig (2008). The failure of models that predict failure: distance, incentives and defaults. Working paper, London Business School.

Schwarz, K. (2009). Mind the gap: widening risk spreads explained by new measures of credit and liquidity. Working paper, Wharton School.

Stern, G. H. and R. J. Feldman (2004). *Too Big to Fail: The Hazards of Bank Bailouts*. Washington, D.C.: Brookings Institution Press.

Wallison, P. J. and C. W. Calomiris (2009). The last trillion-dollar commitment: the destruction of Fannie Mae and Freddie Mac. *Journal of Structured Finance*, Spring, 71–80.

The Role of the Financial Sector in the Great Recession

Michael Mussa*
Peterson Institute for International Economics

In the story of the "Great Recession" of 2008–2009, the financial sector plays a starring role. Excessive and imprudent expansion of credit, utilizing an array of complex financial instruments, fueled an unsustainable boom, especially in housing in the United States. As the boom started to deflate during 2007, investors began to recognize previously underappreciated risks as well as fear widening losses to themselves and to financial institutions which held claims of increasingly dubious value. As the crisis evolved into 2008, grave doubts arose about the viability of some key institutions with highly leveraged balance sheets and complex connections to much of the financial sector. Government interventions to stabilize threatened institutions, in the United States and elsewhere, and substantial easing of monetary policy by the Federal Reserve (but not initially by most other central banks) helped to stabilize the situation for a time. However, as economic conditions deteriorated worldwide in the spring and summer of 2008, fears about the viability of key institutions re-intensified well beyond their earlier scale. In mid-September 2008, the outright failure of Lehman Brothers and the threatened collapse within days of a number of other key institutions set off a global financial panic, in which even the most creditworthy private borrowers could not roll over their short-term paper and leading banks worldwide stopped lending to each other. Extremely forceful intervention by governments and central banks, passing well beyond the normal tactics of monetary easing, contained the crisis in late 2008 and increasingly restored more normal functioning to financial markets during the early months of 2009.

* Michael Mussa is a senior fellow at the Peterson Institute for International Economics.

Nevertheless, the entire world economy suffered massive damage from the disruption of global financial markets. On a monthly basis, worldwide industrial production shrank at annual rates of 10–25% from October 2008 to April 2009, and many countries saw peak annualized rates of decline of 30–60%. The value and volume of world trade collapsed, with annualized monthly rates of decline in the value of world merchandise exports escalating from 30% in October 2008 to 60% in January 2009 before abating to 30% by April 2009. Estimates of the broadest measure of economic activity, world real GDP (using purchasing power parity (PPP) weights), show annual rates of decline of over 6% in both the final quarter of 2008 and the first quarter of 2009. For many individual countries, these two quarters saw the steepest declines in real GDP of the entire postwar era.

In examining this economic tragedy, I shall attempt to develop two almost contradictory main points. First, problems in the financial sector were not the only important cause of the great global recession of 2008–2009 and further deep reforms of the financial sector are not essential preconditions for a moderately vigorous economic recovery. Second, the problems in the financial sector that did contribute importantly to the great global recession are very deep-seated and have been seriously exacerbated by actions taken to contain the recent crisis. If we are to contain the risk of another, even deeper financial crisis and recession sometime in the next two or three decades, then we must either move back to a regime of financial repression similar to that installed during the Great Depression or fundamentally reconfigure the market-oriented financial system that has evolved out of financial repression since the mid-1960s. In particular, capital levels at the key financial institutions whose continuous functioning is essential to the operation of the entire economic system should be raised very substantially to the levels that would prevail if there were no prospect of public support for these institutions, except in the most dire economic circumstances.

1. A Classic Boom/Bust Cycle

The alternative explanation for the great global recession of 2008–2009 does not deny a key causal role of problems in the financial sector (especially in the United States and some other advanced economies), but it does emphasize that other important forces were also at work. The main storyline is as follows.

Since 2002, the world economy has seen a classic boom/bust cycle wherein relatively easy monetary policies around much of the world helped to promote a robust global economic expansion that continued until early 2008. This expansion ultimately led to a global upsurge of inflation, which was particularly visible in commodity prices. In classic fashion, monetary policies were tightened to contain economic overheating, beginning in the United States in mid-2005 and starting later in most other countries. By the spring of 2008, most of the world economy was in recession, partly in response to tighter monetary policies, partly due to surging oil prices, and partly as a result of the evolving financial crisis that started with problems arising from subprime mortgages in the United States. The world recession then deepened severely and suddenly with the unprecedented freezing up of key global credit markets in the autumn of 2008. This last event, however, was not uniquely caused by the unwinding of excessive risks concentrated in the U.S. mortgage market that led to the actual or threatened failure of a couple of U.S. key financial institutions, but was also partly the consequence of broader forces that were already pushing the global economy into recession.

The evidence supporting this broader diagnosis of the causes of the great global recession is abundant. Economic growth was remarkably rapid across most of the world economy from the middle of 2003 through early 2008, with growth rates of global real GDP, as estimated by the International Monetary Fund (IMF), generally running above 4.5%. Monetary policies were relaxed to very easy stances in most of the industrial countries during the global growth slowdown of 2001–2003; except for Australia, Canada, Sweden, and the United Kingdom, these policies remained quite accommodative through 2004 and 2005, and then were tightened at a relatively leisurely pace. Many developing and emerging market economies also maintained quite accommodative monetary policies during this period. The global inflation rate, as measured by the 12-month change in consumer prices, rose from a low of 3.2% in 2002 to reach 6.5% by the summer of 2008. The upsurge in commodity prices was particularly dramatic in 2007–2008, with world oil prices reaching a peak of US$147 per barrel in mid-July 2008. As inflation surged upward in 2007–2008, monetary policies were tightened substantially (except in the few countries that had already done so). Real GDP began to decline in much of Western Europe, Japan, and some emerging market countries in the spring of 2008, and the rate of decline generally accelerated during the summer quarter before the sudden freezing up of global credit markets.

The role of the United States in these global developments deserves special attention. The housing boom reached its peak in late 2005, with real residential investment having doubled from its trough in early 1991. According to the Case–Shiller index, house prices peaked a little later in the summer of 2006. With the downturn in real residential investment, the rate of growth of real domestic demand in the United States slowed significantly after the first quarter of 2006, averaging only 1.2% annualized growth through the end of 2007. Real GDP growth also slowed significantly, down to 2.1% at an annualized rate. However, the slowdown in output growth was cushioned by a significant improvement in U.S. real net exports. Thus, the global adjustment process that many of us had called for was clearly in operation during 2006–2007. The U.S. real trade deficit was gradually being reduced by the combination of slower domestic demand growth in the U.S., continued strong demand growth in the rest of the world, and the downward correction in the real effective foreign exchange rate of the U.S. dollar since its peak in early 2002.

Moreover, slowdown of domestic demand growth in the U.S. meant that the United States was operating as a damper on rising global inflation at a time when this was becoming a serious problem. Indeed, looking ahead to developments during 2008, it was certainly not robust growth of the U.S. economy nor of U.S. demand for oil and other commodities that drove their prices skyward and thereby contributed both to surging inflation and to the adverse effects of rising commodity prices on global economic activity. The United States was undoubtedly a leading actor in the tragedy of the great global recession, but it clearly was not the only one on the stage.

2. The Financial Sector in the Global Recovery

Where there can be no real dispute about the central role of the United States in the great global recession is regarding developments in the financial sector. Some other countries (including the United Kingdom, Ireland, and tiny Iceland) clearly had financial-sector problems of their own making, and many other countries effectively chose to participate in the global financial crisis through their decisions to invest in various U.S. securities. Nevertheless, it is clear that (1) problems arising from mortgage-related assets in the United States were the most important initial cause of global financial problems beginning in 2007 and deepening into 2008; and

(2) the freezing up of key credit markets in the autumn of 2008, which massively accelerated the global recession, was largely (if not entirely) the consequence of developments in or emanating from the United States.

Rather than dwelling further on the much-discussed issue of the role of the U.S. financial-sector developments in causing the great global recession, I shall turn to the now-salient issue of what effect continuing problems in the financial sector may have on the global economic recovery currently under way. The predominant conclusion of most analysts who have examined this issue (as summarized in the IMF's *World Economic Outlook* and *Financial Stability Report*) is that deep problems remain unresolved and substantial losses remain unrecognized in the financial sectors of several advanced economies, and these problems and losses are likely to weigh heavily on the prospects for even moderately vigorous economic recovery. In particular, it is argued that previous economic downturns where financial-sector problems have played a leading role have tended to be unusually deep and prolonged, and recoveries have tended to be unusually tepid. As financial-sector problems have clearly played a leading role in the present global economic downturn, the same should be expected this time. More specifically, key financial institutions in the United States and, perhaps even more so, in some European countries have large volumes of troubled assets still on their balance sheets and face the possible need to recognize hundreds of billions of dollars of additional losses. The worry is that, because of these weaknesses, key financial institutions will be unable or unwilling to supply adequate credit to support a meaningful economic recovery and, if crises were to re-emerge in the financial sector, could even tip the world economy into renewed recession.

No doubt, weaknesses in the financial sector and especially acute financial crises that paralyze key financial markets have played a key role in severe recessions. In some cases, as at present, financial excesses and their unwinding have preceded and been a key cause of the subsequent recession. In other cases, stress in financial sectors has been more the consequence than the initiating cause of the economic downturn. In all cases of deep recession, severe stress in the financial sector has interacted with the general weakening of economic activity to exacerbate the downturn. Also in all of these cases, it has generally been necessary to stabilize conditions in the financial sector — usually with the aid of substantial government intervention — in order to end the downturn and lay the foundation for recovery.

It has not been true, however, in virtually any case, that deep reforms have restored financial sectors to robust health as a precondition for vigorous economic recovery or often even as an accompaniment to the initial stages of such recovery. Instead, the regularity has been that, once reasonable stability is achieved in the financial sector, economic recovery proceeds and, in the reverse of the process that operates during the downturn, it is primarily the economic recovery that restores reasonably good health to the financial system. Some examples will usefully illustrate this important point.

The Great Depression in the United States in the 1930s certainly qualifies as a very deep recession in which problems in the financial sector played a leading role, both as a cause and an effect of other developments in the severe economic downturn from 1929 to 1933. Using annual data, U.S. real GDP fell by 26% between 1929 and 1933, and it was not until 1936 that real GDP recovered its 1929 level. If quarterly data were available, they would show that real GDP declined by more than 30% between mid-1929 and mid-1933 and then recovered to its mid-1929 level by mid-1936. By any reckoning, the Great Depression from peak to trough and back to the pre-contraction level took seven long years. Nevertheless, the Great Depression is an outstanding example of the Zarnowitz rule: it took four years for real GDP to collapse by 30%, but it took only three years of very steep recovery for that lost ground to be regained.

What was the role of the financial sector in all of this? Economists from Milton Friedman and Anna Schwartz (1963) to Ben Bernanke (2000) agree that the massive contraction of money and credit as well as the deep disruption of the financial system between 1929 and the spring of 1933 contributed much to the depth of the Great Depression. With the "Bank Holiday" of March 1933, the introduction of deposit insurance, and other government interventions, financial conditions were more or less stabilized by the summer of 1933. It is not the case, however, that the financial system was massively reformed and restored to robust health by the summer of 1933 or any time soon thereafter. Depositors remained nervous about banks. Banks were very cautious about lending, and held large excess reserves as protection against runs and as reassurance to depositors. Thus, the great recovery of real GDP beginning in the summer of 1933 was achieved with a banking and financial system that had been stabilized but was not robust.

The great recovery restored real GDP to its 1929 level, but it was still well below its trend growth path when another sharp recession hit the U.S.

economy in 1937. Quarterly data (if they were available) would show that this recession was deeper than any in the postwar era. In accord with the Zarnowitz rule, recovery was also steep, with economic activity reaching its pre-recession level within a year of the recession trough.

Was this recession the consequence of financial-sector weaknesses left over from the Great Depression? Not really. Even with the great recovery following the Great Depression, banks wanted to hold large excess reserves. By 1936, the Federal Reserve increasingly regarded these large excess reserves as posing significant inflationary risks. It was feared that banks might suddenly decide to make better use of these reserves by lending them out in a massive expansion of bank credit. To forestall this possibility, the Fed sharply raised reserve requirements. The banks, which wanted to hold large excess reserves as protection against bank runs and as reassurance to their depositors, responded by cutting back lending to restore excess reserves to desired levels. The result, as Friedman and Schwartz (1963) argue persuasively, was a policy-induced contraction in money and credit that precipitated the 1937–1938 recession; this was not a case where a crisis in the financial system induced a recession (the tightening of fiscal policy by the Roosevelt administration probably also contributed). Clear recognition of the history of these policy mistakes by senior officials at the Federal Reserve and in the Obama administration indicates that their repetition in the present circumstances is highly unlikely.

All of this points to one clear conclusion. No reasonable lesson can be drawn from U.S. experience during the Great Depression that supports the notion that recovery from the deep recession of 2008–2009 should be expected to be either exceptionally sluggish or critically dependent upon further deep reforms of the financial system.

More recently, the deep U.S. recessions of 1973–1975 and 1980–1982, and even the relatively mild recession of 1990–1991, were associated with considerable financial stress (even though the imprudence of financial institutions themselves may not have been a leading cause of these recessions). At the depth of these recessions, many leading financial institutions would have been substantially insolvent if their balance sheets had been valued comprehensively on a mark-to-market basis, but these *de facto* insolvencies were effectively concealed by the historical-value accounting applied to most assets. Nevertheless, many financial institutions were under great stress, as investors were well aware that the situation of many financial institutions was not nearly as secure as their official balance sheets purported to show.

As the recoveries began from these earlier recessions, the major financial institutions were almost surely in worse condition, properly measured, than major U.S. financial institutions are today (when the situation is already much improved from late 2008 and early 2009). In these earlier episodes, little was done explicitly to restructure or recapitalize troubled institutions during the recessions or even well into the recoveries. The Continental Illinois National Bank was intervened only in 1984, when the exceptionally vigorous Reagan recovery was well under way. The deep problems of the savings and loan industry were not comprehensively acknowledged and addressed until 1989. Nonetheless, recoveries proceeded and were quite vigorous in the two cases of deep recessions of 1973–1975 and 1980–1982.

In the present case, especially in the United States and the United Kingdom, very vigorous actions have already been taken to close, restructure, and recapitalize weak financial institutions. This has been important for re-establishing reasonable financial stability and will be helpful for economic recovery. Undoubtedly, though, further deep reforms of the financial sector are needed to reduce the risk of future crises. However, experience with past recoveries from deep recessions does not indicate that such reforms are an essential precondition for moderately vigorous recovery from the 2008–2009 recession.

Japan in the 1990s is usually cited as a key example where continuing weaknesses in the financial sector contributed importantly to protracted economic weakness. This is probably correct, at least up to a point. In my former role at the IMF, I was among those who, as early as 1994, were urging the Japanese authorities to be more forthright in recognizing and dealing with substantial weaknesses in the banking system. However, it is not accurate to say that the relatively mild recession that Japan experienced in 1992–1993 was largely the result of weaknesses in the banking system or failure to pursue financial-sector reforms. Rather, the recession was primarily a result of the huge decline in equity values and real estate prices and the collapse of the "bubble economy" that began 2–3 years before the recession. Similarly, the relatively tepid recovery from the 1992–1993 recession was not importantly a consequence of weaknesses in Japanese banks, but instead was mainly attributable to (1) the slowdown of potential growth in Japan; (2) the fact that the recession was relatively mild (making the Zarnowitz rule irrelevant); and (3) the policies of the Japanese government that blunted the immediate negative economic impact of the collapse of the "bubble economy", but had the effect of spreading that impact over a longer period of years rather than precipitating a sharp and deep recession followed by a strong recovery.

This last point is similar to the phenomenon in the 2001 (non)recession in the United States. Strong monetary and fiscal policy stimulus from Fed easing and the Bush tax cuts blunted the downward economic impetus from the sharp drop in stock prices after their March 2000 peak. The result was nearly three years of very sluggish GDP growth, from mid-2000 through the first quarter of 2003, during which the unemployment rate moved up from under 4% to over 6% (in the most recently revised data, U.S. real GDP registered only two, non-consecutive quarters of very modest decline during the period of recession recognized by the National Bureau of Economic Research). The Zarnowitz rule did not apply in this case because there was no deep recession to be followed by a steep recovery.

Returning to Japan, in 1996–1997, the Hashimoto government arguably made a serious mistake when it continued to refuse to recognize and deal with deepening problems in Japanese banks and chose instead to pursue aggressive fiscal consolidation. The Japanese recession that began in 1997 was mainly the consequence of this stupidity, the effect of which was seriously compounded by the onset of the Asian crisis. Fortunately, determined actions were eventually taken to restructure Japanese banks, and the much-sounder banking system that subsequently emerged supported the sustained economic expansion which followed the 2001 recession.

What is the current relevance of this Japanese experience? In Japan, we have recently seen a very deep recession, unlike the relatively mild Japanese recession of 1992–1993. Correspondingly, we should reasonably expect the Zarnowitz rule to apply now, even if it did not apply in Japan in the 1990s. Moreover, on this occasion, in contrast to the 1990s, Japanese banks are not suffering intense difficulties. Hence, the concern that financial-sector difficulties will forestall recovery, whatever its relevance elsewhere, is now not very relevant for Japan.

Two other cases that have attracted much attention are the financial crises in Sweden and Finland in the early 1990s. In both cases, excessive credit expansions that fueled unsustainable real estate booms played key roles in creating the conditions from which the crises ensued. The recessions that followed were deep and quite prolonged, beginning early in 1990 and extending through most of 1993. This was despite constructive measures taken at a relatively early stage — in comparison with the U.S. response to the savings and loan problems in the 1980s and Japan's dilatory response to the banking-sector problems in the 1990s — to correct problems in the financial sector. The suggestion is that these episodes point to the likelihood of a long recession and weak recovery from the present global recession.

This suggestion, however, is based on a misreading of the relevant economic history. The recessions in Sweden and Finland in the early 1990s were deep and prolonged because, as these economies were beginning to recover from the consequences of their domestic financial crises, they were hit with severe external economic shocks in 1991–1992. For Finland, the collapse of the Soviet empire brought a sharp drop in exports. For both Sweden and Finland, the linkage of their currencies to the Deutsche Mark through the Exchange Rate Mechanism (ERM) of the European Monetary Union compelled sharp increases in domestic interest rates, beginning in 1991, as the Bundesbank tightened German monetary policy to combat rising inflation in the aftermath of German unification. This situation was exacerbated during the ERM crisis, beginning in the spring of 1992 when efforts to defend exchange rate parities led to large increases in domestic interest rates, with the Swedish Riksbank pushing the overnight bank rate to 400% in September 1992. Exit from the ERM, exchange rate depreciation, and substantial easing of domestic short-term interest rates brought some relief to Finland and Sweden by late 1992, but the general recession in much of Western Europe that extended well into 1993 continued to weigh down on the Scandinavian economies.

There are many examples where deep recessions have been associated with important financial crises in emerging market economies, recently including Mexico in 1995; Indonesia, Malaysia, South Korea, and Thailand in 1997–1998; and Argentina in 2001. In all of these cases, financial-sector problems were deeply involved in the crises, with pre-existing financial-sector weaknesses often playing an important (if not dominant) causative role. In all of these cases, recovery was quite brisk once financial stability had been restored, but the financial sectors were not comprehensively restructured and restored to good health as precursors to economic recovery.

3. Availability of Adequate Financing

Beyond the general concern that continuing difficulties in the financial sector and the danger of renewed crisis will undermine prospects for even a moderately vigorous recovery, there is the more specific concern about the availability of financing for recovery. In particular, there have been complaints, especially in the United States, that large banks which have received substantial government support have not been expanding their lending. In my view, both these specific complaints and the more general concern about availability of financing are overdone.

Last autumn, after the collapse of Lehman Brothers, key global credit markets froze, and even the most creditworthy private borrowers as well as major banks could not obtain even short-term financing. The situation was very grave, and the possibility of a downward spiral of credit destruction and economic collapse, as occurred in the Great Depression, was very real. Governments and central banks recognized the threat, and acted quickly and vigorously to countervail it with massive support to financial institutions under pressure, broad guarantees of the liabilities of financial institutions, and direct lending into financial markets that had become dysfunctional. Disaster was averted, but significant economic damage was done, as reflected in the steep declines in economic activity late last year and early this year.

While massive contraction of bank credit was avoided, credit extended through financial markets in the form of asset-backed securities has suffered significant and sustained setbacks. Official efforts to rejuvenate these markets have so far met only partial success. Hence, greater reliance on bank credit would seem to be essential to finance an economic recovery. But, for the United States, total bank credit has been essentially flat since 2008 despite substantial reduction of financial market turmoil. Also, reports indicate that banks have been tightening their credit standards for existing and potential future borrowers. This raises the question: will the supply of bank credit be adequate to meet the needs of recovery?

The answer is, almost surely, yes. Focusing on the United States, it is essential to recognize that the failure of bank credit to expand over the past year (through end-June 2009) reflects a weakness in the demand for bank credit as well as constraints on supply. The demand for bank credit is presumably linked to nominal GDP and especially to some specific components of nominal GDP. During the year from mid-2008 to mid-2009, nominal GDP fell by US$354 billion or 2.4%, the first decline (lasting more than one quarter) in 55 years. The components of nominal GDP most closely related to credit demand showed particularly large declines. In nominal terms, residential investment was down US$148 billion; inventory investment was down US$126 billion;

business investment in equipment and software and in non-residential structures was down US$332 billion; and exports and imports, which both use considerable credit, were down US$409 billion and US$809 billion, respectively. In addition, the volume and value of existing home sales, where the mortgage taken out by the purchaser is typically larger than the one repaid by the seller, were down substantially. Mortgage refinancing enjoyed a rebound after the government and the Federal Reserve acted to depress mortgage interest rates for conventional loans, but with house prices down and still falling, money taken out in the new mortgage was — in contrast to previous refinancing booms — typically not much greater than the old mortgage. Thus, from the demand side, it is not surprising that there has not been much buoyancy in bank credit over the past year.

Looking ahead, it is inevitable that, in a moderately vigorous recovery where nominal GDP and its credit-intensive components are rising, the demand for credit will rise. What about the supply? Non-bank sources of credit are likely to remain constrained, so banks should be willing and able to fill in the gap. Official measures of the capital that banks require in order to expand lending are ample, and market measures of bank capital have improved considerably in recent months. Banks also have large liquid resources ready to fund expanded lending, notably in the form of about US$800 billion of excess reserves at the Federal Reserve. Banks earn an interest of only 0.25% on these excess reserves. As opportunities to lend to reasonably qualified borrowers at far higher interest rates (e.g., at a prime rate of 3.25%) expand during the recovery, banks will leap at the chance to expand their earnings at relatively low risk. This is the way in which banks with a legacy of bad assets typically earn their way out of trouble and into prosperity.

When one bank draws down its excess reserves to make new loans, most of these funds flow back into the reserves of the banking system (less a small fraction that drains into currency). Thus, aggregate excess reserves of US$800 billion potentially support expanded bank lending of many times that figure. Of course, if bank lending expands too much too fast, the Federal Reserve will, at some point, become concerned about the inflationary consequences and will rein in the process by contracting the asset side of its balance sheet (or by encouraging banks to hold onto excess reserves by raising the interest rate paid on such reserves). But, such monetary policy tightening will not occur at an early stage of the recovery. The Federal Reserve wants banks to expand their lending to support economic recovery, to fill gaps in financing created by the continuing impairment of markets for asset-backed credit instruments, and to take over much of the credit to the private sector recently extended by the government and the central bank.

This does not mean that we will soon return to the heady days of the credit boom that preceded the 2008–2009 recession. Some who easily obtained relatively cheap credit then will find that credit is more difficult (if not impossible) to obtain now, and the price of credit for those who get it will be higher (relative to the cost of funds to banks). Nevertheless, the supply of credit should be ample to support a moderately vigorous recovery. In particular, my recent forecast of a moderately vigorous recovery involving a 6.8% rise in U.S. real GDP between mid-2009 and end-2010 — about two thirds of the average strength of recoveries following the recessions of the 1950s–1980s — envisions increased lending to cover the following: (1) an increase in inventory investment to barely positive levels; (2) a rise in residential investment that regains about one-third of the decline since late 2005; (3) a rise in business fixed investment that is less than half of the decline during the recession; and (4) a rebound of sales of automobiles and light trucks by end-2010 to about 13 million units at an annual rate, still well below the 16+ million annual rate that characterized the years leading up to 2008. The U.S. financial system has both the means and the profit incentive to meet these rising credit demands.

For other countries, the story about the likely availability of adequate credit to support recovery varies somewhat from that of the United States, but the general conclusion is the same. A few small countries, such as tiny Iceland, will face prolonged processes of restoring their financial systems to reasonably good health, and economic recoveries may well suffer as a result. For the large advanced economies of Western Europe and Japan, and for most of the major emerging market economies, banking systems are in sufficiently good shape and/or enjoy sufficient official support such that adequate flows of new lending are likely to be available to meet rising demands for credit needed to sustain moderately vigorous recoveries.

4. The Long-Term Need for Deep Financial-Sector Reform

To be clear, the arguments just advanced are not intended to support the conclusion that further important reforms in the financial sector are not needed in the longer term to guard against the risk of future deep and damaging financial crises as well as against the financial excesses that often precede such crises. For this purpose, merely achieving a reasonable degree of stability in the financial sector is not nearly enough. Indeed, a clear danger is that the means of achieving this stability in the present episode, by providing massive bailouts to the financial sector through explicit government assistance and through disguised assistance in the form of exceptional easing of monetary policies, have seriously increased problems of moral hazard and substantially escalated risks of future and deeper crises. Such crises, however, are likely some distance down the road — after memories of the bitter experiences of the recent crisis fade. On the one hand, this is reassuring in suggesting that reasonably vigorous recovery need not be preceded by further deep reforms of the financial sector. On the other hand, it is worrying in implying that the political impetus to undertake necessary but controversial reforms may fade before the task is accomplished.

5. The Inherent Instability of Banking

To understand the need for deep reforms of the U.S. financial sector as an essential safeguard against future crises, it is important to recognize what economists since Adam Smith have well understood: banking, and market-based financial systems more generally, is inherently unstable.[1]

Banks and similar institutions live and earn profits based on a half-truth — that their liabilities can be consistently more liquid than their assets. Holders of bank liabilities value them more highly because of their supposed liquidity; that is, the ability to convert them rapidly, at low cost, and with substantial certainty of value, into the widely accepted medium of exchange. The classic fractional-reserve bank performs this magic by holding a small reserve of cash against a large volume of deposits and (in olden times) banknotes, and by promising to pay cash against these liabilities on demand or at short notice. Meanwhile, the bank makes a profit because it earns more on its relatively illiquid assets than it has to pay to holders of its supposedly liquid liabilities.

A modern financial conglomerate employs essentially the same principle of banking when it uses the "originate and distribute" model to sell

[1] I examine Adam Smith's thinking about banking and financial crises, and its relevance to recent events, in Mussa (2009).

packages of relatively illiquid financial claims to investors (perhaps including itself).[2] The liquidity of these packages is enhanced by the explicit or implicit promise that a ready market will be maintained, in which claims to these packages can be readily resold at low cost and with substantial certainty of value. The enhanced liquidity enables the originating institution to profit by selling the packages of illiquid assets for more than the prices at which these assets are acquired.

In a fractional-reserve banking system, the crunch comes when depositors fear that a bank is about to exhaust the cash available to meet incoming claims and a bank run ensues. A more general banking panic arises when it is feared that many banks may be falling into this situation — a circumstance that is likely to arise because the economic and financial conditions that weaken one bank are often reasonably suspected of weakening others. In a modern financial system, the same problem essentially arises when holders of supposedly liquid financial claims begin to doubt the value of the underlying assets and liquidity in the market for these claims suddenly dries up. When this happens in the market for one set of claims, holders of similar claims are likely to be alerted to the danger.

Inevitably, the crunch does come because this is an essential element of the mechanism that constrains what would otherwise become a completely undisciplined and unsustainable expansion of liquidity. Indeed, profit maximization requires that banks and bank-like institutions take on some risk that they will be unable to meet their commitments to maintain the liquidity of their liabilities. Especially for limited-liability corporations, the optimal level of such risk from the perspective of the bank or institution is necessarily positive. Accordingly, from time to time, this risk must materialize as holders of supposedly liquid claims run to cash them in before it is too late.

An individual bank or institution may survive a run by selling off some of its assets, perhaps at somewhat reduced prices, to other institutions with available cash. However, runs on individual institutions tend to occur when general economic conditions are weak and many financial institutions are under stress. Accordingly, many financial institutions become reluctant to release cash they may need for their own survival, and they may curtail their lending or even call in existing loans to raise

[2] James Tobin (1963) is particularly insightful in recognizing that money and banks are not unique, and that a broad array of financial instruments created by various financial institutions and markets share some of the essential features of money and banks.

cash. Thus, a run can turn into a general financial panic in which the prices of assets are driven down precipitously, some financial institutions and many non-financial businesses fail, and the economy falls into recession.

The damage done in such episodes typically spreads well beyond the financial institutions initially responsible for (what turns out to be) imprudent risk taking. Accordingly, public-sector interventions have appropriately been developed to help contain the risk of and damage from financial runs and panics. Such interventions, however, are generally not fully effective in overcoming the inherent instability of the financial system and often create other problems, including contributing to the dangers of financial crises.

6. Financial Repression, Financial Liberalization, and Moral Hazard

The inherent instability of banking is reflected in the long history of financial crises and related economic distress in the United States (and other countries) — a history that has featured important crises about once per decade, culminating in the Great Depression of the early 1930s. A regime of financial repression was adopted in the United States in the midst of the Great Depression, in response to public outrage about the malfunctioning of the financial system. Competition among banks was severely curtailed by limits on interest paid to depositors, restrictions on branching, and denial of most new banking licenses. Substantial barriers were erected between the activities permitted for commercial banks (e.g., taking deposits and making commercial loans primarily funded by these deposits) and other types of financial institutions, notably investment bankers who underwrote new securities issues and operated as broker-dealers in these securities.

The essential idea of this system of financial repression was that the core of the financial system — commercial banks which maintained the payments system and the essential flow of short-term credit — needed to be protected from potential disruption in a financial crisis. Thus, banks were allowed a protected domain of operation, in which they were virtually assured of earning modest profits but precluded from engaging in higher-risk activities that might generate higher rewards. Deposit insurance helped to stabilize the funding for banks by assuring most depositors that their funds were protected. If a bank got into difficulty, the market value of its franchise (which was reflected in its protected monopoly position) was generally sufficient to motivate a takeover of the troubled institution without significant cost to the government.

In contrast, investment bankers took on considerable risks from securities held in their investment and trading portfolios as well as from their activities as underwriters and broker-dealers. Sometimes they earned high returns, and sometimes they went bust — but without threatening the core of the financial system. Indeed, from the 1970s to the 1990s, a number of leading investment houses went under, including Drexel Burnham Lambert, which was driven out of business by the government. Investors in the securities underwritten by investment banks, unlike depositors in banks, were afforded no government guarantee of the value of their claims.

This regime of financial repression effectively suppressed financial crises for more than three decades from the mid-1930s through the 1960s, by far the longest period in U.S. history without a significant financial crisis. There was a significant cost, however, in terms of the efficiency of the financial sector, including low returns paid to bank depositors. This regime became increasingly distortionary and ultimately untenable as inflation accelerated in the late 1960s and 1970s. Financial repression was gradually relaxed from the mid-1960s through the 1990s both by explicit actions of financial deregulation (passed by Congress, implemented by the regulatory authorities, or decided by the courts) and by the powerful effects of financial innovation (enabled by rapidly advancing information processing and communication technologies). As a consequence, the efficiency of the financial sector was undoubtedly improved, but the risk of financial crises was also substantially increased. The latter effect was seriously augmented by egregious and, in many cases, self-interested misunderstandings of the risk taking that were being tolerated in the less regulated financial system and by the inevitable expansion of the role of public policies in providing support to troubled financial institutions.[3]

When substantial financial-sector problems did arise (in the mid-1970s, 1980s, and early 1990s), they were disguised by antiquated accounting practices that failed to recognize promptly substantial movements in the

---

[3] As discussed by Diaz-Alejandro (1985), there is a long history of cases where the relaxation of regimes of financial repression has been followed by financial crises. The United States has also had considerable experience with this phenomenon, as is discussed in a very entertaining way by Mayer (1997).

fair-market value of assets and liabilities on (and off) the balance sheets of financial institutions. When even these proved inadequate, new accounting gimmicks (e.g., "regulatory accounting principles" and "net worth certificates") were introduced to prolong the deception. In addition, monetary policy was used aggressively, on several critical occasions, to cut the cost of funds to financial institutions and install positively sloped yield curves to boost bank profitability — at the expense of the general public who held large volumes of short-term claims issued by banks and other financial institutions. Indeed, the present and former head of the Federal Reserve (as well as other Governors) affirmed the principle that monetary policy could and should be used to combat financial turbulence that was driving down asset prices, but it should never be used to attempt to forestall upsurges in asset prices that appeared likely to be unsustainable. Ultimately, in the extraordinary crisis of the autumn of 2008, when all of these indirect and disguised means of supporting the financial sector proved inadequate, direct transfers of capital from the government to threatened financial institutions became necessary — with, of course, the explanation that such actions were necessary to protect the economy and were not intended to benefit the shareholders or managers of particular institutions, including those whose imprudent risk taking had helped bring on the crisis.

Notwithstanding the truth of this last assertion, there can be no doubt that a system which allows core financial institutions to undertake substantial risks and predictably provides public support when these institutions come under stress will promote those activities that tend to generate such stress. This, of course, is the problem of "moral hazard".

7. The Investor of Last Resort

The fact that mechanisms of public support for financial institutions under stress inevitably generate some moral hazard is not sufficient reason to suppress all mechanisms. Up to a point, public support to financial institutions under stress, especially the "lender of last resort" function of central banks, is desirable to limit the risk of and damage from financial crises that arise out of the inherent instability of banking. The problem is that we have extended such mechanisms of support so far that costs of the moral hazard they generate threaten to overwhelm the good that they are supposed to do.

Indeed, the extension of mechanisms of public support may usefully be summarized in the notion that we have moved from using the central bank as the *lender* of last resort to calling upon the general public to serve involuntarily as the *investor* of last resort. The difference is that a lender of last resort provides funds to a distressed institution on the security of high-quality collateral and therefore undertakes little or no risk in providing the funds. In contrast, an investor of last resort provides funds that are substantially at risk if the recipient should prove incapable of repayment or effectively has no obligation to repay.

There are many ways in which the general public is called upon as the investor of last resort, including at least the following: (1) when the central bank forces short-term interest rates to very low levels during a financial crisis, allowing financial institutions to profit from very low-cost financing at the expense of the general public; (2) when the central bank absorbs the cost of support to financial institutions by providing credit on risky collateral without charging an adequate risk premium; (3) when the government or some public agency explicitly pays out funds to cover losses incurred by distressed institutions, including the use of tax breaks or other mechanisms to achieve this result; (4) when the government or some public agency provides capital to a distressed institution without charging an appropriate risk premium, including the provision of guarantees or the use of gimmicks such as "net worth certificates"; (5) when the government or the financial regulatory authorities allow financial institutions to operate with negative net worth on a fair-market accounting basis and thereby effectively supply public capital without charge; and (6) when the government or some public agency provides, or causes others to provide, valuable support that enables the debtors to financial institutions to make payments on these debts that otherwise might not be made.

In the present crisis, all of these mechanisms have been used and their cumulative use has been very substantial. The ultimate cost is not only the actual amount of explicit and implicit support provided, but also the likely economic damage from future financial crises that the provision of this support has made more likely.

8. The Fundamental Need for More Capital

How can the problem of the increased moral hazard created by the actions taken in this and earlier financial crises effectively be reduced? If we could move back to a regime of financial repression similar to that established during the Great Depression, we have good reason to believe that this would do it. However, due partly to enormous and irreversible advances in the information processing and communication technologies relevant to the financial services industry and to innovations in financial services themselves, there is no way realistically that we can go back to the 1930s or even the 1970s.

Too bad! It would be nice to redo the process of financial deregulation and get it right. This would require that significant restraints be re-imposed on the risk-taking activities of the core institutions of the financial system, and likewise that non-core institutions be effectively precluded from competing with core institutions in those activities essential to the functioning of the payments system (including the market for shorter-term commercial credit). For example, money market funds that compete directly with banks for transaction deposits and as sources of short-term commercial credit would be banned. Also, as under the Glass–Steagall Act, commercial banks at the core of the financial system (and their holding companies) would be excluded from many investment banking activities, including those pursued under the "originate and distribute" model which is effectively equivalent to securities underwriting performed by investment banks. Of course, this is not going to happen. Political opposition from the financial sector is too strong, and public outrage against the financial sector is not at the level reached in the calamity of the Great Depression.

Short of re-establishing a regime of mild but appropriate financial repression, two reforms are essential. First, core financial institutions whose continuous functioning is essential to the operation of the entire economy need to hold much more capital and need to be restrained from activities that put their capital at undue risk. Second, non-core financial institutions need to be effectively prevented from taking on too large a role in the essential functions of core institutions, unless they too satisfy the capital requirements and other key safeguards imposed on core institutions.

In considering the key issue of how much capital core financial institutions should normally hold, it is important to keep in mind four fundamental points. First, the capital of banks and other financial institutions is risk-absorbing, but not resource-using. Bank capital is not a factor of production like machinery, factories, or houses. Augmenting bank capital does not require a sacrifice of real resources that might be used for other productive purposes. Additions to bank capital are not part of gross private domestic investment recorded in the national income and product accounts. Instead, bank capital, like the equity of businesses more generally, corresponds to the commitment of its owners to absorb any losses from the bank's operations after payment of the claims of the bank's creditors, up to the level of that capital, in exchange for the right to accrue gains from the bank's operations after the payment of creditors. Thus, bank capital can be expanded without curtailing in any way the physical capital devoted to economic production. Indeed, bank capital (like the equity capital more generally) appears on the liability side of the balance sheet, along with the claims of the bank's creditors (depositors and others). Holding the assets of a bank constant, raising bank capital simply involves issuing more equity and correspondingly reducing the level of bank debt. There is no effect on the allocation of the economy's real productive resources entailed in such an operation.

Second, the owners of bank capital and bank managers are, of course, concerned about the amount of capital that a bank holds. For a bank to be profitable, it must earn more on its assets (and from various fees) than it pays to its creditors (and spends on its operations). Ignoring the income from fees and the costs of operating the bank, the spread between the interest paid to bank creditors and the return earned on bank assets, divided by the amount of bank capital, determines the rate of return to the owners of bank capital. Holding the spread constant (at a positive level), a higher leverage ratio — the ratio of credit to capital on the liability side of the balance sheet — implies a higher expected rate of return on bank capital. Hence, there appears to be a strong incentive toward higher leverage and less capital relative to assets and to credit liabilities.

Third, this appearance of a strong incentive for high leverage and low capital is somewhat deceptive, but nevertheless very important. Presumably, it should operate in the same way and to a similar extent for all businesses. But, most non-financial businesses avoid high leverage and maintain substantial equity capital. This is because higher leverage generally implies not only a higher expected return for equity owners, but also higher risk. Also, higher leverage generally means that creditors are exposed to greater risk and, accordingly, demand higher interest rates for the credit they supply. These normal forces operating against excessive leverage and low capital, however, do not function with their normal effectiveness for financial institutions, especially large, systemically critical institutions whose liabilities are perceived to be at least partially guaranteed by the government. Insured depositors and many other creditors of banks and some other financial institutions know that when trouble comes, the government is likely to step in and shield them from at least an important part of their potential losses, especially in circumstances of general financial stress. This is exactly what happened — on a grand scale — in the recent crisis, and it is reasonable for people to assume that it would happen again in any similar crisis.

Fourth, contrary to the general presumption that competition is good, the effect of competition among banks and similar financial institutions is to exacerbate the problem of excessive leverage and too little capital. When banks have an important degree of monopoly power, as tends to be the case under regimes of financial repression, they have an interest to protect their monopoly rents by avoiding excessive leverage. In contrast, when competition among banks is fairly intense, a bank that refuses to use high leverage must either suffer a lower expected return on its equity capital and/or raise its spreads and give up a great deal of business to its competitors. Moreover, when most banks are competing and using high leverage, the likelihood of government support for bank creditors generally goes up because, if one bank gets into trouble, most other banks are likely not to be far behind. This phenomenon was clearly revealed in the crisis of last autumn.

9. An Adequate Level of Bank Capital

Given the powerful incentives that banks have to use high leverage and hold too little capital, how may we judge the appropriate level of bank capital from a public policy perspective? A credible answer is that, taking account of the risks to which banks are exposed (on and off the balance sheet as well as with their liabilities and assets), banks should normally be required to hold at least twice as much capital as has been the case over the past 40 years. The argument for this conclusion is straightforward.[4]

---

[4] Unfortunately, the question of how to impose more rigorous capital standards at the technical level is not straightforward. It is clear that capital standards, such as those of Basel I and Basel II, which focus exclusively on the asset side of the balance sheet are idiocy. Capital standards that rely heavily on historical-cost accounting have proven highly unsatisfactory. But, capital standards that rely exclusively on mark-to-market accounting would likely exacerbate financial-sector instability. A mixed approach, which looks at both assets and liabilities and which guards against serious insolvencies on a mark-to-market basis, is needed. The capital standards and associated accounting rules should allow for the possibility that, in extreme crisis situations, financial institutions would be allowed to continue operating even if full valuation of their on- and off-balance-sheet assets and liabilities on a mark-to-market basis revealed technical insolvency. The option of allowing systemically important financial institutions to continue to operate when insolvent on a mark-to-market basis, however, should not be exercised on a regular basis once every decade or so.

On four occasions in the past 40 years, systemically important U.S. financial institutions have operated in situations where their equity capital, evaluated on the basis of fair-market accounting, has been significantly negative. This happened during the recessions and financial turbulence of 1974–1975, 1980–1982, 1990–1991, and 2008–2009. On the first three of these occasions, and very likely on the fourth, the combination of public support and, ultimately, economic recovery avoided outright bankruptcy of most of the institutions that became temporarily insolvent on a fair-market valuation basis. However, while catastrophe was avoided, the costs to the public were substantial, including, for example, the cost of cleaning up the savings and loan mess.

More importantly, the economic damage that can be done when key financial institutions become even temporarily insolvent on a fair-market basis is very great. In the deep recessions of the mid-1970s and early 1980s, severe distress in the financial sector (which was not accurately reflected in the accounting values of bank balance sheets) contributed to the depth of the economic downturns. In the recovery from the relatively mild recession of 1990–1991, "headwinds" arising from continuing weaknesses in the banking sector were often cited as a reason for the relatively sluggish economic recovery. In the crisis of last autumn, when serious doubts arose about the solvency of key financial institutions on a fair-market basis, credit markets froze and economic activity plummeted, creating the deepest global recession of the postwar era. The fact that official accounting statements showed that most key financial institutions were substantially solvent was not particularly reassuring until governments and central banks demonstrated that they were prepared to back these evaluations with whatever amount of cash might be needed.

Surely, this is not an experience that we want to repeat very often. The essential protection against this possibility is a level of bank capital sufficiently high in normal times so that bank capital measured on a fair-market basis does not go negative, even in times of substantial financial and economic stress such as that associated with postwar U.S. recessions. Levels of capital normally held by key financial institutions in recent decades have fallen far short of this standard.

Indeed, there is a strong argument that core financial institutions should normally have capital well in excess of the level needed to absorb declines in the fair-market value of their equity in a deep crisis. The reason is that we require these institutions to be able to support recovery from a deep crisis. They are not in a sound position to accomplish this unless they have substantial capital remaining after absorbing the effects of a deep crisis. As I used to explain this issue to my MBA students in classes on money and banking, the logic here is essentially the same as the logic governing the size of our nuclear retaliatory force: not only must it be sufficiently large to inflict unacceptable damage on an enemy who might attack us, but it must also be sufficiently large and well protected so that it can absorb the enemy's first strike and still be able to inflict unacceptable damage on the enemy.

References

Bernanke, B. S. (2000). *Essays on the Great Depression.* Princeton, NJ: Princeton University Press.

Diaz-Alejandro, C. (1985). Good-bye financial repression, hello financial crash. *Journal of Development Economics*, 19, 1–24.

Friedman, M. and A. J. Schwartz (1963). *A Monetary History of the United States.* Princeton, NJ: Princeton University Press (for the National Bureau of Economic Research).

Mayer, M. (1997). *The Bankers: The Next Generation.* New York: Truman Talley Books/Dutton.

Mussa, M. (2009). Adam Smith and the political economy of a modern financial crisis. *Business Economics*, 44(1), 3–16.

Tobin, J. (1963). Commercial banks as creators of "money". Reprinted in Tobin, J. (1971), *Essays in Economics, Vol. 1: Macroeconomics*, Chicago: Markham Publishing Co.

What Broke? The Root Causes of the Crisis

Edwin M. Truman*
Peterson Institute for International Economics

It is a pleasure to participate once again in an International Banking Conference at the Federal Reserve Bank of Chicago.

Charles Calomiris wrote in his chapter, "It is ... important, in the interest of shaping desirable reform, to get our story straight about what happened to cause the recent crisis" (see p. 74 of this book). I agree, and would add that doing so is equally important with respect to other lessons that should affect policies but might not necessarily rise to the level of reforms requiring Congressional action (for example, monetary policy).

There is no paucity of potential candidates as root causes of the crisis of 2007–2009. The number is probably larger than the 4 or 5 presented in the Calomiris chapter, or the 4 or 5 largely implicit in the Mussa chapter, and less than the 10 or 12 presented in the Baily–Elliott chapter. However, the intersection of these lists of causes is essentially a null set, aside from a common theme of the housing boom.

These observations illustrate the reality that even today, more than two years after this crisis broke in August 2007, there is no agreement about its root causes. This is unfortunate if we want to learn the lessons and apply them in policy reforms, but it gives me free rein in my commentary.

Conventionally, the identified causes of the global financial crisis that has affected the world economy and financial system for two-plus years fall into four broad categories:

(1) Failures of macroeconomic policies, which have three subcategories — monetary and fiscal policies, global imbalances, and the housing boom;

---

* Edwin M. Truman is a senior fellow at the Peterson Institute for International Economics.

(2) Failures of financial-sector supervision and regulatory policies and practices, which have innumerable subcategories;
(3) Excesses of poorly understood financial engineering innovations, which have several subcategories; and
(4) Excesses (or imprudence) of large private financial institutions, in particular those with a global reach.

In the first category (macroeconomic policies), Calomiris includes lax U.S. monetary policy and global imbalances that flattened the U.S. yield curve. Baily and Elliott largely absolve Federal Reserve policies, but do not absolve global imbalances; they also include government policies that encouraged a boom in housing construction. Mussa is less explicit under the macroeconomic heading. Mussa does not absolve the Federal Reserve and other central banks, but his only mention of global imbalances is to note that the U.S. imbalance was declining in advance of the crisis; he mentions housing as well.

In the second category (financial supervision and regulation), Calomiris includes four items: (1) U.S. government policies to promote subprime risk taking, (2) excessive reliance on credit rating agencies, (3) U.S. "too big to fail" policies, and (4) U.S. government policies to limit stock ownership. The chapter is unclear about the relevance of the fourth item, but I assume he is hinting at a limitation on outside influence on corporate governance.

Baily and Elliott agree on the first two of Calomiris' items, but as far as I could tell they do not agree on the third and fourth items. They add, by my count, five items in this category: (1) a general erosion of lending and regulatory standards, (2) flaws in the "originate and distribute" model, (3) lack of a U.S. comprehensive supervisory system, (4) mark-to-market accounting, and (5) inadequate capital cushions.

Mussa focuses explicitly on the "too big to fail" policies in his concern about moral hazard in the wake of the crisis and implicitly as a contributor to the crisis, but I suspect that his indictment is not fully consistent with that of Calomiris. He also, in passing, refers to financial excesses. However, he basically traces the causes of the financial crisis to the business cycle and to financial-sector developments over several decades that got ahead of the regulators.

In the third category (financial engineering), Calomiris includes the liquidity risk and complexity associated with new instruments that added uncertainty to the system. Baily and Elliott do not entirely disagree, but they point to three specific items: (1) the new securitization model, (2) excessive leverage, and (3) credit insurance. Mussa does not mention this category beyond a few oblique hints.

In the final category (behavior of large financial institutions), Calomiris as well as Baily and Elliott are together in citing poor risk management practices, but do not entirely agree on the reasons. Mussa shares the view that imprudent risk taking was involved. For the record, Calomiris pays more attention to compensation policies and practices; the word "compensation" does not appear in the first part of the Baily–Elliott chapter or in Mussa's chapter.

In the context of an international banking conference, my major criticism of these analyses, with the limited exception of Mussa's chapter, is that they treat what is clearly a global financial (and economic) crisis as if it were solely a U.S. event caused by U.S. regulatory and policy failures. Much of the rest of the world would like to believe that we deserve all of the blame for the crisis. Perhaps we do, but being the epicenter is not the same as being the sole cause. I remain to be convinced that policies in the rest of the world were irrelevant to the crisis.

Baily and Elliott do note that housing prices rose rapidly in many countries and state that this fact points to a global driver of what happened, which they hint had something to do with low interest rates. However, when they come to discussing low interest rates, they do not blame the Federal Reserve (or other central banks). They do cite global imbalances, but only in connection with flattening the U.S. yield curve. Moreover, the drivers of the U.S. crisis in the Baily–Elliott list of causes, as well as in the Calomiris list, are almost exclusively U.S.-centric in that other jurisdictions did not share most of the shortcomings that they identify, such as the tax deductibility of mortgage interest payments.

So what do I think? What is my narrative for the root causes of the crisis? In my view, macroeconomic policies in the United States and the rest of the fully developed world were — to a substantial degree, much more than in the conventional stories — jointly responsible for the crisis, though they had help from supervisory sins (largely of omission).

In the United States, fiscal policy contributed to a decline in the U.S. savings rate and monetary policy was too easy for too long, fueling the global credit boom. In Japan, the mix of monetary and fiscal policies distorted the global economy and financial system; monetary policy was too easy for too long, also fueling the global credit boom. Many other countries also had very easy monetary policies in recent years, including other

Asian countries, energy and commodity exporters, and, in effective terms, a number of countries within the euro area as well as the United Kingdom and Switzerland.

The impressive accumulation of foreign exchange reserves by many countries distorted the international adjustment process, and took some pressure off the macroeconomic policies of the United States and other countries. However, I am in the minority of economists who believe that the phenomenon of global imbalances played little or no role in causing the economic and financial crisis. Instead, the imbalances and the crisis were jointly caused by flaws in the design and implementation of macroeconomic policies and the resulting global credit boom.

I do not have the time to argue this point in great detail, but I would cite two facts. First, we have had at least two other periods of large global imbalances, in the late 1970s and 1980s, but they did not lead to financial excesses at all like those we have experienced. Second, the "global savings glut" hypothesis is a flawed analysis not only because it was really a global investment dearth, as was demonstrated by International Monetary Fund (IMF) staff at the time, but also because the analysis focused, in its simplest form, on net inflows and gross official inflows. The reality is that from 2002 to 2007, on average, official inflows to the United States were less than 25% of total gross inflows. The peak years were 2003 at 32% and 2004 at 26% — before the boom year of 2005. Moreover, the Chinese current account surpluses (the net flow to the rest of the world, which is the relevant metric in terms of the savings glut) were only US$69 billion and US$161 billion in 2004 and 2005, respectively; the rest of China's reserve accumulation in gross terms amounted to a recycling of capital inflows. The net savings from China amounted to about 3% of net global savings in the latter year.[1] It is a stretch to think that a flow of net savings of this size added significant downward pressure on the U.S. and other yield curves around the world that could not have been resisted by central banks.

Baily and Elliott are careful not to blame the foreigners for our problems, which is more than I can say for many other U.S. observers and officials past and present. However, their basic argument, and that of Calomiris, about the influence of capital inflows, though common in the

[1] Gross global savings in 2005 was US$10.4 trillion, based on the IMF's World Economic Outlook (WEO) database. Assuming generously that net global savings was half that amount produces a figure for the share of China's current account surplus in net savings of 3.1%.

literature, lacks a factual or analytical base. We do not know what would have happened if global imbalances had been smaller, but the presumption is that U.S. interest rates would have been higher, starting with the federal funds rate. It follows, I would think, that if the foreigners can push U.S. interest rates down or up, the Federal Reserve should have been able to push them up as well.

We had a global credit boom. Monetary policies have something to do with credit booms, with the size of balance sheets, and with "aggregate liquidity" in the Baily–Elliott terminology. The credit boom did not just fuel a housing boom in the United States, but also housing booms in many other countries, some to a greater extent than in the United States. However, in addition to housing booms, the credit boom fueled increases in the prices of equities and many other manifestations of financial excess. We are not talking here about pricking "bubbles"; we are talking about fueling a global credit boom and about the associated pricing of risk.

Financial-sector supervision and regulation, or the lack thereof, also played a role in the crisis. But, the many sins of omission and few sins of commission were committed over several decades, not primarily during the past 10 years. As is reported in the Mussa chapter, they started in the 1960s. Moreover, without the benign economic and financial conditions that prevailed in the wake of the dot-com boom and the associated belief that "this time it is different", this crisis would have taken a different form. Benign conditions lead to lax lending and credit standards, just as night follows day, as Calomiris hints. In principle, financial-sector supervision could have helped to curb the excesses, but it did not do so in the United States or in many other countries around the world.

In some cases, including importantly the United States in this regard but also elsewhere, regulation and supervision were incomplete. The rise of what is now known as the "shadow financial system" had been going on for decades in many countries; this included non-bank financial institutions such as money market mutual funds, special-purpose investment vehicles, hedge funds, private equity firms, etc. In many cases, these entities were highly leveraged and/or used short-term funding to finance longer-term investments, contributing to Mussa's "inherent instabilities". We saw a gradual shift in financial intermediation from traditional banks to other types of financial institutions that were less well capitalized and subject to less close supervision. Traditional banks gradually, but radically, transformed their business models in order to compete with the less-regulated institutions. The global financial system thus became overleveraged, particularly but not exclusively the U.S. financial system. When confidence finally and fully drained from the system a year ago, funding dried up and financial institutions collapsed.

New forms of financial engineering were part of the story, but innovations have been a feature of domestic and international finance for decades. In many cases, the associated innovations were poorly understood, resulting in a failure of risk recognition, which is a necessary precondition for good risk management. Financial engineering helped to distort incentives facing financial institutions and contributed to the market dynamics once the crisis got underway, but it was not a cause (let alone a major root cause) of the crisis.

Finally, on the imprudence of large private financial institutions, in particular those with a global reach, we can agree that they were imprudent in many dimensions. Size has been a problem, and complexity has led to some decisions to rescue particular institutions in whole or in part. However, the global scope of the operations of these institutions was not a major contributing factor to the crisis *per se*.

Thus, in my view, the two major sources of the global financial crisis of 2007–2009 were failures in macroeconomic policies and in financial supervision and regulation. I would assign principal blame to failures in macroeconomic policies by a small margin, which is more blame than is assigned by most observers, including the four authors on which I am commenting. I do not see this as inconsistent with the view that there were structural flaws in national and global financial regulatory and supervisory systems, which had been building for years and should be addressed in the wake of the crisis. It may well be that a crisis of this magnitude was necessary to uncover those flaws. Whether they would have been revealed without the macroeconomic failures is at least a debatable question.

I would like to offer one final thought in which I draw upon my three-plus decades of experience with financial crises in this country and around the world. The only other global economic and financial crisis of the post-World War II period was the crisis in the early 1980s, centered on 1982. That crisis was also, in many respects, made in the United States. U.S. macroeconomic policy mistakes produced a rip-roaring inflation and an extended period of negative real short-term and long-term U.S. dollar interest rates that fueled a global credit boom, in particular credit to emerging market economies. The Federal Reserve finally began to address the U.S. inflation problem in late 1979. We had a brief six-month recession associated with a flirtation with credit controls. The recession was followed by a brief 12-month recovery and expansion, before we plunged back into a recession in mid-1981 that lasted 16 months.[2] The U.S. recession of 1981–1982 coincided with a global recession centered on 1982, with global growth that year of less than 1%.

1982 was the year in which the global debt crisis broke out. The debt crisis was a consequence of the reversal of U.S. financial conditions from negative real interest rates to positive rates — macroeconomic causes — and the excesses of international bank lending in originating loans and syndicating them to smaller banks around the world. By the end of 1982, most international banks in the United States and other major industrial countries were insolvent on a mark-to-market basis. However, at the time, the secondary market in sovereign loans was fortunately underdeveloped. In the wake of the debt crisis, blame was heaped upon the international banks for causing the crisis through their reckless lending. A number of reforms were instituted, including the U.S. requirement that syndication fees be spread over the life of loans as well as the Basel I capital standards which were agreed later in the decade.

Thus, in many respects, the crisis of the early 1980s was a lot like this crisis, including the fact that the global financial system was blamed for the crisis and came under tremendous strain. Its causes included principally a volatile mix of macroeconomic as well as financial supervisory and regulatory components.

---

[2] It is likely that the National Bureau of Economic Research (NBER) will date this recession as only slightly longer, perhaps 18 months from December 2007 to June 2009.

III. CONTAINING A SYSTEMIC CRISIS: IS THERE REALLY NO PLAYBOOK?

Regulating Systemic Risk

Masahiro Kawai*
Asian Development Bank Institute

Michael Pomerleano
World Bank

1. Introduction

With a few notable exceptions, central bankers, financial supervisors/regulators, other policymakers, international organizations, the private sector, and academic economists failed to predict the current global financial crisis and underestimated its severity. Such a dramatic failure of the entire financial community warrants soul searching: is it possible to prevent a systemic crisis? In this paper, we argue that this is indeed possible and that the best way to prevent a financial crisis is to identify and act on systemic risk or sources of financial instability.

Using a new database, developed by Laeven and Valencia (2008), on the occurrence of systemic banking crises and policy responses to resolve them, one can see that all of the crises have two elements in common. First, virtually all of the countries that suffered a crisis had made serious policy mistakes and accumulated significant structural vulnerabilities and financial imbalances. Second, in virtually all instances, the crisis was slow to unfold and could have been "spotted" in its early stages and managed better. In all instances, there were underlying vulnerabilities. The financial markets were very forgiving and often provided policymakers

* Masahiro Kawai is Dean of the Asian Development Bank Institute; Michael Pomerleano is an Advisor at the World Bank. The authors are thankful to Charles Calomiris, David Mayes, Larry Wall, and other conference participants for comments, and to Barnard Helman for excellent editorial assistance. The findings, interpretations, and conclusions expressed in the paper are entirely those of the authors and do not necessarily represent the views of the Asian Development Bank, its Institute, the World Bank, their respective executive directors, or the countries they represent.

with the benefit of doubt. When it became obvious that policymakers were unable or unwilling to address the underlying problems, the financial markets were damaged by a loss of confidence, which eventually led to crises.

The devastating global financial crisis of 2007–2009 offers a set of initial lessons. The new lessons learned are more substantial than those learned in the past, as what were considered as the best financial systems — those of the U.S., the U.K., and continental Europe — all went wrong. The objective of this paper is to explore how to spot signs of systemic risk and prevent a financial crisis. We argue that an effective framework for systemic stability regulation should be established in each country, but that such a national effort would not be sufficient without the U.S. and the U.K. — hosts to global financial centers and where the crisis originated — making a full political commitment to systemic stability regulation.

The paper is organized as follows. In Section 2, we discuss the importance of crisis prevention and argue that effective macroprudential supervision — a "top-down" approach, complemented by "bottom-up" microprudential supervision — can effectively spot and prevent crises. In Section 3, we provide basic principles in establishing a systemic financial regulator from the perspectives of objectives and mandates, resources, implementation, and structure. Section 4 reviews recent reform proposals considered nationally and internationally to address systemic risk, and recommends that each country create a framework for systemic stability regulation or even an independent financial stability regulator. Section 5 concludes with recommendations for future action.

2. Importance of Crisis Prevention

2.1 *Policy mistakes behind the global financial crisis*

The root cause of the global financial crisis of 2007–2009 can be traced back to the build-up of excessive optimism — created by a long period of worldwide high economic growth, low real interest rates, and subdued volatility of financial prices — as well as the flood of liquidity. With these benign macroeconomic and financial environments, investors around the world were prompted to search for yield and underestimated the risks of investment, especially those in new financial products. From this perspective, the International Monetary Fund (IMF) (2009a) summarizes causes of the global financial crisis in three dimensions: flaws in financial regulation and supervision, failure of monetary policy to address the build-up of systemic risk, and a weak global financial architecture.

2.1.1 *Flaws in financial regulation and supervision*

Several excellent reviews of what went wrong in financial regulation (Group of Thirty, 2009; Brunnermeier *et al.*, 2009; de Larosière Group, 2009) point to the fact that there were regulatory and supervisory deficiencies, including inadequate macroprudential supervision. Essentially, national financial regulators and supervisors failed to see the large build-up of systemic risks. In the U.S., the regulatory and supervisory framework was highly fragmented, and its scope was narrowly focused on insured deposit-taking institutions and did not cover all financial activities that posed economy-wide risks. As a result, the "shadow banking system" grew among investment banks, mortgage brokers and originators, special investment vehicles, insurance companies, and other private asset pools, as they had long been lightly regulated by a patchwork of agencies and were generally not supervised prudentially.[1]

Due to the propensity to focus on individual institutions, supervisors around the world failed to recognize interconnections and links across financial firms, sectors, and markets. Because of the lack of a macroprudential approach, supervisors only focused on their own piece of the puzzle, overlooking the larger problem. Shin (2009) points out a fallacy of aggregation: "mis-educated" supervisors and examiners were focused on individual institutions, without regard to the impact on the system. There is thus a growing realization that a macroprudential approach to supervision and an effective systemic stability regulator are needed to complement microprudential measures.

---

[1] Tobias and Shin (2008) estimate that the shadow banking system was as large as US$10.5 trillion, comprising US$4 trillion in assets of the large investment banks, US$2.5 trillion in overnight repos, US$2.2 trillion in structured investment vehicles, and another US$1.8 trillion in hedge fund assets. This should be compared with the US$10 trillion in assets held in the conventional U.S. banking system, which meant that system leverage was at least double what was reported.

2.1.2 *Failure of monetary policy to contain financial imbalances*

The latest IMF analysis points to "macroeconomic policies, which did not take into account building systemic risks" and states that "a key failure during the boom was the inability to spot the big picture threat of a growing asset price bubble" (IMF, 2009b). Clearly, the U.S. Federal Reserve underestimated the build-up of financial imbalances coming from housing price bubbles, high leverage of financial institutions, and interconnections between financial markets. In addition, Taylor (2009) argues that the Federal Reserve policies brought excessive liquidity and low interest rates to the U.S. and that the federal funds rate was kept too low for too long, fueling the housing boom and other economic imbalances. The Federal Reserve may well have assumed that, even if the asset price boom collapsed, the impacts on the financial system and the economy could be mitigated by lower interest rates.[2]

In theory, tighter prudential regulation could have been mobilized to contain systemic risk; but in practice, before the authorities realized it, huge systemic risks had accumulated below the regulators' radar in the shadow banking system. Given the failure of prudential supervisory action to prevent a build-up of systemic risk, the central bank — as a macro-supervisor — should have reacted to credit booms, rising leverage, sharp asset price increases, and the build-up of systemic vulnerabilities by adopting tighter monetary policy.

2.1.3 *Weak global financial architecture*

There were also deficiencies in the global financial architecture — the official structure that facilitates global financial stability and the smooth flow of goods, services, and capital across countries. There are three issues.

First, global institutions — like the IMF, the Bank for International Settlements, and the Financial Stability Forum — failed to conduct effective macroeconomic and financial surveillance of systemically important economies. That is, they did not clearly identify the emerging systemic

---

[2] Wessel (2009) provides a well-documented and insightful account of the thinking of U.S. policymakers during the crisis. The inescapable conclusion is that, for a long time after the start of the crisis, central bankers — Bernanke, King, Trichet, and their colleagues — did not see the crisis coming and for too long ignored the advice of those who did.

risk in the U.S., the U.K., and the euro area; send clear warnings to policymakers; or provide practical policy advice on concrete measures to reduce the systemic risk.[3] Their analysis clearly underestimated the looming risk in the shadow banking system; interconnections across financial institutions, markets, and countries; and global macroeconomic-financial links.

Second, there was considerable discussion of global payments imbalances during 2002–2007. The IMF in particular warned repeatedly, especially through the newly established multilateral consultation process, that global imbalances posed a serious risk to global financial stability. However, the global imbalance discussion may have diverted policymakers' attention away from U.S. domestic financial imbalances, the risk of U.S. dollar collapse, and the need to revalue the Chinese currency.

Third, the crisis has revealed the ineffectiveness of fragmented international arrangements for the regulation, supervision, and resolution of internationally active financial institutions. The problem became particularly acute when such institutions showed signs of failing. Although home-country authorities are mainly responsible for resolving insolvent institutions, host-country authorities were often quick to ring-fence assets in their jurisdictions because of the absence of clear international rules governing burden-sharing mechanisms for losses due to failure of financial firms with cross-border operations.

2.2 *Principles of crisis containment*

The most fundamental approach to a financial crisis should be to prevent one from taking place in the first place. Once a crisis breaks out, however, efficient crisis management and resolution policies become important.

The key principle should be that crisis prevention is better than cure. This entails the prevention or mitigation of the build-up of vulnerabilities

---

[3] The IMF (2009a) admits that "official warnings both within and outside the Fund were insufficiently specific, detailed, or dire to gain traction with policymakers." IMF surveillance often echoed the conventional view that advanced countries, such as the U.S. and the U.K., with relatively low stable inflation together with profitable and well-capitalized banking sectors could withstand the unwinding of the bubble in housing and capital markets.

that could lead to systemic risk and, eventually, a financial crisis. The major preventive mechanisms should include (1) the establishment of effective regulation and supervision that monitors and acts on economy-wide systemic risk; (2) a sound macroeconomic management framework (for monetary, fiscal, and exchange rate policies) that can counteract the build-up of systemic vulnerabilities such as asset price bubbles; and (3) the creation of a strong international financial architecture that can send pointed early warnings and induce effective international policy coordination to reduce systemic risk internationally. In the prevention exercise, the macroprudential approach is becoming increasingly important.

Once a financial crisis breaks out, it is necessary to adopt comprehensive policy measures so that the crisis does not magnify or prolong itself. Crisis management tools include (1) the provision of timely and adequate liquidity; (2) rigorous examination of financial institutions' balance sheets, including thorough stress tests; (3) support for viable but ailing financial institutions through guarantees, non-performing loan removal, and recapitalization; and (4) the adoption of appropriate macroeconomic policies to mitigate the adverse feedback loop between the financial sector and the real economy, reflecting the specific conditions and reality of the economy. An important challenge is how to ensure that such management policies do not create moral hazard problems.

Finally, if a financial crisis evolves into a full-blown economic crisis, with systemic damages to the financial, corporate, and household sectors, it is vital to quickly resolve the problem. Crisis resolution measures include (1) the use of mechanisms for restructuring financial institutions' impaired assets and, hence, corporate and household debt; (2) the use of well-functioning domestic insolvency procedures for non-viable financial institutions; and (3) the use of international mechanisms for resolving non-viable, internationally active financial institutions, including clear burden-sharing mechanisms. Without a clearly defined regime for the resolution of financial institutions domestically and internationally, the crisis management process can create international conflict, such as ring-fencing of foreign bank assets.

It is noted that the nature of a crisis resolution mechanism affects crisis management policies and the degree of moral hazard for financial institutions. Later in this chapter, we summarize the discussion by arguing that a systemic stability regulator with sufficient powers should be established at the national level that focuses on all three dimensions: crisis prevention, management, and resolution. Given that the role of the global stability regulator — the IMF and the Financial Stability Board (FSB) — may be limited, the role of a national stability regulator will be critical.

2.3 *Macroeconomic and financial surveillance and macroprudential supervision*

Several excellent reports that have addressed the need to improve financial regulation and supervision from systemic perspectives agree on the following[4]: the financial regulatory frameworks around the world have paid too little attention to systemic risk; current financial regulations have tended to encourage procyclical risk taking, which increases the likelihood of financial crises and their severity when they occur; and current regulations do not deal adequately with large, complex financial institutions — financial intermediaries engaged in some combination of commercial banking, investment banking, asset management, and insurance — whose failure poses a systemic risk or externality to the financial system as a whole (Haldane, 2009). They also point to the danger induced by implicit "too big to fail" or "too interconnected to fail" problems.

The traditional bottom-up supervision addressing the soundness of individual institutions is founded on the assumption that making each bank safe will make the whole system safe. The focus on individual institutions and the inadequate attention paid to the overall system evident in this approach explains how global finance has become so ripe for contagion without sounding regulatory alarms. Crisis prevention necessitates taking a macroprudential approach to complement the existing microprudential supervisory rules.

To understand the nature of macroprudential supervision, it is useful to consider the examples of a broad agenda to address systemic risk, outlined by Bernanke (2009) and Tarullo (2009). Box 1 lists a set of issues that effective supervisors and regulators should bear in mind. In our view, the financial stability monitoring agenda summarized in Box 1 might be suited to the U.S., but it is too narrow for emerging market economies. The objects of systemic oversight should be broader, including the corporate and household sectors as well as macroeconomic elements (such as capital flows and external debt).

---

[4] These include the Volcker recommendations in the Group of Thirty (2009) report; the 11th Geneva Report on the World Economy (Brunnermeier *et al.*, 2009); the de Larosière Group (2009) report on financial supervision and stability in the European Union; and papers by a group from New York University's Stern School (Acharya and Richardson, 2009).

Box 1: Agenda to Address Systemic Risk

- Undertake consolidated supervision of all systemically important financial firms;
- Monitor large or rapidly increasing exposures, such as exposure to subprime mortgages, across firms and markets rather than only at the level of individual firms or sectors;
- Assess the potential systemic risks implied by evolving risk management practices, broad-based increases in financial leverage, or changes in financial markets or products;
- Analyze possible spillovers between financial firms or between firms and markets, such as the mutual exposures of highly interconnected firms;
- Ensure that each systemically important firm receives oversight commensurate with the risks that its failure would pose to the financial system;
- Provide a resolution mechanism to safely wind down failing, systemically important institutions, such as the development of an orderly resolution of systemically important non-bank financial firms;
- Assign uniform and robust authority for the prudential supervision of systemically important payment and settlement systems to ensure that the critical financial infrastructure — including the institutions which support trading, payments, clearing, and settlement — is robust, such as arrangements for clearing and settling credit default swaps (CDS) and other over-the-counter (OTC) derivatives;
- Mitigate procyclical features of capital regulation and other rules and standards;
- Identify possible regulatory gaps, including gaps in the protection of consumers and investors that pose risks for the system as a whole;
- Limit the risk of sudden stops in capital flows triggering an exchange rate correction with adverse impacts on banks, households, and corporations with large unhedged liabilities;

(*Continued*)

Box 1: (*Continued*)

- Share findings in a regional and global stability forum; and
- Issue periodic reports on the stability of the financial system, in order to ensure market discipline through transparency and informed debate.

Source: Bernanke (2009) and Tarullo (2009).

Essentially, the aim of macroprudential supervision is to preserve systemic financial stability by identifying vulnerabilities in a country's financial system and calling for policy and regulatory actions to address those vulnerabilities in a timely and informed manner so as to prevent a crisis. In contrast to microprudential supervision, which takes a bottom-up approach that focuses on the health and stability of individual institutions, macroprudential supervision takes a top-down approach that focuses on the economy-wide system in which financial market players operate and that helps assess sources of risks and incentives. It requires the integration of detailed information on banks, non-bank financial firms, corporations, households, and financial markets.

3. Systemic Stability Regulation — Principles

We propose that each country should establish an effective, powerful systemic stability regulator to be in charge of crisis prevention, management, and resolution. Using the methodology first presented by Carmichael and Pomerleano (2003) to address the role of a systemic stability regulator, this section presents a rigorous framework that systematically reviews the following four components:

- Objectives and mandates — what the stability regulator expects to achieve;
- Resources — the political backing, legal support, and human and financial resources needed to enable the stability regulator to carry out its objectives and mandates effectively;
- Implementation — the instruments, tools, and techniques that the stability regulator uses to achieve its objectives; and

- Structure and organization — the organizational structure of the stability regulator such that it is able to meet the delegated financial stability responsibilities in the most effective way.

3.1 *Clear objectives and mandates of a systemic stability regulator*

Regulatory objectives and mandates are what the systemic stability regulator expects to achieve. When a systemic crisis takes place, financial authorities are forced to be intensively involved in managing and resolving the crisis. However, those actions take place after the onset of a crisis. One of the most important functions of the systemic stability regulator is to monitor, anticipate, and intervene prior to a crisis. Such an approach and methodology would aim to preserve systemic financial stability by spotting vulnerabilities in a country's financial system, so that, if necessary, actions could be taken in a timely and informed manner to prevent a build-up of systemic risk and an eventual crisis from occurring. The role of the systemic stability regulator would be to strengthen, not displace, examination and supervision focused on individual institutions.

The major objectives and mandates can be summarized as follows:

- *Monitoring* systemic risks, such as large or growing credit exposure to real estate, across firms and markets;
- *Assessing* the potential for deficiencies in risk management practices, broad-based increases in financial leverage, or changes in financial markets and products, creating systemic risk;
- *Analyzing* possible spillovers between financial firms or between firms and markets (for example, through the mutual exposures of highly interconnected firms);
- *Identifying possible regulatory gaps*, including gaps in the legal regime governing the insolvency of financial institutions, that pose risks for the system as a whole;
- *Curtailing systemic risks* across the entire financial system — encompassing corporations, households, and capital inflows as well as arrangements for crisis management and financial institution resolution — through legislative action, prudential measures, advising on monetary policy, and intervention in individual institutions; and
- *Issuing periodic reports* on the stability of the financial system.

The stability regulator needs to have a clear mission mandate addressing expectations and responsibilities. It must conduct a macro-financial surveillance and take a macroprudential approach to supervision that addresses risks to the financial system as a whole, in an effort to enhance economy-wide financial stability and prevent systemic crises. This would include the monitoring of corporate finance and household debt, which have implications for monetary policy and financial stability, as well as monitoring of international banking flows which bear on systemic stability due to the risks of sudden stops.[5] The stability regulator would also organize the immediate response to a crisis, the strategy for coordinated financial and corporate sector restructuring, and the orderly resolution of failed corporations and financial institutions. The stability regulator is thus charged with express responsibility for containing systemic risks in the financial system.

3.2 *Sufficient regulatory resources to fulfill responsibilities*

The systemic stability regulator needs sufficient political, legal, legislative, human, and financial resources to carry out its objectives and mandates effectively. It would need substantial analytical capabilities and resources to identify the types of information needed; collect the required information; analyze the information obtained; and develop and implement the necessary policy, supervisory, and regulatory response. The stability regulator should be allowed to obtain information from assessments and programs of the central bank (if the central bank does not have the full responsibility of systemic stability regulation) and other financial supervisors whenever possible. It would further need broad authority to obtain information — through data collection and reports or, when necessary, examinations — from a range of financial market participants, including banking organizations, securities firms, and key financial market intermediaries.

In some countries, the stability regulator might be able to rely on private companies (for example, credit bureaus and rating agencies) to collect corporate data or might assign this responsibility to bank supervisors. To collect the necessary data, the stability regulator would have to operate in a system that provides the capacity to enforce compliance or

[5] In emerging markets, a corporate sector that is highly leveraged and unprofitable or that is prone to currency mismatches (as in Indonesia and Korea in 1997) can lead to massive problems (see Kawai, 2000).

exact a commensurate penalty when companies are found to be in violation of laws. This includes the authority to craft an orderly resolution of systemically important financial firms and benchmarks to limit leverage. Essentially, the stability regulator would require knowledge and expertise across a wide range of financial firms and markets to offer a comprehensive and multi-faceted approach to systemic risk.

3.3 *Effective implementation by the systemic stability regulator*

The systemic stability regulator should possess the entire implementation arsenal — the instruments, tools, and techniques to be used to achieve its objectives and mandates. These include macroprudential supervisory tools to reduce systemic risk, such as the ability to impose capital and liquidity requirements; limit leverage ratios, loan-to-value ratios, and debt-to-income ratios; set the policy interest rate; and introduce (or revise) legislation concerning insolvency regimes for non-viable financial firms.

The systemic stability regulator would need to set the standards for capital, liquidity, and risk management practices for financial firms, given the importance of these matters for the aggregate level of risk within the financial system. A comprehensive list of macroprudential measures is discussed in Borio and Shim (2007). Box 2 offers a partial list of such measures.

Boris and Shim (2007) suggest that macroprudential actions may be taken in a gradual, sequenced manner in the face of a build-up of vulnerabilities and systemic risk. For example, once a sign of built-up vulnerabilities is identified, a stability regulator would need to issue warnings. When vulnerabilities worsen but the problem is largely limited to a certain sector of the economy — such as commercial real estate and household mortgages — targeted tools could be mobilized, including performing sector-focused stress tests, tightening lending and underwriting standards, and limiting loan-to-value ratios and/or debt-to-income ratios. If the problem were to become more generalized and threaten systemic stability, then raising minimum capital requirements could be called for; and if the problem were built through markets and unregulated institutions, as opposed to banks, then tightening monetary policy by raising policy interest rates could be more effective.

Inadequate information, in part due to limited data capture (inadequate efforts and excessive parsimony in expenditures on human resources and databases), is possibly the biggest obstacle to adequate monitoring, analysis, and macroprudential supervision.

Box 2: Macroprudential Supervisory Measures

Competition regulation

- Limits on the "too big to fail" or "too interconnected to fail" problem

Market conduct regulation

- Enhanced transparency and competition

Macroprudential measures

- Higher standards on capital requirements and risk management for systemically important firms
- Limits on financial firms' leverage, such as setting maximum leverage ratios and/or credit growth
- Efforts to mitigate procyclicality with automatic countercyclical provisioning, such as a form of dynamic provisioning
- Limits on sectoral exposure (corporations, households)

Households

- Loan-to-value (LTV) restrictions for mortgages
- Limits on consumer debt, such as debt-to-income ratios

Corporations

- Limits on leverage, such as limits on debt/equity ratios
- Limits on tax advantages, such as disallowing interest deductibility for leverage exceeding a certain level or foreign currency-denominated loans

External

- Limits on external debt
- Limits on currency and maturity mismatches

Source: Authors' summary.

3.4 *Effective organization of a systemic stability regulator*

The organizational structure of the systemic stability regulator must be designed in the most effective way possible to carry out the delegated responsibilities of financial stability. The focus of the stability regulator should be on the macro-financial surveillance of the system, which is the analysis of an economy's macroeconomic and financial developments, as well as on macroprudential supervision, which is a top-down approach that helps assess sources of economy-wide risks. Such an organization would require political independence, credibility, and transparency, as well as an adequate level of staffing whose members possess knowledge, expertise, and experience across a wide range of financial institutions and markets.

An important issue is whether the systemic stability regulator should be a single entity or a collective effort among different national financial authorities, each with a different specific responsibility. Key financial authorities include the central bank, the financial supervisor(s), and the finance ministry. The central bank is critical to financial stability as the monetary policymaker to set the policy interest rate in response to the emergence of systemic vulnerabilities or the outbreak of a crisis, and as the lender of last resort to protect a country's payments system. The finance ministry should also be involved in stability regulation, as crisis resolution invariably entails fiscal outlays — whose costs should be made transparent and explicitly accounted for in the fiscal budget.

First, a fully consolidated stability regulator that combines all the functions of central banking, financial supervision and regulation, and treasury — as in the case of Singapore — could be an ideal arrangement from the perspective of maintaining financial stability.[6] This option requires the establishment of a new national agency in charge of systemic stability regulation, absorbing all of the macroprudential functions and monetary policy making from other authorities. However, because of the heightened emphasis on central bank independence, this model is not a realistic option for many developed countries.

The second option would be for the central bank to play the systemic stability regulator function by taking over macroprudential supervisory and regulatory powers. However, an argument can be made that the central bank is not in the best position to take sole responsibility of maintaining financial stability, as this responsibility requires a much broader expertise and perspective than traditional central banking. This arrangement could

---

[6] Singapore has not suffered from any significant financial crises. In contrast, Japan experienced a land price bubble in the late 1980s and a systemic banking crisis in the late 1990s, despite the fact that the finance ministry had the power to supervise and regulate banks and the central bank was not independent (see Kawai, 2005). So, the most important element of success or failure may not be in the organizational structure of such a systemic stability regulator, but in how it functions.

also expose the central bank to the risk of political interventions once the eruption of a crisis requires management and resolution policies.

The third option would be to establish a coordinated systemic stability regulatory council, comprising the finance minister, the central bank governor, and the head(s) of national financial supervisors. An independent, powerful working group that supports this council may be chaired by a reputable expert (like former Federal Reserve Chairman Paul Volcker) and may include finance and central bank deputies, the head(s) of supervisors, and other relevant parties as active members, with the authority to engage in crisis prevention, management, and resolution. The working group would provide recommendations for policy actions to the council, which would make the ultimate decision. In this instance, a country's central bank may assume a secretariat role, given its usual advantages in the analysis of macro-financial surveillance for systemic stability.

4. Alternative Models of Systemic Stability Regulation

4.1 *Global practices of central banks in financial stability*

The role of a country's central bank is critical to promote financial stability. There is a view that the central bank should be responsible for financial stability in addition to the usual responsibility of price stability. There are several reasons for making such a recommendation. First, in the U.S., full employment and price stability are the dual mandates conferred by Congress on the Federal Reserve in the conduct of monetary policy; financial stability is an essential element in achieving those objectives. Second, there are important synergies between systemic stability regulation and monetary policy, as insights garnered from performing one of those functions inform the performance of the other. Third, close familiarity with private credit relationships, particularly among the largest financial institutions and through critical payment and settlement systems, enables the central bank to better able anticipate how its actions could affect the economy. Finally, the "lender of last resort" function of the central bank is a natural link between the central bank and the emergence and reduction of systemic risk.

Table 1 summarizes information on the structure of financial supervision and regulation and the role of central banks in prudential supervision. Of the 83 countries listed in the table, 29 have an integrated prudential supervisor, 20 have a supervisory agency in charge of two types of financial intermediaries, and 34 have multiple sectoral supervisors. The central banks

Table 1. Economies with single, semi-integrated, and sectoral prudential supervisory agencies as of 2009.[a]

Single Prudential Supervisor for the Financial System (year of establishment)		Agency Supervising Two Types of Financial Intermediaries			Multiple Sectoral Supervisors (at least one for banks, one for securities firms, and one for insurers)	
		Banks and securities firms	Banks and insurers	Securities firms and insurers		
Australia (1998)	Maldives[c] (1998)	Finland	Canada	Bolivia	Albania[c]	Lithuania[c]
Austria (2002)	Malta[c] (2002)	Luxembourg	Colombia	Bulgaria[c]	Argentina[c]	New Zealand[c]
Bahrain[c] (2002)	Netherlands[c] (2004)	Mexico	Ecuador	Chile	Barbados[c]	Panama
Belgium (2004)	Nicaragua[c] (1999)	Switzerland	El Salvador	Jamaica[c]	Botswana[c]	People's
Bermuda[c] (2002)	Norway (1986)	Uruguay	Guatemala	Mauritius[c]	Brazil[c]	Republic of
Cayman Islands[c]	Republic of Korea		Malaysia[c]	Slovak Republic[b,c]	Croatia[c]	China (PRC)
(1997)	(1997)		Peru	Ukraine[c]	Cyprus[c]	Philippines[c]
Denmark (1988)	Singapore[c] (1984)		Venezuela		Czech Republic[b]	Poland[c]
Estonia (1999)	South Africa[c] (1990)				Dominican Republic[c]	Portugal[c]
Germany (2002)	Sweden (1991)				Egypt[c]	Russia[c]
Gibraltar (1989)	Taiwan, Republic				France[c]	Slovenia[c]
Guernsey (1988)	of China (2004)				Greece[c]	Sri Lanka[c]
Hungary (2002)	United Arab Emirates[c]				Hong Kong SAR[c]	Spain[c]
Iceland (1988)	(2000)				India[c]	Thailand[c]
Ireland[c] (2002)	United Kingdom				Indonesia[c]	The Bahamas[c]
Japan (2001)	(1997)				Israel[c]	Tunisia[c]

(Continued)

Table 1. (*Continued*)

Single Prudential Supervisor for the Financial System (year of establishment)	Agency Supervising Two Types of Financial Intermediaries: Banks and securities firms	Agency Supervising Two Types of Financial Intermediaries: Banks and insurers	Agency Supervising Two Types of Financial Intermediaries: Securities firms and insurers	Multiple Sectoral Supervisors (at least one for banks, one for securities firms, and one for insurers)	
Kazakhstan[c] (1998)				Italy[c]	Uganda[c]
Latvia (1998)				Jordan[c]	United States[c]
Total: 29	**Total: 5**	**Total: 8**	**Total: 7**		**Total: 34**

Notes: [a] The table focuses on prudential supervision, not on business supervision (which can be carried out by the same agency or by a separate agency, even in the integrated model). Also, the table does not consider deposit insurers, even though they play an important role in banking supervision in a number of countries and can do so under any regulatory model.

[b] The authorities in these countries announced plans to integrate prudential supervision in their central banks in 2006.

[c] Banking supervision in these countries is conducted by the central bank.

Source: Čihák and Podpiera (2006). Updated by the authors.

of 49 countries (59% of the total) have the authority of banking supervision; and of these 49 countries, 39 (80%) are developing and emerging economies. It is informative to note that in countries with multiple sectoral supervisors, central banks almost always have this supervisory authority.

Table 2 summarizes the central bank mandates of the G-20 members and a few more Asian economies. In all cases, the central bank is in charge of price stability as well as payment system stability; and in some cases, it is in charge of supervising and regulating securities and insurance firms, in addition to banks. Close to half of the central banks have financial stability committees and most of them do publish financial stability reports, suggesting the presence of their analytical capacity to conduct macro-financial surveillance. Also, the central banks of Saudi Arabia and Singapore hold the responsibility of macroprudential supervision, but the majority of the world's central banks do not.

4.2 *Reform proposals in the U.S., the U.K., and the European Union*

National efforts to address systemic risk and promote financial stability are proceeding in the U.S. and the U.K., while regional efforts are under discussion in the European Union (EU).

4.2.1 *U.S. stability reform plan*

In the U.S., the Obama administration has proposed that the Federal Reserve become the nation's financial stability overseer. The central bank would gain both the power to monitor risks across the financial system and the authority to examine any firm that could threaten financial stability, even though normally the Federal Reserve would not supervise that institution. The nation's biggest and most interconnected firms would be subject to heightened oversight. The Fed would more tightly regulate systemically important financial institutions ("Tier 1 institutions"), even if they are not banks in the traditional sense (such as General Electric). The administration's proposal also calls for a rapid resolution plan. It mandates that systemically important financial firms be required to file a "funeral plan" regularly — a set of instructions for how the institution could be liquidated in an orderly and timely fashion should the need to do so arise. Finally, a new insolvency regime to be

Table 2. Mandates for the world's major central banks.

			Financial System Stability						
			Payment system regulation and supervision	Regulation and supervision of			Macro-prudential surveillance	Financial stability committee	Financial system stability analysis/report
Country/Region	***De jure* Independence**	**Price Stability**		**Banking**	**Securities**	**Insurance**			
Argentina	Yes	Yes	Yes	Yes	—	—	—	—	Yes
Australia	Yes	Yes	Yes	—	—	—	—	Yes	Yes
Brazil	Yes	Yes	Yes	Yes	Yes	—	—	—	Yes
Canada	No	Yes	Yes	—	—	—	—	—	Yes
China (PRC)	No	Yes	Yes	—	—	—	—	Yes	Yes
eurozone	Yes	Yes	Yes	—	—	—	—	Yes	Yes
Hong Kong	No	Yes	Yes	Yes	—	—	—	Yes	Yes
India	No	Yes	Yes	Yes	Yes	Yes	—	Yes	Yes
Indonesia	Yes	Yes	Yes	Yes	—	—	—	—	Yes
Japan	Yes	Yes	Yes	Yes	—	—	—	—	Yes
Malaysia	No	Yes	Yes	Yes	Yes	Yes	—	—	Yes
Mexico	Yes	Yes	Yes	—	—	—	—	—	Yes
Philippines	Yes	Yes	Yes	Yes	—	—	—	Yes	—
Russia	Yes	Yes	Yes	Yes	—	—	—	Yes	—
Saudi Arabia	No	Yes	Yes	Yes	Yes	Yes	Yes	Yes	Yes
Singapore	No	Yes	Yes	Yes	Yes	Yes	Yes	Yes	Yes
South Africa	Yes	Yes	Yes	Yes	—	—	—	—	Yes
South Korea	Yes	Yes	Yes	—	—	—	—	—	Yes

(Continued)

Table 2. (*Continued*)

			Financial System Stability						
				Regulation and supervision of					
Country/Region	***De jure* Independence**	**Price Stability**	**Payment system regulation and supervision**	**Banking**	**Securities**	**Insurance**	**Macro-prudential surveillance**	**Financial stability committee**	**Financial system stability analysis/report**
Switzerland	Yes	Yes	Yes	Yes	Yes	—	—	—	Yes
Thailand	No	Yes	Yes	Yes	Yes	Yes	—	Yes	—
Turkey	Yes	Yes	Yes	—	—	—	—	—	Yes
United Kingdom	Yes	Yes	Yes	—	—	—	—	Yes	Yes
United States	Yes	Yes	Yes	Yes	—	—	—	Yes	—

Note: Information on only the eurozone and the United Kingdom, among the EU members, is provided. "—" means no role or in coordination with other agencies.

Source: Authors' compilation of information from various central bank websites.

introduced will cover all such firms, modeled on the scheme run by the Federal Deposit Insurance Corporation (FDIC) for ordinary banks.

Against this Federal Reserve-led model, there is a competing view that a Financial Services Oversight Council should be created to provide macro-prudential oversight of the system, that is, to oversee systemic risk issues, develop prudential policies, and mitigate systemic risks. This council would include the Federal Reserve, regulators/supervisors, the FDIC, and the Treasury. This model could become effective if the council could clarify its objectives and mandates as well as acquire sufficient resources and implementation tools. Also, the fragmentation of financial regulation and supervision would have to be eliminated by consolidating these functions into a single authority. This would help harmonize prudential regulatory standards for financial institutions, products, and practices so as to prevent regulatory arbitrage, which would tend to increase systemic risk.

4.2.2 *U.K. stability reform plan*

The U.K. Treasury has proposed regulatory reforms as well. A Council for Financial Stability would be created to bring together the Bank of England (BOE), the Financial Services Authority (FSA), and the Treasury. The FSA would be in charge of both macroprudential and microprudential supervision, and would address systemic risks (such as rapid credit surges, for example) by requiring more bank capital. The BOE would have statutory responsibility for financial stability and would be given new powers to deal with troubled banks. However, the BOE objects that it does not have the tools it needs to maintain financial stability.

The Conservative Party makes a very different proposal. It advocates the abolition of the FSA and the enlargement of the BOE mandate to absorb all of the FSA's supervisory functions. Essentially, this would transform the BOE into a key systemic stability regulator, signifying a return to the pre-1998 financial services regulation in the U.K. Prior to 1998, responsibility for banking supervision was with the BOE; the supervisory functions were transferred to the newly established FSA beginning in 1998.

4.2.3 *European Union reforms*

In Europe, forging a robust approach to coordination is a big challenge, in particular on issues related to regional financial and macroeconomic stability. A high-level expert group headed by Jacques de Larosière (de Larosière Group, 2009) proposed establishing two supranational structures to deal with cross-border aspects of financial stability:

- A European System of Financial Supervisors, which would bring together existing national supervisors with three new sectoral EU-level authorities (for banking, insurance, and securities markets); and
- A European Systemic Risk Council, which would monitor systemic risks and address them through coordinated policy responses from EU member states.

The European Commission favors a systemic risk board to sound the alarm when it perceives a critical build-up of risk. It has drafted a proposal to establish a European Systemic Risk Board (ESRB), which would be in charge of EU-level macroprudential regulation and supervision. It would be headed by the president of the European Central Bank (ECB). Although the ESRB would identify risks with a systemic dimension, issue risk warnings, and, if necessary, recommend specific actions to avoid the build-up of wider problems, it would not have any binding power to impose measures on member states; that is, its recommendations would not be legally binding. In addition, the role of monetary policy in financial stability is not clearly specified, particularly when the demands of price stability and financial stability clash. These limitations could significantly weaken the role and performance of the ESRB as Europe's regional systemic stability regulator.

The EU recognized a second problem as well: the system for supervising cross-border banks is flawed, and the question of who should be in charge of Europe-wide bank oversight remains unanswered. The European Commission has drafted a proposal to establish a European supervisory authority to carefully monitor large, cross-border financial institutions. Finally, new EU laws are likely to require banks to strengthen capital cushions, liquidity, and countercyclicality.

4.3 *Alternative models*

There are several models for systemic stability regulation, including a fully integrated model *à la* Singapore, a central bank-led model as in pre-1998 U.K., and a coordinated "council" model. Although the fully integrated model could be ideal from the perspective of promoting financial stability, its establishment is now increasingly difficult due to the rising demand for central banks to be independent from the government and the political process. The central bank-led model is also possible, but it bears the risk of government interference particularly during times of crisis management and resolution, threatening the independence of the central bank. Nevertheless, in countries — particularly in many developing and emerging economies — where the central bank is not independent, this model will likely remain viable.

A realistic approach for most developed countries would be to establish a workable "council" approach in which the national financial authorities (the central bank, supervisor(s), and finance ministry) work collectively, as if they formed a single systemic stability regulator, to perform the stability regulation function. There exist frameworks for financial crisis management in the U.S., the U.K., and Japan (see Table 3). The "council" approach would be, in a sense, an expansion of this framework to address broader issues of crisis containment, including crisis prevention. However, this should not be a mere expansion of the existing frameworks.

For such a "council" approach to function successfully, the collective objectives and mandates as well as the division of labor among the authorities should be clearly defined, sufficient capacities and resources should be provided collectively, and all of the necessary macroprudential tools should be made available for use. Most importantly, a culture of sharing information should be developed and there should be intensive dialogue among the financial authorities.

The central bank has a comparative advantage in macro-financial surveillance and may or may not have macroprudential authority (particularly tools). If the central bank does not have macroprudential authority, then it could still suggest the supervisor(s) to take certain macroprudential actions (such as an increase in capital adequacy ratios, a reduction of loan-to-value ratios, etc.) to contain a build-up of systemic risk. Similarly, the supervisor(s) can suggest that the central bank alter monetary policy to contain systemic risk.

Table 3. Existing frameworks of systemic crisis management in the U.S., the U.K., and Japan.

	United States	United Kingdom	Japan
Key Processes	The following approvals are required to apply the systemic risk exceptions: • 2/3 of the Federal Deposit Insurance Corporation (FDIC) Board; • 2/3 of the Board of Governors of the Federal Reserve System; and • Treasury Secretary after consulting with the President	Based on a memorandum of understanding, Her Majesty's (HM) Treasury, the Financial Services Authority (FSA), and the Bank of England (BOE) shall take coordinated actions for crisis management: • HM Treasury has the authority to nationalize banks; and • HM Treasury shall provide a blanket guarantee of deposits, based on the common law power.	The Prime Minister shall decide if the systemic risk exception (Article 102, Deposit Insurance Law) should be applied, after consulting with the Financial Crisis Management Council (members listed below).
Members	• Treasury Secretary • Chairman of the Federal Reserve • Chairman of the FDIC	• Chancellor of the Exchequer • Governor of the BOE • Chairman of the FSA	• Prime Minister (Chair) • Chief Cabinet Secretary • Minister of Financial Services • Commissioner of the Financial Services Agency (FSA) • Minister of Finance • Governor of the Bank of Japan (BOJ)

Source: Financial Services Agency, Japan.

5. Conclusions

Our starting point is that a financial crisis is not an "unknown unknown", though its precise timing and the magnitude of its severity might be. A crisis builds up over time in response to policy mistakes and investor herd behavior. While markets tend to be forgiving for a long time, the unsustainable imbalance is eventually corrected. By identifying and dealing with systemic risk — or sources of financial vulnerabilities — before it creates critical instability, policymakers could prevent a financial crisis. For this purpose, macro-financial surveillance and macroprudential supervision are vital, and a systemic stability regulator — or relevant financial authorities under a collective framework for systemic stability regulation — must act to avoid the build-up of large vulnerabilities and imbalances in each jurisdiction. In our experience, an inadequate effort to capture and analyze data is a key obstacle to conducting adequate macroprudential supervision.

Several models are possible to choose from in creating a systemic stability regulator, including a fully integrated model *à la* Singapore, a central bank-led model as in pre-1998 U.K., and a coordinated "council" model that has yet to be tested. For most countries, a realistic approach would be to take a "council" model, where (1) all financial authorities (the central bank, supervisors, and finance ministry) work in a coordinated manner, including intensive information exchange and consultation; and (2) the central bank conducts macroeconomic and financial surveillance while the supervisors take macroprudential actions in addition to microprudential supervision. It is highly desirable for supervisors to consolidate their supervision over banks, non-bank financial institutions, and markets.

Even if such a framework for national systemic risk regulation is established, financial stability may be at risk without a global strategy to address financial crisis prevention, management, and resolution. A successful international financial order can be constructed only with a binding set of minimum international standards. In the absence of such standards, the differences in national policies in accounting, information transparency, regulation of leverage, and capital standards will likely lead to a regulatory arbitrage "race to the bottom", with the competition from more pliant jurisdictions undermining more stringent regulatory regimes, and the "export" of financial instability.

In this sense, the Westphalian principles of sovereignty that govern international financial oversight are not suited to the realities of an interconnected financial system in the 21st century. If the financial authorities in major economies — such as the U.S., the U.K., and the euro area — do not make progress in the creation of a binding global financial order, the prospects for attaining global financial stability are limited. The financially integrated world would have to continue to live with regulatory fragmentation, with all of its attendant risk to stability. In order to be successful, the recent reforms at the global level, focusing on the newly created Financial Stability Board, require that the U.S. and the U.K. make strong political commitments to national and international financial stability regulation.

References

Acharya, V. V. and M. Richardson (eds.) (2009). *Restoring Financial Stability*. NYU-Stern Report. Hoboken, NJ: John Wiley & Sons.

Bernanke, B. S. (2009). Financial reform to address systemic risk. Speech at the Council on Foreign Relations, Washington, D.C., March 10.

Borio, C. E. V. and I. Shim (2007). What can (macro-)prudential policy do to support monetary policy? Bank for International Settlements (BIS) Working Paper No. 242, Geneva, December.

Brunnermeier, M., A. Crockett, C. Goodhart, A. Persaud, and H. S. Shin (2009). *The Fundamental Principles of Financial Regulation*. Geneva Report on the World Economy 11. Geneva and London: International Center for Monetary and Banking Studies (ICMB) and Centre for Economic Policy Research (CEPR).

Carmichael, J. and M. Pomerleano (2003). *The Development and Regulation of Non-Bank Financial Institutions*. Washington, D.C.: World Bank.

Čihák, M. and R. Podpiera (2006). Is one watchdog better than three? International experience with integrated financial sector supervision. *Czech Journal of Economics and Finance*, 56(3–4), 102–126.

de Larosière Group (2009). *High-Level Group on Financial Supervision in the EU — Report*. February. Available at http://ec.europa.eu/internal_market/finances/docs/de_larosiere_report_en.pdf/.

Group of Thirty (2009). *Financial Reform: A Framework for Financial Stability*. Washington, D.C., January 15. Available at http://www.group30.org/pubs/reformreport.pdf/.

Haldane, A. G. (2009). Rethinking the financial network. Speech delivered at the Financial Student Association, Amsterdam, April.

International Monetary Fund (IMF) (2009a). Initial lessons of the crisis for the global architecture and the IMF. Paper prepared by the Strategy, Policy, and

Review Department, IMF, Washington, D.C., February. Available at http://www.imf.org/external/np/pp/eng/2009/021809.pdf/.

International Monetary Fund (IMF) (2009b). *Global Financial Stability Report, April 2009.* Washington, D.C.: IMF.

Kawai, M. (2000). The resolution of the East Asian crisis: financial and corporate sector restructuring. *Journal of Asian Economics*, 11, 133–168.

Kawai, M. (2005). Reform of the Japanese banking system. *International Economics and Economic Policy*, 2(4), December, 307–335.

Laeven, L. A. and F. V. Valencia (2008). Systemic banking crises: a new database. International Monetary Fund (IMF) Working Paper WP/08/224, Washington, D.C., September.

Shin, H. S. (2009). It is time for a reappraisal of the basic principles of financial regulation. January 31. Available at http://www.voxeu.org/index.php?q=node/2949/.

Tarullo, D. K. (2009). Modernizing bank supervision and regulation. Statement before the Committee on Banking, Housing, and Urban Affairs, U.S. Senate, Washington, D.C., March 19.

Taylor, J. B. (2009). *Getting Off Track: How Government Actions and Interventions Caused, Prolonged, and Worsened the Financial Crisis.* Stanford, CA: Hoover Institution Press.

Tobias, A. and H. S. Shin (2008). Money, liquidity and monetary policy. Paper for the American Economic Association Meeting, December.

Wessel, D. (2009). *In Fed We Trust: Ben Bernanke's War on the Great Panic.* New York, NY: Crown Business.

Dealing with the Crises in a Globalized World: Challenges and Solutions

Vincent R. Reinhart*
American Enterprise Institute

I was assigned to offer general remarks on three papers — the papers by Baily and Elliott, Kawai and Pomerleano, and Levine — dealing with crises and a globalized world. Looking across them, it is an easier task than I first thought in that there is considerable common ground. They share a sense of the difficulties introduced by the complexity and interconnectedness of the financial system. They are also infused with a frustration that economists have not taken these forces to heart. Indeed, there is an undercurrent that the professional failure is part of the reason we are here.

The recognition of our collective shortcomings need not be as nihilistic as yesterday's proceedings, which sent everyone home believing that we are doomed. Recognition of failure is the first step in recovery, and I am going to try and be uncharacteristically upbeat, but I reserve the right to be churlish toward the end.

These are complicated issues that are best approached from an oblique angle. This may sound surprising at first, but the key to understanding financial regulation comes from lessons taught by two people separated by one and a half centuries: the Victorian theologian and educator, Edwin A. Abbott; and the contemporary American actor, Kevin Bacon. I will consider their contributions in turn and then address how those insights should influence financial reform.

* Vincent R. Reinhart is a resident scholar at the American Enterprise Institute and a former director of the Federal Reserve Board's Division of Monetary Affairs.

1. A Romance of Geometry

Writing as E.A. Square (or EA^2) in 1884, Abbott (1884) provided the most useful metaphor for international financial regulation ever produced with his book, *Flatland*. For all those who only vaguely remember it from high school, *Flatland* endowed geometric concepts with personality.

Imagine that you were a point in a plane. What would life be like? What movements would even be conceivable? What would be your sense of direction and interaction with other points? Consider the plight of a two-dimensional (2D) entity in a plane visited by a three-dimensional (3D) entity, which highlights the difficulties of perspective and projection. A sphere, for example, dropped into a plane first appears as a point and then becomes a circle; the circle grows and grows, shrinks and shrinks, returns to a point, and then disappears. If we only had a 2D conception, it would be very difficult to understand what just happened. Indeed, it would be tempting to talk about an inflating and deflating bubble in a time-series perspective.

Even harder to imagine is when a cube passes through that 2D world. Why? The sequence of events depends on the angle the cube is dropped at. If the unseen prime mover gets it just right, the cube would hit the plane as a straight line, followed by a sequence of expanding then contracting rectangles, and end with the return of a straight line foretelling nothingness. Drop it at another angle and suddenly a family of triangles, and then odder shapes, visits Flatland. Projections are hard.

Why is this relevant? A national financial regulator is a 2D entity observing a slice of a 3D large complex financial institution. The regulator only sees the part in its own national financial market, and it can be very difficult to envision the larger shape from just one slice. Now, further complicating matters, our global system is one in which different regulators observe different slices of the same object taken at oblique angles, and its shape in each country slice depends on the tax system, the regulations, and whether there are "too big to fail" protections. In a real sense, the failure of oversight represents the failure of imagination to visualize a complicated object correctly.

If you think that the shape of a large complex financial institution is very specific to the national slice, it is extremely difficult to imagine the shape of the entire object. In fact, the resulting entity is quite complex in its full dimensionality. It is hard to visualize in a lower dimension and it is quite changeable from a small rotation.

This geometric explanation provides some insight into Stijn Claessens's policy alternatives[1]: coordination through a college of regulators, a converged approach with common frameworks, an international banking charter, or a world financial authority.

What does a college of regulators do? It pools visualizations. Everyone goes to Basel to sit in a conference room. The first regulator says, "I've got a circle." The neighbor says, "Well, I've got a triangle in my local market." Everyone shares their own projections and then the group tries to get a picture of the entire object. What is Citigroup? What is JPMorgan Chase? What is Deutsche Bank?

In a converged approach with common frameworks, each national regulator should enforce a common shape at each cross-section. That is, every firm has to be a rectangle in every national slice. This can be problematic, however, when slices are taken at oblique angles.

What is an international banking charter or, for that matter, a world financial authority? In a bit of reverse creation, people create an entity to explain the order they already formed from the void. Put in those terms, it is easy to imagine how complicated such an assignment is.

2. Six Degrees of Separation

The job of supervisors becomes even harder when there are strains in financial markets. A financial crisis puts these large complex financial institutions into a spinning motion, and a national regulatory authority sees a different shape than what was there yesterday. Suddenly, what matters in Iceland matters in the United Kingdom, and what matters in Ireland matters in the United States. When put into motion, the entities crash at the edges because, as Andrew Sheng points out in his chapter, each firm is close to many other firms. Deterioration in one national market spreads.

Should we really be surprised at this interconnectedness? Not if you have ever played the Kevin Bacon game. In the Kevin Bacon game, the goal is to connect the actor to anyone else who has ever made a film in six or fewer links. This makes operational the idea of "six degrees of separation", or that everyone is interconnected in a limited number of

[1] See the Claessens chapter in this book.

steps. The fact is that you can link Kevin Bacon to 83% of the credited actors in the history of U.S. filmmaking.

Note that the Kevin Bacon game has been played since 1994 and relies on a paper about mathematical chains from 1929. We have also spent a lot of time over the last two days talking about Bagehot's dictum, whose book, *Lombard Street*, was written in 1873. E.A. Square discussed the problem of visualization in 1884. Is that the best we can do in understanding crisis management? International officials have had to learn on the job during this crisis because the profession has not given them robust rules for crisis management.

3. Crises and Learning from the Past

As a last point, one of the most striking results in *This Time Is Different* by Carmen Reinhart and Kenneth Rogoff (2009) is about the time-series and cross-sectional pattern of crises. Some countries never default or they have graduated, in which case default is only a dim memory; other countries default a lot. Some countries never have bouts of high inflation or currency runs; other countries often have frequent bouts of inflation and currency runs. In contrast, every country has banking crises. There really has been no period since the 1800s, with one exception, in which banking crises were not observed in the cross-sections. This raises two issues touched on by Andrew Sheng.

First, as for the exception, in the three decades after World War II there really were no significant financial crises. There were also considerable controls on financial actions. What were the advantages of that immediate postwar experience? The problem, of course, is that it involves a trade-off between what we observe, financial stability, and what we do not observe, innovations which were not done because of constraints. However, it is an open question as to whether we are on the right point on the trade-off between growth and variability of outcomes. Do we really need all countries to be on the same point of that trade-off?

Second, the regularity that defaults and inflation crises are different from financial crises suggests that institutions' rules and social consensus can matter for the honoring of contracts, both by the government and by the central bank. A government can put in rules making it less likely for a country to default, and a central bank can put in rules so that it will be less likely to devalue the currency it produces. But, financial crises are always with us because human nature matters as well as the rule of law. What we observe in financial crises is a combination of greed, fear, and forgetfulness.

4. Conclusion

Simple rules can help, as pretty much everybody on the panel agrees. However, enforcing good behavior and limiting the exercise of greed will not eliminate financial crises. All of those rules have to be obeyed by bankers as interpreted by supervisors, and both groups are human. Strong independence of supervision would help, but we have to recognize that the political economy and human nature are such that we will almost certainly erode the rules and pressure supervisors to enforce them differently over time.

This means that, while we need robust rules for financial regulation, we also need resilient rules for crisis management. To me, the historical tragedy is that we have mismanaged crises so as to increase their amplitude, frequency, and cost of recovery. Another lesson from *This Time Is Different* (Reinhart and Rogoff, 2009) is that the aftermath of a crisis is protracted: what we do has consequences that can last a very long time.

References

Abbott, E. A. (1884). *Flatland: A Romance of Many Dimensions.* London: Seeley & Co.

Bagehot, W. (1873). *Lombard Street: A Description of the Money Market.* London: Henry S. King & Co.

Reinhart, C. and K. Rogoff (2009). *This Time Is Different.* Princeton, NJ: Princeton University Press.

Systemic Risk: Is There a Playbook?

Robert K. Steel*
Wells Fargo & Co.

Thank you very much. It is my pleasure to be here, and let me thank the Chicago Fed and the World Bank for having me here today. As you may know, I have been associated with several different organizations, so let me say that my comments are my own perspective and no one else should be burdened by them.

I feel a bit odd because for most of my life I have been among what you might characterize as poachers as opposed to gamekeepers, yet I am here among lots of gamekeepers. I think my perspective is different from that point of view, but hopefully it is useful and I will do my best to try to answer the question that Vincent Reinhart raised. I was impressed that he had a picture to tell you how he was going to answer the question. I took the question to be, "Is there a playbook?" That is what I want to talk about.

I think we need to frame the issue. First of all, we have to accept that there will be periods when we will need to be responding to crises. Alan Greenspan described it as an unavoidable characteristic of market economies to have these types of events. So, we should get in our minds that we are going to need to be, to use the sporting analogy, in the "ready" position to execute a playbook.

Now I have bad news, but I also have good news. I think the bad news is that historical playbooks are not very useful. We can continue with the American football analogy which Vincent started, as we know that the T-formation replaced the single wing in popularity and basically the formation evolves all the time. So, having an old playbook is not very useful and I think you have to accept that. That is the bad news.

I think the good news is that there are specific characteristics of good playbooks. So, the right idea is to ask, "What do we think the characteristics

---

* Robert K. Steel serves on the Board of Directors of Wells Fargo & Co.

of good playbooks should be?" In that spirit, I would like to tell you that I do not think they are the characteristics we have in our playbook today. However, I have some ideas about what should be in the new playbook, and I think there is some agreement on what everyone should want in their playbooks. I will conclude by making three comments about policy changes that I think are compatible with the idea of improved playbooks.

Again, most of my life was not spent as a gamekeeper, but instead from the other (market) perspective. As a result, I use vocabulary from that perspective. I think that if you look at the playbook and the responsibilities of supervisors and regulators, due to the complexity and the importance of their work, there should be strong collaboration given the distributed nature of the responsibilities. Let me come back to this point.

Second, the one common playbook characteristic of effective organizations is their ability to think ahead. I have known many great leaders and all of them highlighted the need to spend more time considering the downside rather than the upside of an opportunity or situation. It is amazing, if you understand the downside and think ahead, how the upside has a way of taking care of itself. However, if you do not do that, you will end up in a little more of a challenging situation.

The third point I would like to raise deals with transparency and evaluation. What went right and what went wrong? So, if I were designing a playbook for a business for a particular opportunity, or for almost anything, I think these would be some of the basic characteristics: collaboration, thinking ahead, and transparency and evaluation. Now, let us roll through those three ideas and see how we grade our regulatory system through the lens of those three perspectives.

Let us talk about collaboration initially. Vincent and I first met in Washington, D.C., and there was a completely comfortable relationship that developed between the Fed and the Treasury. Every two weeks, we had lunch at the Federal Reserve Board and it was hosted by a Governor. Staff from my section at the Treasury would meet with Board staff. It happened every two weeks and we got to know each other well. We really did not talk about a crisis at the time, but instead we talked about the issues of what could go right and what could go wrong. I believe that, if this was a business that we all owned, we would encourage lots of examples like this. This process has been going on for decades and is a very good thing.

I think a more formal analogy is the 1988 creation of the President's Working Group on Financial Markets. For those of you who watched closely the last couple of years, I really cannot imagine how things would have worked had there not been the President's Working Group. Now you all know what this is, but basically we have four people who get together about every six to eight weeks to talk, share perspectives, and consider different issues. Again, this was not really codified in too formal a manner and there have been periods of time since the creation of the President's Working Group where it has been very inactive. Now, imagine if we had a crisis and these four key regulators were not well connected, were not comfortable with one another, and did not know each other.

Therefore, while it might seem like a small thing, my personal view is that codification of this process, perhaps even in a more elegant way with some type of visibility like the President's Working Group, would be a good thing. Perhaps there would be regular meetings and there would be some form of communication as to what is going on. I think this would be a good thing for the whole system from a systemic perspective. If I were writing a playbook, this would be one characteristic of it.

I think the second characteristic would be a desire to understand the downside possibilities and to have plans on the shelf to think about how to address these possibilities. This is consistent with the vocabulary that people have used earlier this morning of a living will, or a strategy of what you are going to do or not do if things become challenging. It is amazing to me how little of this there is in the system. People do not ask hard questions. What would happen if this happened? What would be the knock-on effect if this happened? So, the idea is to have a much more developed capability in a cross-departmental way among the different regulators/supervisors. There needs to be ongoing discussions about how we would handle a certain type of crisis. Importantly, I think you quickly learn that you cannot predict what the crisis will be. Thus, it is not a matter of understanding exactly what is going to happen. Instead, you start to brainstorm — if this type of issue happened, who would we convene and how would we respond? Who would be the experts we should bring to the table? In my business career, well-managed and well-running departments, divisions, and organizations all have this characteristic of thinking "around the corner" so that they will be on their toes, as opposed to their heels, when something challenging occurs.

I think the third specific characteristic deals with accountability. Vincent is famous for lots of things, but he was always looking over the Fed Chairman's shoulder at Humphrey–Hawkins testimonies. In my perspective, having the equivalent of some type of report to Congress on issues concerning the health of the financial system would be welcomed.

This feedback would be important. As you know, none of us like doing these things when we are doing them, but we all know that the preparation of getting ready for them is a good thing and provides the groundwork to ensure you have the capability to address upcoming issues.

So, I think those are three quite specific examples of where everyone's playbook would be enhanced. Given the issues raised in this panel, what other policy issues are up in the air that are consistent with a better playbook? Which are not consistent with a better playbook? I will emphasize what my mother taught me: focus on the positive things as opposed to the things I am against. She would be proud.

I think the one thing from my perspective that is the most valuable is some type of clear resolution capability. The lack of clarity and consistency which Vincent just highlighted is fair to criticize. I am a strong supporter of Treasury Secretary Paulson and his team, but if we had to do it over, there were things that were not consistently communicated as well as they could have been. I think this is a fair criticism that we have to take on for those of us who were part of that team. So, the idea of having a stronger, clearer resolution process is clearly one of the changes that is required.

I also believe that some kind of systemic risk management capability is needed. You should not infer from this, nor from my comments on the President's Working Group, that I have made a decision as to which group or entity should be the trigger on systemic risk issues. However, my bias is that it should be the Fed. Let me clarify that. I do believe that systemic risk is the key issue, and I agree with the point made this morning that it is too crude to simply say "more capital"; it really is a matter of more capital on a risk-adjusted basis. You have to get that second part right. I think it is too blunt and too expensive to the system to basically just say that there has to be more capital for everyone. We are going to have to apply this in a pretty tailored way to be sure that we get it right, and it will be a complex process.

I think those are the three things from my perspective that are consistent with a better playbook. These include a strong resolution authority, some type of systemic risk manager, and also acceptance of the fact that regulators and supervisors should be pushing back as businesses push to have less capital.

When I worked in my previous jobs, I always thought capital was this balance between friction and insurance as a business manager. During positive times, you would prefer to run with less friction and less insurance, and that means less capital. However, you have to have the supervisors and regulators push back. They have to say, "I am sorry, but you are going to have to take a bit more friction to pay for the insurance." That is the responsibility of regulators — to get that balance right on a risk-adjusted basis.

Thank you.

IV. DEALING WITH THE CRISIS: THE ROLE OF THE STATE

Banking on the State

Piergiorgio Alessandri*
Bank of England

Andrew G. Haldane
Bank of England

1. Introduction

Historically, the link between the state and the banking system has been umbilical. Starting with the first Italian banking houses in the 13th century, banks were financiers of the sovereign. Sovereign need was often greatest following war. The Bank of England was established at the end of the 17th century for just this purpose, financing the war debts of King William III.

From the earliest times, the relationship between banks and the state was often rocky. Sovereign default on loans was an everyday hazard for the banks, especially among states vanquished in war. Indeed, through the ages, sovereign default has been the single biggest cause of banking collapse.[1] It led to the downfall of many of the founding Italian banks, including the Medici Bank of Florence. As awareness of sovereign risk grew, banks began to charge higher loan rates to the sovereign than to commercial entities. In the 15th century, King Charles VIII of France paid up to 100% on war loans to Italian banks, which were at the same time charging Italian merchants 5–10% (Homer and Sylla, 2005). The Bank of

---

* Piergiorgio Alessandri is an economist in the Risk Assessment Division of the Bank of England; Andrew G. Haldane is Executive Director of the Financial Stability area of the Bank of England. Contributions and comments were provided by Paul Doran, Marius Jurgilas, Samuel Knott, Salina Ladha, Ouarda Merrouche, Filipa Sa, William Speller, Aron Toth, Matthew Willison, and Nick Vause.

[1] Reinhart and Rogoff (2009) provide an outstanding history of financial crises over the past 800 years.

England's first loan to the government carried an interest rate of 8% — double the rate at which the Bank discounted trade bills.

Over the past two centuries, however, the tables have progressively turned. The state has instead become the last-resort financier of the banks. As with the state, banks' needs have typically been greatest during times of financial crisis; and like the state, last-resort financing has not always been repaid in full and on time. The Great Depression marked a regime shift in state support to the banking system. The credit crisis of the past two years may well mark another.

Table 1 provides a snapshot of the scale of intervention to support banks in the U.K., the U.S., and the euro area during the current crisis. This totals over US$14 trillion, or almost a quarter of global GDP. It dwarfs any previous state support of the banking system. These interventions have been as imaginative as they have been large, including liquidity and capital injections, debt guarantees, deposit insurance, and asset purchase. The costs of this intervention are already being felt. As in the Middle Ages, perceived risks from lending to the state are larger than to some corporations. The price of default insurance is higher for some G7 governments than for McDonald's or the Campbell Soup Company. Yet, there is one key difference between the situation today and that in the Middle Ages. Back then, the biggest risk to the banks was from the sovereign; today, perhaps the biggest risk to the sovereign comes from the banks. Causality has reversed.

State support is one side of the "social contract" between banks and the state (Tucker, 2009). State regulation of banks is the other. Table 1 suggests that the terms of this social contract have recently worsened. That should come as no surprise. At least over the past century, there is evidence of an upward ratchet in the scale and scope of state support of the banking system. Whenever banking crises strike, the safety net has bulged; like overstretched elastic, it has remained distended.

What explains this ratchet? All contracts are incomplete.[2] Contractual relationships, like personal ones, often break down due to commitment problems. Social contracts between the state and the banks are no exception. This generates a time-consistency problem for the authorities when dealing with crises — a tendency to talk tough but act weak. This explains historical hysteresis in the safety net.

[2] Indeed, contract incompleteness is one of the reasons banks exist in the first place (Rajan, 1998).

Table 1. Support packages.

	U.K. (US$ trillion)	U.S. (US$ trillion)	euro area (US$ trillion)
Central Bank			
— Money creation	0.32	3.76	0.98
— Collateral swaps	0.30	0.20	0.00
Government			
— Guarantees	0.64	2.08	>1.68
— Insurance	0.33	3.74	0.00
— Capital	0.12	0.70	0.31
Total (% GDP)	74%	73%	18%

Source: Bank of England (2009). Figures for the U.K. updated to November 4, 2009.
Notes: We use a Euro/U.S. dollar exchange rate of 0.710 and a pound sterling/U.S. dollar exchange rate of 0.613. Money creation includes both monetary and financial stability operations.

So what can be done? There are many reform proposals on the table.[3] Two sets of initiatives are discussed here: changes to the regulation of banks' risk taking, and changes to the terms of the social safety net to improve its time consistency. It is too early to know whether these measures will be sufficient, but recent events suggest some mix of these measures is surely necessary.

2. Evolution in the Banking Safety Net

The three longest-standing state insurance devices for the banking system are *liquidity insurance*, *deposit insurance*, and *capital insurance*. These offer protection to different parts of banks' capital structure: wholesale deposits, retail deposits, and equity, respectively. So, how have risks to banks' balance sheets — in effect, the "insurable interests" of the state — evolved over time? And how, in turn, has this evolution shaped the design of the banking safety net?

The U.K. provides a useful historical case study. Figure 1 plots U.K. banks' balance sheets against GDP since 1880. The ratio was flat for

[3] See, for example, King (2009).

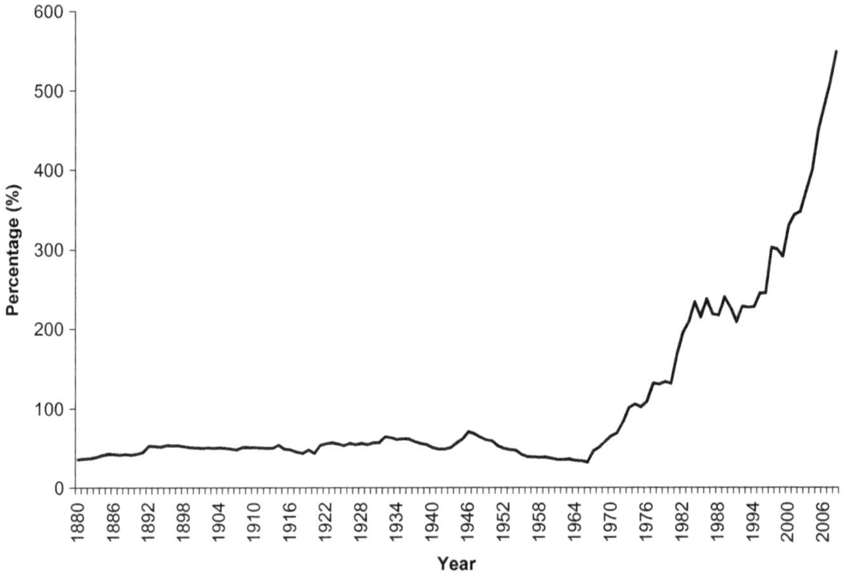

Figure 1. U.K. banking sector assets as percentage of GDP.

Sources: Sheppard (1971) and Bank of England.

Note: The definition of U.K. banking sector assets used in the series is broader after 1966, but using a narrower definition throughout gives the same growth profile.

almost a century, at around 50%. Over this period, banks' assets grew roughly in line with money spending. But from the early 1970s, the pattern changed dramatically. By the start of this century, bank balance sheets were more than five times the size of annual U.K. GDP. Within the space of a generation, the insurable interests of the state had risen 10-fold.

By itself, this expansion of balance sheets need not imply that the state was bearing greater implicit risk. For example, banks could have self-insured by holding larger buffers of capital and liquidity. In practice, however, the opposite happened (Figures 2 and 3). Capital and liquidity ratios have fallen secularly in the U.K. and the U.S. for over a century. Since the start of the 20th century, capital ratios have fallen by a factor of around five in the U.S. and the U.K.; liquidity ratios have fallen by roughly the same amount in half that time. Taken together, these balance sheet trends indicate a pronounced rise in banking system risk and, hence, in potential demand for state insurance. They have also affected the returns required by bank shareholders.

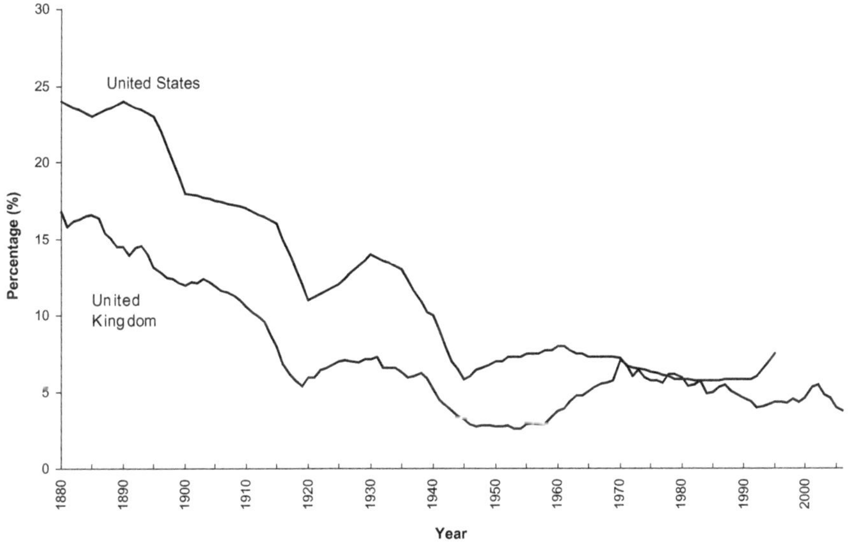

Figure 2. Capital ratios for U.K. and U.S. banks.

Sources: U.S.: Berger *et al.* (1995); U.K.: Sheppard (1971), British Bankers' Association, published accounts, and Bank of England calculations.

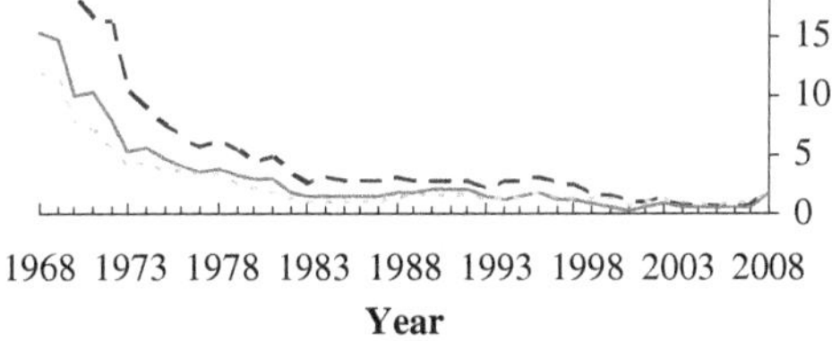

Figure 3. Pound sterling liquid assets relative to total assets.

Sources: Bank of England and Bank of England calculations.

[a] Cash + Bank of England balances + money at call + eligible bills + U.K. gilts.

[b] Proxied by: Bank of England balances + money at call + eligible bills.

[c] Cash + Bank of England balances + eligible bills.

As banks have moved up the risk spectrum, the return required by shareholders has predictably increased. Between 1920 and 1970, the return on U.K. banks' equity averaged below 10% per annum, with low volatility of around 2% per year (Figure 4). This was roughly in line with risks and returns in the non-financial economy. However, the 1970s signaled a sea change. Since then, returns on U.K. banks' equity have averaged over 20%. Immediately prior to the crisis, returns were close to 30%. The natural bedfellow to higher return is higher risk; and so it was, with the volatility of U.K. banks' returns having trebled over the past 40 years.

This regime shift upwards in the risk and return profile of U.K. banks can be explained by the fall in their capital ratios. Higher leverage boosts required returns on equity because it simultaneously makes the banking system's balance sheet more fragile. There is unlikely to be a better case study of these dynamics at play than the events over the past decade.

So, how has the state's safety net evolved in response? The element of the safety net with the longest historical pedigree is *liquidity insurance*,

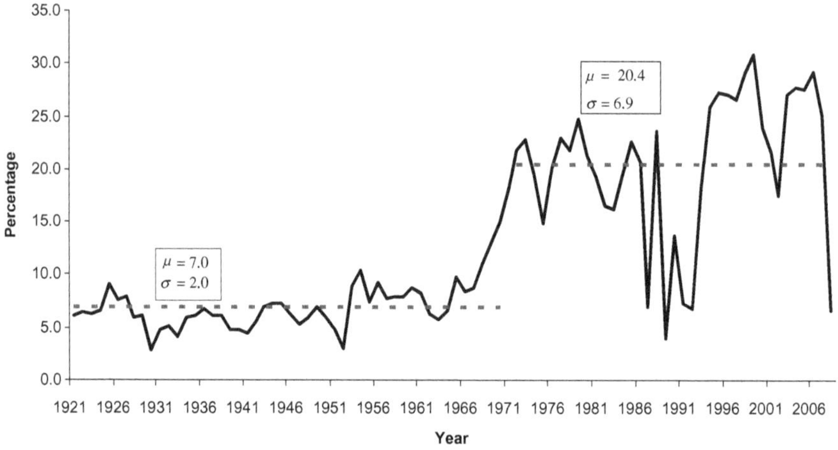

Figure 4. Return on equity for U.K. banks.

Sources: Capie and Billings (2004), British Bankers' Association, and Bank of England calculations.

Notes: μ and σ denote mean and standard deviation, respectively. There is a definitional change in the sample in 1967; the latter period has a slightly larger sample of banks and returns on equity are calculated somewhat differently, including being pre-tax.

typically provided by the central bank in the form of last-resort lending. The principles behind last-resort lending were first articulated by Henry Thornton at the beginning of the 19th century and were subsequently elaborated by Walter Bagehot (Thornton, 1802; Bagehot, 1873). Last-resort lending was, in practice, often rather less elegant than the theory. Writing at the time of the 1825 banking crisis, Jeremiah Harman, a director of the Bank of England, described it thus:

> We lent [money] by every possible means and in modes we have never adopted before; we took in stock on security, we purchased Exchequer bills, we made advances on Exchequer bills, we not only discounted outright, but we made advances on the deposit of bills of exchange to an immense amount, in short, by every possible means consistent with the safety of the Bank. . . . Seeing the dreadful state in which the public were, we rendered every assistance in our power. [Quoted in Bagehot (1873)]

Figure 5 plots the Bank of England's balance sheet in relation to GDP since 1830. Stripping out the effects of the two World Wars, this ratio declined fairly steadily, from around 15% in 1830 to around 5% at the start of this century. Financial panics over this period did little to interrupt the downward trend. However, events of the past two years have dramatically altered that picture. In relation to GDP, base money in the U.K. has risen by a factor of four — easily the highest financial crisis multiplier ever.[4] It has reached a peak last witnessed almost two centuries ago. Past liquidity crises are foothills by comparison with recent Himalayan heights.

Measures of central bank balance sheet expansion underestimate the scale of liquidity support provided during this crisis. As in Harman's time, there has been a widening of the collateral taken by most central banks in their operations (Committee on the Global Financial System, 2008). The taking of imaginative forms of collateral has a history which predates central banking: in the 12th century, King Baldwin II of Jerusalem secured a loan using his beard as collateral. Nonetheless, recent efforts are probably unprecedented in scope. Collateral swaps, typically not involving beards but often requiring haircuts, have also played a significant role during this crisis. They too do not expand base money, but do liquefy banks' balance sheets. Guarantees of wholesale liabilities have similarly served as an

[4] The sample in Figure 5 ends before quantitative easing began, so base money growth is not affected by recent monetary policy actions in the U.K.

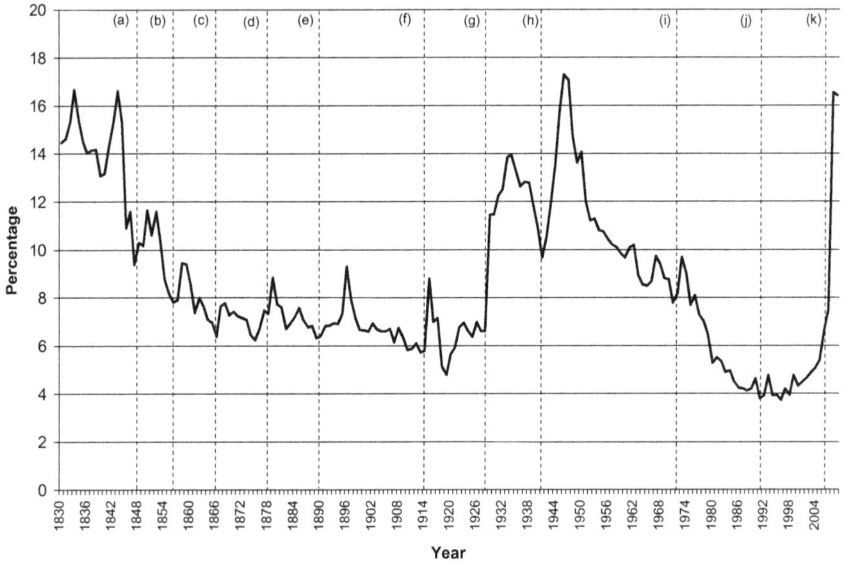

Figure 5. Bank of England's balance sheet as percentage of GDP.

Source: Bank of England.

Note: (a) Famine/End of railroad boom (1847); (b) Overextension of credit from 1855 to 1866; (c) Failure of Overend, Gurney & Co. (1866); (d) Failure of City of Glasgow Bank (1878); (e) Support for Barings Bank (1890); (f) WWI (1914); (g) Currency and Bank Notes Act (1928); (h) World War II (1941); (i) Secondary banking crisis (1973); (j) Small banks' crisis (1991); (k) Current crisis (2007).

important liquidity insurance device for a number of countries. Together, these two instruments have totaled between 10% and 40% of GDP across the U.K., the U.S., and the euro area.

Plainly, there has been a dramatic expansion in both the scale and scope of state liquidity insurance to the banking system. This pattern has been repeated in the majority of recent systemic banking crises. In a study of 42 systemic banking crises between 1970 and 2007, Laeven and Valencia (2009) found a peak liquidity provision of almost 30% of total deposits. Drastic times clearly call for drastic measures. Harman's description of last-resort lending in 1825 would not look out of place today, except that, crucially, the decimal point would have changed place.

Deposit insurance and capital insurance have a shorter history. *Deposit insurance* was first introduced in the U.S. in 1934 to protect retail depositors scorched by the experience of the Great Depression. It failed to catch on internationally. By the early 1960s, the U.S. was still the only developed country with an explicit deposit insurance scheme. Since then, there has been a steady rise in the number of adopting countries (Figure 6). By 2009, almost 100 countries globally had such a regime.

Typically, the introduction and extension of deposit insurance regimes has been a response to banking crises. This time's crisis has been no exception. Australia and New Zealand have both introduced deposit guarantee schemes, and more than 40 countries have increased the coverage limits of their existing schemes (including in the U.K., the U.S., and Germany). In a few countries, such as Germany and Ireland, deposit insurance limits have temporarily been removed; in many others, they have been removed implicitly. This, too, is a familiar pattern during times of crisis. Laeven and Valencia (2009) found that coverage limits for deposit insurance schemes increase fourfold, on average, in relation to

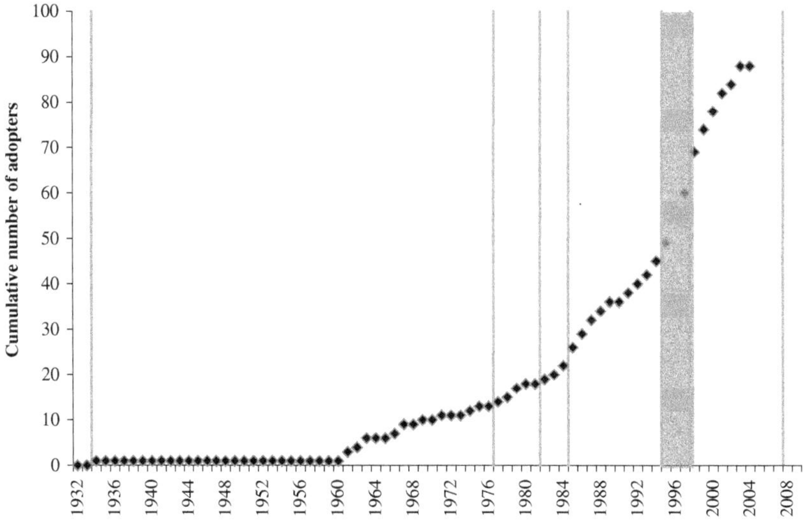

Figure 6. Number of deposit insurance schemes and crises.

Note: 1934 — Great Depression (U.S.); 1977 — Banking crisis (Spain); 1982 — Banking crisis (Kuwait); 1985 — Banking crisis (Kenya); 1995 — Banking crises (Brazil, Bulgaria); 1996 — Banking crises (Belarus, Lithuania); 1996–1998 — Asian crisis (Indonesia, Korea, Malaysia, Thailand); 1998 — Banking crisis (Ukraine).

GDP after systemic crises. As with liquidity insurance, there has been a secular expansion in the scope and scale of deposit insurance.

Finally, explicit *capital insurance* of the banking system appears to have been a more recent phenomenon. In the U.S., the Reconstruction Finance Corporation was established in 1932 at the height of the Great Depression, and it played a key role in recapitalizing U.S. banks through injections of preferred stock. More recently, recapitalization of banks has accompanied the banking crises in Scandinavia, Japan, Asia, and Latin America. Historically, capital injections into the U.K. banking system have tended to be small and bespoke — for example, at the time of the secondary banking crisis in the 1970s and the small banks' crisis in the early 1990s (Table 2; Logan, 2000). In terms of scale, capital injections during this crisis knock these interventions into a cocked hat, so to speak. Once again, the decimal point has changed place. This pattern is replicated in studies of recent systemic banking crises. Since the 1970s, capital injections to the banking system have averaged around 8% of GDP at crisis times (Laeven and Valencia, 2009).

Taken together, this evidence paints a consistent picture: a progressive rise in banking risk and an accompanying widening and deepening of the state safety net. There is an upward ratchet. This ratchet is evidence of a policy time-consistency problem.

3. The Time-Consistency Problem and the Banking Safety Net

What explains this time inconsistency? A simple framework is developed to explain the existence of, and upward ratchet in, the safety net. It focuses on the incentive structures facing owners of banks and the risk strategies they pursue. The run-up to the present crisis provides several examples of those incentives and strategies at work.

Take the payoff profile facing a bank shareholder. Assume that the sensitivity of the bank's assets to aggregate risk — in the language of finance, its "beta" — equals 0.1. So, for every 10% movement in the market as a whole, the bank's assets move by 1%. Assume too that the beta of the bank's deposits is zero and that the bank has an equity capital ratio of 10%. While arbitrary, these numbers are broadly plausible. Conveniently, under those assumptions, the beta of the bank's equity equals 1. Figure 7 shows the payoff profile facing owners of the bank.

Table 2. Capital provision in past U.K. crises.

Date	Crisis	Support recipient(s)	Reason for capital provision	Did U.K. clearing banks receive direct capital support?	Authority providing capital support	Percentage (%) of GDP at the time
1977	Secondary banks	Slater Walker	Orderly resolution (wind down)	✗	Bank of England	<0.1
1984	Johnson Matthey	Johnson Matthey	Orderly resolution (wind down)	✗	Bank of England	<0.1
1994	Small banks	National Mortgage Bank	Orderly resolution (wind down)	✗	Bank of England	<0.1
2008	Current crisis	Royal Bank of Scotland, Lloyds Banking Group, Northern Rock	Mitigate systemic risk and promote lending	✓	Treasury	~4

Source: Bank of England.

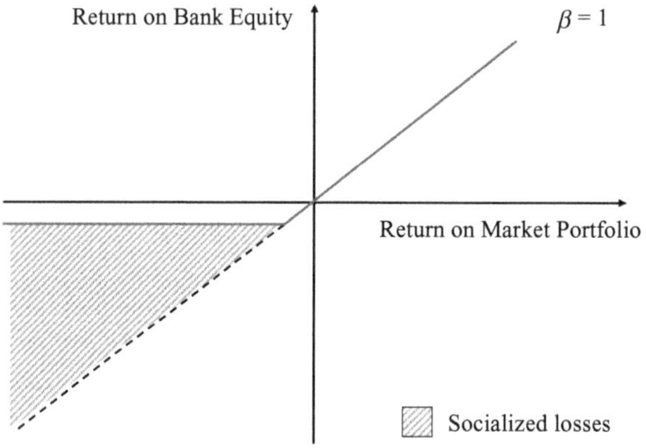

Figure 7. Payoff profile for bank equity.

As shown in Figure 7, the return on a bank's equity lies on a 45° line when market returns are positive. Gains to shareholders are potentially unlimited. But, the same is not true in bad states of the world. The reason is limited liability, which constrains the losses of shareholders to around zero. Losses beyond that point are borne by other parts of banks' capital structure — i.e., wholesale and retail depositors. Therein lies the problem.

If protection of depositors is felt to be a public good, these losses risk being borne by the state instead, either in the form of equity injections from the government (capital insurance), payouts to retail depositors (deposit insurance), or liquidity support to wholesale funders (liquidity insurance). The gains risk being privatized and the losses socialized. Evidence suggests that this is a repeated historical pattern.

Socialized losses are doubly bad for society. Taxes may not only be higher on average; they may also need to rise when they are likely to be most painful to taxpayers, namely in the aftermath of a crisis. Therefore, tax profiles will be spiky rather than smooth and will spike when the chips are down. This is the opposite of what tax theory would tell us is optimal (Barro, 1979).

So far, so bad. But it is about to get worse, for this tells only half the story. This is a repeated game. State support stokes future risk-taking incentives, as owners of banks adapt their strategies to maximize expected profits. So it was in the run-up to the present crisis. In particular, five such strategies were clearly in evidence:

Higher leverage. The simplest way of exploiting the asymmetry of payoffs arising from limited liability is to increase leverage. For example, if the capital ratio of the hypothetical bank were to halve from 10% to 5%, the beta of the bank's equity would double (Figure 8). In that event, the imbalance between privatized gains (above the zero-axis) and socialized losses (below the zero-axis) would increase. Private investors would harvest more of the upside and export more of the downside. Indeed, there is clear evidence of this strategy being pursued over long sweeps of history (see Figure 2).

Figure 9 looks at the behavior of U.K. banks over the past decade; it plots their leverage against the riskiness of their assets. U.K. banks have migrated northwest over the past 10 years, with balance sheet expansion financed by higher leverage. Because U.K. and European banks were not subject to any regulatory restriction on simple leverage, there was no effective brake on this leverage-fueled expansion.

Higher leverage fully accounts for the rise in U.K. banks' returns on equity up until 2007. It also fully accounts for the subsequent collapse in these returns. The high-leverage strategy pursued by U.K. and European banks rather effectively privatized gains and socialized losses.

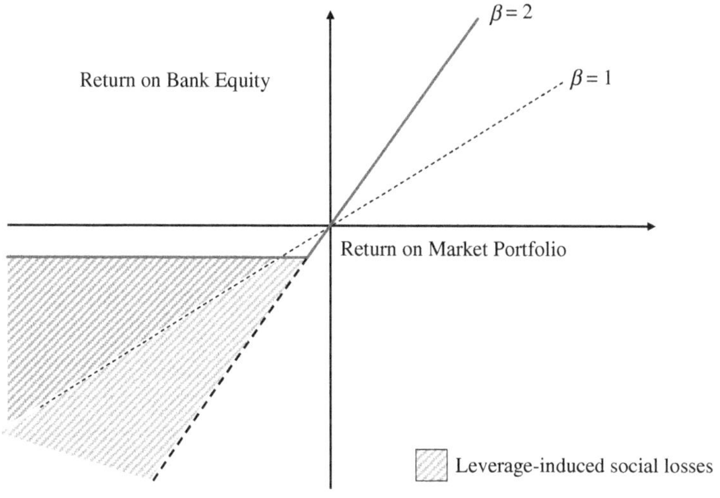

Figure 8. Payoff profiles for bank equity.

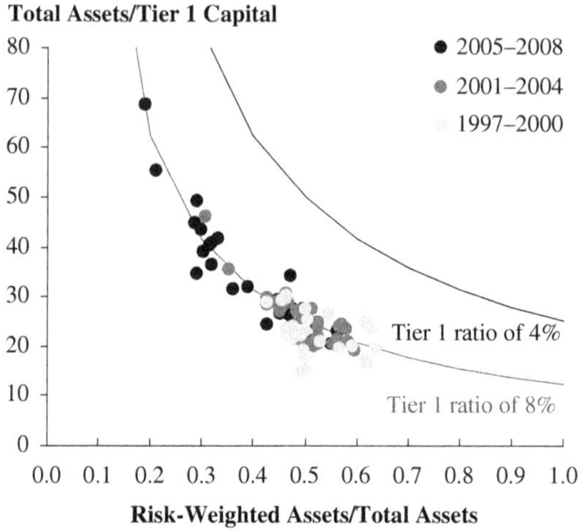

Figure 9. Leverage and risk taking in U.K. banks.
Sources: Published accounts and Bank of England calculations.

Higher trading assets. An alternative means of replicating the effects of higher leverage is to increase the proportion of assets held in banks' trading books. Trading assets are marked to market prices, thereby increasing their sensitivity to aggregate market fluctuations (beta). To illustrate, assume that a bank holds 90% of its assets in the banking book (with a beta of 0) and the remainder in the trading book (with a beta of 1). This gives an asset beta of 0.1 and an equity beta of unity (see Figure 7). However, if the size of the trading book is doubled to 20% of assets, this doubles the equity beta of the bank (see Figure 8).

Figure 10 plots a cross-section of global banks' trading assets as a fraction of their total assets against their leverage. It suggests that efforts to expand balance sheets through higher leverage were focused on trading assets. In the first part of this decade, rising asset prices delivered mark-to-market gains on banks' expanding trading assets. This boosted their profitability and returns on equity. As long as asset prices rose, this created an "Alice in Wonderland" world in which everybody had won and all had prizes. But when asset prices fell, reality returned. The same institutions suffered enormous mark-to-market trading book losses. Across global banks, trading book losses since the start of the crisis total over US$900 billion. In a number of cases, these losses necessitated state

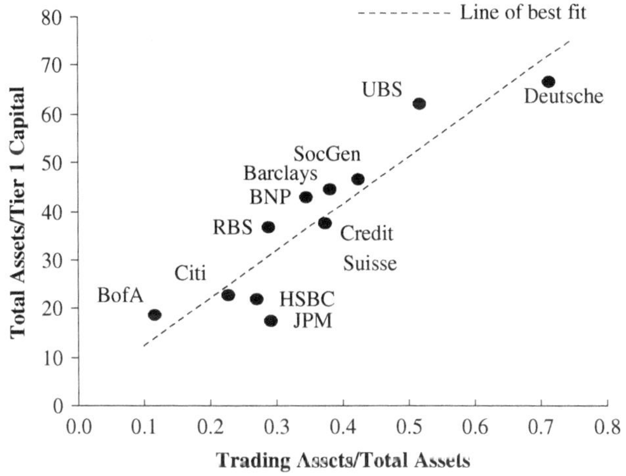

Figure 10. Large and complex financial institutions' (LCFIs') trading portfolios and financial leverage as of 2007.

Sources: Published accounts and Bank of England calculations.

support. Trading book expansion also allowed banks to import the upside and export some of the downside.

Business line diversification. A third strategy pursued by many financial institutions in the run-up to the present crisis was diversification of their business lines. For banks individually, this made sense, as it helped reduce the idiosyncratic risk from individual business lines. Pre-crisis, this strategy seemed the epitome of sound banking.

In fact, it epitomized Keynes' (1931) description of a sound banker: "One who, when he is ruined, is ruined in a conventional and orthodox way with his fellows, so that no-one can really blame him." For risk across the system as a whole, this strategy has systemically dangerous consequences. By increasing the similarity of banks' asset portfolios, it increases the system's sensitivity to aggregate fluctuations. Although diversification may purge idiosyncratic risk, it simultaneously reduces diversity and thereby increases systemic risk (Haldane, 2009; Beale *et al.*, 2009). It also increases the risk of adversity being socialized and prosperity privatized.

High-default assets. A fourth strategy for exploiting the asymmetry of equity payoffs is to originate assets which themselves have asymmetric returns. High-risk loans are one example. These assets yield a

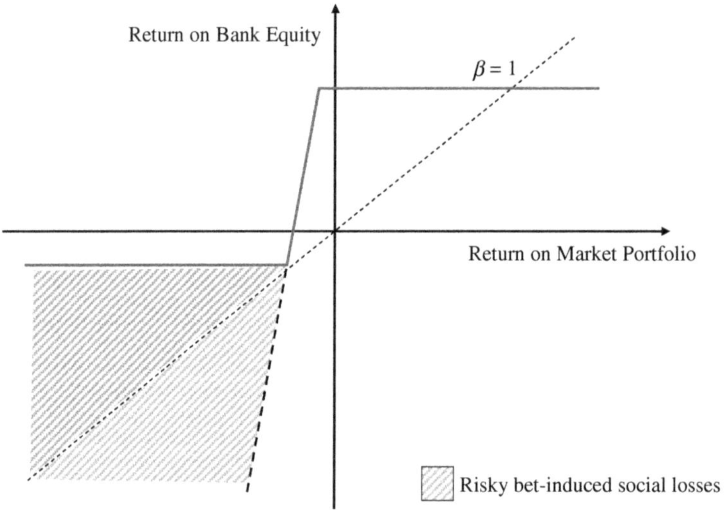

Figure 11. Payoff profile for bank equity.

high, fixed payoff in good states of the world; but in bad states they default, generating large losses. Because losses are bunched in the tail, the result is that more of the gain is privatized and more of the loss socialized (Figure 11).

This was the strategy pursued by U.S. banks in the run-up to the present crisis. Unlike banks in Europe, U.S. banks were effectively constrained from expanding their balance sheets by a regulatory leverage ratio. So instead, they did the next worst thing: they sought higher return on equity by increasing the riskiness of their asset pool. This explains their venture into subprime and leveraged lending as well as various kinds of securitized exotica.

Figure 12 looks at the leverage and risk positions of European versus U.S. banks. European banks lie in the northwest, as they exploited the absence of a leverage constraint to expand their balance sheets in search of higher return on equity. U.S. banks, by contrast, located themselves in the southeast with lower leverage but higher risk per unit of assets. For U.S. banks, this was a best-response strategy for boosting shareholder payoffs. When the risk on these high-default assets materialized, however, the result was the same as for European banks — deep losses, often cushioned by the state.

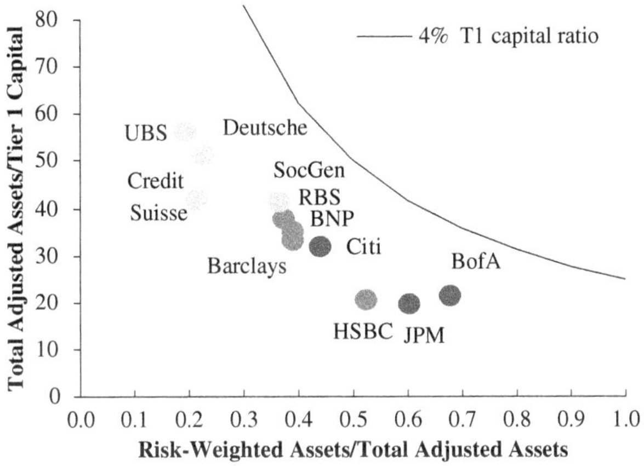

Figure 12. Leverage and risk taking in international banks as of 2007.

Sources: Published accounts and Bank of England calculations.

Note: These adjustments aim to ensure a common accounting treatment of exposures between U.S. and European banks.

Out-of-the-money options. The payoffs to high-risk lending can be replicated using an alternative strategy of writing deep out-of-the-money options. This can be achieved, for example, by selling protection in the credit default swap (CDS) market. The writer of that protection receives an insurance premium and, thus, a steady source of income in good states of the world. Because of that, this strategy appears to generate "alpha" — excess returns — during the good times.

In fact, this strategy is a "wolf in sheep's clothing"; it is beta dressed up as alpha. In the event of a bad state of the world — default by the reference entity, in a CDS context — the writers of the insurance suffer a significantly negative payoff, eliminating the apparent alpha earned in good states (see Figure 11). This was, in effect, the AIG strategy. AIG is believed to have written around US$1.0 trillion of CDS protection. This strategy delivered large apparent alpha returns during the disco years; but when the music ceased and the true beta was revealed, AIG required state support of around US$180 billion.

These five strategies are the latest incarnation of efforts by the banking system to boost shareholder returns and, whether by accident or by design, game the state. For the authorities, it poses a dilemma. *Ex ante* they may well say "never again", but the *ex post* costs of crises mean that such a statement lacks credibility. Knowing this, the rational response by market participants is to double their bets. This adds to the cost of future crises; and the larger these costs, the lower the credibility of "never again" announcements. This is a "doom loop".

The St. Petersburg paradox explains how a gambling strategy which starts small but then doubles up in the event of a loss can yield positive (indeed, potentially infinite) expected returns, provided, that is, the gambler has the resources to double up in the face of a losing streak. The St. Petersburg lottery has many similarities with the game played between the state and the banks over the past century or so. The banks have repeatedly doubled up, and the state has underwritten any losing streak. Clearer practical examples of a policy time-consistency problem are unlikely to exist.

4. Resolving the Time-Consistency Problem

In addressing this time-consistency problem, two broad approaches are possible: redesign of the financial system to reduce the scale of insurable risks, and redesign of the social safety net to make it less susceptible to gaming.

4.1 *Redesigning the financial system*

What options best tackle excessive risk-taking incentives? A number suggest themselves, some of which are modest and others more radical.

4.1.1 *Introducing leverage limits*

One simple means of altering the rules of the asymmetric game between banks and the state is to place heavier restrictions on leverage. European banks were not subject to a regulatory leverage ratio in the run-up to the present crisis, and so they exploited that loophole. Closing it would bring about a clockwise rotation in banks' payoff schedules, lowering the beta of banks' equity returns and reducing risk-taking incentives.

This is an easy win. Simple leverage ratios already operate in countries such as the U.S. and Canada, where they appear to have helped slow debt-fueled balance sheet inflation. The Basel Committee on Banking Supervision is now seeking to introduce leverage ratios internationally. To be effective, it is important that leverage rules bite. They need to be robust to the seductive, but ultimately siren, voices claiming that this time is different. This suggests that they should operate as a regulatory rule (Pillar 1), rather than being left to supervisory discretion (Pillar 2). It is also important that leverage limits are set at the right level. Such limits need to be fundamentally re-evaluated.

We have sleepwalked into a world in which leverage of 20 or 30 times capital is the rule rather than the exception. Now is a good time to wake up. Evidence from the not-too-distant past suggests that there may be less to fear from materially higher capital ratios — say, a multiple of current ratios — than some would suggest (see Figure 2).

4.1.2 *Recalibrating risk weights*

With hindsight, the capital assigned to certain categories of high-risk and off-balance-sheet transactions by Basel rules was far too low. Those miscalibrations were then arbitraged by the banks in ways which included inflated trading books and an overexpansion into high-risk loans and securitized assets. The Basel Committee has already set about trying to correct some of the more obvious of these defects. For example, materially higher risk weights are set to be introduced for trading book assets from the end of 2010. This will include, importantly, securitized and re-securitized products, whose payoff profiles too closely resemble deep out-of-the-money options (see Figure 11). New risk weights should better reflect the tail risk these products embody.

These reforms will close a regulatory loophole and thereby lower the beta of, and hence systemic risk in, the banking system. At the same time, they leave open some rather more fundamental questions, which the Basel Committee is also considering. These include whether the distinction between banking and trading books as well as the re-securitization of assets are necessary in the first place. If a robust financial and regulatory system is one which is parsimonious and transparent, the answer might be that they are not. It may be time to take Occam's razor to regulatory rulebooks.

4.1.3 *Rethinking capital structure*

The asymmetry of payoffs risks excessive risk taking. The source of this asymmetry is limited liability. It is revealing that limited liability was first introduced into banking in the U.K. in the mid-19th century, as that was roughly the time state support for banks took shape. This is unlikely to have been serendipity. So, could the distortions from limited liability be tackled at the source?

In the early days of banking, liability was not just unlimited — it was often as much personal as financial. In 1360, a Barcelona banker was executed in front of his failed bank, presumably as a way of discouraging generations of future bankers from excessive risk taking (Caprio and Honohan, 2008); however, it was not conspicuously successful. From the Middle Ages, debtor prisons replaced the gallows. They were a common feature of many developed countries, including the U.S. and the U.K., right up until the 19th century. The switch to limited liability at that time was a conscious attempt to encourage risk capital into the banking system to help finance growth. In essence, this meant trading off financial risk against future productivity. At first, equity in banks often carried "double liability", with shareholders liable for losses on the purchase price of their shares plus their par value at issuance. Among state banks in the U.S. during the 19th and early 20th centuries, double liability is believed to have helped constrain risk taking (Grossman, 2001). However, this practice was ended at the time of the Great Depression in the U.S.

Given the likely need to rebuild bank equity in the future, now may not be the time to return to unlimited liability. Fortunately, there are two alternative approaches to adapting capital structure that alter the balance of risk-taking incentives without jeopardizing the flow of risk capital. Both involve operating not on equity, but on debt; and both involve making debt, like equity, a more loss-absorbing instrument in stress events.

First, contingent capital is a means of automatically converting debt instruments into equity in the event of a capital top-up being needed. The capital structure of banks thereby becomes more malleable. There has been recent interest in contingent capital instruments as a means of providing banks with an extra degree of freedom in stress situations (King, 2009; Dudley, 2009). The benefits, in principle, seem clear. The difficulties in practice include whether there is likely to be sufficient investor demand for such hybrid instruments.

Second, wholesale debt instruments at present rank equally with retail deposits in the U.K. in the event of a wind-up. But in the U.S., depositor preference has operated nationally since 1993, with retail deposits ranking ahead of wholesale debt. There are benefits to depositor preference both *ex ante* (by heightening debtor incentives to monitor risk) and *ex post* (by facilitating resolution). There are also some potential downsides, including causing unsecured creditors to run sooner. It may be a good time to re-weigh these arguments in the U.K.

4.1.4 *Reconsidering the industrial organization of banking*

Over the past few decades, the global banking system has evolved into a particular organizational form, with a small number of large banks, a high degree of concentration, and relatively low rates of entry and exit. Events of the past two years have accelerated these trends. In 1998, the five largest global banks had around 8% of global banking assets; by 2008, this fraction had doubled to around 16% (Figure 13).

These structural trends worsen the time-consistency problem for the authorities, increasing the pressure for state support to "too important to fail" banks. This has heightened recent interest in rethinking the industrial organization of finance (King, 2009). There are a number of potential

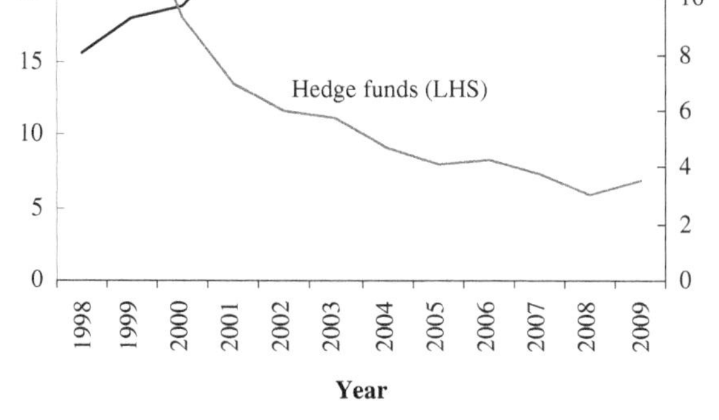

Figure 13. Bank and hedge fund concentration.

Sources: TASS and *The Banker*.

forms such a restructuring could take.[5] In weighing these options, there may be lessons from an, on the face of it, unlikely corner of finance: hedge funds.

Hedge funds started this crisis in the doghouse, yet they are the dog that has not barked. Their industrial structure may explain why. Unlike banking, the hedge fund sector does not comprise a small number of large players, but rather a large number of relatively small players. The largest hedge funds typically have assets under management of less than US$40 billion, whereas the largest banks have assets in excess of US$3 trillion. Also unlike banking, concentration in the hedge fund sector is low and has been falling. The top 5 hedge funds comprise around 8% of total assets, down from 30% a decade ago (Figure 13). Moreover, the business models of hedge funds are typically specialized rather than diversified, and entry and exit rates from the hedge fund industry are both high. The annual average attrition rate for hedge funds is around 5%; at present, it is around double that figure. Among U.S. banks, in contrast, the average attrition rate over the past few decades has been less than 0.1%; it has not come close to hitting 5% at any point since the Great Depression.

It may be coincidence that the structure of the hedge fund sector emerged in the absence of state regulation and state support. It may be coincidence that the majority of hedge funds operate as partnerships with unlimited liability. It may be coincidence that, despite their moniker of "highly leveraged institutions", most hedge funds today operate with leverage less than a tenth that of the largest global banks. Or, perhaps it might be that the structure of this sector delivered greater systemic robustness than could be achieved through prudential regulation. If so, this is an important lesson for other parts of the financial system.

4.2 *Redesigning the safety net*

4.2.1 *A framework for the banking safety net*

Even with systemic risk reduced, the state is unlikely to be able to credibly stand aside when future tail risks eventuate, as they are sure to do. Some

---

[5] For example, see Kay (2009) and Group of Thirty (2009).

bulwark is needed. As in other public policy arenas, a pre-defined and transparent regime can help to reinforce the credibility of *ex post* actions, serving as a pre-commitment device.

Currently, only some of the ingredients of such an *ex ante* framework exist. Internationally, deposit insurance frameworks tend to be fairly well defined and liquidity insurance frameworks somewhat less so, but both are much better defined than frameworks for capital insurance. A well-articulated framework for the banking safety net would not only provide greater clarity on each of these pieces; it would also set out interactions and interdependencies between them — when and how the different insurance strands come together to avert crises. At present, no such *ex ante* map exists. Having one in the future would increase, but not guarantee, the chances of it being adhered to.

4.2.2 *Time-consistent liquidity insurance*

Almost all central banks have flexed their liquidity insurance frameworks during the course of this crisis, and rightly so. In many cases, this has meant a combination of longer-maturity lending to a broader range of financial institutions against a wider set of collateral. Pre-crisis liquidity insurance frameworks were shown during the crisis to lack time consistency. How can we best guard against a recurrence?

Two elements are key. The first involves a greater degree of self-insurance by banks to lower the probability of central bank resources needing to be drawn. In practice, this means that liquidity regulation needs to be tightened, reversing the secular fall in liquidity ratios (see Figure 3). In the language of insurance, the excess on the central bank policy needs to be raised materially. The Financial Services Authority's (2009) proposed new liquidity regulation provides a good starting point. Second, central bank liquidity insurance frameworks need to explicitly recognize the possibility of drastic times requiring drastic measures. The key is to prevent such drastic action from becoming disorderly, on the one hand, and permanent, on the other.

The first element can be achieved by having a pre-defined framework that recognizes the need for abnormal liquidity provision, whether in size, collateral quality, or term. The second element can be achieved by setting prices (fees and collateral haircuts) for liquidity provision that discourage abnormalities from becoming regularities. The Bank of England's (2008) new Sterling Monetary Framework, announced last October, seeks to apply those principles in practice.

4.2.3 *Time-consistent deposit insurance*

Deposit insurance schemes have been stretched in many countries to the point of offering blanket coverage of retail deposits. Those actions are already damping the risk senses of depositors, who have rationally reacted by seeking out the highest-yielding accounts. This has contributed to a competitive frenzy in the retail deposit market. In the U.K., retail deposit rates have risen over the past year from 100 basis points below the base rate to 100 basis points above the base rate.

In general insurance markets, distorted risk choices are guarded against by sharing the risk between insurer and insuree, *ex ante* (through risk-based premia) or *ex post* (through co-insurance devices). Deposit insurance regimes in some, but not all, countries have such features. In the U.K., deposit insurance premia are not risk-based. Private risk incentives would be better aligned with the public good if the U.K.'s deposit insurance regime had such a feature.

4.2.4 *Time-consistent capital insurance*

In historical terms, capital insurance to the banking system is the newest of the state support mechanisms for banks. Partly for that reason, its framework is least well advanced. Indeed, give or take, there is no framework at present. Whether a framework is needed will depend importantly on the levels of private capital held in the future by the banking system, i.e., the degree of self-insurance. That debate has some distance still to travel. However, there are complementary measures which could serve a similar purpose. For example, some academics have proposed private-sector capital insurance schemes, funded *ex ante* by levies on banks (Kashyap *et al.*, 2008; NYU Stern School of Business, 2008); so, too, have some policymakers (Tucker, 2009). These schemes are, in many respects, similar to existing deposit insurance regimes. Like them, such schemes would ideally set risk-based premia and be pre-funded to ensure they were time-consistent.

One potential benefit of private-sector contingent capital proposals is that they allow a mutualization of risk. This lowers the aggregate pool of capital that might be needed by the banking system. If this pool of capital is large enough to accommodate future crisis needs, private-sector capital insurance may offer a better cost/risk trade-off than self-insurance. As history shows, however, this is a not inconsiderable "if". Further work would be needed to establish what size insurance scheme would genuinely augment the capital pool.

5. Conclusion

Over the course of the past 800 years, the terms of trade between the state and the banks have first swung decisively one way and then the other. For the majority of this period, the state was reliant on the deep pockets of banks to finance periodic fiscal crises. But for at least the past century, the pendulum has swung back, with the state often needing to dig deep to keep crisis-prone banks afloat.

Events of the past two years have tested even the deep pockets of many states. In so doing, they have added momentum to the century-long pendulum swing. Reversing the direction will not be easy. It is likely to require a financial-sector reform effort that is every bit as radical as that which followed the Great Depression. It is an open question whether reform efforts to date, while slowing the swing, can bring about that change of direction.

References

Bagehot, W. (1873). *Lombard Street: A Description of the Money Market.* London: Henry S. King & Co.

Bank of England (2008). The development of the Bank of England's market operations: a consultative paper by the Bank of England. Available at http://www.bankofengland.co.uk/markets/money/publications/condococt08.pdf/.

Bank of England (2009). *Financial Stability Report*. June.

Barro, R. J. (1979). On the determination of the public debt. *Journal of Political Economy*, 87(5), 940–971.

Beale, N., D. Rand, N. Arinaminpathy, and R. M. May (2009). Conflicts between individual and systemic risk in banking and other systems. Unpublished manuscript.

Berger, A., R. Herring, and G. Szegö (1995). The role of capital in financial institutions. *Journal of Banking and Finance*, 19, 393–430.
Capie, F. and M. Billings (2004). Evidence on competition in English commercial banking, 1920–1970. *Financial History Review*, 11, 69–103.
Caprio, G. Jr. and P. Honohan (2008). Banking crises. CDE Working Paper Series.
Committee on the Global Financial System (2008). Central bank operations in response to the financial turmoil. CGFS Paper No. 31.
Dudley, W. C. (2009). Some lessons from the crisis. Remarks at the Institute of International Bankers Membership Luncheon, New York City.
Financial Services Authority (2009). Strengthening liquidity standards — including feedback on CP08/22, CP09/13, CP09/1. Policy Statement 09/16. Available at http://www.fsa.gov.uk/pubs/policy/ps09_16.pdf/.
Grossman, R. S. (2001). Double liability and bank risk taking. *Journal of Money, Credit and Banking*, 33(2), 143–159.
Group of Thirty (2009). *Financial Reform: A Framework for Financial Stability*. Available at http://www.group30.org/pubs/reformreport.pdf/.
Haldane, A. G. (2009). Rethinking the financial network. Available at http://www.bankofengland.co.uk/publications/speeches/2009/speech386.pdf/.
Homer, S. and R. Sylla (2005). *A History of Interest Rates*, 4th ed. New York: John Wiley & Sons.
Kashyap, A. K., R. G. Raghuram, and J. C. Stein (2008). Rethinking capital regulation. Paper prepared for the Federal Reserve Bank of Kansas City Symposium on "Maintaining Stability in a Changing Financial System."
Kay, J. (2009). *Narrow Banking: The Reform of Banking Regulation*. London: Centre for the Study of Financial Innovation.
Keynes, J. M. (1931). The consequences to the banks of the collapse of money values. In *Essays in Persuasion*, London: Macmillan.
King, M. (2009). Speech to Scottish business organisations, Edinburgh. Available at http://www.bankofengland.co.uk/publications/speeches/2009/speech406.pdf/.
Laeven, L. and F. V. Valencia (2009). Systemic banking crises: a new database. IMF Working Paper No. 08/224.
Logan, A. (2000). The early 1990s small banks' crisis: leading indicators. Bank of England Financial Stability Review Issue 09.
NYU Stern School of Business (2008). Project on "Repairing the U.S. Financial Architecture: An Independent View."
Rajan, R. (1998). The past and future of commercial banking viewed through an incomplete contract lens. *Journal of Money, Credit and Banking*, 30(3), 524–550.
Reinhart, C. M. and K. Rogoff (2009). *This Time Is Different: Eight Centuries of Financial Folly*. Princeton, NJ: Princeton University Press.

Sheppard, D. K. (1971). *The Growth and Role of U.K. Financial Institutions, 1880–1962*. London: Methuen.

Thornton, H. (1802). *An Inquiry into the Nature and Effects of the Paper Credit of Great Britain*. London: J. Hatchard.

Tucker, P. (2009). Regimes for handling bank failures: redrawing the banking social contract. Available at http://www.bankofengland.co.uk/publications/speeches/2009/speech396.pdf/.

Liquidity Risk and Central Bank Actions During the 2007–2009 Crisis

Francesco Papadia*
European Central Bank
Tuomas Välimäki
Suomen Pankki

1. Introduction

This paper looks at one aspect of the 2007–2009 financial crisis — namely, its liquidity component — and specifically addresses the actions taken by the Bank of England, the Bank of Japan, the European Central Bank (ECB), and the Federal Reserve System of the United States to deal with this aspect of the crisis.

In order to look at this issue with the proper perspective, the paper first illustrates the approach to implementing monetary policy before the crisis. It then focuses on the liquidity component of the financial crisis and considers the actions that central banks adopted to deal with it, illustrating, in particular, the effect these actions had on the size and composition of their balance sheets. Finally, the paper tries to reach some conclusions about the effectiveness of central bank actions.

---

* Francesco Papadia is General Director of Market Operations at the European Central Bank; Tuomas Välimäki is Head of Market Operations at Suomen Pankki. The views expressed are those of the authors and do not necessarily correspond to those of the institutions to which they are affiliated. The authors gratefully acknowledge the contributions from Jens Eisenschmidt, Jens Tapking, Dana Schäfer, Simone Manganelli, Dimitrios Rakitzis, and Christophe Marchal. The material presented in this article will be part of a book to be published by Oxford University Press and due by December 2010.

2. The Implementation of Monetary Policy in Major Central Banks Before the Crisis

A short reference to the situation prevailing before the crisis is useful so as to have a firm point of departure for interpreting what happened during the crisis. Before August 2007, a substantial convergence in monetary policy had taken place among the most important central banks.

In strategy terms, monetary policy had simplified to the relationship between one objective, price stability, and one instrument, a short rate of interest. While much is made about the difference between the single objective (price stability) of, for instance, the ECB and the double objective (price stability and growth) of the Fed, in practical terms the difference is not so relevant, considering that the two objectives are, particularly over the relevant medium term, highly collinear.

In implementation terms, there was a clear convergence towards the corridor approach — that is, towards steering the interbank overnight rate to a target level consistent with the policy objective, with the boundaries for the movements of the rate set by an interest rate corridor within which the rate would be controlled by adjusting the net supply of liquidity by open market operations. However, the corridor approach was implemented according to two different variants: the "narrow variant" applied by the Federal Reserve and the "broad variant" used by the ECB and the Bank of Japan, with the Bank of England having something of an intermediate variant. The narrow variant foresaw a small liquidity deficit, a restricted collateral framework, and few counterparties; whereas the broad variant was wider in all three aspects (a large liquidity deficit, variegated collateral, and numerous counterparties).

One salient aspect of the narrow variant of the Federal Reserve, i.e., the small liquidity deficit, can be seen in Figure 1. Before the crisis, the size of its monetary policy instrument on the liabilities side (reserves) was much smaller, in relative terms, than for other central banks; correspondingly, its balance sheet was very lean in relation to both banknotes and GDP. In terms of counterparties for monetary policy operations, the Fed had only about 20, against the hundreds of the ECB and the numerous ones of the Bank of Japan. Also, the collateral of the Fed was very restricted, as only Treasury paper, mortgage-backed securities, and agency paper were accepted for refinancing operations; in contrast, the range of collateral was much wider in the case of the ECB and the Bank of Japan.

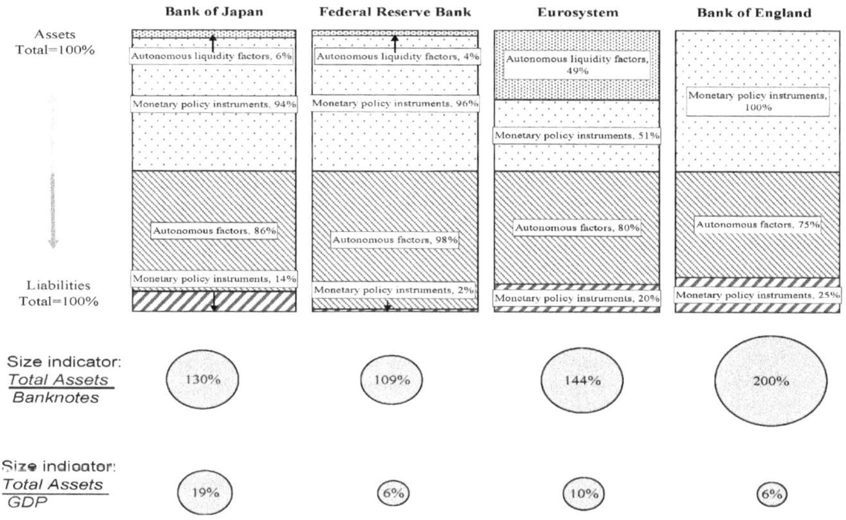

Figure 1. Balance sheets of the ECB, the Federal Reserve, the Bank of Japan, and the Bank of England as of June 2007.

The origin of a narrow or a broad variant resulted not only from historical developments and differences in the institutional setups, but also from differences in preferences for market neutrality. Despite their clear dissimilarities, however, the broad and the narrow variants were indistinguishable in their main function to stabilize short-term interest rates around the policy rate, as can be seen in Figure 2. The case of Japan is not reported in Figure 2 since, with interest rates very close to zero for a good part of the period considered in the figure, there was just no room for any deviation of rates around the target. For the other three central banks, the deviations of the overnight rate from the target before the start of the crisis in 2007 were very limited and approximately the same, with the exception of the Bank of England before the adjustments in 2005 and the overall reform of its monetary policy framework in 2006.

Then, on August 9, 2007, the crisis started. One very important component of this crisis was the liquidity component. As aptly noted by Goodhart (2008), liquidity is an eminently ambiguous concept and there are at least three interpretations of it: market liquidity, funding liquidity, and central bank liquidity. The first one has to do with the ease with which assets are exchanged for cash, and is often measured by the bid/ask spread.

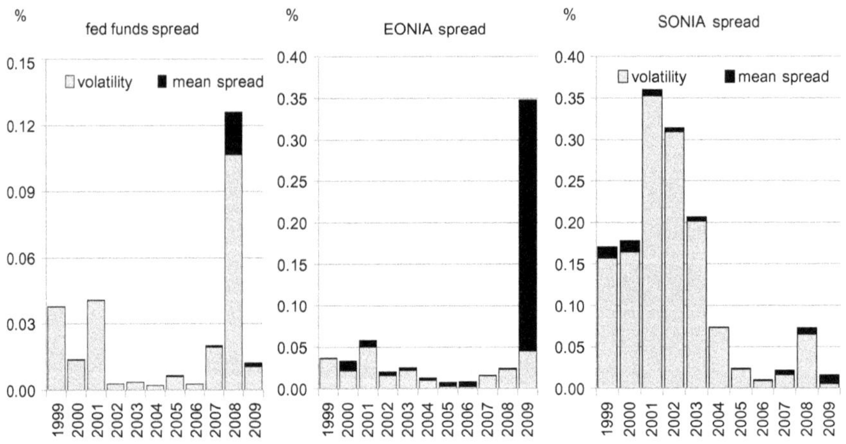

Figure 2. Volatility and mean spread of short-term rates in the U.S. (left), the euro area (middle), and the U.K. (right).

The second one relates to the ability of a bank to fund the gap in its balance sheet deriving from its maturity transformation, and the third one essentially corresponds to the reserves a bank holds with the central bank.

3. The Liquidity Component of the 2007–2009 Crisis

The liquidity aspect of the crisis can be visualized in a sequential manner. First, market liquidity dried out, which had a dramatic effect on funding liquidity. Consequently, banks made a massive recourse to central bank liquidity to remedy the impairment of the two other forms of liquidity.

Two parameters help in visualizing the liquidity crisis. The first parameter is the deviation of the overnight rate from the policy rate. As can be seen in Figure 2, the deviations in 2008 (the first full year of the crisis) were, in all jurisdictions considered, much higher than in the preceding years. In 2009, a kind of Japanese syndrome appeared: with rates very close to zero, there was hardly any rate deviation in the U.S. and the U.K. In the case of the euro area, however, the average rate was, for a long period, well below the policy rate, thus significantly contributing to the deviation between the policy rate and the market rate. The second parameter characterizing the liquidity crisis is the spread between unsecured (Euribor or Libor) and secured (Eurepo) interbank lending rates. This has

Figure 3. Spread between secured interbank rate and overnight indexed swap (OIS) rate for the euro (12-month maturity).

a very similar behavior to that of the spread between the secured rate and the overnight indexed swap (OIS) rate, even if, as shown in Figure 3, some deviations between the two rates appeared during the climax of the crisis at the turn of 2008.

The spread between the unsecured (Euribor) and secured (Eurepo) rates for the euro is reported in Figure 4. Of course, the much higher credit risk was an important determinant of the higher spread during the crisis. To capture this variable, a credit default swap (CDS) index of 20 banks is added to the figure. The figure, however, immediately shows two problems if one wants to explain the spread with credit risk as measured by the CDS index. First, the 20 banks' CDS spread is, in some periods, too high, as it explains more than 100% (indeed, 200%!) of the unsecured–secured spread. Second, the pattern of the unsecured–secured spread is very different from the pattern of the CDS index; in particular, at the turn of 2008, after the failure of Lehman Brothers, the explosion of the unsecured–secured spread is not explained by the CDS index.

To deal with the first problem, following Eisenschmidt and Tapking (2009) and consistently with the definition of Euribor that refers to lending

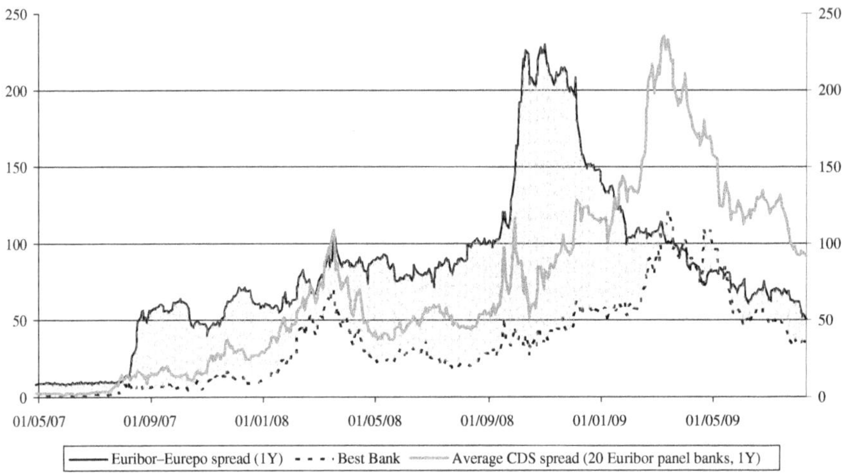

Figure 4. Spread between unsecured (Euribor) and secured (Eurepo) rates for the euro (12-month maturity).

between banks with prime credit, the CDS spread of the bank with the lowest CDS (best bank), and not the average of 20 banks, is also presented in Figure 4. The difference between the unsecured–secured spread and the best bank CDS spread is shown by the shaded area between the two curves. This substantially avoids the problem of a credit risk exceeding the unsecured–secured spread. To deal with the second problem, a closer look is necessary at the part of the unsecured–secured spread not explained by credit risk. This is illustrated in the shaded area in Figure 4, which can be dubbed "liquidity risk premium" for reasons presented below.

The work of Eisenschmidt and Tapking (2009) helps to explain why the residual between the total unsecured–secured spread and its credit component can be interpreted as liquidity risk premium. These authors show that if there were no liquidity difference between secured and unsecured lending, the interest rate spread between the two would be brought by arbitrage to coincide with the credit risk premium: lending unsecured and buying protection by purchasing CDS contracts would be equivalent to lending secured, and the return on the two operations should be the same. But if there is a liquidity difference, the arbitrage condition no longer holds. Hence, the component of the unsecured–secured spread that is not explained by credit risk can be interpreted as liquidity risk premium. The estimate of the liquidity risk premium obtained using the CDS spread of the "best bank" will be looked at more closely below. Before coming to this, however, an overall interpretation of the actions of central banks during the crisis is attempted.

4. An Overall Interpretation of the Actions of Central Banks During the Crisis

Monetary policy has two sides: interest rate control, which is visible; and financial intermediation, which is normally hidden. The central bank inevitably carries out some form of intermediation while implementing monetary policy, as it gets some assets from banks as collateral for its refinancing operations and provides central bank liquidity in return. This intermediation, however, is normally limited and is only a side effect of the provision of the net amount of liquidity which is necessary to control interest rates, not an activity autonomously carried out with some specific macroeconomic objective in mind. The secondary nature of the intermediation side of monetary policy was particularly evident in the narrow variant of the corridor approach, as practiced for instance by the Federal Reserve, but was also clearly detectable in the broad variant, as applied for instance by the ECB.

However, during the crisis, the situation changed radically and central bank intermediation became an integral and quantitatively very important part of central bank actions to deal with the liquidity consequences of the crisis. Indeed, focusing on intermediation allows an overall interpretation of the actions of central banks during the crisis, as the amount of intermediation that the impaired private sector became unable to conduct was shifted onto the central bank. The impairment was, in turn, determined by a dramatic worsening of the ratio between the risk of the banks' balance sheets and their capital: the former grew enormously, while the latter was severely dented by the losses which banks suffered. Dudley (2008) refers to this phenomenon as "banks' balance sheet pressure". This "pressure" forced banks to a salvage de-leveraging which, if not compensated, would have caused even larger damages to the economy. In these distressed conditions, central banks complemented the impaired private-sector intermediation, and the broad variant to monetary policy of the ECB proved more robust than the narrow one. In fact, the Federal Reserve broadened its approach dramatically to make it even broader than that of the ECB.

Empirically, if this interpretation is correct, one should see, in particular, a move of part of the outstanding stock of interbank intermediation to the asset and liability side of the central banks' balance sheets. Checking precisely whether this transfer took place is difficult, but there are two facts about the European experience that match it. The first fact is that turnover in the unsecured interbank market, especially on the term sector, decreased during the crisis (ECB, 2009): turnover fell by 26% in April 2009 with respect to April 2008, after a decline of 12% in the previous year. In 2009, the decline in turnover was even more dramatic in the 3–12-month term, at 46%, while there had been an increase of 12% in 2008. The second fact is that central banks' balance sheets swelled, as discussed below.

Also, the unprecedented lending by central banks in foreign currency — supported by a net of swaps, the most important of which were with the Federal Reserve — fits well into this overall interpretation. As long as only the net provision of central bank liquidity was relevant, it did not matter how this was supplied. When central banks had to substitute, at least in part, interbank intermediation with their own intermediation, they had to do this in the many forms in which private intermediation takes place: different maturities, different currencies, and, in some cases, different markets — hence, the much more variegated nature, in addition to the much larger size, of central banks' balance sheets.

It should be noted that the increased intermediation of the International Monetary Fund (IMF), other multinational institutions, and even governments, in terms of larger deficits and "loans" to the private sector, constitutes other aspects of the same trend. Nevertheless, what happened on central banks' balance sheets was the most obvious manifestation of the general phenomenon of the shift of intermediation from the private sector to the public sector. The effects of credit easing and quantitative easing on the balance sheets of central banks have been dramatic (Figures 5–9).

The sudden and dramatic quantitative increase of the balance sheet is obvious in the case of the Federal Reserve and the Bank of England. It is also clear in the case of the ECB, even if it is less extreme and an increase of autonomous factors (in addition to more abundant liquidity provision) contributed to this result. The increased scale of intermediation by the ECB is also evidenced by an increase in the number of

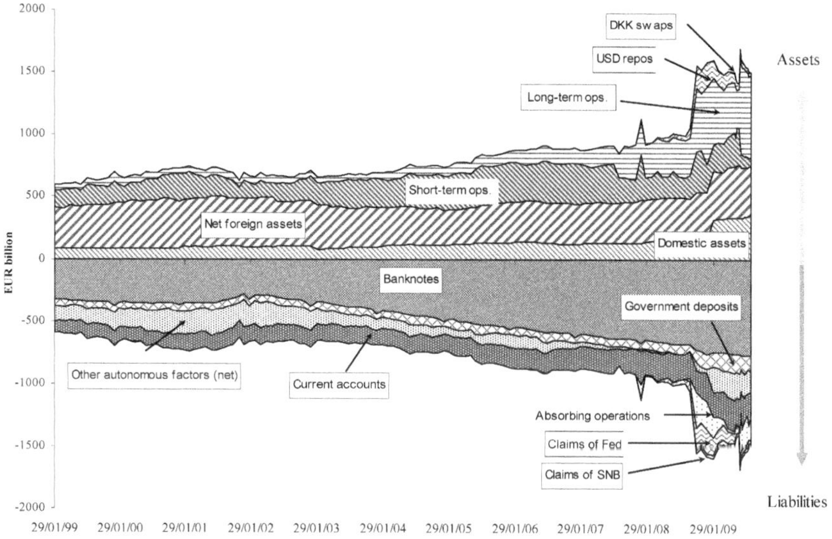

Figure 5. Selected items of the ECB's balance sheet, January 1999–August 2009.

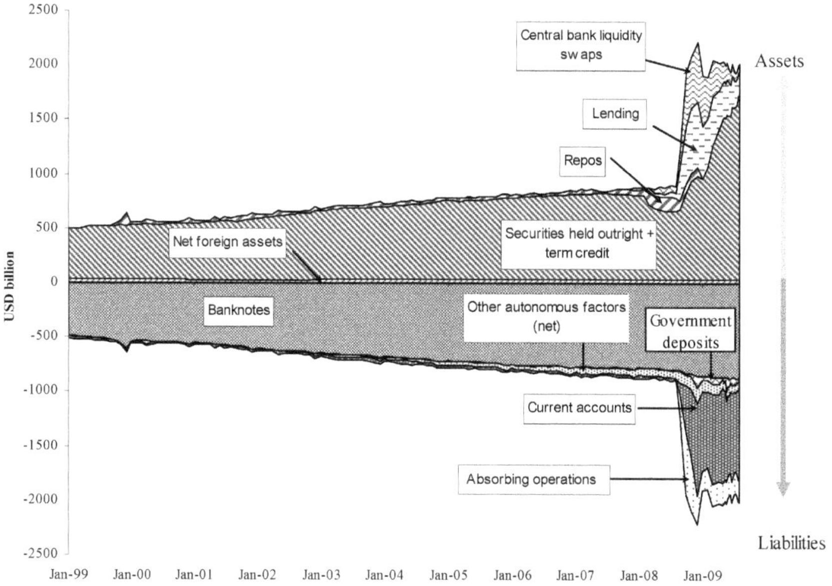

Figure 6. Selected items of the U.S. Federal Reserve's balance sheet, January 1999–August 2009.

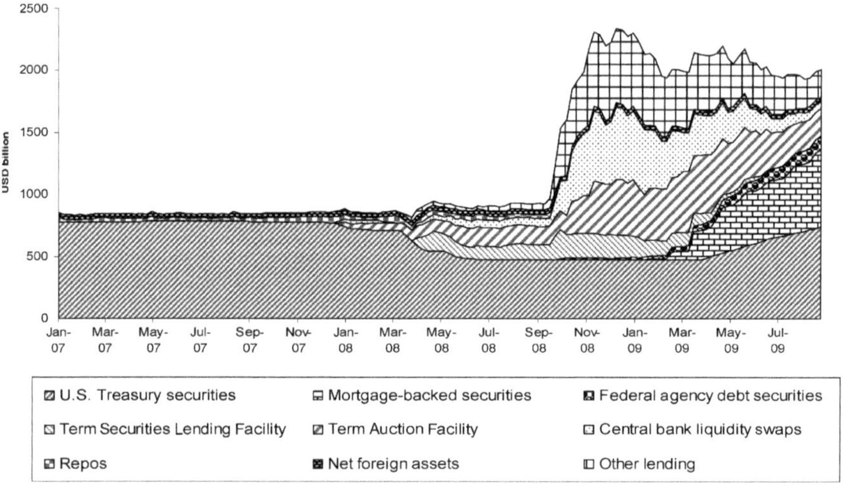

Figure 7. Composition of the asset side of the Federal Reserve's balance sheet, January 2007–August 2009.

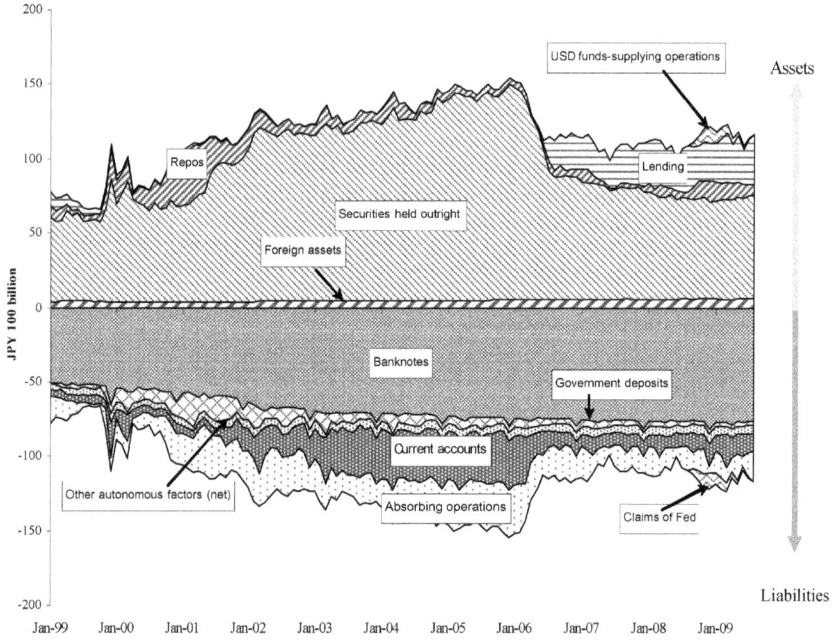

Figure 8. Selected items of the Bank of Japan's balance sheet, January 1999–August 2009.

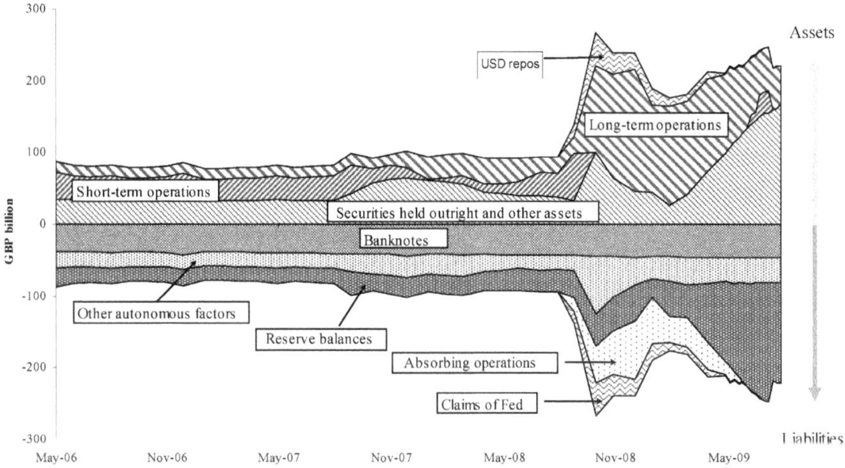

Figure 9. Selected items of the Bank of England's balance sheet, May 2006–August 2009.

counterparties seeking refinancing from it after the beginning of the crisis — from below 400 before the crisis to a peak of more than 800 in the case of main refinancing operations, and from less than 200 to more than 1,000 for longer-term refinancing operations. In the case of the Bank of Japan, there is no equivalent increase of the balance sheet, as this country was not hit with the same degree of violence by the phenomenon and had let its balance sheet swell well before the crisis because of its quantitative easing policy. Furthermore, the extreme diversification of the asset side of the balance sheet, due to central bank intermediation, is obvious in the balance sheet of the Federal Reserve and, in lesser measure, in the balance sheets of the ECB and the Bank of England.

The differences in scale and kind of the actions of the different central banks result largely from differences in financial intermediation between the Anglo-American economies and that of continental Europe. That is, bank lending is dominant in Europe, whereas the role played by direct financing and money market funds is much higher in the U.S. and the U.K. In practice, all of the credit easing actions taken by the ECB worked their way through banks. This is also the basic reason why the ECB has labeled its actions as "enhanced credit support".

5. An Assessment of the Effectiveness of Central Bank Actions

This section assesses the effectiveness of the central bank actions in fighting the consequences of the crisis. It should be stressed that here only the proximate effectiveness of the measures will be considered, concentrating on the money market and in particular on the unsecured–secured spread. An assessment of the effectiveness for the wider financial market, and even more for the real economy, would require a different treatment which probably cannot be written as yet.

Different empirical exercises have been carried out to ascertain whether central bank actions have been effective, in particular when it comes to reducing the spread between unsecured and secured lending (Taylor and Williams, 2008; McAndrews *et al.*, 2008; Čihák *et al.*, 2009; Donati, 2009). The studies do not, however, draw the same conclusions. Moreover, some econometric tests carried out by the authors of this paper to see whether introducing the measures from central banks as dummy variables would identify a reduction in the spread were inconclusive, given that the relevant time series are highly irregular and tend to be dominated by a few extreme observations. In these conditions, a visual analysis, concentrating on the ECB case, is carried out below.

Figure 10 shows the liquidity component of the unsecured–secured spread, measured from the CDS of the best bank and not from the CDS index of 20 banks, together with vertical solid lines indicating the negative events which led to much higher spreads and dotted vertical lines indicating the most important ECB actions. The evidence is suggestive that all of the measures considered, with the exception of the 1-year repo in June 2009, were followed by lower liquidity risk. It should be stressed, however, that when the 1-year repo was allotted, the estimated liquidity risk premium had already withered away. Overall, this is an encouraging sign about the effectiveness of the ECB actions.

As a sort of robustness check, in Figures 11 and 12 another visual analysis is carried out, looking at the experience of the Fed as well as the ECB, where the entire unsecured–secured spread and not only its liquidity component is used. This can be seen as a robustness check, admittedly paid by lower precision, because the liquidity risk premium reported above is, of course, estimated with some unknown error. In addition, and more fundamentally, it is not sure that liquidity risk and credit risk are really additive and separable; in particular, during a crisis they may be correlated.

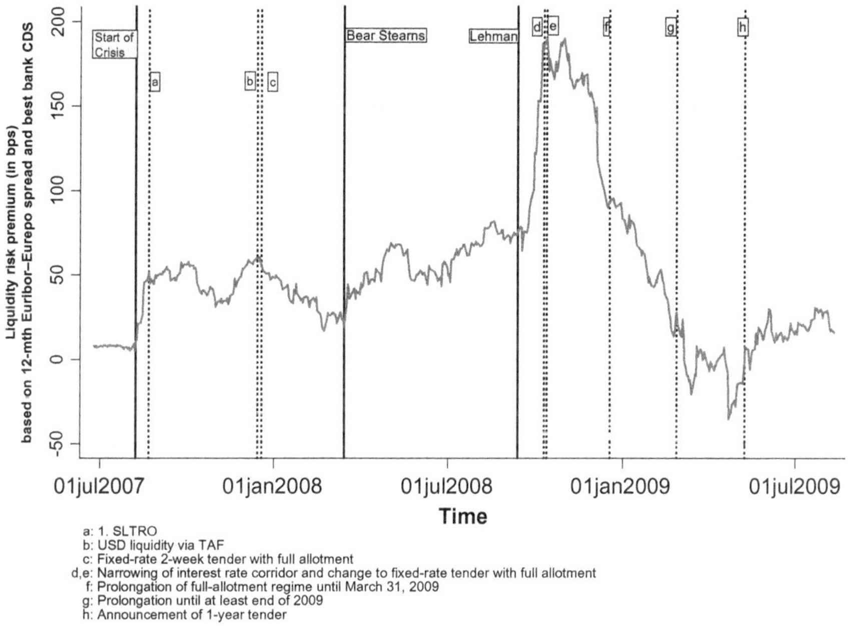

Figure 10. One-year Euribor–OIS spread liquidity component and relevant ECB actions.

The results obtained here are broadly comparable to those obtained by looking only at the liquidity risk: the actions of the Federal Reserve as well as those of the ECB seem to have led to lower spreads. More generally, and less rigorously, the spread reached enormous levels at the turn of 2008, but both the Federal Reserve and the ECB have taken extreme measures in terms of remedying the dysfunctioning of bank intermediation, and the spreads have come down to much lower levels (even if they ended the period covered in the figures at levels still higher than those prevailing before the crisis). These latter levels, however, should not be taken as the norm, given that experience has confirmed that there was a substantial amount of underestimation and underpricing of risk before August 2007. Indeed, if normality is not meant by reference to historical values, the levels reached by the unsecured–secured spreads at the end of the period covered in the figures look closer to normal than those prevailing before August 2007.

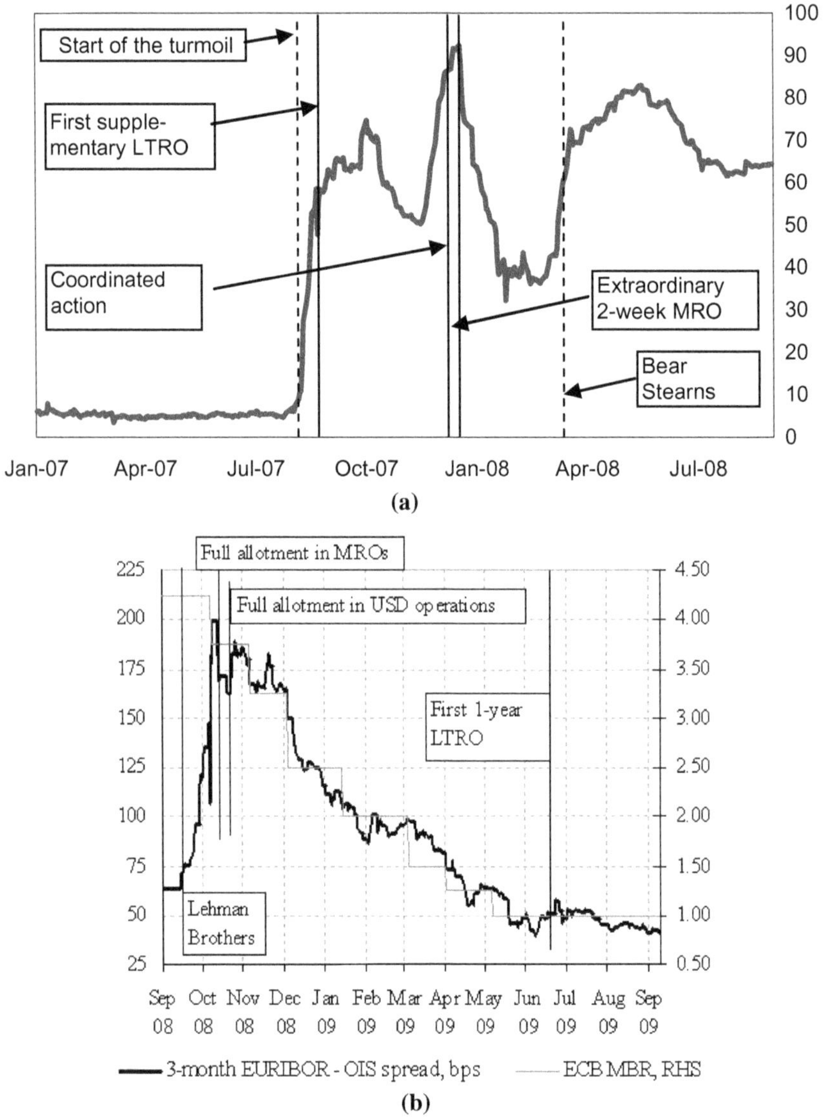

Figure 11. Three-month Libor/Euribor–OIS spreads (in basis points) and ECB actions, (a) January 2007–August 2008 and (b) September 2008–September 2009.

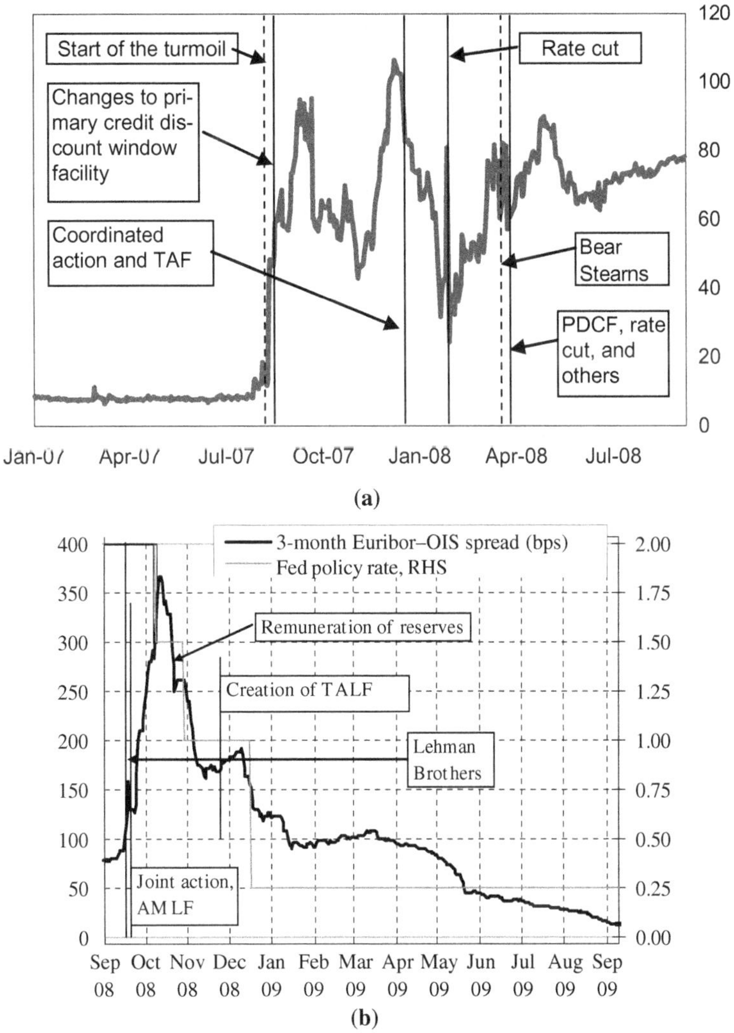

Figure 12. Three-month Libor/Euribor–OIS spreads (in basis points) and Federal Reserve actions, (a) January 2007–August 2008 and (b) September 2008–September 2009.

6. Conclusion

This paper advances the general conclusion that, confronted with extreme market dislocations, central banks have reacted with extreme measures which have had a good amount of success, at least with regard to the money market. As of the time of writing, the jury is still out to assess the effectiveness of central bank actions as far as the wider financial market and the real economy are concerned. Nevertheless, the omens are also favorable on this front, given the developments which have taken place since March 2009 in the financial market and in the real economy.

References

Čihák, M., T. Harjes, and E. Stavrev (2009). Euro area monetary policy in uncharted waters. IMF Working Paper WP/09/185, August.

Donati, P. (2009). The effect of conventional and unconventional monetary policy on the money market spreads in the euro area. ECB working paper, September.

Dudley, W. C. (2008). Remarks at the Federal Reserve Bank of Chicago's 44th Annual Conference on Bank Structure and Competition. Speech, May.

ECB (2009). *Euro Money Market Survey 2009*. September.

Eisenschmidt, J. and J. Tapking (2009). Liquidity risk premia in unsecured interbank money markets. ECB Working Paper No. 1025.

Goodhart, C. (2008). Liquidity risk management. *Banque de France — Financial Stability Review*, 11, 39–44.

McAndrews, J., A. Sarkar, and Z. Wang (2008). The effect of the Term Auction Facility on the London Inter-Bank Offered Rate. Staff Report No. 335, Federal Reserve Bank of New York, July.

Taylor, J. B. and J. C. Williams (2008). Further results on a black swan in the money market. SIEPR Discussion Paper No. 07-46, May.

The Role of the State in a Crisis

Phillip L. Swagel*
Georgetown University

1. Introduction

In addressing the role of the state in a crisis, this paper discusses what the government — the state — should do to help resolve a crisis (I leave the role of the state in *creating* a crisis for the discussant, Peter Wallison). The focus here is on fiscal policy, which is natural since I was Assistant Secretary for Economic Policy at the Treasury Department from December 2006 to January 2009.

I first consider the "playbook" of steps to stabilize the financial system in a crisis, and then compare this with the actions actually taken during 2007–2009. In looking at the crisis, I focus first on the most severe stage of the crisis in mid-September 2008 following the collapse of Lehman Brothers, and then consider more broadly actions taken at other times or actions that could have been taken but were not. Several constraints account for the differences between the list of what should have been done and that of what was done, notably legal and (especially) political constraints.

In considering these constraints and the topic of what might have been done earlier to prevent the economic catastrophe of fall 2008, a general point is that the political situation plays an enormous role in shaping the feasible options with which to address a crisis. Some potential actions that might be desirable to take could be politically impossible, notably including injecting public funds to deal with the crisis while it was still mounting in

---

* Phillip L. Swagel is a visiting professor and director of the Capital Markets Research Center at Georgetown University's McDonough School of Business.

March 2008 rather than after the financial system was in turmoil in September 2008. Unfortunately, the problem of political constraints is probably not one that can be "solved", but is simply a fact of life that crisis management must take into account. With this in mind, I then consider what might have been done during this crisis that was not tried and that might have been feasible (albeit not for sure): a massive (and massively unfair) housing bailout. The paper concludes by drawing some lessons for the management of future crises.

2. The "Playbook" for Dealing with a Financial Crisis

As discussed in Swagel (2009), there is something of a "playbook" by which to address a financial crisis. The eventual goal is for the government to exit from any interventions, including selling off financial stakes accumulated in firms or assets purchased from firms. As we well understood at the Treasury, successful efforts to deal with past crises such as that in Sweden in the early 1990s typically involved such substantial involvements in the financial sector. The broad steps involved in dealing with a crisis are as follows:

- *Stabilize the financial system.* This includes stopping runs on core financial institutions that might otherwise be solvent but for the effects of the panic. Such panic-induced distress might reflect, for example, the impact on net worth of a fire sale of assets resulting from a drying up of liquidity such as the collapse of the repo funding market.

  Guarantees on bank funding or on claims by bank counterparties, while anathema in normal circumstances, could play prominent roles in ending a severe panic. Guarantees might be seen as a sledgehammer-type intervention in markets to get ahead of an unfolding crisis and end a run on markets, as opposed to undertaking a series of more limited steps in an escalating sequence such as by starting with partial guarantees.
- *Winnow insolvent banks.* Insolvent financial institutions — so-called "zombie" banks — hunker down and attempt to ride out the financial crisis in the hope of regaining solvency as asset prices stabilize and rebound. Such banks absorb resources that might otherwise be put to work by other financial intermediaries to support lending. Shutting down insolvent banks is thus an important step to restore the flow of

credit and avoid the dissipation of resources. Acquisitions can play a useful role as part of a consolidation process, since having a strong bank take over a weak one would be expected to lead to increased lending and thus support economic activity.

- *Ensure the viability of surviving banks.* The financial system must have sufficient capital buffers to withstand expected further losses. This step is aimed at providing market participants with assurances about the viability of the financial system — eventually to facilitate a government exit and a return of private capital. The government does not need to guarantee every individual bank, but instead ensure that the system as a whole is solvent.
- *Provide policy certainty.* This is also aimed at facilitating a return of private capital to replace public resources. Private investors will naturally hesitate if they see a possibility of wholesale nationalization of banks.

Therefore, this playbook first stanches any panicked flight from banks, and then cleanses the surviving firms so that any government stakes can be sold off. This is not to rule out nationalization as a potential policy measure — indeed, the point of winnowing insolvent banks is precisely for the government to take over failed banks — but only to make clear that potential investors must see an end to nationalization if the goal is to eventually have a private banking system (and this has certainly been the goal in the United States across administrations).

3. The Plays Run During This Financial Crisis

As discussed by Gorton and Metrick (2009), the financial crisis from August 2007 onwards can be seen as a form of bank run from the securitized banking system funded by repurchase agreements (rather than a run from the traditional deposit-taking banking system). In the wake of the collapse of Lehman Brothers on September 14, 2008, the run broadened to include money markets and commercial paper, as short-term credit markets locked up in the wake of the Reserve Primary Fund (a money market mutual fund) "breaking the buck" as a result of losses on Lehman securities. In the end, the problems in money market mutual funds were idiosyncratic to the Reserve Primary Fund and a few others with particular exposures to Lehman securities (some of which received support from a corporate parent to avoid "breaking the buck"); however, this was not apparent at the time, so the problems at the Reserve Primary Fund appeared to have led market participants to question the stability of money market mutual funds as a whole.

As discussed by Bernanke (2009), large-scale withdrawals from money market funds led fund managers to hoard cash in anticipation of withdrawals. This in turn led to problems in commercial paper markets, with commercial paper issuers finding a paucity of demand as money market mutual funds sat on the sidelines. While one would normally expect the market to clear with simply an increase in yields needed to bring customers back to buying commercial paper, market participants were reporting to the Treasury that this was not happening and that it was increasingly difficult for them to fund. With short-term credit markets seized, large non-financial corporations were faced with liquidity challenges. The crisis was spilling over dramatically to affect the broad economy.

This was the sequence of events that led to the request for the Troubled Asset Relief Program (TARP) — not the direct impact of Lehman's bankruptcy *per se*, but rather the unintended and indirect impact through the problems at the Reserve Primary Fund appearing to lead toward a cascading shutdown of short-term credit markets. From the perspective of the Treasury, this appeared to be a broad panic — a run on the financial system. This then threatened to have a massive impact on the broad economy, with large non-financial companies telling officials at the Treasury that they were unable to roll their commercial paper and faced liquidity problems.[1]

The policy response included a guarantee on money market mutual funds (Treasury) as well as a series of facilities aimed at stabilizing money markets and commercial paper (Federal Reserve), along with the proposal to purchase illiquid assets using the TARP. With markets continuing to deteriorate after the TARP legislation was proposed, this was then followed by capital injections into banks using the Treasury's TARP authority and loan guarantees for senior bank debt by the Federal Deposit Insurance Corporation (FDIC). Swagel (2009) provides a discussion of the circumstances behind these decisions. These actions coincide, in part, with the list of actions to take during a crisis, as explained below.

---

[1] As noted in Swagel (2009), the norm would be to expect that commercial paper would roll over at *some* interest rate, albeit perhaps a substantially higher one.

3.1 *Stabilize the financial system*

Providing stability in the face of a panic was the aim of the guarantee on money market mutual funds and (later) the three-year FDIC guarantees on senior bank loans. Federal Reserve facilities to extend liquidity to money market mutual funds and commercial paper issuers were similarly targeted at the part of the credit market that was overtaken by panic in the week of September 14, 2008. Finally, the TARP capital injections could also be seen as an effort to stabilize the financial system by assuring market participants that firms would have the ability to withstand further losses, including asset write-downs.

While guarantees are far from a desirable policy under normal circumstances, they were likely essential for stopping the panic that began in the wake of the failure of Lehman Brothers and the "breaking of the buck" by the Reserve Primary Fund. It is possible in theory that the guarantees and liquidity facilities, even without the TARP, would have been sufficient to address the crisis, since the FDIC guarantees on senior bank debt essentially provided a breathing space of three years in which banks could be assured of financing. In reality, however, the FDIC loan guarantees would not have been put into place without the TARP capital injections being proposed at the same time to provide a Treasury capital buffer ahead of the FDIC (notwithstanding the underlying fact that there is only one public balance sheet and that the FDIC and the Treasury are both part of it).

3.2 *Winnow insolvent banks*

This step was essentially not taken in the current crisis, or at least not intentionally taken. More than 100 banks have failed in this economic cycle, but this was not part of a strategy to winnow out insolvent banks; rather, it was a consequence of the economic environment and the legacy of past lending decisions. Indeed, political circumstances would have made it impossible in practice to implement a strategy to winnow out weak banks were one to have been considered (which it was not).

This can be seen in the political reactions in the fall of 2008 to bank consolidation, notably the October 2008 acquisition of the National City Corporation (NatCity) by the PNC Financial Services Group. NatCity did not receive approval from the federal banking regulators for its application for the TARP Capital Purchase Program (CPP), and without this approval the bank's application for a capital injection did not proceed for consideration by the Treasury. The ensuing takeover of NatCity by PNC was met with a firestorm of criticism that taxpayer money was being used to fund acquisitions when it was meant to be used for banks to lend. The irony was that it is generally beneficial when a weak bank is absorbed by a strong one; after all, a weak bank does not lend, while a strong one would be expected to do so and thus better support the economy in the regions with the failing bank. The complaint that banks were not using TARP funds to support lending is equally misleading. The TARP funds were meant to stabilize the banking system and assure market participants that the system was viable; as a result of this increased stability, lending would be higher than otherwise (although it is difficult to show the impact of a crisis that was averted). Regardless of these points, the criticism over bank acquisitions meant that there was little prospect for any winnowing out of the banking system, even had this been on the minds of policymakers.

3.3 *Ensure viability*

The policy steps taken on Columbus Day (October 13) 2008 — capital injections and the FDIC loan guarantees — eventually proved successful in stabilizing the financial system and providing market participants with a measure of assurance about the viability of major banks. This sense of certainty was not complete, however, until the results of the stress tests (the Supervisory Capital Assessment Program) were unveiled in May 2009 and it became clear to market participants that the government would not seek to nationalize the weaker of the large banks (notably Citibank).

3.4 *Provide policy certainty*

Giving market participants a sense of future policy steps is especially difficult in the middle of a financial crisis when events are moving rapidly. This was certainly the case in the fall of 2008, when the Treasury first switched from the planned TARP purpose of buying assets to injecting capital, and then canceled the asset purchases outright. As discussed in Swagel (2009), these steps were taken for reasonable purposes (even if inevitably there will be disagreement about them), but there is no denying that the changes in direction created uncertainty as market participants had a hard time understanding what policy steps would come in response to future market developments.

The impact of policy uncertainty can also be seen in the reaction of credit markets to Treasury Secretary Timothy Geithner's February 10, 2009 speech in which he unveiled the administration's Financial Stability Plan (FSP). Subsequent events have shown that this speech indeed discussed the policy steps subsequently followed by the Treasury, including the stress tests, additional capital raising, and implementation and expansion of the Term Asset-Backed Securities Loan Facility (TALF) aimed at boosting securitization. However, the speech was widely criticized at the time for a lack of specifics, particularly after President Obama had appeared the night before to suggest that details would be forthcoming. The impact of this uncertainty can be seen in the upward spike in credit default swap (CDS) spreads of six major banks, as shown in Figure 1 (taken from a September 2009 Treasury report), perhaps reflecting market participants' concerns that the new administration would not take effective steps to continue to stabilize the financial sector. This concern

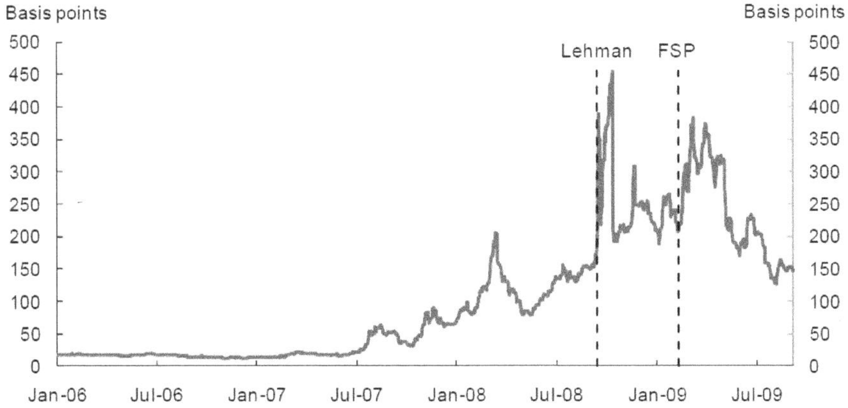

Figure 1. Average CDS spreads of selected financial institutions (in basis points).

Source: Bloomberg.

Note: Includes BAC, C, GS, JPM, MS, and WFC.

was unfounded, but the graphical depiction in the Treasury's own report illustrates the impact of policy uncertainty.

In addition, policy uncertainty was created by the events surrounding the public discussion in the middle of March 2009 of bonuses to certain staff at AIG. The reaction of the top administration officials to public criticism regarding these bonuses led some banks which had accepted public capital to seek to repay the TARP funds, notwithstanding the possibility that the stabilization of the financial sector remained unclear. This uncertainty, however, was eventually dispelled by the announcement of the stress test results and the subsequent ability of major banks to raise capital.

3.5 *Provide clarity on balance sheets*

The original purpose of the TARP to buy illiquid assets mainly would have performed the function of helping to clarify the status of firms' balance sheets, both those whose illiquid assets were purchased and hopefully others for which pricing clarity was gained through government actions. In principle, government actions to help provide clarity on firms' balance sheets could involve purchasing illiquid assets or simply insuring them. Both of these possibilities require a pricing mechanism. One such mechanism was developed at the Treasury in the fall of 2008, i.e., a system of reverse auctions that took into account the heterogeneity of the illiquid mortgage-backed securities (MBS). However, it remains to be seen how effective this would have been in practice in terms of resulting in prices that were accepted by the market, as the asset purchases were abandoned in November 2008 at a time when it appeared that the remaining TARP resources would need to be husbanded for additional capital injections. As part of the Obama administration's Financial Stability Plan, the Public-Private Investment Program (PPIP) is meant to help provide this clarity, but as of fall 2009 remains a work in progress. In the meantime, a steep yield curve is acting in a way to help recapitalize banks through earnings.

As of late 2009, the end goal of allowing the government to sell off its stakes in firms and dispose of assets accumulated during the crisis also remains a work in progress. A number of banks have bought themselves out of the confines of the TARP, but the government stake in other firms — notably Citigroup and GMAC — remains sizable.

4. Alternative Steps to Those Taken in Fall 2008

A comparison of the steps taken against those in the playbook shows that the response during the worst phase of the crisis in the fall of 2008 broadly went in the right direction, but with considerable uncertainty created along the way. Whether this was inevitable or avoidable awaits judgment with the benefit of greater hindsight. In the meantime, however, it is possible to discuss several alternatives to the steps that were taken. These alternatives are drawn from academic critiques of the TARP-related actions. A lesson in considering these alternatives is that the political situation has considerable impact in terms of the ability of the government to act.

The first alternative would be to inject capital from the start rather than proposing to purchase assets. Cochrane and Zingales (2009) assert that the original proposal to purchase illiquid assets was itself a concern to market participants: "It did not help that the TARP was such a transparently bad idea. The Fed and Treasury soon figured that out, settling on equity 'injections' and a bank-debt guarantee instead. Floating a bad idea does not instill confidence." As noted above, the Treasury did in fact switch to capital injections in October 2008, as markets continued to deteriorate after the TARP was proposed and then enacted as the Emergency Economic Stabilization Act of 2008. The problem with the criticism of Cochrane and Zingales, however, is that it would have been impossible to start with capital injections. A proposal for the government to buy 20% of the banking system would not have passed the House of Representatives. This was a hard political constraint. With this in mind, the comparison of buying assets against injecting capital is then flawed in that it pits a feasible option (buying assets) against an infeasible alternative (injecting capital from the start). The real choice in September 2008 was between proposing the TARP as originally envisioned for the purpose of buying illiquid MBS versus the (feasible) alternative of not having any TARP and thus not having the ability to switch to capital injections as financial market conditions deteriorated in the ensuing weeks.

The second alternative would be to put in place the Fed liquidity measures and the FDIC loan guarantees, but not the TARP. An advantage of this alternative compared to the TARP is that it did not require Congressional action: the Fed was able to proceed under its emergency authorities, while the FDIC loan guarantees were permitted through the use of the systemic risk exception in the Federal Deposit Insurance Corporation Improvement Act (FDICIA). This combination of steps might well have succeeded in stabilizing markets while avoiding the uncertainties that resulted from the difficulty in obtaining Congressional approval for the TARP; after all, the FDIC loan guarantees, if extended widely, would have assured market participants of the viability of firms for at least the three-year duration of the guarantees. As noted above, however, this alternative was also likely infeasible in that the FDIC was not keen to extend the loan guarantees in the first place. In the circumstances of last fall, it is unlikely that the guarantees would have taken place on their own without the accompanying TARP capital injections to stand in front of the FDIC deposit insurance fund.

The third alternative would be to obtain non-bank resolution authority before September 2008. Before the TARP was provided by Congress in late 2008, the Treasury did not have legal authority to commit public resources to intervene in a failing institution such as Lehman Brothers. The Federal Reserve judged that Lehman Brothers did not possess suitable collateral against which it could lend, while the FDIC was similarly unable to support Lehman since the company was not a bank. The period from the collapse of Bear Stearns in March 2008 to the collapse of Lehman Brothers in September 2008, however, represents a time in which one could imagine the Treasury seeking to obtain authority to intervene in a failing non-bank firm and then being in a position to prevent or cushion the impact of Lehman's failure.

Unfortunately, this alternative also ignores the political reality — in particular, the difficulty of enacting such extraordinary powers before a crisis is apparent (that is, before an acute crisis takes place). Economic growth was still positive in March 2008 and throughout the first half of 2008, even though job growth was negative (as would be expected with the economy growing at a rate below potential). Moreover, the Economic Stimulus Act of 2008, enacted in February 2008, provided for US$100 billion in stimulus payments to American households, although these stimulus checks had yet to go out. Even the failure of Bear Stearns, while definitely a wake-up call that a run on a non-financial institution could happen virtually overnight, did not have an acute knock-on impact on other firms, and the subsequent action by the Federal Reserve to allow broker-dealers to access discount window liquidity through the Primary Dealer Credit Facility appeared to ensure that a similar funding run would not take place against another firm like Bear Stearns (notably Lehman Brothers).

In sum, the economic situation was worrisome, but by far not at the point of the collapse which ensued in the fall of 2008 and into 2009. For better or worse, the simple political reality is that it would have been hard to obtain authority from Congress for a rescue fund such as the TARP to be placed at the discretion of the executive branch of government. Similarly, it is unimaginable that Congress would have granted non-bank resolution authority to the Treasury or other executive branch agencies in 2008 — even in 2009, such authority has been difficult for the Obama administration to obtain from a skeptical Congress. Moreover, this is without the difficulties of a divided government and election-year politics that would have been faced by the Bush administration in 2008.

5. Conclusion: What Could Have Been Done That Was Not Attempted?

While the discussion above relates to the difficulty of obtaining authority to deploy public resources ahead of the collapse of Lehman Brothers, one policy alternative that was much discussed but never attempted was a massive bailout of homeowners facing foreclosure. There were many calls throughout 2007 and 2008 for the Bush administration to do more to prevent foreclosures, but, as discussed in Swagel (2009), these were largely rhetoric. Programs to avoid foreclosures could help many sympathetic homeowners, including families who ended up in an unaffordable mortgage through predatory lending. The reality, however, is that such programs will also inevitably result in as many undeserving families receiving assistance. Despite all the best intentions and efforts at policy design, people who were responsible and did not buy a larger house than they could afford will end up paying in part for assistance to homeowners who took risks and acted irresponsibly — and efforts to limit this horizontal inequity will reduce the number of people receiving assistance. The simple reality is that it is much easier to say that more needs to be done to avoid foreclosures than it is to actually propose a plan that is both effective and politically feasible.

In retrospect, however, a housing bailout carried out in sufficient scope could have improved the performance of assets (such as MBS) by enough to avert the crisis of last fall and the ensuing economic calamity. An effective program would have been indiscriminate, with deserving and undeserving homeowners alike receiving enough public assistance to stay in their homes. To put the program in place quickly would have required doing without the inherent delays in attempting to sort out deserving homeowners from undeserving homeowners and then attempting to calibrate the necessary financial assistance to each family's situation. Mortgages generally cannot be purchased out of an MBS for less than par, so the policy would have involved the government making lenders and investors in mortgages whole and then providing the necessary subsidy to refinance home buyers into mortgages they could afford.

Such a housing program would have been massively unfair and wildly unpopular if done in a transparent fashion. It would have involved a bailout of the banks that had made irresponsible loans, the investors who purchased the MBS into which those loans were securitized, and the people who speculated on their homes (including people who could have afforded a smaller house than they purchased). This unfairness means that such a program was unlikely to have been politically feasible. Indeed, Senator John McCain, in his run for President, put forward a housing proposal that involved similar steps, including buying mortgage loans at par and then modifying them to avoid foreclosures — only for his proposal to be roundly criticized for being irresponsible.

A key lesson of the policy response to the financial crisis is that the political and economic situation inevitably weighs heavily on the ability of the fiscal authority to take steps to address a worsening financial market ahead of a crisis. Simply put, it is likely unrealistic in the United States for massive public resources to be deployed before the economic impact of a financial crisis is widely felt, even though it may likely be too late to fully address the situation. The prospect for the executive branch of government to obtain radical authorities to be used "just in case" they are needed is limited, as is the prospect for any administration to somehow resist pressures to use public resources when they are made available.

References

Bernanke, B. S. (2009). Reflections on a year of crisis. Speech delivered at the Federal Reserve Bank of Kansas City's Annual Economic Symposium, Jackson Hole, Wyoming, August 21.

Cochrane, J. and L. Zingales (2009). Lehman and the financial crisis. *Wall Street Journal*, September 15.

Gorton, G. and A. Metrick (2009). Securitized banking and the run on the repo. NBER Working Paper No. 15223.

Swagel, P. (2009). The financial crisis: an inside view. *Brookings Papers on Economic Activity*, Spring(1), 1–63.

Comments: Panel on the Role of the State

Peter J. Wallison*
American Enterprise Institute

We all understand that the role the state plays in the financial system can be helpful or harmful. In the current crisis, the historical consensus is likely to be that the extraordinary actions of the Fed and of the government generally — particularly after the collapse of Lehman Brothers — were helpful. However, a more important question is not what was done, but rather how we got into a position where they *had* to be done. Here, I think, the role of the state — at least in the U.S. — was harmful; and if that role had not been carried out as it was, we might not be talking about this subject today.

The fundamental question about the current financial crisis is whether what happened in 2008 was *sui generis* — an artifact, say, of government policy itself — or the result of a defect in our financial and regulatory system (some would say a defect in capitalism itself). As a political matter, those who believe that the financial crisis provides an opportunity for the government to take a greater role in the financial system and in the economy generally would tend to see the crisis as the result of inherent flaws in the financial system. On the other hand, those who are less admiring of the government and of its role in the economy would tend to see the government and its policies as at least one of the major causes of the crisis.

However, the issue is more important than the politics. Whether we believe that the crisis is the result of government policy or the result of inherent problems in the financial system will determine the nature of our proposals for reform — or whether we advance any major reforms at all.

What I am about to say implicates the responsibilities of the recently established Financial Crisis Inquiry Commission, of which I am a

---

* Peter J. Wallison holds the Arthur F. Burns Chair in Financial Policy Studies and is Co-Director of the American Enterprise Institute's program on Financial Policy Studies.

member. Our role is to discover (as best as we can) the causes of the financial crisis, and to report our conclusions to Congress, the President, and the American people. I have pledged to the Chairman and other members of the Commission that I will follow the evidence wherever it leads. My work up to now — which has involved a close study of Fannie Mae and Freddie Mac and of government housing policies in general — suggests to me that ill-advised housing policies of the U.S. government were the principal cause of the financial crisis.

The causal relationships seem fairly clear. Because of government requirements, the Federal Housing Administration (FHA) as well as Fannie Mae and Freddie Mac bought trillions of dollars of affordable housing loans — loans to people at or below the median income. Furthermore, large banks, in order to gain regulatory approval for mergers and other expansion, made trillions of dollars in mortgage loans that qualified under the Community Reinvestment Act because they were made to people at 80% of the median income or below. All told, as of the end of 2008, there were 26 million subprime and other non-prime (Alt-A) loans in the U.S. financial system, or 47% of all outstanding mortgages. Of this group, about two-thirds were on the balance sheets of (or had been guaranteed as mortgage-backed securities (MBS) by) the FHA and Fannie and Freddie, or were held as whole loans on the balance sheets of the four largest U.S. banks. This is pretty strong evidence that the housing policies of the U.S. government were responsible for the enormous number of subprime and Alt-A loans, which were the source of the mortgage meltdown and the financial panic that followed.

The fact that almost 50% of all U.S. mortgages were subprime or otherwise weak has never happened before — not even close. There had always been a subprime market in the United States, but only at a fraction of this size. When these loans started to default at unprecedented rates in 2007, the shocking losses on supposedly AAA securities backed by these loans caused the asset-backed market to simply shut down. The collapse of a whole market was also unprecedented, and distinguishes this asset bubble and this crisis from all others. It also accounts for the global aspect of the crisis, since the asset-backed market was a global market. The shutdown of this major source of financing and liquidity subsequently caused the collapse of many other companies, including, first, Bear Stearns and then Lehman Brothers and AIG. These financial failures, in my view, caused the financial crisis and ultimately the recession that the United States is still experiencing.

If this is a correct diagnosis of what happened, the government interventions that occurred starting in 2008 were simply required to mop up the mess that was created by the earlier distortions of the housing finance market. In other words, if the housing bubble had not been almost half-full of bad mortgages, the financial crisis would never have occurred. As Charles Calomiris said this morning, but for the housing bubble we would not be here today.

If government policy is what lawyers would call the precipitating cause of the financial crisis, then the crisis was *not* the result of a flaw in our financial system or in our system of regulation. This is not to say that our financial and regulatory system is flawless, but only that the financial crisis is not likely to occur again provided we do not make major changes in the regulatory structure. All we have to do is stop the government from adopting policies that distort the financial system. Indeed, major changes could have serious unintended consequences if they mean imposing bank-like controls on all large financial companies. It would increase costs and reduce innovation and risk taking, adversely affecting economic growth. It would also introduce moral hazard, which would require yet more government intervention in regulating financial institutions.

On the other hand, many people apparently assume that the financial crisis *was* the result of flaws in our financial or regulatory system. If so, it would also be reasonable to assume that a similar financial crisis might occur again, and soon, unless we do something to forestall it. This approach would give rise to all kinds of proposals for greater control over financial institutions in order to prevent a recurrence of a financial crisis. The administration's proposals for regulating all systemically significant firms, and setting up a mechanism to resolve or rescue them if they fail, are explicitly based on the notion that a financial crisis could occur again if we do not act now. As Treasury Secretary Geithner said in his recent House testimony, "Make no mistake, the flaws in our financial system and regulatory framework that allowed this crisis to occur, and in many ways helped to cause it, are still in place." All of the various proposals for new regulations are based on the same premise.

There is nothing wrong with the reform proposals; indeed, they might even be prudent if they are right. Nonetheless, it is important to keep in mind that what we eventually conclude was the cause of the crisis should influence the remedies we select, or whether we need any remedies at all. It is also important to note that one of the unique elements of this financial crisis is that it was characterized by an investor panic. Not only did the asset-backed market shut down because investors had lost confidence in the ratings on asset-backed securities; in part because of this shutdown, no one even knew with confidence which financial institutions were insolvent or unstable due to their holdings of poor-quality mortgages. This lack of information gave rise to the panic, which was heightened after Lehman Brothers' failure demonstrated that the U.S. government was not going to rescue every major financial institution that might be in trouble.

Accordingly, in reviewing the three papers in this set, it is important to consider not only whether the remedies they suggest would be appropriate for a financial crisis, but whether they would also be appropriate for a financial panic — a massive loss of investor confidence in banks and non-banks alike.

Of the three presentations in this panel, one — the Alessandri–Haldane paper — directly addresses the question of modifying the regulatory system to help prevent a future financial crisis. The authors point out that deposit insurance and regulation have made it possible for banks to use more leverage (by reducing their capital) and take more risks. They note that, as a political matter, government intervention cannot be reversed; deposit insurance, once provided, cannot be withdrawn. So, the problem for policymakers is to develop a regulatory structure that is effective in dealing with the lower capital levels, reduced liquidity, higher leverage, and greater risk taking that will inevitably follow from the government's willingness to assure depositors that their funds are safe. As they note, all of the weaknesses in the banking system can be traced back to a successful effort by the banks to "game the state" by exploiting the benefits the government has showered on them. They suggest a number of important, original, and interesting ways to address this problem through setting leverage limits, recalibrating risk weights, placing more risks on shareholders by modifying limited liability rules, reducing concentration in banking, and introducing risk-based premia for deposit insurance and capital insurance.

The practicality of some of these ideas is questionable. Properly assessing the risk created by an individual institution so as to require it to pay the correct amount to a pre-funded insurance system has proven difficult in the past. Also, modifying shareholder liability could mean that banks would have to become smaller such that their ability to serve the needs of large multinational corporations would be in doubt.

A more significant question is whether any of these changes would actually stop an investor panic of the kind that we faced in 2008. By definition, a panic is irrational. The fact that banks have paid into a better and more efficient deposit insurance system — or are taking fewer risks, holding more capital, and maintaining higher liquidity — may not avail them much if investors have lost confidence in whether they are solvent. It is important to remember that almost all of the largest U.S. banks were considered well capitalized before the crisis began. If, in the future, we again have a situation in which large numbers of financial institutions are invested in the same assets and those assets turn out to have a serious, previously unrecognized deficiency, is there anything in the Alessandri–Haldane formula that will prevent runs? I doubt it. Better regulation of individual banks is not a prescription for preventing a common shock to the system as a whole. Indeed, to the extent that better and more comprehensive regulation might channel banks into the same investment and management patterns, it might then enhance the possibility of a common shock rather than reduce it.

Papadia and Välimäki make a more-than-tentative case for the proposition that unprecedented central bank liquidity provisions in the midst of the crisis were effective in reducing the severity of the crisis and the panic. First, they argue that there was a major liquidity risk in the crisis, and then that the central banks provided enough liquidity to make up for the lack of liquidity from the private banks. They show that liquidity supplied by the European Central Bank and the Fed was followed by a reduction in the spread of Libor over the overnight indexed swap (OIS). This does not necessarily mean cause and effect, but it is a good *prima facie* case. The authors are careful to point out that the data speak only to the money markets and not to the other elements of the panic. Nevertheless, in terms of the role of the state, their paper suggests that the actions of central banks can have a palliative effect in easing at least part of a financial crisis.

The other side of the coin — which Papadia and Välimäki do not address — is the risk that central banks were taking in ballooning their balance sheets. The authors point out that at first the European Central Bank had a more open standard than the Fed on the collateral it would accept in exchange for its liquidity provisions, but later the Fed went further than the ECB. Indeed, in its loan to AIG, the Fed went so far as to take as collateral the equity of a company that it deemed — on what basis we do not know — sufficiently strong to repay the loan. As this is being written, the Fed is now paying dearly for this boldness. There is first the question of whether bailing out AIG was necessary, and then the question of whether the collateral the Fed received was adequate. Its willingness to take equity in AIG as collateral raised questions about the Fed's later argument that it could not find sufficient collateral in Lehman Brothers to rescue that firm.

Although the Fed received a lot of praise for its bold and decisive action — action that Papadia and Välimäki argue resulted in a salutary reduction in liquidity risk in the money markets — the U.S. Congress seems to have been alarmed by what it saw. The idea that an independent agency could put out over a trillion dollars without any Congressional approval was a shock that has caused many (perhaps a majority) in Congress to favor restrictions on the Fed and a reduction in its non-monetary authority.

It would be unfortunate if, as a result of its actions in this crisis, the Fed's ability to lend generally to the market (rather than to individual companies) in the event of a future crisis or panic were to be restricted. Despite the fact that Papadia and Välimäki limited the scope of their analysis to the money markets, the calming of those markets would inevitably have a calming effect on a panic. After all, the traditional way to deal with a panic is to flood the market with liquidity, so that investors, creditors, and others believe that they will be able to get their funds when they ask for them. Admittedly, it is difficult to know whether a particular institution is insolvent or merely illiquid, but this perennial problem would not be solved by creating a resolution system of the kind the Obama administration has proposed. In any event, as long as a stricken and threatened company has collateral, the Fed should be able to provide it with liquidity.

Finally, Swagel's presentation focuses on the difficulty of dealing with a financial crisis when all you have are ad hoc tools. Was it better to buy the bad assets from the banks or recapitalize them? The answer as a matter of policy is irrelevant, says Swagel, who was there. Congress would not have given the Treasury the funds to recapitalize the banks anyway.

At first, this seems to be an argument for a comprehensive resolution system for financial institutions. Swagel points out, for example, that if the Treasury had gone to Congress with a request for funds to recapitalize the nation's largest banks, it would not have gotten the TARP funds it actually got. Congress, he says, was willing to allow the Treasury to buy bad assets from the banks, but would not have permitted investments in their equity. Nevertheless, since there were no restrictions on the use of the TARP funds for recapitalizing banks, that is what was ultimately done when it turned out that buying their toxic assets was too difficult. What he seems to be suggesting is that the administration in office should have the authority in advance to take the necessary actions to stem a panic without having to return to Congress.

But, in fact, Swagel is arguing the opposite: there are real drawbacks in authorizing the government to take actions that, if employed injudiciously, could have a major adverse effect on our financial system and economy. These powers should be granted to the state only when we are sure that they are necessary to prevent something worse.

This brings us back to the original question: was the financial crisis the inevitable spawn of a volatile and inherently unstable financial system (which may need better regulation), or was it caused by an exogenous and unique factor, i.e., government policy that distorted the financial system by allocating trillions of dollars for the creation of fatally weak mortgage loans? Until we know the real cause of the financial crisis and the ensuing panic, it would be sensible to hold off providing any new authority to this or any future administration. My view is that, in policy as in medicine, we should wait for a thorough diagnosis before we settle on a prescription. There is also another medical maxim worth mentioning — first, do no harm.

V. WHAT TO DO ABOUT BUBBLES: MONETARY POLICY AND MACROPRUDENTIAL REGULATION

Financial Instability and Macroeconomics: Bridging the Gulf

Claudio Borio*
Bank for International Settlements

Mathias Drehmann
Bank for International Settlements

1. Introduction[1]

Mental habits die hard, and our minds often work in separate compartments. Maybe this is what Darwinian evolution is all about. What does not work gets weaned out in the relentless pursuit of efficiency. No doubt, habit and compartmentalization reduce the degree of energy spent in performing tasks. They protect our mental machines from overheating: low energy, low maintenance. But, all of this comes at a cost. We may, at times, fail to see critical interconnections and similarities between tasks. Important gains may simply go unnoticed as we mechanically go about our daily activities — until, of course, something goes badly wrong.

Let us now turn to the approaches to macroeconomics and financial stability that have prevailed for so long. The parallels are striking. In each case, there have been some unquestioned "truths". Moreover, while the two approaches share some common features, they have proceeded along quite separate tracks.

* Claudio Borio is the Deputy Head of the Monetary and Economic Department and Director of Research & Statistics at the Bank for International Settlements. Mathias Drehmann is a Senior Economist at the Bank for International Settlements.

[1] This paper was prepared for the 12th Annual International Banking Conference, "The International Financial Crisis: Have the Rules of Finance Changed?", September 24–25, 2009, co-sponsored by the Federal Reserve Bank of Chicago and the World Bank. The views expressed in this paper are those of the authors, and do not necessarily represent those of the Bank for International Settlements.

Consider first the prevailing approach to macroeconomics. The macroeconomy is mostly well behaved and self-correcting. The economic system is buffeted by continuous shocks, but converges quickly to equilibrium. Make a few additional standard assumptions and a monetary policy that focuses exclusively on delivering short-term price stability works best, as it stabilizes the real economy. If financial instability materializes, it must be the result of an outsized, very improbable shock; but even then, it is unlikely to have a large macroeconomic effect. Thus, either way, it is not worth incorporating the financial sector into the framework. In fact, financial factors may be dispensed with altogether.

Consider next the approach to financial (in)stability. The financial system can be fragile and is not self-correcting. Small shocks can generate large effects — the very essence of financial instability. The system need not return to equilibrium. Make a few additional assumptions and a prudential policy that focuses exclusively on individual institutions works best, as it stabilizes the system. Even if macroeconomic instability triggers (or results from) financial instability, its role is inconsequential, given that so much of the action takes place within the financial system anyway. Thus, it is not worth incorporating the macroeconomy into the framework, and monetary factors may be dispensed with altogether.

Clearly, this portrayal is intentionally highly stylized, but it does contain an important kernel of truth. We are confronted with the same economic system, and yet look at it through completely different eyes. To be sure, efforts to bridge this gulf have been under way for some time; and at the Bank for International Settlements (BIS), we have been among those pushing in this direction more vigorously. Yet, in the big scheme of things, the road ahead is much longer than that already traveled. The recent financial crisis — what *has* gone badly wrong — holds forth the promise of changing mindsets. This process has gained momentum. However, it is still hard to say how far it will proceed.

This paper is intended as a small contribution to efforts to bridge the gulf between approaches to financial stability and macroeconomics. There are many possible starting points for this exercise. Here, we begin the intellectual journey from a practical question: how can financial (in)stability be defined and measured? Measurement betrays perspectives. It brings out what we know and do not know. It is also a precondition for operational policy frameworks. It is, therefore, a good candidate to highlight differences in approaches and areas for possible reconciliation.

We argue that three steps can help to bridge the gulf between the two approaches. First, it is important to make a clear distinction between financial instability, on the one hand, and financial distress (or financial crises), on the other. Financial instability is a property of the financial system; financial distress is an event. The system may be unstable for long periods, even if financial distress does not materialize. The lag between the two is critical. Second, it is best to build on the endogenous-cycle view of financial instability. This view highlights the mutually reinforcing dynamic interplay between the financial sector and the macroeconomy ("procyclicality") as well as the boom–bust nature of business fluctuations. It has significant implications for measurement and modeling. Finally, policies should be adjusted to take into account the close interactions between the financial sector and the macroeconomy. We argue for a macrofinancial stability framework, in which the macroprudential orientation of financial policy would be strengthened and monetary policy would lean against the build-up of financial imbalances and associated risks, even if near-term inflation was under control (BIS, 2008).

The paper is organized as follows. Section 2 briefly defines financial (in)stability and financial distress. Section 3 explores current measurement technologies and highlights the parallels and differences between frameworks designed to deliver price and macroeconomic stability, ending with a call for a marriage between the two traditions. Section 4 draws out the policy implications of the analysis. The last section considers future prospects.

2. Financial (In)Stability: Definition[2]

Ever since financial stability as a public policy objective has risen to prominence, efforts to define it have multiplied. Even so, a generally agreed definition that could be the basis for an operational framework has remained elusive.

Most definitions of financial stability share three useful elements. First, they focus on the financial system as a whole, as opposed to individual institutions. Second, they do not consider the financial system in isolation, but ultimately measure the economic (welfare)

[2] This and the next section draw heavily on Borio and Drehmann (2009a).

benefits and costs in terms of the real economy (output foregone). Third, they make an explicit reference to financial instability — the converse of stability — which is seen as more concrete and observable than financial stability.

At the same time, differences abound. Some definitions are very broad, including any allocative distortions arising from financial "frictions" relative to an ideal benchmark (Haldane, 2004); others are more restrictive, focusing on the absence of episodes of acute distress and significant disruptions to the functioning of the system (Mishkin, 1999). Some highlight the robustness of the financial system to external shocks (Allen and Wood 2006; Padoa-Schioppa, 2003); others see the financial system as a possible source of shocks (Schinasi, 2004). Some tie the definition closely to the equally common but elusive notion of "systemic risk" (Group of Ten, 2001; De Bandt and Hartmann, 2000); others avoid it.

For the purposes of developing an operational framework, some definitions are more helpful than others. Broad definitions unnecessarily widen the policy objective and hinder accountability. Furthermore, definitions that rule out the possibility of the financial system being a source of shocks risk being too restrictive and misleading.

In this paper, we will use the following terminology. We define *financial distress/a financial crisis* as an event in which substantial losses at financial institutions and/or the failure of these institutions cause, or threaten to cause, serious dislocations to the real economy, measured in terms of output foregone. We define financial *in*stability as a set of conditions that is sufficient to result in the emergence of financial distress/crises in response to normal-sized shocks; these shocks could originate either in the real economy or in the financial system itself. Financial stability is then defined as the converse of financial instability.

Although the definition above is very rough, it provides a reasonable starting point for our analysis. Three characteristics of this definition are worth noting. First, it is pragmatic in that the scope is narrowed to the performance of financial institutions. It goes without saying that large fluctuations in asset prices and in the exchange rate — or problems in the balance sheets of governments, households, and non-financial enterprises — can by themselves have a sizable impact on output, even if the financial sector is not seriously disrupted. Pure sovereign and exchange rate crises are examples of the genre. But, including them would arguably broaden the definition too much from an operational perspective.

Financial stability mandates are probably best defined narrowly in terms of the financial sector so as to avoid broadening the scope of regulation too far.[3]

Second, the definition distinguishes episodes of financial distress as *events* from financial instability/stability as *properties* of the financial system. By their nature, properties are harder to identify than events, as they may involve the appeal to a counterfactual. For example, the system can be unstable even if no financial distress materializes for quite some time (see below).

Finally, it is crucial that financial distress is generated in response to a shock that is not of extraordinary size, for it is unreasonable to expect the financial system to function effectively regardless of the size of exogenous shocks that hit it (Goodhart, 2006). Moreover, all analytical approaches to financial instability share this characteristic, i.e., a normal-sized shock can generate financial distress through the amplifying mechanisms in the system. At one end of the spectrum, in models that stress self-fulfilling processes, there is a multiplicity of equilibria without a clear basis to choose among them; in this sense, the shock is not even well defined (Diamond and Dybvig, 1983). At the other end, according to the endogenous-cycle view of financial instability, the shock itself is largely seen as one stage in a bigger dynamic process — the financial cycle, where the boom generates the subsequent bust (Kindleberger, 1996; Minsky, 1982). In between the two extremes, other models describe how small shocks can have large effects, given the inherent fragility of the system. This is true regardless of whether the models stress the role of aggregate or systemic shocks, which affect all institutions (Allen and Gale, 2004), or the role of contagion, as idiosyncratic shocks ripple through the system owing to the informational and balance-sheet linkages that keep it together (Rochet and Tirole, 1996).[4]

---

[3] This, of course, does not imply that authorities should not consider carefully the implications of developments outside the financial sector for its stability. Far from it! Moreover, the broader macroeconomic consequences of strains in the balance sheets of other sectors that do not impinge on the financial sector's stability can be taken into account through other policies, not least monetary policy.

[4] For a discussion of different analytical perspectives on financial stability, see, e.g., Borio and Drehmann (2009a) and Wagner (2010).

3. Financial (In)Stability: Measurement and Modeling

3.1 *Role of measurement*

Any operational framework designed to secure financial stability requires a mapping of the definition of the goal into a measurable, or at least observable, yardstick. Measurement performs two quite distinct roles: it helps ensure the *accountability* of the authorities responsible for performing the task, and it supports the *implementation* of the strategy to achieve the goal in real time. The former calls for *ex post* measurement of financial instability, i.e., assessments of whether financial instability prevailed or not at some point in the past. The latter relies on *ex ante* measurement, i.e., assessments of whether the financial system is fragile or not today. While both *ex ante* and *ex post* measurement are "fuzzy", the challenges in supporting strategy implementation are tougher. Here, the distinction between episodes of financial distress (events) and financial instability (a property) is critical and often overlooked.

If an episode of financial distress has occurred within any given window, *ex post* measurement difficulties are challenging but manageable. In order to conclude that the system was unstable, policymakers should be able to (1) recognize financial distress *ex post*; and (2) reach a judgment that the distress was out of proportion with the original exogenous (unavoidable) shock, i.e., that financial distress was the result of financial instability rather than an extreme shock. To be sure, even this assessment can involve considerable fuzziness. How large should be the losses among financial intermediaries and the associated costs for the real economy before the episode can qualify as one of "financial distress"? How large should the "shock" be? Nevertheless, overcoming this fuzziness should not be too hard.[5]

Given the lead–lag relationships involved, such measures would also be good thermometers of financial distress. By contrast, if financial distress has not emerged, *ex post* measurement would be much harder. The main drawback is that the system may actually be unstable (fragile) even if no financial distress has materialized. Episodes of financial distress are rare, and the window during which the system may be fragile without experiencing a financial crisis may last years. As a result, it can be hard to judge how well the authorities are performing for quite a long time.

[5] This fuzziness is apparent when comparing papers that identify financial crises *ex post*; see, e.g., Reinhart and Rogoff (2008) and Laeven and Valencia (2008).

Judging whether the system was unstable during any given recent tranquil period requires policymakers to answer the same kind of counterfactual as for real-time implementation, and hence for *ex ante* measurement: what would have happened had the system been hit by a shock? Or, in the endogenous-cycle view of financial instability, were imbalances building up that simply happened not to unwind during the period? In effect, during tranquil periods, the demands on *ex ante* and *ex post* measurement are qualitatively equivalent.

While qualitatively equivalent, the demands on *ex ante* measurement are tougher. Implementing the chosen strategy in real time requires that real-time proxies for financial instability be developed. This is necessary to take remedial action well before the episode of distress materializes, so as to reduce its likelihood.[6] Another way of highlighting the challenges in *ex ante* measurement is to consider its implications for the measures of properties of financial instability. *Ex ante* measurement calls for good leading, as opposed to contemporaneous, measures of episodes of financial distress — i.e., for good barometers rather than thermometers of instability. That is, *ex ante* measurement must be able to capture the financial system's fragility *before* financial distress actually emerges.

As we shall see, a key challenge here is what might be called the "paradox of instability": the financial system can appear strongest precisely when it is most fragile. This puts a premium on the policymakers' ability to read the "tea leaves" correctly (Knight, 2007).

3.2 *A taxonomy*

In considering the possible range of measurement tools, it might be helpful to start from what an ideal measure would be. This measure would be the output of a fully structural model of the economy, mapping instruments into the goal. More precisely, it could be written as follows:

$$M \leftarrow f(X, I, u),$$

where the measure of financial (in)stability M is some transformation of the output of a structural model of the economy, $f(.)$, linking a set of

[6] At the same time, the demands may vary depending on how far the system is based on rules or discretion (see below).

variables X to policy instruments I and exogenous shocks u. Such a model would permit the *ex post* identification of financial instability by decomposing the past into "shocks" and the endogenous response of the system. It could also be used to generate the *ex ante* probability distribution of outcomes, and hence of financial distress, through the simulation of the shocks. It could be the basis for generating scenarios, by tracing the behavior of the system conditional on specific shocks; or it could be relied upon to design appropriate policies, by seeing how the system would behave under different configurations of the instruments. For example, ideally the tools would generate an "expected cost of financial distress" metric over a specific horizon, combining the likelihood of financial distress with its cost in terms of economic activity. The authorities could then use this measure as the basis for the calibration of both automatic stabilizers and discretionary actions aimed at keeping it within a desired range.

The obvious parallel with the way monetary policy is carried out is no coincidence. Recall that the costs of financial instability are defined in terms of output; we are, therefore, ultimately dealing with the same goal variable. But beyond this, the two worlds could not appear to be further apart. In fact, rightly or wrongly, monetary policy frameworks are often indicated as the Nirvana to which financial stability frameworks should aspire. In monetary policy, the quantitative side of the job is much more extensive. Policymakers have models that link instruments to the goal (some varying combination of inflation and output), and routinely use them to make forecasts and carry out policy simulations (Nelson, 2008). Typically, not just one but a variety of such tools are employed, exploiting their relative strengths and weaknesses in forecasting and policy analysis. The tools are seen as helpful in disciplining the inevitable and crucial role of judgment. They can be used to keep measures of price stability, such as a point estimate for inflation over a given horizon, within desired ranges. This is what is typically done in inflation-targeting regimes.

By contrast, the picture appears quite different in financial stability analysis. There are no satisfactory models of the economy as a whole linking balance sheets in the financial sector to macroeconomic variables. Even the empirical modeling of financial instability within the financial sector, for given (exogenous) macroeconomic factors, is often very primitive, hardly going beyond rather mechanical exercises with very limited behavioral content (e.g., Upper, 2007).[7] If an instrument is included in the model at all, this is the interest rate, whose primary function is to achieve price stability. All of this makes it virtually impossible to do meaningful risk analysis and policy simulations within a single framework. Policymakers need to fall back on a variety of much more limited quantitative tools that put little discipline on judgment.

As we will discuss later, such a sharp contrast between sophistication and success, on the one hand, and coarseness and failure, on the other, may be partly deceptive. Not everything that shines is gold. Nevertheless, the perception has been quite real.

In order to assess the state of measurement in financial stability analysis, we next survey the landscape of the tools used. It is useful to classify them along three dimensions. First, how far do they provide leading, as opposed to contemporaneous, measures of episodes of financial distress? In other words, how far do they act as barometers rather than thermometers of financial distress? This is important for the use to which those measures can be put. Second, how far do the tools take into account, directly or indirectly, the behavioral interactions that underlie episodes of financial distress? Failure to capture such interactions, i.e., the endogenous nature of aggregate risk with respect to collective behavior, can easily underestimate the likelihood of financial distress. Third, how far do the tools actually "tell a story" about the transmission mechanism of financial distress?[8] Being able to tell a convincing story can influence their effectiveness in communicating risks and can give more confidence in the measures. However, sometimes a trade-off may exist between the granularity and degree of detail needed for storytelling and the accuracy in measurement.

---

[7] The workstream by Goodhart *et al.* (2004) provides an interesting exception. However, given its inherent complexity, it still falls short of satisfactory implementation. Moreover, since the models are based on "endowment" economies, they rule out feedback effects on output.

[8] This is close to the distinction between structural and reduced-form models. The term "structural model" is often used to refer to models whose parameters are invariant with respect to policy interventions ("deep parameters"), so that policy simulations can be properly carried out. Given the state of modeling of financial stability, this would simply mean setting the bar too high. We return to this issue in the next section, where we discuss briefly the implications for monetary policy of the inability to model financial distress satisfactorily.

We focus on tools that are actually used at present in policy institutions. We start with a variety of indicators, ranging from traditional balance sheet variables and market prices at one end to more ambitious early warning indicators at the other. We then discuss vector autoregressions (VARs), which amount to very simple representations of the economy and could, in principle, perform both risk and policy analyses. We finally consider current system-wide, multi-module measurement models, with macro stress tests being the prime example.

3.2.1 *From balance sheet to market price indicators*

The simplest type of indicator comprises statistics based on *balance sheet items*. These include, for example, measures of banks' capitalization, non-performing loans, loan loss provisions, balance sheet items of households and corporations, etc. Most of the International Monetary Fund's (IMF's) "Financial Soundness Indicators" fall into this category (IMF, 2008). In addition, national authorities would have data for individual institutions at a more granular level.

Clearly, at best, these variables can be used as inputs into a richer analysis of vulnerabilities (e.g., Carson and Ingves, 2003). Crucially, given accounting rules, variables such as loan loss provisions, non-performing loans, and levels of capitalization are rather backward-looking. At best, they are contemporaneous rather than leading indicators of financial distress, i.e., thermometers rather than barometers. Indeed, profits tend to be rather high, and provisions low, when risk is taken on; the recent experience has been no different in this respect (Figure 1). The same is true for variables such as balance sheet and income leverage.[9] By construction, similar limitations apply to indices which combine balance sheet variables into a single number to generate an index of stress (e.g., Bordo *et al.*, 2000).

Ratings for individual borrowers go one step beyond balance sheet variables. Relative to balance sheet variables, ratings have the advantages of combining information into a single statistic and of being designed to be forward-looking, providing estimates of the probability of default or

[9] In order to become useful from a forward-looking perspective, the variables need to be embedded in a "theory" of the dynamics of instability, such as the endogenous-cycle view, that links them explicitly to future episodes of financial distress (see below).

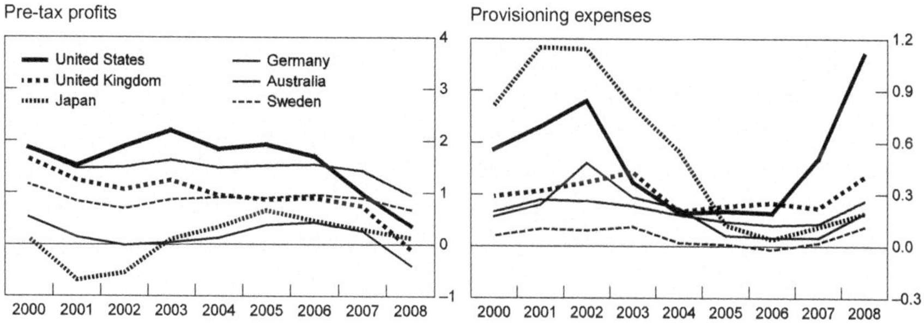

Figure 1. Profits and provisioning (as a percentage of total average assets).
Source: BIS annual reports from 2003 to 2009.

expected loss. Their most important limitation is that they relate to individual institutions taken in isolation. Thus, a measure of the strength of the financial system as a whole requires the bottom-up aggregation of ratings that do not take a systemic account of similar exposures and interactions. Questions also arise regarding their reliability as truly leading indicators of financial distress, at least for credit agencies' ratings. In practice, downgrades tend to be rather "sticky" compared with the arrival of information.

An alternative procedure is to build indicators of financial distress from *market prices*. There are various possibilities. At one end, raw indicators can be considered either in isolation or combined, with little or no theoretical restrictions, such as volatilities and quality spreads. More ambitiously, by imposing some structure, prices of fixed-income securities and equities can be used to derive estimates of probabilities of default or expected losses for individual institutions[10] and, by taking into account correlations, for sectors as a whole.

On the face of it, such indicators have a number of advantages over those discussed so far. They are forward-looking measures that incorporate all of the information available to market participants at a particular point in time, i.e., they are comprehensive, point-in-time measures of risk. They

[10] To do so, one needs to rely on a pricing model that reverse-engineers the various outputs, based on some assumptions. For example, so-called expected default frequencies (EDFs) — in effect, probabilities of default — can be obtained from equity prices, recalling that equity can be regarded as a call on the firm's assets just as its debt is a put on them (Merton, 1974).

therefore also implicitly embed views about any similarities in exposures and interactions that may exist within the sector covered. They are also available at high frequencies. However, they have drawbacks too. The most important one is that any biases in the market's assessment are embedded in the estimates. If, as seems natural, excessive risk taking is the source of financial instability, then estimates of risk derived from market prices would tend to be unusually low as vulnerabilities build up and would tend to behave more like contemporaneous indicators of financial distress.

Available evidence tends to confirm that the lead with which market prices point to distress is uncomfortably short for policy. For example, unusually low volatilities and narrow spreads prevailed across a broad spectrum of asset classes until the turmoil started in the summer of 2007, when they finally rose sharply (BIS, 2009a; see also Figure 2). As discussed in Borio and Drehmann (2009a), these drawbacks are also naturally reflected in more sophisticated measures that combine indicators based on market prices (e.g., Illing and Liu, 2006; Tarashev and Zhu, 2008).

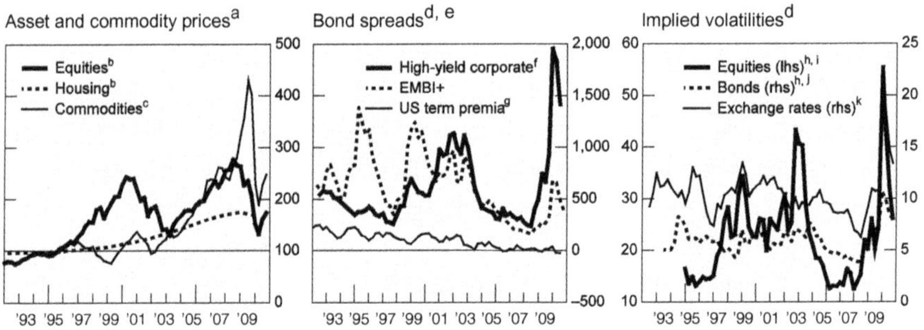

Figure 2. Buoyant asset markets.

[a] 1995 = 100. [b] Sixteen OECD countries; weighted averages based on 2005 GDP and PPP exchange rates. [c] Goldman Sachs Commodity Index, in U.S. dollar terms. [d] Quarterly averages. [e] In basis points. [f] JPM Global High Yield; spread to worst. [g] Estimated for 10-year zero-coupon Treasuries. [h] Simple average of the United States and Germany. [i] Derived from the price of call option contracts on stock market indices. [j] Price volatility implied by the price of call options on 10-year government bond futures contracts. [k] JPMorgan benchmark index for the level of G7 currencies' implied volatility.

Sources: OECD; Bloomberg; Datastream; Merrill Lynch; JPMorgan Chase; national data.

3.2.2 *Early warning indicators*

One possible way of overcoming these limitations is to develop formal *early warning indicators* (EWIs) of financial distress. These are specifically designed to identify episodes of financial distress in advance. There has been a growing literature on EWIs. Although most of it was initially concerned with exchange rate and sovereign crises, banking crises have been attracting growing attention (e.g., Bell and Pain, 2000; Demirgüç-Kunt and Detragiache, 2005; Davis and Karim, 2008). The basic approach consists of using reduced-form relationships linking a set of explanatory variables to a "financial distress" index, often a zero/one variable.[11]

Potentially, EWIs have some attractive features. They represent statistically rigorous attempts to identify basic relationships in the historical data. They are explicitly forward-looking. They implicitly capture any interactions that have existed in previous episodes. As long as their structure is not purely data-driven but inspired by some analytical view of distress, they might be able to help frame broad stories about financial instability.

Their performance so far, however, has also revealed shortcomings. The forecasting horizon is often quite short (typically not exceeding one year and sometimes as short as one month), which is more relevant for investors than policymakers. The prediction may include information that is actually not available at the time the prediction is made (e.g., Kaminsky and Reinhart, 1999). The choice of independent variables may be excessively data-driven, such that the "story" is not obvious and there may be a risk of overfitting at the cost of out-of-sample performance. EWIs have a tendency to produce too many false positives — i.e., predicting crises that do not occur — and their performance tends to be rather poor (Bell and Pain, 2000). More generally, they are open to the criticism that there is no guarantee that past relationships will hold in the future.[12]

---

[11] The statistical methodology varies, ranging from threshold models calibrated based on noise-to-signal ratios (Kaminsky and Reinhart, 1999) to multivariate logit or probit models (Demirgüç-Kunt and Detragiache, 1998, 2005). Mixtures of the two are also possible (Borio and Lowe, 2004).

[12] Likewise, EWIs cannot be used consistently to generate counterfactual stories based on alternative policy responses, as they normally do not include instruments *I*. In fact, changes in policy regimes may be one reason why past relationships need not hold in the future.

In research with colleagues at the BIS, we have sought to develop simple indicators that overcome some of these limitations (Borio and Lowe, 2002a, 2002b). The indicators aim to predict banking crises over horizons that, depending on the calibration, range from one to four years ahead. They rely exclusively on information that is available at the time the predictions are made, i.e., they are truly real-time. They are quite parsimonious, being based on two (or at most three) variables, as they draw heavily on the endogenous-cycle view of financial instability. The basic idea is that the co-existence of unusually rapid credit expansion and asset price increases points to the build-up of financial imbalances which, at some point, are likely to unwind. The indicators are intended to measure the co-existence of asset price misalignments with a limited capacity of the system to absorb the asset price reversal. Misalignments are simply captured by deviations of asset prices from a (one-sided) trend: the absorption capacity of the system by deviations of the ratio of private-sector debt to GDP from a similar trend, both exceeding certain thresholds. The precise timing of the unwinding is impossible to predict — hence, the use of flexible, long horizons.

Our work indicates that these indicators perform rather well both in and out of sample (Borio and Drehmann, 2009b). In sample, they exhibit a comparatively low noise-to-signal ratio despite their parsimony, alleviating the false-positive problem. Out of sample, they do a rather good job in detecting the general build-up of risks ahead of the current crisis.

The out-of-sample analysis suggests at least two conclusions. First, the indicator does identify, with a lead of at least a couple of years, the emergence of problems in the United States, the country at the epicenter of the crisis. This is shown in Figure 3. Based on the credit-to-GDP and property price gaps jointly exceeding critical thresholds, signs of the build-up of risk emerged in the early to mid-2000s, depending on the precise property price index and thresholds used. Second, the indicator picks up most of the countries that have taken measures to prop up their banking systems, but it misses those where the problems have originated exclusively in foreign exposures, in this case to strains in the United States. This highlights an obvious limitation in an increasingly globalized world: it is implicitly assumed that the banks resident in one country are only exposed to financial cycles in that country. In Borio and Drehmann (2009b), we suggest how this shortcoming can be addressed by using information on cross-border exposures.

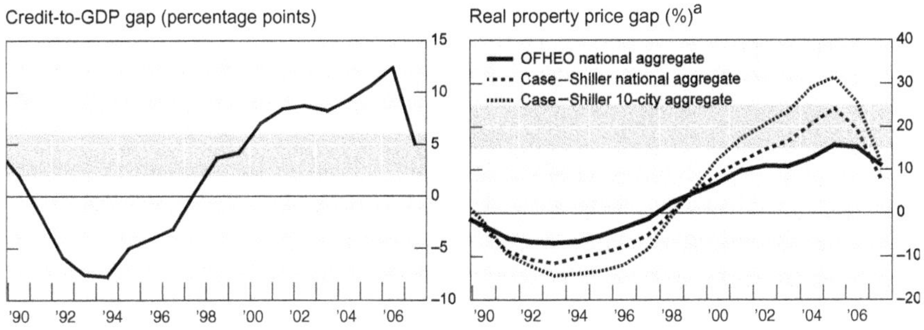

Figure 3. Out-of-sample performance: estimated gaps for the U.S.

Note: Out-of-sample performance of indicators of financial distress. The indicators are estimated over the period 1980–2003 and tested out of sample over the period 2003–2008. Data are quarterly. Gaps are estimated using a one-sided rolling Hodrick–Prescott filter with lambda set to 1600. The shaded areas refer to the threshold values for the indicators: 2–6 percentage points for the credit/GDP gap, and 15–25% for the real property price gap. Both thresholds need to be exceeded for the signal to be on. The estimates for 2008 are based on partial data (up to the third quarter).

[a]Weighted average of residential and commercial property prices, with weights corresponding to estimates of their share in overall property wealth. The legend refers to the residential property price component.

Source: Borio and Drehmann (2009b).

3.2.3 *Single-module measures: VARs*

In the absence of structural econometric models, a potentially useful tool to carry out stability analysis is *vector autoregressions* (VARs). VARs are largely data-driven representations of the economy, with few theoretical restrictions. Typically, a rather small set of variables is allowed to interact dynamically, with the dynamics ultimately driven by a set of exogenous shocks. If financial distress could be defined in terms of some of those variables (e.g., as financial institutions' losses exceeding a certain threshold), the tool could be rather versatile. Through simulations, it could generate a probability distribution of outcomes for the endogenous variables, and hence a measure of the probability of distress over any given horizon. It would also allow for the computation of value-at-risk metrics or the simulation of stress tests.

In principle, VARs are quite appealing. Depending on the horizon over which the forecasts are made, they should act as barometers rather than as thermometers of financial distress. They take into account interactions between variables and, hence, feedback effects. Moreover, they can provide the basis for some storytelling, tracing the impact of propagation of shocks through the system, although the parameters of the VARs are not amenable to a structural interpretation.

In practice, however, VARs fall well short of this promise. Data limitation is a problem. The variables typically used to capture financial distress, such as non-performing loans or aggregate defaults in the corporate sector, are rather rudimentary and are poorly modeled. The representation of the financial sector is cut to the bone and the range of possible shocks is quite limited; the models have to be kept manageable for estimation, and often exclude asset prices or proxies for liquidity. The lack of structure implies that the models have very little to say about the dynamics of distress. In addition, the assumptions on which the models are built make it very hard to detect any fundamental nonlinearities associated with them.[13] By construction, given their very nature and the estimation methods, the models capture average relationships among the data series, rather than how the series interact under stress, and are unable to incorporate boom–bust cycles.[14]

3.2.4 *Multiple-module measures: macro stress tests*

The absence of fully fledged structural models and the limitations of VARs have encouraged the use of multiple-module approaches to the assessment of financial distress. So-called *macro stress tests* generally fall into this category. By analogy with the stress tests for the portfolios of

---

[13] Specifically, the models generally assume that the underlying relationships interact in a (log)linear fashion, so that, say, a three-standard-deviation shock has exactly the same impact as three times a one-standard-deviation shock. This assumption would be acceptable if the underlying data-generating process was linear or if the VAR was used to study the impact of small shocks around the equilibrium of the process. However, stress tests do not consider small shocks, and it is not likely that the relevant data-generating processes are all log-linear over the relevant range. Nonetheless, some papers have channeled this assumption (e.g., Drehmann *et al.*, 2006; Misina and Tessier, 2008).

[14] See Borio and Drehmann (2009a) for representative examples.

individual institutions, macro stress tests are designed to form a view of how the system as a whole would behave under exceptional but plausible adverse circumstances, i.e., in response to negative "shocks" drawn from the tail of the underlying probability distribution (IMF and World Bank, 2003).[15] These measures are thus inspired by the "negative exogenous shock amplification" view of financial instability. They effectively seek to replicate for the financial system the stress tests individual firms carry out on their portfolios.

Despite considerable differences, all macro stress tests share some characteristics (Drehmann, 2009).[16] A macro engine — be this a VAR (Pesaran *et al.*, 2006), a traditional macro model (Bunn *et al.*, 2005), or a macro model linked to market risk drivers (Elsinger *et al.*, 2006) — is used to generate the shock and/or to trace out a scenario for macroeconomic variables, i.e., the change in the assumed "systematic risk factors". These are then used to shock the balance sheets of the relevant sector so as to assess more precisely their impact on its financial strength, measured in a variety of ways (Čihák, 2007).

Just like the stress tests for individual institutions, macro stress tests have become quite popular. They are explicitly forward-looking. They have the potential to cover a broad range of scenarios, not constrained by the probability distributions derived from historical relationships. They are quite helpful in tracing the propagation mechanism from shock to outcome, and hence in storytelling and communicating concerns. Above all, they can be much more granular than other approaches, relating scenarios to features of individual balance sheets. For example, information about interlinkages in the banking sector can be used to calculate knock-on effects from losses at individual institutions (Elsinger *et al.*, 2006). The ultimate measures of distress, therefore, are closer to those that capture the concerns of policymakers, such as the erosion in the degree of capitalization in the banking system.

Even so, their limitations should not be underestimated. Some of these have to do with the shortcomings of the individual modules; for example, as already noted, the macroeconomic modules do a very poor job of incorporating financial variables. Others relate to how the modules are linked. For one, the modular structure can easily result in internal

---

[15] This view can take the form of a point forecast conditional on some unusually large shocks, or of a whole probability distribution with its tail representing the outcomes of interest (e.g., a value-at-risk (VaR) measure).

[16] For surveys of the range of practices, see Sorge (2004) and Drehmann (2008, 2009).

inconsistencies, both conceptual and empirical, such as those that can arise from piecewise estimation. Moreover, there is a clear danger of excessive complexity, undermining robustness and ease of communication both within the organization and with the public.

Most importantly, greater granularity and relevance are bought at the expense of ruling out interactions and feedback effects.[17] After all, it is these interactions, both within the financial system as well as between the financial system and the real economy, that lie at the heart of the dynamics of financial distress. This is especially serious when the horizon of the simulation exceeds one period, as it realistically should. The very fact that unusually large shocks are needed to produce any action suggests that the current generation of macro stress tests is missing essential elements of financial instability. As a result, there is a serious risk that, as carried out now, macro stress tests may underestimate the likelihood of financial distress and its potential magnitude.

This is consistent with recent experience. To our knowledge, all of the macro stress tests carried out before the recent financial turmoil failed to anticipate it as a possible relevant outcome. The tests indicated that the capital buffers in the system were perfectly adequate, and yet they came under considerable strain once the turmoil erupted.

3.3 *Overall assessment: from a financial stability to a macroeconomics perspective*

The discussion of quantitative measurement tools points to a number of conclusions. First, the technology to measure the likelihood of financial distress in real time is still rather rudimentary. The tools generally provide little comfort in the estimates and, with rare exceptions, the lead with which distress is assessed is insufficient to take remedial action. Most behave more like thermometers than true barometers of distress and/or risk lulling policymakers into a false sense of security. Stress tests, as currently conceived, are no exception. Their inability to capture interactions and endogenous feedback effects is a major stumbling block.

Second, that said, those EWIs rooted in the endogenous-cycle view of financial instability appear comparatively more promising. The key insight is using market prices and rapid credit expansion as contrarian

[17] Current research is precisely seeking to incorporate these effects; see Aikman *et al.* (2009).

indicators of financial instability. This turns the paradox of financial instability to the policymakers' advantage: the system looks most robust precisely when it is most fragile. At that point, market prices are not an indication of unusually *low risk*, but of unusually *high risk taking*.

Third, structural models of financial instability are in their infancy. Analytical models of financial instability have not gone much beyond stylized characterizations of the dynamics of financial distress. Most of these are in the exogenous-shock amplification tradition, which fails to capture the dynamic build-up of vulnerabilities during the boom phase (i.e., the essence of the more promising financial cycle tradition). They are equally unable to model the interactions between the financial system and the real economy. At the same time, the financial cycle view, while intellectually compelling, has as yet failed to provide canonical formal models that are considered acceptable by the prevailing standards of the profession.

Finally, if financial instability models are unable to reach out to macroeconomic models, the trip in the opposite direction is hardly more successful. One reason why the modeling of interactions between the financial system and the real economy is so poor is that the current generation of macroeconomic models has very little to say about financial instability (Table 1). Recall the key features of those models (e.g., Borio, 2006; Borio and Zhu, 2008; Leijonhufvud, 2008; Buiter, 2009). Financial factors are

Table 1. Two stylized paradigms for economic fluctuations.

	Prevailing Paradigm	Alternative
Price Stability for Economic Stability	Sufficient	Not sufficient
Role of Financial Factors	Peripheral	Core
Financial Imbalances/ Instability	Little importance	Critical
Business Cycle	Exogenous shocks — rapid convergence to equilibrium	Endogenous shocks — self-perpetuating cycles
Nonlinearities	Unimportant	Critical
Changing Risk Tolerance	Unimportant	Critical
Rational Expectations	Standard	Too constraining

Source: Borio (2006).

hardly captured; in fact, money and credit are often excluded altogether. When the modeling is done, it is generally grafted onto a core structure that sees the business cycle as largely the result of shocks hitting a system that quickly returns to its steady-state equilibrium. Time-varying risk premia are dispensed with. There are no coordination failures, either across economic agents at a point in time or intertemporally. As a rule, expectations are model-consistent. Even when default is included, its impact is trivialized. By construction, these models cannot accommodate financial instability. It is simply not in their genetic code.

There is, of course, a natural argument to defend the current focus of macroeconomic models. After all, episodes of financial distress are infrequent. Why should one adapt models that are seen to work, say, 99.9% of the time in order to capture developments that are expected to occur only 0.1% of the time? The cost/benefit calculus seems self-evident. Moreover, any lingering doubts would be dispelled by the inherent difficulties of modeling financial instability, with its complex nonlinearities, especially if one was to build on microfoundations.

We do not find this argument convincing. It is not just that the episodes that occur so rarely are particularly costly, or that they have in fact become less rare owing to deep-seated structural forces (Borio, 2006). The idea that it is possible to have two separate models — one for fair weather and the other for turbulent conditions — is dubious. It relies on the notion that what occurs in good times is not causally related to what occurs in bad times. It fits quite comfortably with the stylized exogenous-shock propagation paradigm so prevalent in current thinking, but it fits very uneasily with what one observes in reality: it is unchecked aggressive risk taking in good times that sows the seeds of the bad times. The boom does not just precede the bust; it prepares the ground for it. Decisions in good times determine the likelihood and costs of bad times, and they do so with a typically very long fuse. As we shall see next, all of this has important implications for policy frameworks.

4. Financial (In)Stability: Policy

Bearing in mind the tight interrelationship between the financial system and the macroeconomy, what policies are most conducive to sustainable financial and macroeconomic stability? In analysis at the BIS, we have argued for a long time that this calls for mutually reinforcing adjustments in both prudential and monetary frameworks — what has been sometimes referred to as a new "macrofinancial stability framework" (BIS, 2008). What follows takes each of the two frameworks in turn and reiterates why action on the two fronts appears desirable.

4.1 *Towards a macroprudential framework of regulation and supervision*

The key adjustment in prudential frameworks is to strengthen their macroprudential orientation (Crockett, 2000; Borio, 2003, 2009; Knight, 2006; BIS, 2009a). A macroprudential approach has two distinguishing features: it focuses on the financial system as a whole, with the objective of limiting the macroeconomic costs of episodes of financial distress; and it treats aggregate risk as dependent on the collective behavior of financial institutions (i.e., as partly endogenous). This contrasts sharply with how individual agents treat aggregate risk: they regard asset prices, market/credit conditions, and economic activity as unaffected by their decisions, since, taken individually, agents are too small to affect them. It also contrasts with the predominant features of existing regulatory and supervisory arrangements, which tend to focus on individual institutions.

For present purposes, the most important dimension of a macroprudential approach is how it deals with the evolution of aggregate risk in the financial system over time: the "time dimension".[18] The key concern, highlighted in the previous analysis, is precisely that system-wide risk can be amplified by interactions within the financial system as well as between the financial system and the real economy — the core of the financial-cycle view of instability. This is what procyclicality is all about (Crockett, 2000; Borio *et al.*, 2001; BIS, 2001; Brunnermeier *et al.*, 2009). Feedback effects are of the essence. During expansions, the mutually reinforcing process between declining risk perceptions, rising risk tolerance, weakening financing constraints, rising leverage, higher market liquidity, and booming asset prices and expenditures feeds onto itself, potentially leading to the overextension of balance sheets. This process, then, operates in reverse (and more abruptly) as financial

[18] The macroprudential approach also has a cross-sectional dimension, which deals with the way in which system-wide risk is distributed within the financial system as a point in time; see Borio (2003, 2009).

strains emerge, amplifying financial distress. All along this sequence of events, actions that are rational and compelling for individual economic agents may result in undesirable aggregate outcomes, destabilizing the whole system. Coordination failures, across agents and over time, are of the essence.

The guiding principle to dampen procyclicality is to calibrate policy tools in order to encourage the build-up of buffers during good times so that they can be drawn down as strains materialize. By allowing the system to absorb the shock better, this would help to limit the costs of incipient financial distress. Moreover, the build-up of the buffers, to the extent that they act as a kind of dragging anchor or "soft" speed limit, could also help to restrain the build-up of risk taking during the expansion phase. As a result, it would also limit the risk of financial distress in the first place.

Three guidelines could inform the implementation of a macroprudential orientation. First, a holistic approach is needed. The self-reinforcing mechanisms are multifaceted, and so are the contributing factors. Much attention has been paid to the role of capital requirements. How far can they be structured so as to induce countercyclical capital buffers? But, many aspects of financial policy have a material impact on the degree of procyclicality of the financial system (BIS, 2009b). Liquidity, underwriting standards, as well as margining and collateral practices (including loan-to-value restrictions) could be made less procyclical or countercyclical. Accounting standards could be made more consistent with sound risk management; here, the adoption of more forward-looking loan provisioning and a critical review of certain aspects of fair value accounting, such as the recognition of day 1 profits, are essential (e.g., CGFS, 2009). Deposit insurance schemes could be pre-funded. In addition, resolution procedures could be tailored to the system-wide implications of distress.

Second, the approach should rely as far as possible, but no more, on rules rather than discretion. Automatic stabilizers are essential. For one, as long as they are not too ambitious, they would help address the limitations in the measurement of aggregate risks in real time, which can make discretionary action error-prone. The objective here is simply to edge the system in the right direction, not to strive for optimality. Dynamic provisions are a good such example. Above all, however, automatic stabilizers can act as effective pre-commitment devices. They reduce the huge political economy pressures on supervisors to refrain from acting during booms — pressures that are greatly magnified by the paradox of financial instability. At the same time, discretion has a role to play whenever effective rules cannot be developed, and it can help tailor intervention to the varying features of the financial cycle.

Third, careful thought should be given to the institutional setup. It is crucial to align goals, know-how, and control over instruments. The dispersion of responsibilities for financial stability as well as deep-seated differences in perspective complicate this task. The institutional setup should be based on clear mandates and hold policymakers accountable. It calls for close cooperation between central banks and supervisory authorities. Furthermore, it needs to secure a degree of operational autonomy from the government, i.e., it is so critical to "take away the punchbowl just when the party gets going", as risks build up.[19] At the same time, fuzziness in the measurement of financial stability and long lags between the accumulation of risks and their materialization add to the difficulties involved in holding the authorities to account.

4.2 *Towards a more preemptive monetary policy*

The key adjustment to monetary policy frameworks is to allow for the possibility of tightening policy, leaning against the build-up of risks and associated financial imbalances, even if near-term inflation appears under control — the "response option". Otherwise, the danger is that monetary policy could inadvertently accommodate the build-up of risks. Indeed, as argued elsewhere, it could positively encourage it, to the extent that interest rates which are low relative to equilibrium norms induce risk taking — an element of the "risk-taking channel" of monetary policy, arguably an underappreciated aspect of the transmission mechanism (Borio and Zhu, 2008).[20] In turn, the unwinding of the financial imbalances could cripple the effectiveness of monetary policy or, at a minimum, greatly complicate

---

[19] It is critical here to make a distinction between crisis prevention and crisis management. A degree of autonomy from the government is essential in crisis prevention, to take restraining action during the boom phase. Close coordination is both desirable and inevitable in crisis management, whenever dealing with the bust involves the use of public money.

[20] For empirical evidence on this channel, see Jiménez *et al.* (2009), Ioannidou *et al.* (2009), and Altunbas *et al.* (2009).

it. The Japanese experience and the recent adoption of so-called unconventional monetary policies have hammered this message home (Borio and Disyatat, 2009).

Implementing the response option calls for two modifications to the frameworks (Borio and Lowe, 2002a). One is to lengthen the operational policy horizon beyond the 1–2 years typical of some inflation-targeting regimes. The key concept here is *sustainable* price stability. The other is to pay more attention to the medium-term balance of risks to the outlook. The lags between the accumulation of risks and their materialization are quite long and variable. The cumulative processes take time to unfold, and the timing of their unwinding is highly uncertain. Given the obvious forecasting difficulties, the longer horizon should primarily be seen as a device to assess the balance of risks facing the economy in a more meaningful and structured way, not as a mechanical extension of point forecasts.

Four further points are worth highlighting. First, implementing these adjustments does not require the explicit inclusion of financial stability in central bank mandates. As defined at the outset, the costs of financial instability are measured in terms of output foregone. This is no different from standard concerns with macroeconomic stability.[21] That is the ultimate metric to judge the success or failure of policy. At this level, the issue is equivalent to that of how to address any potential trade-offs between price and output stability over different horizons. Whether mandates are helpful or not depends on how they might affect the central bank's perspective, the operational strategy chosen, communication, and, above all, political economy constraints (such as the central bank's relation to the government). This is likely to vary across countries and circumstances. The lens through which the central bank views the workings of the economy is more important than the mandates. Past experience points to little correlation between the nature of broad mandates and the central bank's willingness to lean against the wind of financial imbalances (Borio, 2006).

Second, to characterize the response option as "pricking bubbles" or "targeting asset prices" is misleading. The real issue is how to respond to

[21] Not surprisingly, Borio and Lowe (2004) show that the composite indicators of financial distress based on credit and asset prices also have leading information content for output and inflation, even controlling for the past behavior of these variables; the horizon varies between two and four years ahead.

the build-up of risks in the financial system that could derail the real economy. Unusually high asset prices and low risk premia are one symptom of such a build-up. But, the unusually rapid expansion of credit and leverage is a critical, and probably even more important, element (Borio and Lowe, 2004). The co-existence of the two provides the most reliable signal of growing danger.

Third, while justified, objections couched in terms of the exceedingly demanding informational requirements for successful implementation appear overdone. The empirical evidence suggests that the build-up of risks can be identified, albeit fuzzingly. Moreover, the comfort policymakers have with their current tools is partly illusory. It reflects more the force of habit and repetition than the underlying reality. The margin of uncertainty surrounding unobservable concepts such as economic slack (output gaps), underlying productivity growth, natural unemployment rates, and natural interest rates is simply huge; but as long as things do not go badly wrong, we turn a blind eye and learn to live with it. We are all creatures of habit, and we create intellectual norms to seek comfort in our daily struggle with uncertainty.

Finally, relying exclusively on macroprudential tools to address procyclicality is not prudent. In our view, it is simply too much to ask from the prudential framework to take on the whole burden. There may be circumstances in which problems in the balance sheets of the non-financial sector are serious enough to cause crippling macroeconomic instability, even if the financial sector does not experience a major financial crisis. Also, the ultimate anchor on credit creation is the central bank's reaction function; thus, prudential tools may not be enough if they have to fight against a monetary tide. Tinbergen's (1952) dictum — "two goals, two instruments" — is often invoked out of context.[22] His point was not that one should have tools exclusively devoted to a single objective, but that the *interrelationships* between objectives arising from the single economic structure have to be taken fully into account. A balance in the use of instruments is called for. The task is simply too large for any single one to do the trick on its own. Moreover, it is often argued that the interest rate tool is too blunt. However, in sophisticated and open financial systems, where the scope for regulatory arbitrage is high, the interest rate has the merit of setting the universal price of leverage. It reaches parts that other instruments cannot reach.

[22] On this, see also Shirakawa (2009).

4.3 *Towards a common research agenda*

We are now essentially back to the observation that prompted our intellectual journey. We are dealing with a single economic structure and tightly intertwined phenomena — financial and macroeconomic instability. Yet, until recently, there has been a tendency to approach them from very different perspectives. Better policy requires better analysis. What are the implications for the research agenda?

For one, there is an urgent need to develop models of the workings of the economy that fully incorporate the interplay between financial factors and the macroeconomy. These models should help to focus and discipline our thinking as well as inform quantitative judgments about the strength of the various relationships at work. This does not mean that the models should be all-encompassing and complex. On the contrary, ideally they would be parsimonious, would drill down to the core of the interrelationships, and would be tightly targeted. As an aside, we tend to be skeptical of the prevailing approach, which consists of adding yet another friction to a neoclassical underlying structure, as done in the dynamic stochastic general equilibrium (DSGE) tradition.[23] As noted earlier, this structure is ill suited to capture what we regard as the key cumulative disequilibrium processes involved. In addition, to help calibration, models should explicitly bring the various instruments into the picture. It would be very useful, in particular, to examine the extent to which prudential and monetary policy instruments can substitute or complement each other. This may also call for the exploration of new perspectives on old questions, such as the influence of monetary policy on risk perceptions and attitudes — the risk-taking channel of monetary policy.

Beyond this, certain specific analytical tools deserve special attention. Real-time measures of financial instability are a case in point. These can guide both monetary and prudential policies. Improving macro stress test methodologies is worth pursuing. At the same time, we would caution against the risk of excessive complexity. The very nature of financial

[23] The corresponding literature is expanding very fast; see Borio and Zhu (2008) for references. See also Cecchetti *et al.* (2009). To be clear, adding the financial sector into DSGE models is a very helpful step that should be encouraged and pursued (e.g., Goodfriend and McCallum, 2007; Christiano *et al.*, 2008). The point here is that, given the underlying basic structure of the models, we are skeptical that the essence of the processes at the heart of financial instability can be captured.

instability — small shocks trigger large responses — suggests to us that there is something fundamentally amiss with the stress testing approach. If so, adding layers of complexity in an attempt to model feedback effects may not be the most promising way to go. By contrast, given their simplicity, transparency, and track record so far, refining the basic structure of EWIs based on the endogenous-cycle view of financial instability may yield a higher payoff. Potential avenues include the systematic inclusion of cross-border exposures, common global factors, and a refined treatment of risk premia.

5. Conclusion

Approaches to financial and macroeconomic stability have been worlds apart for far too long. It is high time they were brought together again. The financial crisis has given momentum to a process that hitherto had only proceeded very timidly and hesitantly. Policymakers have become much more keenly aware of the need to adjust policies to capture the tight and possibly destabilizing interplay between financial factors and real economy factors. Since the crisis, addressing procyclicality head-on has become a priority of the international policy community (e.g., FSF, 2009; Group of Twenty, 2009; de Larosière, 2009). By the same token, the need to strengthen the macroprudential orientation of financial regulatory and supervisory frameworks has become widely accepted; several efforts are under way to make this shift operational. Monetary policymakers are also reconsidering the merits of leaning against the build-up of risk and financial imbalances, even if near-term inflation appears under control (e.g., Carney, 2009; Trichet, 2009; Shirakawa, 2009). However, better policy requires better analysis, and this has lagged behind. The road ahead is still a long one.

References

Aikman, D., P. Alessandri, B. Eklund, P. Gai, S. Kapadia, E. Martin, N. Mora, G. Stern, and M. Willison (2009). Funding liquidity risk in a quantitative model of systemic stability. Bank of England Working Paper No. 372, June.

Allen, F. and D. Gale (2004). Financial fragility, liquidity and asset prices. *Journal of the European Economic Association*, 2, 1015–1084.

Allen, W. and G. Wood (2006). Defining and achieving financial stability. *Journal of Financial Stability*, 2(2), 152–172.

Altunbas, Y., L. Gambacorta, and D. Marques-Ibanez (2009). An econometric assessment of the risk-taking channel. Paper presented at the BIS–ECB Joint Workshop on "Monetary Policy and Financial Stability", Basel, Switzerland, September 10–11.

Bell, J. and D. Pain (2000). Leading indicator models of banking crises — a critical review. *Bank of England Financial Stability Review*, December, 113–129.

BIS (2001). *71st Annual Report*. June.

BIS (2008). *78th Annual Report*. June.

BIS (2009a). *79th Annual Report*. June.

BIS (2009b). Addressing financial system procyclicality: a possible framework. Note for the FSF Working Group on Market and Institutional Resilience, April.

Bordo, M., M. J. Dueker, and D. C. Wheelock (2000). Aggregate price shocks and financial instability: an historical analysis. NBER Working Paper No. 7652, April.

Borio, C. (2003). Towards a macroprudential framework for financial supervision and regulation? *CESifo Economic Studies*, 49(2), 181–216. Also available as BIS Working Paper No. 128, February.

Borio, C. (2006). Monetary and prudential policies at a crossroads? New challenges in the new century. *Moneda y Crédito*, 224, 63–101. Also available as BIS Working Paper No. 216, September.

Borio, C. (2009). Implementing the macroprudential approach to financial regulation and supervision. *Banque de France — Financial Stability Review*, September, 31–41.

Borio, C. and P. Disyatat (2009). Unconventional monetary policies: an appraisal. Keynote lecture at the Money, Macro and Finance Research Group Annual Conference, Bradford, Leeds, September 9–11.

Borio, C. and M. Drehmann (2009a). Towards an operational framework for financial stability: "fuzzy" measurement and its consequences. BIS Working Paper No. 284. Also forthcoming in *Financial Stability, Monetary Policy, and Central Banking*, Conference proceedings for the 12th Annual Conference of the Central Bank of Chile, Santiago, November 6–7, 2008.

Borio, C. and M. Drehmann (2009b). Assessing the risk of banking crises — revisited. *BIS Quarterly Review*, March, 30–46.

Borio, C., C. Furfine, and P. Lowe (2001). Procyclicality of the financial system and financial stability: issues and policy options. In *Marrying the Macro- and Micro-Prudential Dimensions of Financial Stability*, BIS Papers, No. 1, March, 1–57.

Borio, C. and P. Lowe (2002a). Asset prices, financial and monetary stability: exploring the nexus. BIS Working Paper No. 114, July. An abridged version of this paper was released as "Imbalances or 'bubbles'? Implications for monetary and financial stability," in Hunter, W., G. Kaufman, and M. Pomerleano (eds.) (2003), *Asset Price Bubbles: The Implications for Monetary, Regulatory, and International Policies*, Cambridge, MA: MIT Press, 247–270.

Borio, C. and P. Lowe (2002b). Assessing the risk of banking crises. *BIS Quarterly Review*, December, 43–54.

Borio, C. and P. Lowe (2004). Securing sustainable price stability: should credit come back from the wilderness? BIS Working Paper No. 157, July.

Borio, C. and H. Zhu (2008). Capital regulation, risk-taking and monetary policy: a missing link in the transmission mechanism? BIS Working Paper No. 268, December.

Brunnermeier, M., A. Crockett, C. Goodhart, M. Hellwig, A. Persaud, and H. Shim (2009). *The Fundamental Principles of Financial Regulation*. Geneva Report on the World Economy 11. London: CEPR.

Buiter, W. (2009). The unfortunate uselessness of most "state of the art" monetary economics. Available at http://blogs.ft.com/maverecon/, March 3.

Bunn, P., A. Cunningham, and M. Drehmann (2005). Stress testing as a tool for assessing systemic risks. *Bank of England Financial Stability Review*, June, 116–126.

Carney, M. (2009). Some considerations on using monetary policy to stabilize economic activity. Remarks at the Symposium on "Financial Stability and Macroeconomic Policy", sponsored by the Federal Reserve Bank of Kansas City, Jackson Hole, Wyoming, August 22.

Carson, C. S. and S. Ingves (2003). Financial soundness indicators. IMF board paper, May 14.

Cecchetti, S., P. Disyatat, and M. Kohler (2009). Integrating financial stability: new models for a new challenge. Essay prepared for the BIS–ECB Workshop on "Monetary Policy and Financial Stability", Basel, September 10–11.

CGFS (2009). *The Role of Valuation and Leverage in Procyclicality*. CGFS Publication No. 34, April.

Christiano, L., R. Motto, and M. Rostagno (2008). Monetary policy and stock market boom–bust cycles. ECB Working Paper No. 955, October.

Čihák, M. (2007). Introduction to applied stress testing. IMF Working Paper No. 07/59.

Crockett, A. (2000). Marrying the micro- and macroprudential dimensions of financial stability. BIS speech, September 21.

Davis, E. P. and D. Karim (2008). Comparing early warning systems for banking crises. *Journal of Financial Stability*, 4(2), 89–120.

De Bandt, O. and P. Hartmann (2000). Systemic risk: a survey. ECB Working Paper No. 35, January.

de Larosière, J. (2009). *The High-Level Group Report on Financial Supervision in the EU*. February 25.

Demirgüç-Kunt, A. and E. Detragiache (1998). The determinants of banking crises: evidence from developing and developed countries. *IMF Staff Papers*, 45, 81–109.

Demirgüç-Kunt, A. and E. Detragiache (2005). Cross-country empirical studies of systemic bank distress: a survey. IMF Working Paper No. 05/96, May.

Diamond, D. and P. Dybvig (1983). Bank runs, deposit insurance and liquidity. *Journal of Political Economy*, 91, 401–419.

Drehmann, M. (2008). Stress tests: objectives, challenges and modelling choices. *Sveriges Riksbank Economic Review*, June(2), 60–92.

Drehmann, M. (2009). Macroeconomic stress testing banks: a survey of methodologies. In Quagliariello, M. (ed.), *Stress Testing the Banking System: Methodologies and Applications*, Cambridge: Cambridge University Press.

Drehmann, M., A. Patton, and S. Sorensen (2006). Corporate defaults and macroeconomic shocks: non-linearities and uncertainty. Mimeo, Bank of England.

Elsinger, H., A. Lehar, and M. Summer (2006). Risk assessment for banking systems. *Management Science*, 52(9), September, 1301–1341.

FSF (2009). *Report of the Financial Stability Forum on Addressing Procyclicality in the Financial System*. Basel, April.

Goodfriend, M. and B. McCallum (2007). Banking and interest rates in monetary policy analysis: a quantitative exploration. *Journal of Monetary Economics*, 54(5), 1480–1507.

Goodhart, C. A. E. (2006). A framework for assessing financial stability? *Journal of Banking and Finance*, 30(12), December, 3415–3422.

Goodhart, C. A. E., P. Sunirand, and D. P. Tsomocos (2004). A model to analyse financial fragility: applications. *Journal of Financial Stability*, 1(1), 1–30.

Group of Ten (2001). *Consolidation in the Financial Sector*. Basel: Bank for International Settlements.

Group of Twenty (2009). *G20 Working Group 1: Enhancing Sound Regulation and Strengthening Transparency — Final Report*. March 25.

Haldane, A. (2004). Defining monetary and financial stability. Unpublished paper, Bank of England, London.

Illing, M. and Y. Liu (2006). Measuring financial stress in a developed country: an application to Canada. *Journal of Financial Stability*, 2(3), 243–265.

IMF (2008). *Financial Soundness Indicators*. Washington, D.C.: IMF.

IMF and World Bank (2003). Analytical tools of the Financial Sector Assessment Program. February 24.

Ioannidou, V. P., S. Ongena, and J. L. Peydró (2009). Monetary policy and subprime lending: a tall tale of low federal funds rates, hazardous loans and reduced loan spreads. European Banking Center Discussion Paper No. 2009-04S.

Jiménez, G., S. Ongena, J. L. Peydró, and J. Saurina (2009). Hazardous times for monetary policy: what do twenty-three million bank loans say about the effects of monetary policy on credit risk-taking? Banco de Espana Working Paper No. 0833.

Kaminsky, G. L. and C. M. Reinhart (1999). The twin crises: the causes of banking and balance-of-payments problems. *American Economic Review*, 89(3), 473–500.

Kindleberger, C. (1996). *Manias, Panics and Crashes*, 3rd ed. Cambridge: Cambridge University Press.

Knight, M. D. (2006). Marrying the micro- and macroprudential dimensions of financial stability: six years on. Speech delivered at the 14th International Conference of Banking Supervisors, October.

Knight, M. D. (2007). Now you see it, now you don't: risk in the small and in the large. Speech delivered at the Eighth Annual Risk Management Convention of the Global Association of Risk Professionals, February 27–28.

Laeven, L. and F. Valencia (2008). Systemic banking crises: a new database. IMF Working Paper WP/08/224.

Leijonhufvud, A. (2008). Keynes and the crisis. CEPR Policy Insight No. 23, May.

Merton, R. C. (1974). On the pricing of corporate debt: the risk structure of interest rates. *Journal of Finance*, 29, 449–470.

Minsky, H. P. (1982). *Can "It" Happen Again? Essays on Instability and Finance*. Armonk, NY: M.E. Sharpe.

Mishkin, F. (1999). Global financial stability: framework, events, issues. *Journal of Economic Perspectives*, 13, Fall, 3–20.

Misina, M. and D. Tessier (2008). Non-linearities, model uncertainty, and macro stress testing. Bank of Canada Working Paper No. 08-30.

Nelson, W. (2008). Monetary policy decisions: preparing the inputs and communicating the outcomes. BIS Paper No. 37, February.

Padoa-Schioppa, T. (2003). Central banks and financial stability: exploring the land in between. In Gaspar, V., P. Hartmann, and O. Sleijpen (eds.), *The Transmission of the European Financial System*. Frankfurt: European Central Bank.

Pesaran, M. H., T. Schuerman, B. J. Treutler, and S. M. Weiner (2006). Macroeconomic dynamics and credit risk: a global perspective. *Journal of Money, Credit and Banking*, 38(5), 1211–1262.

Reinhart, C. M. and K. Rogoff (2008). Banking crises: an equal opportunity menace. NBER Working Paper No. 14587.

Rochet, J. and J. Tirole (1996). Interbank lending and systemic risk. *Journal of Money, Credit and Banking*, 28, 733–762.

Schinasi, G. (2004). *Safeguarding Financial Stability: Theory and Practice*. Washington, D.C.: International Monetary Fund.

Shirakawa, M. (2009). Some thoughts on incentives at micro- and macro-level for crisis prevention. Remarks at the Eighth BIS Annual Conference on "Financial and Macroeconomic Resilience — Revisited", Basel, June.

Sorge, M. (2004). Stress-testing financial systems: an overview of current methodologies. BIS Working Paper No. 165, December.

Tarashev, N. and H. Zhu (2008). Market perceptions of systemic risk in the banking industry. *BIS Quarterly Review*, March, 6–8.

Tinbergen, J. (1952). On the theory of economic policy. In Tinbergen, J., P. J. Verdoorn, and H. J. Witteveen (eds.), *Contributions to Economic Analysis*, Amsterdam: North-Holland Publishing Company.

Trichet, J. C. (2009). Credible alertness revisited. Speech delivered at the Symposium on "Financial Stability and Macroeconomic Policy", sponsored by the Federal Reserve Bank of Kansas City, Jackson Hole, Wyoming, August 22.

Upper, C. (2007). Using counterfactual simulations to assess the danger of contagion in interbank markets. BIS Working Paper No. 234, August.

Wagner, W. (2010). In the quest of systemic externalities: a review of the literature. *CESifo Economic Studies*, 56(1), 96–111.

Is a Less Procyclical Financial System an Achievable Goal?*

Charles A. E. Goodhart[†]
London School of Economics

1. Introduction

Banking — indeed, financial intermediation as a whole — is inherently procyclical. Profitability and asset prices rise during upturns, while defaults and non-performing loans decline. Volatility and risk appear, as currently measured (e.g., by value-at-risk estimates), to go down; and credit ratings get revised upwards. Inevitably, banks (and other financial intermediaries or OFIs) seek to expand and put on additional leverage. The reverse happens in downturns, albeit often with greater ferocity, as has been seen recently.

The inability of banks, or indeed of policymakers and regulators, to iron out financial cycles is often attributed to myopia and/or to recurring cycles of greed followed by fear. However, the future is unknowable and cycles do not have a regular periodicity. In the U.K., for example, every single quarter from the end of 1992 until 2008 Q2 experienced relatively steady growth. The timing of turning points is remarkably hard to predict, whether by economic forecasters, market practitioners, or anyone else.

---

* This paper was initially presented at a conference organized by the Central Bank of Argentina in Buenos Aires on August 30–September 1, 2009. The author thanks the Central Bank of Argentina for allowing him to present it again at the Federal Reserve Bank of Chicago's International Banking Conference, and to publish it in this conference proceedings volume.
[†] Charles A. E. Goodhart is a member of the Financial Markets Group at the London School of Economics.

So, the best estimate of the future is some combination of a continuation of current trends together with a mild tendency for reversion to the mean equilibrium (wherever that may be) (Goodhart and Lim, 2009). Therefore, the behavior of banks (and almost everyone else) that seems largely based on the extrapolation of recent trends, and hence reinforces the cycle, is not driven by irrationality. It is the best that can be done.

Cyclicality in banking and finance is thus inevitable, but it can also exacerbate the amplitude of economic cycles, as is now the case. There is a need to avoid policy actions that do harm by enhancing the natural procyclicality of the financial system. Despite the best of intentions, policymakers around the world have, in recent decades, adopted measures that have unwittingly done just this. Section 2 outlines a number of these steps, which have served to increase the virulence of such procyclicality.

In Section 3, we move on to current proposals for mitigating such procyclicality, touching on countercyclical macroprudential measures, direct constraints on (bank) size or function, proposals for banks (and OFIs) to self-insure, etc. One characteristic of banking — and of financial intermediation more generally — is that it is much more closely linked to the property market, both for residential housing and for commercial property, than to any other sector of the economy. A much larger proportion of bank lending is for the purpose of purchasing property than for any other purpose, and the most common source of collateral for securing such lending (whether for buying such property or for other purposes) is also property. This does not lessen the general concordance between banking (and financial intermediation more broadly) and general economic cycles, a common cyclicality, since cycles in the housing market and in the broader economy are closely intertwined (Leamer, 2007). But it does mean that policy measures that influence the amplitude of cycles in the housing market are, by the same token, likely to have a similar effect on banking cycles. Thus, in addition to examining policies that may enhance or retard such banking cycles, we shall also review measures that have similar effects in housing markets.

If policies to restrain financial cyclicality were easy to devise and were without serious side effects (costs), they would already have been introduced (as per the efficient regulator hypothesis). Section 4 outlines some of the problems behind such policies. One notable implication is that they (or some of them) may raise the costs of bank intermediation. We end by discussing the implication of that for the future structure and development of the banking sector, and of financial intermediation, around the world.

2. Measures That Enhanced Procyclicality

2.1 *Assessment of capital adequacy*

One of the purposes of Basel II was to align capital requirements to risk, and in particular to the internal risk estimates of the commercial banks themselves, more closely than Basel I had done. However, such risk measurements, and market and model measures of risk, are based primarily on current (and recent past) values of key variables, mainly of profitability, volatility, and correlation. Profitability rises in a boom, while volatility and correlation typically go down. It is not until a crisis strikes that all of this reverses sharply. So, (market) risk-based measures are typically far more procyclical than the broad-brush, and somewhat naive, risk buckets established in Basel I.

The problem is, of course, that the future is unknowable and uncertain. There are certain conditions that make a financial crisis more likely, such as sharply rising asset (housing) prices, a rapid expansion in and high levels of leverage, etc., but it is difficult to put well-defined estimates of probability to the likelihood or scale of any resultant downturn. In this context, accountants are likely to be very averse to using (somewhat subjective) estimates of future values (such as those involved in the Spanish dynamic pre-provisioning approach), and would rather use measures of current values as the best available yardstick.

So long as markets functioned well, and so long as the efficient market hypothesis was believed to hold, there seemed to be no problem. Of course, the future is unknowable, but efficient arbitrage should keep the current market value of an asset in line with the present value of the expected discounted future cash flows from the asset. Surely the future is unknowable and markets can be, and are, mistaken, but what could be a better measure? Turning points cannot be easily predicted (if at all), so the default market prediction tends to extrapolate recent developments. This is bound to involve market overshooting both towards the end of a boom and in a bust.

So, mark-to-market accounting tends to be procyclical, exaggerating both profits (losses) and capital strength (weakness) in a boom (bust), but what alternative is better? Problems, however, arise when market failures and dysfunctionality occur in a bust, particularly when market prices get driven down by forced, panic sales; and uncertainty (Uhlig, 2009), or bad publicity (who would buy toxic assets?), or short-termism (waiting for a "bottom" to develop) prevents prices from being restored to their present discounted cash flow values. It is widely believed that, over much of the field of mortgage-backed securities, current market values have fallen far below their present discounted cash flow values in the recent turmoil. Indeed, this belief has lain behind many of the policy steps proposed to revitalize the banking sector, notably the Troubled Asset Relief Program (TARP) in the U.S.

But, if and when markets become dysfunctional, how should accounting procedures respond? My colleague, Avi Persaud, in our Geneva Report, *The Fundamental Principles of Financial Regulation* (Brunnermeier *et al.*, 2009), has advocated relating the accounting procedure to the liability structure of the financial intermediary. Assuming markets become dysfunctional, when the liabilities backing an asset are long-term, then the intermediary can wait out the crisis and the asset could be valued in terms of its present discounted cash flow. But in cases where the liabilities are predominantly short-term (such as Northern Rock, Bear Stearns, and Lehman Brothers), the intermediary would be more likely to be forced into an immediate sale, so their assets' current market price would be the correct yardstick.

Whatever the analytical validity of this approach, there are practical problems in hypothecating particular liabilities to particular assets, since all liabilities jointly and severally support all assets. If this route towards accounting reform, therefore, proves unattractive or impossible, the accounting profession will be forced to come up with some other suggestions for dealing with market failures and dysfunctions. We will see what they propose.

Nevertheless, except for such special cases, mark-to-market, fair-value accounting will and should remain the yardstick. So, the best current methods of assessing individual bank risk — Basel II — and of valuing assets — via the International Financial Reporting Standards (IFRS) with its emphasis on mark-to-market, fair-value accounting methods — involve greater procyclicality than their predecessors, Basel I and historical cost accounting, respectively. We should not deal with that by reverting to worse measures again. Instead, we should offset such extra procyclicality by the application of new, focused countercyclical instruments.

2.2 *Liquidity*

The list of financial failures generally included those institutions which combined dubious assets, so their solvency was in question, with an excessive reliance on short-dated, wholesale funds. When the latter could not be rolled over, owing to fears of insolvency, these firms faced immediate illiquidity. They did not have sufficient liquid assets — or, in the case of U.S. broker-dealers, access to Fed lending, prior to the revisions in spring 2008 — to cope.

Some 30 or 40 years ago, most commercial banks held large proportions of their portfolios in domestic government bonds, which had liquid markets and little or no credit risk. But, being less risky, they had lower yields. Over the years since then, such holdings of low-risk, low-yield assets have been systematically run down by commercial banks almost everywhere and replaced by higher-yielding, riskier assets, largely property- and house mortgage-related.

As a result, banks and OFIs turned for liquidity, and to finance leverage that outstripped the available retail deposit base, to funding from short-term wholesale markets. So, funding liquidity came to replace asset liquidity. The idea was that, so long as bank capital sufficiency was assured, which adherence to Basel II was supposed to achieve, then banks could always rely on access to these large, efficient wholesale markets (such as the interbank and commercial paper markets). Unfortunately, Basel II failed to provide such assurance; it was "gamed" and manipulated by banks such as UBS and Northern Rock. Even more important, the large wholesale markets collapsed after August 9, 2007, and are still moribund.

The Basel Committee on Banking Supervision (BCBS) had attempted in the mid-1980s to put together an accord on banking liquidity as a supplement to the Capital Accord of 1988. But when that initiative failed for a variety of reasons, no individual country regulator felt able to halt (let alone reverse) the developing trend away from asset liquidity. Thus, when short-term wholesale markets collapsed after August 9, 2007, banks were left with little internal asset liquidity with which to ride out the storm. This then forced central banks, kicking and screaming, to expand "lender of last resort" facilities to an ever-widening group of financial intermediaries against the collateral of ever lower-quality assets for ever-longer maturities.

Although central banks did, under extreme pressure, come up with numerous innovative responses, it was an uncomfortable exercise. So, there is now another international BCBS attempt to revisit the question of regulatory oversight of liquidity management. The main difficulty on this occasion will probably be, with respect to large, international cross-border banks, the relative powers and responsibilities of the host regulator/supervisor *vis-à-vis* the home regulator/supervisor.

2.3 *Remuneration*

Perhaps the worst theory in the field of finance governance to have been promulgated in recent decades was that it was desirable to align the incentives of bank executives, who make the key decisions, with those of bank shareholders. As can be seen in Figure 1, bank shareholders will always prefer a riskier option with the same mean expected return (50% chance of A; 50% chance of B) to the safe outcome (C).

In effect, shareholders have a put option to give the bank back to its other creditors. The structure of most bank executive remuneration packages is equivalent to having a much more leveraged option, encouraging ever-greater risk seeking. Insofar as bank losses could be or were internalized, by imposing such losses on subordinated debt holders and/or on depositors, there was some (but probably not a great) chance of having such creditors' actions restrain bank executive decisions. However, the externalities or contagion costs of the failure of large, interconnected financial intermediaries are (or are perceived to be, especially after the Lehman Brothers failure) so great that national authorities around the world have

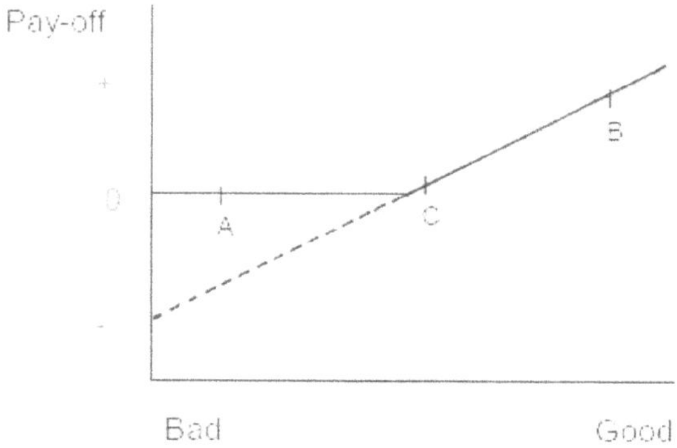

Figure 1. Payoff structure for (bank) shareholders.

now guaranteed *all* debt liabilities, both deposits and subordinated debt, of such creditors.

Who then picks up the bill for any such failures? As demonstrated, it falls on the taxpayer. One implication is that any step requiring banks to raise new capital raises the cost of funding to such banks (in contrast to the Modigliani–Miller theorem), since it reduces the value of the (unpriced) put option against the taxpayer. Another implication is that the government and the regulatory authorities do, and should, have a direct concern in adjusting the structure of bank executive incentives and remuneration.

Present measures towards such a realignment mostly involve trying to extend the averaging period over which bonus payments become payable. However, insofar as much risk taking involves small, steady receipts during normal, good times against a small likelihood of a much larger payout in occasional bad times, such as using carry-trade strategies, writing credit default swap (CDS) insurance, etc., this only scratches the surface. It will still be an optimal strategy for an executive to lever up, and to underprice risk, during normal times since the probability of a bad outcome is low enough; and should the latter occur, there would still be limited liability.

2.4 *Direct constraints*

Insofar as there remained direct functional constraints on the financial operations of banks during the last couple of decades, such as the Glass–Steagall Act in the U.S., these tended to be relaxed. The general ethos was that markets, and financial intermediaries within them, worked sufficiently well to allow for light-touch, principles-based regulation; and when a problem in asset/financial markets did occur, then a central bank (and especially the Fed) could, so it was thought, restore equilibrium by a judiciously aggressive lowering of interest rates. The credibility of such a "Greenspan put" response was enhanced by its apparent success on October 19, 1987; in October 1998; on September 11, 2001; and in general response to the 2000/2001 NASDAQ/IT bust. As Hy Minsky (1977, 1982) analyzed, this very belief in greater, permanent stability encouraged reductions in the price of risk and the overextension of leverage, thus leading to instability. The proximate cause of the crisis was a generalized belief amongst not only the credit rating agencies but almost all those operating in the U.S. housing market that, because aggregate housing prices diversified across the whole of the U.S. had not fallen significantly for the past 50 years, the probability of them doing so over the next 10 years was vanishingly small. With the benefit of hindsight, this belief now seems ludicrous, but it was the cornerstone on which the huge subprime edifice was erected. There was no need to limit mortgage extension to no-income, no-job, no-asset applicants if the house itself provided perfect surety and collateral for the loan.

Therefore, there was much delusion, and self-delusion, about the true riskiness of many of these assets, reinforced by the use of models whose parameters were drawn from a period of unusual calm in developed countries — the "Great Moderation". So much of the excessive extension of leverage was due to an unwitting misreading of conditions. Nevertheless, such extension was not entirely unwitting by any means. When the regulators allowed it, banks and OFIs took advantage of their ability to increase leverage in the pursuit of short-term profits. In Europe, which had rejected simple leverage ratios as too naive, banks took on huge volumes of highly rated (i.e., AAA and super senior) mortgage-backed securities, with such low risk weights that they did not impact on their Basel II capital adequacy ratios (CARs), in order to raise their leverage ratios; often, these reached levels of 50 to 1, or worse, levels at which they would have been assessed in the U.S. under the Federal Deposit Insurance Corporation (FDIC) Improvement Act of 1991 as critically undercapitalized (and shut down unless they raised more capital quickly). In the U.S., the Securities and Exchange Commission (SEC) relaxed the limits on the leverage ratios of the broker-dealers, the large U.S. investment houses, in effect by imposing Basel II CARs on them (Halloran, 2009); not surprisingly, they took full advantage of that dispensation.

As late as May 2007, Northern Rock — which collapsed the following September — was the darling of the London Stock Exchange, largely because of (not despite) its sky-high leverage ratio, aggressive expansion, and reliance on wholesale funding. When times are good, the market applauds the aggressive use of capital. But that is just when regulators would prefer to see financial intermediaries rebuilding capital buffers for use in a subsequent downturn. *Per contra*, in a crisis, when regulators would like to see financial intermediaries actually using their capital and liquidity base to undertake more lending to support the wider economy, the market will be more fearful of default and/or of government recapitalization, and thereby applaud de-leveraging and hoarding of capital/liquidity.

The idea that the market will help regulators to sustain stability over the boom/bust cycle is fallacious. Unfortunately, financial regulators will very often find themselves having to row against the inherent tides of the market. This will limit and constrain the ability of the regulators, and influence the way that regulation/supervision needs to be done.

2.5 *Housing*

House ownership is often perceived as a public good. Hence, governments are prone to support it by a variety of measures, with both direct and indirect subsidies. These include mortgage interest deductibility, preferential treatment for capital gains, provision of mortgage guarantees, encouragement of securitization, non-recourse terms in case of default, etc. Insofar as this raises housing price levels, it will generate an increased supply of housing so that the ratio of houses to potential house owners shifts. Similarly, it will encourage, as it is meant to do, a weaker and less stable fringe of house owners into the market.

During good, normal times, competition will lead to ever more generous loan-to-value and loan-to-income ratios. During crises or bad times, these will be severely scaled back. Moreover, owing to inertia and lags, house price changes are strongly auto-correlated and such auto-correlation may well get extended by extrapolative expectations. For all such reasons, there have been a number of severe boom/bust cycles both in housing markets and in commercial property markets; for example, there have been three such major cycles in the U.K. since 1970. Because of the close links between the real estate market (and its financing) and the financial sector, there has been a close concordance, with causal relationships in both directions, between housing and banking cycles.

Little or nothing has been done to restrain such cycles in housing and property markets. Indeed, it has been argued that political support for the subprime market (until the bubble burst) in the U.S. helped to worsen the intensity of the recent cycle there. Furthermore, these cycles are so long that prior experience seems no antidote. The history of housing bubbles in the U.K. in 1972–1973 and 1988–1990 had little effect, as far as can be seen, in restraining enthusiasm for housing purchases in 2003–2006.

2.6 *Moral hazard*

Around the world, the recent crisis has seen the authorities provide liquidity on ever-wider and more generous terms, while recapitalizing banks and guaranteeing the par value of almost all non-equity debt. The safety net has become both larger and more comfortable for the financial sector. As a result, moral hazard will have risen sharply. One must expect executives in banks and OFIs to take full advantage. As mentioned in Section 2.3, the incentive is to do just that.

So, what is to be done?

3. Countermeasures

3.1 *Direct constraints on bank activity*

One natural response to our present difficulties is to try to reset the structure so that we can return to the status quo ante, in which the state would no longer play a role as general guarantor, and in which the fear of bankruptcy and private-sector loss would again provide some (enough?) discipline against excessive risk taking. There are several versions of this proposal, most of which have a slightly quaint flavor of seeking to revert to an unspoilt, earlier, and simpler arcadian age, before the wiles and innovations of investment bankers fouled the nest.

The first approach is the call to break up big banks, so that they can be more easily shut down. "If banks are too big to fail, they are too big," Mervyn King has said, and he has the support of Paul Volcker. Whereas it is true that some banks are now too big to fail on their own even with zero contagion, the key systemic problem is contagion. Contagion depends on the (perceived) similarities between a failing bank and its confreres, and on the interconnections between them. Northern Rock, IKB, and Sachsen were not large; but if Northern Rock had been allowed to fail, there would have been a run on Bradford & Bingley and Cheltenham & Gloucester the day after and on HBOS the day after that.[1] If a large bank were broken up

[1] The skeptic will note that all of these banks did eventually fail and have to be taken over, but crisis resolution is, in some large part, about playing for time and seeking to avert panic. If such time is not well used, one may then just get a slower-moving collapse. The difficulty in 2007–2008 was that the basic concern was ultimately about solvency/capital adequacy, yet this was not really addressed until after the Lehman Brothers failure.

into segments that were just smaller-scale mirror images of the original, then the contagion/systemic problem would remain almost as bad.[2] As several economists such as W. Wagner (2007, 2008) and V. Acharya (2009) have noted, contagion is a positive function of similarities between banks. The microprudential supervisor wants diversification *within* each individual bank; the macroprudential supervisor should want diversification *between* banks. A danger of microprudential regulation is that it forces all of the regulated banks into the same mold.

So, apart from the legal issues of whether the government should override private property contracts by enforcing a break-up, there are doubts as to whether having many smaller banks would help to ease contagious crises. Recall that it was the myriad of small banks that failed in the U.S. in 1929–1933, whereas the more oligopolistic systems in some other countries (e.g., Canada and the U.K.) were more resistant. A more realistic approach is to try to assess how far the larger banks involve greater systemic risk and then impose additional offsetting charges (as discussed further below).

A second approach is to try to limit the range of institutions/functions to which the safety net applies. This theme goes under several headings, such as narrow banking or bringing back the Glass–Steagall Act, with the associated populist phrase that current banking combines "a casino with a utility". This has obtained surprising traction, even in the august pages of the *Financial Times*, given how silly the idea is. Perhaps the worst error of the crisis was to allow Lehman Brothers to fail, but it had no retail deposits; in the populist jargon, Lehman, AIG, and Bear Stearns were casinos, not utilities. For reasons set out in my paper (Goodhart, 2008), regulatory constraints on the protected, narrow sector will drive business to the unregulated sector during normal times, but provoke a flight back to safety during crises, thereby worsening the crisis.

Banking is about risk taking, e.g., with maturity mismatch. Securitization and derivatives are used to lessen and hedge such risks. A narrow bank that has to hold all of its assets (unhedged) to maturity can be very risky; for example, is a 15-year fixed-rate mortgage loan a suitable asset for a bank or a specialized building society (savings and loan association) to hold? What exactly do the proponents of narrow

[2] However, this approach might at least allow the first small bank to run into difficulties to go bankrupt, *pour encourager les autres*, even if runs on similar banks are then vigorously rebuffed. When Barings was allowed to fail in 1995, the Bank of England prepared prophylactic measures to support the remaining British merchant banks.

banking suggest in the case of relationships with industry? Relationship banking, as practiced in Asia and in Europe, places these banks far more at risk to the changing fortunes of their major clients than in the more arm's-length, capital-market-integrated Anglo-Saxon model.

3.2 *Remuneration and risk taking*

The recent crisis suggests that banks (and OFIs) took on excessive risk. Was this because they were fools, and did so unwittingly? Their regulators, who allowed them to do so, were probably fooled by the opacity of the shadow banking system, by the use of fancy mathematical risk models, and by the gaming of Basel II. But if the bankers were also fooled, they hardly deserve their over-the-top remuneration packages.

More likely, as outlined in Section 2.3, they took on more risk because it was in their own self-interest to do so; that is, they were (social) knaves. A right-wing maxim states, "Guns do not kill people; people kill people." Transformed into financial terms, this could be rephrased as thus: "Excessive leverage does not kill banks; chief executives kill banks." Decisions on how to run banks are generally made by a handful of top executives, with occasional input from large equity investors. The most important determinant of the risk profile of a bank is not, therefore, going to be the regulations on CARs, but the incentives facing top management.

Moral hazard arises when those making decisions are insured against failure, since there will then be an incentive to gamble. The public fury against the rewards, bonuses, and pensions for those in charge of failing banks is partly a witch hunt. However, it is also grounded in the perception that the expectation of such high returns, whatever the outturn, was not only partly responsible for the genesis of this crisis, but will lead to the next one as well.

Perhaps there could be two classes of equity, with limited liability for all outside investors and *unlimited* liability for senior executives. The latter would then each be forcibly vested with an unlimited liability share upon reaching a top executive position, and would have to continue holding it (non-transferable) until their death or the termination of their bank. Had this been the case, people like Sir Fred Goodwin and Dick Fuld would now be paupers. Might that, however, make bank executives too cautious and risk-averse?

Perhaps we should start from the other end. Exactly how risk-averse do we want our banking CEOs to be? How might we start to think about this question? If we knew how risk-averse we want our bank executives to be, could we then engineer their remuneration package to achieve the desired level of risk aversion, always remembering that those who get to the top of the tree are likely to be supremely self-confident in the first place?

Regulators have hesitated to become involved in remuneration issues for obvious reasons. But if this is where the fundamental moral hazard resides, perhaps they should overcome their cold feet.

3.3 *Insurance*

I doubt if much traction will be obtained with (1) the attempt to turn back the clock towards a simpler world, because that is essentially misconceived; or (2) the attempt to reset the incentives of bank executives via intervening in remuneration, because that is difficult to accomplish and is a political hot potato. This leaves us with two main sets of proposals. The first, which has greater support in the U.S., is to reassess the relationship between the public authorities — i.e., the ministry of finance, the central bank, and the regulators/supervisors — and the commercial banks (and OFIs) as being one of insurer/insured, rather than of banker/client, and then to ask how such insurance might best be priced and provided.

The new reality, post the Lehman Brothers failure, is that the public sector — the state — has become the ultimate guarantor of both the liquidity and the continued viability (solvency) of all the systemic parts of the financial sector. In other words, the public sector insures the systemic parts of the financial sector. Once upon a time, the relationship followed a banking paradigm. Just as a commercial bank assessed the potential solvency (creditworthiness) and the quality of collateral offered by the bank's client, so a central bank was supposed to assess the solvency and the quality of collateral of a commercial bank coming to it for "lender of last resort" assistance. If these were not good enough, the commercial bank should be let go and allowed to fail (Bagehot, 1873). Under the pressure of recent events, however, this latter paradigm has been abandoned in favor of broader insurance of the liquidity and solvency of all systemic financial institutions. Liquidity assistance has been provided to an ever-widening range of financial intermediaries on ever more dubious collateral for ever-lengthening durations. Similarly, apart from equity holders, most bank creditors have been guaranteed. In effect, the public sector *is* insuring the core, systemic financial system.

Seen in this light, the potential for moral hazard and, hence, of costs to the insurer — in this case, the taxpayer — is immense. The question, then, is how to price and provide such insurance in order to reduce (minimize) the costs whilst still retaining the benefits. One strand of thought is to try to require the insured to take out considerable self-insurance (co-insurance) as a precondition. A suggestion (Kashyap *et al.*, 2008) is to require all such systemic financial intermediaries to issue debt instruments, which could be forcibly switched to equity, at the fiat of the authorities, whenever a financial crisis is (in the opinion of those same authorities?) called. A second suggestion (Hart and Zingales, 2009) is to require any bank whose CDS price moves too high for too long to either raise more capital or be taken over by the authorities.[3] The implications of such ideas for the cost and availability of capital to the banking sector have yet to be assessed.

A second strand of thought considers the price, or premium, at which the public sector might provide such insurance. An article of faith amongst American economists — but not reciprocated by European policymakers — is that the private sector is far superior to the authorities in price discovery, and so premiums (the price for insurance) should be set by private-sector insurers. But, "*Quis custodiet ipsos custodies*?" If the systemic financial sector cannot be allowed to fail, neither can its (private-sector) insurers (N.B. AIG!). A compromise solution, suggested by the economists at New York University (see Acharya and Richardson, 2009, Ch. 13), is to require private-sector insurers to take on a small proportion of all such insurance, say 5% — big enough for them to price the risk carefully, but small enough for them to survive calls if and when a crisis occurs. The public sector would then provide the remaining bulk (95%) of the insurance, piggybacking on the price set by the private-sector insurers.

3.4 *Countercyclical regulation*

One reason why (some) Americans have been pushing the insurance approach is that it may be designed to give a greater role to private-sector

[3] Oddly enough, Hart and Zingales (2009) do not appear to have recognized that exactly the same idea lay at the heart of the Prompt Corrective Action feature of the FDIC Improvement Act of 1991, and yet that failed to work in 2007–2009.

markets. They tend to regard the phrase "smart regulation" as an oxymoron, and there is considerable evidence to support that position. Nevertheless, the main thrust of proposals within Europe, of which our Geneva Report on *The Fundamental Principles of Financial Regulation* (Brunnermeier *et al.*, 2009) is a good example, has been to try to mitigate the procyclical effects of recent regulation (Basel II and IFRS mark-to-market accounting) by introducing time- and state-varying countercyclical capital charges in response to cycles in leverage and in asset prices. This represents the second main set of proposals.

One of the main defects of the BCBS approach, at least up until now, is that it has not been willing to recommend, or even discuss, a ladder of sanctions. This is because it has no legal standing for doing so on constitutional grounds. Consequently, any proposed target or standard that it has proposed normally transmutes into a reputational minimum; this makes infra-minimal holdings effectively unusable, while leaving the size of the effective buffer (above the minimum) entirely at the discretion of the regulated. This must change, and any proposal for countercyclical capital or liquidity requirements needs to be supported and bolstered by an accompanying ladder of sanctions, as in the FDIC Improvement Act of 1991.

The general desirability of countercyclical regulatory requirements has been broadly accepted in Europe, though less so in the U.S., as outlined above. The problem lies much more in the details, though this applies to some considerable extent to both approaches. For example, just how does one assess which institutions are systemic? Closely aligned with that query, just how does one measure the systemic risk that the failure of an institution would generate? Regulators should only be concerned with externalities, not with (the risk of) such losses as can be internalized. The measurement problems are severe; some academic work has been undertaken to seek to answer these questions (Adrian and Brunnermeier, 2008; Segoviano and Goodhart, 2009), but it remains in its infancy.

3.5 *Housing*

The close interlinkages between banking and the property (housing) market have been stressed several times in this paper. Insofar as it is arguably sensible and appropriate to impose countercyclical regulations on banks and on other systemic financial intermediaries, by exactly the same set of arguments one would also advocate introducing countercyclical regulatory controls on the mortgage market. These could take the form of limits on loan-to-value or loan-to-income ratios that would tighten (weaken) as the housing cycle fluctuated. The penchant in several (small European) countries for borrowing in foreign currencies should also be controlled. There are obvious ways of trying to avoid such controls, but there are (legal) steps that can be taken to make such measures effective.

4. Future Outcomes?

In any interface between bankers and regulators/supervisors, the bankers are always likely to come out on top. They have far more resources, and hence can hire better-skilled employees, and will normally have more political clout. If they do not capture the regulators, they will subdue them. This has several implications. The first is that the structure and form of the underlying incentives facing the bankers themselves, including social norms, will be at least as (if not more) important as the details of the regulations and the efficiency of the supervisors. The second is that the attempts by regulators/supervisors to constrain bankers — after all, effective regulation is intended to do so — will be a losing battle. Bankers will innovate around regulations, and regulators will tend to lag behind in the dialectic dance. Since financial supervision is, therefore, such an inherently unrewarding exercise, in which failure is all too obvious and success goes unnoticed, there are good reasons for a central bank to delegate as much of the process as is consistent with the maintenance of systemic financial stability to a notionally independent agency. Otherwise, it may suffer damaging reputational contagion.

Nevertheless, in the aftermath of the current financial crisis, something will have to be done. Bankers took on excessive leverage in the boom; and so when the bust came, they cut back so sharply that markets collapsed, trade declined sharply, and economies fell into depression despite frantic countervailing efforts by the authorities. Although the key driving force lies in the incentives facing the bankers (and their remuneration has, not surprisingly, been the main focus of public anger), it is unlikely that much will be done to directly constrain the form of such remuneration. To do so runs contrary to the basic tenets of capitalism; the bankers would fight any such proposals, and the threat of transferring business to more accommodating sites would be credibly deployed.

Instead, what is more likely to happen is that banks will be faced with greater restrictions on expansion and leverage during upturns. At a minimum, the Europeans are likely to introduce a maximum leverage ratio, as the Swiss National Bank has already done (and as the U.S. had in place via the FDIC Improvement Act of 1991), and will probably make it adjustable (downwards) at the discretion of their macroprudential regulator. Whether European regulators will go further down the road of requiring countercyclical CARs or Spanish-style dynamic provisioning is unclear. The latter is inconsistent with the IFRS, while the technical details of establishing the former are complex.

Moreover, the banks see countercyclical requirements as a bit of a con trick. Such requirements will bite in booms, but during recessions the market will require an ever-higher buffer on top of the lower official requirements. So, the bankers will see countercyclical requirements as more simply equivalent to higher capital charges at all times.

What will happen to the debate in the U.S. — i.e., whether they will go for the (self)insurance route or the countercyclical route, or a mixture of both — is as yet unclear. Banks will, naturally, give their support to whichever seems best and least arduous for themselves. Once again, there could be divisions in approach between the U.S. and the Europeans, though that remains to be seen because the political and Congressional timetable in the U.S. has been, and remains, so long drawn out. If such divisions develop, it will further complicate the process of reaching international agreement at the BCBS and the Financial Stability Board (FSB).

In addition, the whole exercise is becoming diverted from the central, more important subject of *what* should be done, with what instrument, to mitigate financial boom/bust cycles, towards the subsidiary, less important question of *which agencies* should have the powers/responsibilities. In other words, the whole exercise is being deflected into "turf wars". In the U.K., such a turf war on the relative responsibilities of the specialist supervisor — the Financial Services Authority (FSA) — and of the Bank of England is in full swing, with the current Labour government favoring the FSA and the prospective future governing party, the Conservatives, favoring the Bank of England. The battle lines over turf in the U.S. are even more convoluted, as others can describe better.

Furthermore, the process of reaching international agreement has already been made more difficult by differences in viewpoint over the relative responsibilities of *home* and *host* regulators. The large international banks and the Institute of International Finance argue vehemently for centralizing regulation/supervision with the home regulator, in order to maximize operational efficiency and minimize the administrative costs of compliance with supervision, using the argument of the need for a "level playing field". Against that, crisis resolution has, during the recent turmoil, been entirely national in character and very expensive. Since the national taxpayer has borne the brunt of such resolution (with international banks being "international in life, but national in death", and with legal insolvency regimes that vary from country to country), there is an opposing groundswell amongst many national regulators for a transfer of more regulatory powers back to host regulators. Eurozone countries are, however, ambivalent, since most (federally minded Europeans) would prefer to centralize regulation/supervision to some central federal bodies, without having the fiscal powers to undertake crisis resolution at the central federal level.

Thus, the outcome of current (international) efforts to re-regulate remains obscure. The most likely outcome will be a generalized introduction of a leverage ratio (adjustable at local discretion), the promulgation of some form of (internationally agreed) liquidity ratio, and a tightening of capital adequacy requirements, though whether with or without countercyclical characteristics remains to be seen. The effect of all this will be to raise the cost of capital against banks. In response, banks will have to raise the spread between their deposit and loan rates; this spread marks the cost of bank intermediation. As the cost of intermediation via banks rises, financial intermediation will become diverted, possibly via securitization again, into other channels. What these channels may be, what risks they will entail, and how the next major financial crisis will unfold will be a subject for the next generation to discover.

References

Acharya, V. V. (2009). A theory of systemic risk and design of prudential bank regulation. *Journal of Financial Stability*, 5(3), September, 224–255.

Acharya, V. and M. Richardson (eds.) (2009). *Restoring Financial Stability: How to Repair a Failed System*. Hoboken, NJ: Wiley.

Adrian, T. and M. K. Brunnermeier (2008). CoVaR. Working paper, Princeton University and Federal Reserve Bank of New York. Available at http://www.princeton.edu/~markus/research/papers/CoVaR/.

Bagehot, W. (1873). *Lombard Street*. New York: Scribner, Armstrong & Co. Republished in 1999, Chichester, U.K.: John Wiley & Sons.

Brunnermeier, M. K., A. Crockett, C. A. E. Goodhart, A. Persaud, and H. S. Shin (2009). *The Fundamental Principles of Financial Regulation*. Geneva Report on the World Economy 11. Geneva and London: International Center for Monetary and Banking Studies (ICMB) and Centre for Economic Policy Research (CEPR).

Goodhart, C. A. E. (2008). The boundary problem in financial regulation. *National Institute Economic Review*, 206(1), October, 48–55. Also available as Appendix in Brunnermeier *et al.* (2009).

Goodhart, C. A. E. and W. B. Lim (2009). Interest rate forecasts: a pathology. Financial Markets Group, London School of Economics, Special Paper No. 185, April.

Halloran, M. J. (2009). Systemic risks and the Bear Stearns crisis. In Ciorciari, J. D. and J. B. Taylor (eds.), *The Road Ahead for the Fed*, Stanford, CA: Hoover Institution Press, Ch. 10.

Hart, O. and L. Zingales (2009). A new capital regulation for large financial institutions. CEPR Discussion Paper No. DP7298.

Kashyap, A. K., R. G. Rajan, and J. C. Stein (2008). Rethinking capital regulation. In *Maintaining Stability in a Changing Financial System*, Proceedings of the Federal Reserve Bank of Kansas City Symposium, Jackson Hole, Wyoming, August 21–23.

Leamer, E. (2007). Housing IS the business cycle. In *Housing, Housing Finance, and Monetary Policy*, Proceedings of the Federal Reserve Bank of Kansas City Symposium, Jackson Hole, Wyoming, August 30–September 1.

Minsky, H. P. (1977). A theory of systemic fragility. In Altman, E. I. and A. W. Sametz (eds.), *Financial Crises*, New York: Wiley.

Minsky, H. P. (1982). *Can "It" Happen Again? Essays on Instability and Finance*. Armonk, NY: M.E. Sharpe, Inc.

Segoviano, M. and C. A. E. Goodhart (2009). Banking stability measures. IMF Working Paper No. 09/04.

Uhlig, H. (2009). A model of a systemic bank run. NBER Working Paper No. 15072, June.

Wagner, W. (2007). Diversification at financial institutions and systemic crises. University of Tilburg Discussion Paper No. 71. Also available in *Journal of Financial Intermediation* (2010), 19(3), 373–386.

Wagner, W. (2008). The homogenization of the financial system and financial crises. *Journal of Financial Intermediation*, 17(3), 330–356.

Bubbles?

Allan H. Meltzer*
Carnegie Mellon University

What is a financial bubble? As with many popular terms, it is not entirely clear what the user means. Economic theory gives a precise definition, but it does not fit what users of the term have in mind. I will start with the economist's term because it helps to clarify some issues. Then, I will claim that the wide use of "bubbles" to describe market events hides consideration of systemic problems that we should want to correct.

1. Economic Bubbles

In a standard dynamic general equilibrium model of trade and exchange, expectations of higher prices can generate an increase in price brought about solely to satisfy the expectation. No changes in taste or technology occur. Economists call the resulting price increase a "bubble".

No transactions occur; the model does not admit transactions. This assumption bypasses a problem that arises when the model is used to interpret actual events. Let me grant for this purpose that actual buyers hold bullish expectations about price and are willing to wager that the price will rise. What about the sellers? Their presence poses a problem, for they are not present in the standard model; the model has only a representative agent. The model abstracts from buyers and sellers. Actual sellers must believe that prices will not rise.

The presence of buyers and sellers with different beliefs or expectations makes the economic model of bubbles inapplicable. A few years ago at this conference, I developed the same points about bubbles in a paper on the dot-com expansion. I pointed out that the economic model

---

* Allan H. Meltzer is the Allan H. Meltzer University Professor of Political Economy at Carnegie Mellon University and a visiting scholar at the American Enterprise Institute.

of bubbles did not apply. Not only did it not account for the seller's willingness to sell, but it also neglected observed differences between companies that sold online and those that did not. A comparison of Amazon and Borders showed that the stock market gave much greater valuation to future earnings of online companies even if they had no earnings at the time.

I proposed an alternative explanation that I believe better fits the facts. Some investors became convinced that online sales represented a new, very profitable technology. After a few quarters of data showed that few companies would earn high profits and that some were unlikely to profit, share prices fell. Ten years later, we know that many of the companies failed. Few, if any, online companies' share prices have revisited their 1999 values.

2. Revisiting Bubbles

The housing market is the most recent market in which prices are alleged to have increased solely or mainly based on expectations of further increases and no decline. Unlike the alleged dot-com bubble, many of the sellers were builders, so a larger part of the supply was new production. Of course, prices of existing houses also rose in regions experiencing rising prices of new homes.

Expectations were active and relevant. But, this does not establish that there was an economic bubble, nor does the evidence that many people claimed that price would never fall. Bubble expectations must be self-fulfilling. This is a much harder claim to establish; it is not sufficient to point to the rapid increase in selling prices. Other factors were at work.

Chief among the other factors were the changes in housing and mortgage markets over the previous decade. The U.S. government already had many programs to encourage and subsidize home ownership. The Federal Home Loan Banks (FHLBs) date from the early 1930s, and the Federal National Mortgage Association (FNMA) from 1937. The FHLBs began as a source of loans to home lending institutions like the thrift institutions. The FNMA made loans and purchased mortgages from the mortgage market institutions. Also in the 1930s, the federal government established the Federal Housing Administration (FHA) to guarantee loans to borrowers who did not have an established or qualified credit rating. The borrower paid a fee to the FHA.

Governments of both major political parties defend support for housing as supplying a public good. Homeownership, they claim, increases social stability and community pride. Beginning in the late 1990s, past programs greatly expanded. The federal government encouraged zero-down-payment loans, loans that lacked past credit history, and loans that were sold on the expectation that the borrower would make a capital gain without making any equity investment. Repeated warnings of a crisis ahead by Peter Wallison, Bill Poole, Alan Greenspan, and others had no effect. Congressman Barney Frank, Chairman of the House Financial Services Committee, dismissed the critics. Was it irrational to believe that housing subsidies would increase?

In rapidly expanding housing markets, loan-to-value ratios rose close to 100% for all defaulted loans with negative equity. In Denver, the average loan-to-value ratio on such loans reached 99%; in Atlanta, Boston, and New York, the average was 98% (Haughwout and Okah, 2009, p. 38). Loans with positive equity in the same four areas were 82%, 80%, 72%, and 75%, respectively. For all areas as a group, loan-to-value ratios for houses with negative and positive equity were 91% and 73%, respectively. The conclusion I draw is that reducing down payments to nearly zero was a regulatory failure that made a major contribution to housing and financial distress.

Congress made a major contribution to exuberance, but it was not alone. For at least 30 years, the Federal Reserve prevented failures of large banks and not-so-large financial firms like Long-Term Capital Management. It was not irrational to believe that bankers who bought risky loans would profit, as failures would be bailed out. Loose talk about a "Greenspan put" reflected the market belief that the Federal Reserve would limit the spread of failures. When the Treasury and the Fed prevented fallout from Bear Stearns and Merrill Lynch, money managers believed and said that the worst was over. Losses would be shifted to the taxpayers.

The shock to expectations came when Lehman Brothers failed. I strongly favor an end to "too big to fail" policies. However, changing that policy, which had held for 30 years, without prior warning in the middle of a recession was a major error. In fact, it was calamitous. Rational money managers rushed to hold cash and Treasury bills, and uncertainty rose. Treasury Secretary Paulson's inability to announce and follow a consistent policy further heightened uncertainty. A serious recession threatened to become a major disaster.

Words have implications. The implication of "bubbles" is that a near-disaster occurred because irrational beliefs brought us an irrational result. This claim does not lead to a correct view of what has to change. It neglects the role of policies and institutions. We cannot prevent irrational beliefs, nor can we eliminate all financial crises as long as lenders borrow short and lend long. But, we can reduce the size and frequency of periods of financial failure by changing policy.

Since the Federal Reserve rescued First Pennsylvania in the 1970s, it has followed a "too big to fail" policy. It has repeatedly tried to rescue failing banks and firms. This policy gives the profits to the bankers and the losses to the public. It encourages some bankers to take excessive risk, as many did in 2005–2007. It is based on the mistaken premise that regulators protect the public by protecting bankers from their mistakes.

In 1991, Congress noticed that Federal Reserve loans to failing banks increased the size of losses and threatened the solvency of the Deposit Insurance Fund. It passed a modified version of the proposal for structured early intervention offered by George Benston and George Kaufman. The Federal Deposit Insurance Corporation (FDIC) Improvement Act tried to lower the cost to the FDIC and the public. However, has anyone heard of the FDIC Improvement Act? The regulators ignored it and continued the "too big to fail" policy.

To limit future losses, we require different policies — policies that change both bankers' and the Federal Reserve's responsibilities and incentives. Bankers should be told that the "too big to fail" policy has ended. They must become responsible for what they put on their balance sheet. To limit bank size, I propose that, beyond some moderate size, a bank must increase capital reserves more than in proportion to its increase in size. The reason is that society does not gain enough from economies of scope and scale to compensate for the loss from bailouts and failures. Instead of protecting bankers, regulators should protect the public.

Permitting failure implies that other financial firms will face losses. To prevent the spread of failures, the Federal Reserve must announce a "lender of last resort" rule that commits the Fed to lend against collateral to protect the market. Recognizing political reality, I believe the "lender of last resort" rule should be accepted by Congress.

Bagehot's rule is a good place to start. When the Bank of England followed that rule, banks failed but Britain avoided financial crises. That is a much better result than what the Federal Reserve achieved with the "too big to fail" policy and no explicit rule for lending in a financial panic.

In addition, Congress should close Fannie Mae and Freddie Mac. All housing and other mortgage and credit subsidies should be on the budget.

Finally, let me concede to those who claim to have seen "bubbles" that they do not mean what economic theory says. What they mean is less clear. It has the disadvantage of preventing more careful consideration of the sources of financial problems and the government policies that have been responsible for the recent housing boom. It should surprise no one that combining a loan with zero down payment and a poor credit rating leads to failures and defaults. Add a "too big to fail" policy to that, and we should expect financial exuberance.

Reference

Haughwout, A. F. and E. Okah (2009). Below the line: estimates of negative equity among nonprime mortgage borrowers. *Economic Policy Review*, 15, July, 31–43.

What to Do About Bubbles: Monetary Policy and Macroprudential Regulation

Marvin Goodfriend*
Carnegie Mellon University

A few years ago, I argued at this conference that it is impractical for interest rate policy to act directly against extreme asset price appreciations. Among other things, I pointed out that there is unlikely to be a window of opportunity to act because, once policymakers agree that asset prices are unsustainably high, they would also agree that an aggressive interest rate action could cause asset prices to crash; and policymakers would not want to precipitate a disorderly adjustment in asset prices.

Today, I am going to reinforce my point with a story that could not be told a few years ago. Alan Greenspan is famous for calling the U.S. equity market irrationally exuberant in the autumn of 1996 after the Dow broke through three millennium marks — 4,000, 5,000, and 6,000 — in just over a year and a half. This certainly seemed a reasonable judgment at the time. In retrospect, however, one would have to say that Greenspan was wrong. The market went higher. The Dow did not peak until five years later, and has fluctuated around 10,000 since then.

Fast-forward to the extreme house price appreciation of the mid-2000s. One might imagine that, having misjudged the sustainability of the Dow appreciation of the mid-1990s, Greenspan would be less inclined to second-guess the house price appreciation of the mid-2000s. As the saying goes, "Once burned, twice shy." Indeed, it seems fair to say Greenspan was less inclined to argue that house prices were unsustainably high in the mid-2000s.

It might be said that Greenspan was "0 for 2." But that is not my point. Efficient market theory has long taught that it is difficult to forecast the

---

* Marvin Goodfriend is Professor of Economics and Chairman of the Gailliot Center for Public Policy, Tepper School of Business, Carnegie Mellon University.

direction of asset prices. Even someone as well informed as the Fed Chairman can get it wrong. It is hard for anyone to judge correctly when asset prices are too high. In statistical time-series terms, asset prices are hard to forecast because they embody a highly persistent, near-random-walk component. It is hard to tell whether a price that evolves in part as a near random walk is going to rise or fall in the future, regardless of whether it has moved up or down sharply in the recent past.

Moving on, recent years have seen great changes in monetary policy analysis, as economists in central banks and academia have come together on an analytical approach known alternatively as the new neoclassical synthesis or the new Keynesian model. I believe that recent work represents a major improvement over the practice typical 20 years ago, inasmuch as the approach features rules for monetary policy conducted in models that are based on private optimizing behavior with specifications designed to be structural and quantifiable, and thereby usable (in principle) for policy analysis. However, I am also sympathetic to the view that the most commonly used mainstream new Keynesian model of monetary policy is deficient because it ignores the monetary aggregates, financial intermediation, or distinctions among various short-term interest rates that play different roles in the transmission mechanism. In fact, the mainstream model with a single short-term interest rate is silent on the widening of interest rate spreads in banking and short-term non-bank credit markets that is the hallmark of the current credit turmoil.

In response to the credit turmoil, monetary economists are busy modifying the mainstream model to address the causes and consequences of time-varying credit spreads. My own work prior to the credit turmoil, alone and with Bennett McCallum, integrates money and banking into the mainstream model of monetary policy in order to account for time-varying interest spreads between the interbank rate, the bank loan rate, the Treasury bill rate, and the risk-adjusted return on physical capital (Goodfriend and McCallum, 2007).

According to that work, the key to modeling such spreads is to recognize that the returns observed in markets reflect only a part of the total yield on assets. Observable interest rates reflect only the pecuniary yield, but assets also have an implicit collateral services yield. In competitive equilibrium, banks pass on to borrowers the marginal savings in monitoring loans made possible by the posting of collateral. In effect, the deduction in the loan rate charged by banks for borrowers posting collateral is the implicit collateral services yield on the asset serving as collateral. Since all assets earn the same risk-adjusted yield in equilibrium, the model regards observed interest rate spreads as reflecting different implicit collateral services yields among assets. For instance, because the value of a factory is more costly than a Treasury bill to monitor, the Treasury bill provides more services as collateral than a factory; hence, theory predicts that, risk-adjusted, the pecuniary return on a Treasury bill will be far below the pecuniary yield on a factory. By explicitly valuing assets in our model inclusive of pecuniary and implicit yields, we can account for spreads among various interest rates.

Thus, our model links asset markets and monetary policy through money and banking, and gets at some issues that appear to be at the core of the credit turmoil. That said, the enormous widening of interest rate spreads and the collapse of credit markets in the credit turmoil appear to have been associated with a shortage of financial capital in banks and default, which remain to be introduced into the mainstream model.

Moving on once again, I want to say something about the political economy of central bank last-resort lending. Walter Bagehot recommended long ago that a central bank should support the banking system in a panic by lending freely against good collateral at a penalty interest rate. Bagehot's rule is certainly a good place to start in the implementation of last-resort lending by central banks. The point I want to make about Bagehot's rule is this: its effectiveness as a stand-alone prescription for last-resort lending depends on the political economy context in which it is placed. Bagehot's prescription for the Bank of England in the 19th century worked because the Bank of England was a private institution. It did not have access to public funds, nor could its earnings be appropriated by the public sector. Hence, the Bank of England had an incentive to lend only on good collateral and at a penalty rate to protect itself and its profits, too. It was in its own interest to provide last-resort lending services to the financial system in times of panic, in return for monopoly privileges accorded to the Bank of England by the government.

Modern central banks like the Federal Reserve are not private institutions. In particular, the seigniorage or profit after expenses earned by modern central banks from the monopoly on high-powered money is transferred routinely to the fiscal authorities. Moreover, losses made on assets acquired by a modern central bank can be recouped by withholding transfers that would have otherwise gone to the fiscal authorities, or by an infusion of funds from the fiscal authorities. Either way, modern central banks are tied to fiscal authorities. For instance, the Federal Reserve has taken losses on some of the assets that it acquired to facilitate the purchase of Bear Stearns by JPMorgan Chase in 2008, and the U.S. Treasury agreed to indemnify the Fed against those losses. Bagehot's rule is not as enforceable as it was for the Bank of England in the 19th century. The problem is that a modern central bank can be persuaded to lower its collateral standards if it believes that it can get indemnification for losses from the fiscal authorities.

Furthermore, unlike in 19th-century Great Britain, today there is deposit insurance and, in the current credit turmoil, government-guaranteed bank debt. In such circumstances, central bank last-resort loans expose taxpayers to losses even if the central bank protects itself with good collateral. This is the case if a bank fails while a last-resort loan is outstanding, and thus deprives the failed bank of collateral that might otherwise be needed to cover insured deposits or guaranteed debt. In contrast, if the Bank of England took good collateral and the bank that it lent to failed subsequently, the Bank of England would be made whole without putting the taxpayer at risk because there were then no deposit insurance or government-guaranteed bank liabilities.

Moving on once more, there is a lot of talk in the United States about creating a "pinnacle" systemic financial oversight council. Some proposals imagine putting the pinnacle council in the Federal Reserve. I would say that doing so is not compatible with Federal Reserve independence. The reason is straightforward. The pinnacle council must have the power to call on taxpayer funding to resolve or recapitalize banks in an emergency, or to deny the use of taxpayer funding in such circumstances. Either way, it must be empowered to make what is essentially a fiscal-policy decision. Therefore, the pinnacle council must be lodged in a part of the government with the authority to make the political decision to spend or not to spend taxpayer dollars to support the financial system. The pinnacle council could be put under the Treasury or in an arm of Congress, but not in an independent central bank like the Federal Reserve. To preserve the Federal Reserve's independence on monetary policy, it is essential that these political decisions be made elsewhere. Through its representative on the pinnacle council, of course, the Fed could provide technical input to the council and share responsibility for the council's decision to authorize or deny fiscal resources in support of a financial system in turmoil.

By the way, if we have a pinnacle council, say, under the Treasury, then the pinnacle council should authorize *ex ante* all Federal Reserve last-resort lending beyond temporary loans to depository institutions that are deemed well capitalized. Prior authorization is needed to assure that taxpayers are represented in the decision by their political representatives and are willing to assume the risk that they might be called upon to make if collateral pledged against central bank last-resort loans is unavailable to finance deposit insurance or government debt guarantees.

In my remaining time, I want to talk about regulation. A hallmark of the unprecedented credit turmoil is that many customers of financial markets — borrowers, lenders, and investors alike — have been badly hurt. This has led me to think that regulation as protection is false promise. Let me explain.

The Madoff swindle is an extreme example of what I have in mind. Bernie Madoff defrauded some of the most sophisticated people in America. The parents and grandparents of Madoff's clients would have been exceedingly careful with their life savings. How could the current generation have made such foolhardy financial decisions, placing large sums in the hands of a man without verification of his investments?

High promised and apparent actual returns such as those delivered by Madoff's Ponzi scheme will always attract some investors. But, I believe the scale of Madoff's swindle was possible in large part because his clients thought, implicitly if not explicitly, "How bad could it get? This is the United States!" There is no other way to understand the letting down of the imperative to "watch your funds" by those who should have known better.

What I mean is that regulation as protection crowds out due diligence by investors. The promised financial system stability drives some investors to seek higher returns outside the regulated sector. One might conclude that Madoff's firm should have been regulated. My response is that there is no way to prevent funds from being invested beyond the reach of regulation. In fact, the more extensive the regulated sector, the greater the incentive to place funds through unregulated private financial firms, at home or by going abroad, to benefit from systemic stability without paying the regulatory cost. Any effort to rethink regulation should take this fact into account: regulation that promises systemic stability creates an incentive for finance to "free ride" on that promise by moving beyond the regulated sector, thus undermining both the firm-specific and systemic protection that regulation promises.

I would say that regulation should lower its sights. We should recognize that regulation cannot protect us from ourselves. Regulation creates the counterproductive dynamic discussed above. Moreover, the political economy of regulation reinforces the problem. Regulations promise to protect the public. The financial sector goes along knowing that, over time, it can circumvent whatever regulations are put in place. Thus, politicians get the credit, the public feels secure, and the public is less demanding of financial offerings and is consequently exposed to greater losses in one way or another — as a borrower, lender, investor, or taxpayer.

Instead of promising protection *per se*, regulations should help to make customers more demanding of finance, whether as lenders, borrowers, or investors. Regulation should make households better comparative shoppers, so to speak. Elsewhere in the economy, households protect themselves and discipline industries by behaving as well-informed and demanding customers in competitive markets. Households routinely compare alternative products in conversations with friends and neighbors at meals and in other gatherings. In large part, households acquire the confidence to become demanding consumers by word of mouth.

The same must be true if households are to become demanding customers of financial offerings. However, the perceived protection afforded by financial regulation short-circuits the development of an equilibrium in which households become demanding customers in personal financial matters. It is costly for a household by itself to become an informed financial customer, given a relative lack of understanding among friends and neighbors. Informed conversations with friends and neighbors at meals and in other gatherings are few. The equilibrium is one that blocks the spread among households of common knowledge necessary to create confident, demanding customers in personal finance.

For the most part, a household's financial needs can be satisfied reasonably well with a relatively simple menu of financial services and products, whether households are borrowers, lenders, or investing their life savings. Households do not need sophisticated technical knowledge of finance any more than they need technical knowledge of most non-financial products to be demanding customers in those markets. Households need only to be made confident of the fundamentals of personal finance in order to make intelligent choices among a menu of "plain vanilla" financial products and services. Unfortunately, the current equilibrium appears to fall short of providing households with either the confidence to make good financial choices or a menu to choose from. In short, it seems that we are in a bad equilibrium in which the common knowledge needed to make households effective financial customers is stuck at a low level.

As I see it, a good part of the reason that our financial markets are in this bad equilibrium is that regulation as protection is false promise. Regulations should be employed less as a way of protecting households *directly* and more as a *means* of moving financial markets from a bad to a good equilibrium in which households can protect themselves by becoming knowledgeable, confident, and demanding borrowers, lenders, and investors. At a minimum, regulators should publish a menu of standardized financial products designed so that their returns and terms can be compared easily between each other and across firms. Regulators should also encourage firms to offer these standardized products so that households can become demanding financial customers. By standardizing the production and sale of basic financial offerings in competitive private markets, regulation would provide a much-needed public good that would empower households to protect themselves as well as help to discipline the financial system.

Reference

Goodfriend, M. and B. T. McCallum (2007). Banking and interest rates in monetary policy analysis: a quantitative exploration. *Journal of Monetary Economics*, 54, 1480–1503.

VI. DEALING WITH CRISES IN A GLOBALIZED WORLD: CHALLENGES AND SOLUTIONS

Dealing with Crises in a Globalized World: Challenges and Solutions

Athanasios Orphanides*
Central Bank of Cyprus

A year has already passed since the peak of the worst financial crisis the world has experienced since the Great Depression of the 1930s. This extreme episode of financial instability has led to a severe and truly globalized economic downturn, and has highlighted the worldwide devastation that can result from a disturbance in just one area of the world with a highly interconnected financial system. The emerging signs of recovery are welcome, though unusually high uncertainty persists. The crisis has revealed a number of weaknesses in the global architecture of financial regulation and supervision, as well as gaps in the toolkit available to policymakers for crisis management. An intense discussion on dealing with future crises is essential, and it is reassuring to see that it is taking place in various international forums. Against this background, I would like to thank the organizers of this conference for their invitation to participate in this panel on challenges and solutions for dealing with crises in a globalized world. I will use this opportunity to share with you some reflections on three areas where I believe progress is needed for promoting financial stability at the global level: international cooperation and convergence, simplicity in regulation, and the role of central banks in promoting financial stability. The views I express are my own and do not necessarily reflect the views of my colleagues on the Governing Council of the European Central Bank.

This has been a crisis of the global regulatory framework. The fact that supposedly well-regulated financial institutions have been the major source of problems is an embarrassment for the international community

* Athanasios Orphanides serves as Governor of the Central Bank of Cyprus.

of regulators and supervisors. The financial turmoil has revealed serious gaps in the crisis resolution framework at the global level and has highlighted the lack of coordination and harmonization in accounting, regulation, and supervision, even within common economic areas such as the United States and the European Union (EU). It is an inescapable conclusion that these deficiencies have contributed to the severity of the crisis, which points to the urgent need for enhanced cross-border cooperation to establish consistent rules in all of these areas.

The greater the heterogeneity across jurisdictions in accounting, regulation, supervision, and crisis resolution practices, the greater the potential threat of regulatory arbitrage by financial institutions operating in multiple jurisdictions and thus the greater the pressure on local regulators and the risk of regulatory capture. International harmonization and convergence is a practical way to minimize this risk.

Consider the continuing differences in accounting standards across borders that hinder international comparisons of banking institutions. The absence of a level playing field in the application of accounting standards creates an anomaly in international finance. The same rules and concepts need to apply globally, which requires urgent work to be done. It should be recalled that one of the aims of the creation of the International Accounting Standards Board (IASB) was precisely to achieve the goal of introducing a single set of standards across the globe and improving the governance of the standard-setting process. Progress has been slower than desirable.

There is also a clear need for a harmonized regulatory framework across all major jurisdictions and markets. The lack of a consistent set of rules is bound to lead to competitive distortions among financial institutions and encourage regulatory arbitrage. Although the lack of a harmonized set of rules — for example, in the definition of capital — at the global level is more than evident, regulatory inconsistencies even in the case of a single financial market such as the EU exist and are problematic. As noted in the de Larosière (2009) report, the present regulatory framework in Europe lacks cohesiveness mainly due to the options provided to EU members in the enforcement of common directives. These options lead to a wide diversity of national transpositions related to local traditions, legislation, and practices.

That said, as a result of the crisis, progress is being made. At the EU level, the Council of the European Union (2009) decided in June to establish a European System of Financial Supervisors (ESFS), comprising three new European supervisory authorities to succeed the current three Level 3 Committees, namely the Committee of European Banking Supervisors (CEBS), the Committee of European Securities Regulators (CESR), and the Committee of European Insurance and Occupational Pensions Supervisors (CEIOPS). These new bodies are expected to upgrade the quality and consistency of national supervision, strengthen oversight of cross-border groups through the setting up of supervisory colleges, and create a European single rule book applicable to all financial institutions in the single market.

Another area that requires greater convergence in practice is the imposition of sanctions. Supervision cannot be effective with weak and highly divergent sanctioning regimes. It is essential that all supervisors across the world are able to deploy sanctioning regimes that are sufficiently convergent and strict, thus acting as a deterrence. This is far from being the case now. The same exercise should be initiated with respect to supervisory powers, which also differ greatly from one country to another and cannot be conducive to coherent and effective supervision.

As regards cross-border bank resolution and insolvency, once the financial crisis hit, weaknesses and differences in national and international approaches in these areas came to a head, mainly as a result of different resolution tools and safety nets applicable across the globe. Differences in bankruptcy legislation for financial institutions across countries and the absence of *ex ante* rules governing cross-border bank resolution present a serious problem that has proven to be very costly during the crisis. Without common bank resolution rules or modes of collaboration, supervisors' obligations to their own taxpayers have led them to minimize liabilities to non-residents and maximize control of assets. For example, in the face of an imminent collapse of Icelandic bank branches under the authority of Icelandic supervisors, and in the absence of assurances that U.K. bank liabilities would be covered (or guaranteed), U.K. supervisors ring-fenced Icelandic bank assets; the failure of Lehman Brothers also triggered discriminatory and potentially inefficient ring-fencing of assets outside the U.S.

Measures to improve cross-border crisis resolution should focus on introducing compatible legal frameworks for bank resolution. In this respect, a key issue is the convergence of banking legislation by home and host countries of the cross-border firms along a number of fronts. Specifically, early remedial actions should be taken, including common criteria on the triggers and timing of resolution or the bankruptcy procedures of a global firm; resolution tools to allow quick and well-synchronized action by the relevant authorities across countries in order to preserve the failing firm's franchise value and ensure fair treatment of all creditors; and deposit and investor protection schemes to ensure that depositors/investors are covered by the scheme prevailing in each jurisdiction, regardless of whether the entity is a subsidiary or a branch.

To achieve these objectives, there will need to be more active and effective multilateral mechanisms for cross-border regulation and supervision. These mechanisms could build on the existing frameworks of the Financial Stability Board (FSB), the Basel Committee on Banking Supervision, and other standard setters. The International Monetary Fund (IMF) could also play an important role, for instance, in developing guidelines for dealing with cross-border bank supervision and resolution. This could address best practices in such areas as triggers and deposit protection. Moreover, the IMF's Financial Sector Assessment Program (FSAP) could provide a platform for evaluating the adequacy of countries' oversight of cross-border financial firms.

It is encouraging that, on this front, two international initiatives on bank resolution frameworks are making progress. Earlier this month, the Basel Committee published the report and recommendations of its Cross-Border Bank Resolution Group, which includes recommendations for authorities on effective crisis management and resolution processes for large cross-border institutions (Basel Committee on Banking Supervision, 2009). The IMF and World Bank initiative on the legal, institutional, and regulatory framework for national bank insolvency regimes is also expected to produce a final report in the spring of 2010, which will review the principal impediments to effective resolution of a cross-border financial institution (Financial Stability Board, 2009).

This has been a crisis of the global supervisory framework. Numerous examples suggest what, after the fact, was recognized to be lax or non-existent supervision. How can supervision become more foolproof? One way is to reduce the complexity of the supervisory process.

In the years leading to the crisis, some financial institutions developed and traded highly complex derivatives. In retrospect, some of these derivative products added little or no social value, but imposed a burden on regulation as the difficulty in their evaluation resulted in systematic mispricings.

A perennial issue in regulation and supervision is that, given any set of rules (regulation), profit-seeking financial firms may always attempt to find ways to circumvent the rules in a manner that would let them maximize the return on their capital. Supervision — that is, the monitoring and enforcement of the letter and the spirit of the rules — is more successful the easier it is to verify compliance, and this can be done more easily when the rules are simple. In other words, there is a trade-off between complexity in regulation and its effectiveness. Complexity makes supervision harder to implement and risks introducing gaps between the presumed and actual effectiveness of regulation. For that reason, regulation must, in principle, discourage complexity. Simple rules are harder to circumvent and render their supervision more effective.

In the lead-up to the crisis, the tendency was to move away from simple rules and towards more refined (and more complex) regulatory frameworks. Consider, for example, the Basel II international capital framework for banks. It was aimed at aligning regulatory capital requirements more closely with the underlying risks that banks face, but the added complexity imposed additional demands on supervisors to assess and verify the trustworthiness and accuracy of the associated banks' internal risk assessments. As events from the current crisis have demonstrated, the potential for mistakes is very real and the consequences can be very costly.

Simple rules such as leverage ratios, liquidity ratios, or loan-to-value ratios in lending practices may appear overly restrictive to bank managers who, based on their internal risk management systems, might wish to push the envelope of their activities a bit further. However, they can help improve the robustness of the regulatory and supervisory framework and render the financial system more stable.

There is a parallel with the design of rules for monetary policy. Simple rules may appear deficient to a theorist who could proclaim that they cannot deliver the most efficient or theoretically optimum outcomes. But, achieving a theoretical ideal is not a good guide to policy, in light of our imperfect understanding of economic behavior. Appropriately designed, simple rules can serve as robust guides and help avert major mistakes.

There is now a growing consensus that the excessive leverage of many banks was a major contributing factor to the global financial crisis. Moreover, the inevitable de-leveraging currently taking place is imposing further stress on the system. To enhance the longer-term resilience of the financial system, effective regulation to curtail banks' build-up of leverage is required. Not surprisingly, this has brought under the spotlight the use of a simple measure of leverage that complements the more complex, risk-sensitive capital requirements in an attempt to put a lower bound on banks' leverage. This will effectively serve as a safety valve against the weaknesses and shortcomings of the Basel II capital requirements. A supplementary leverage ratio ensures a minimum capital buffer that protects banks against unexpected losses and underestimation of risk. As we have learnt from the current crisis, the failure of risk models may quickly turn banks that seem adequately capitalized into ones which are poorly capitalized. Adding a simple leverage ratio to Basel II should reinforce banks' capital, strengthen capital regulation, and contribute to a more stable international financial system.

There are a number of benefits of a gross leverage ratio. The most direct is that it helps limit balance sheet size. The current risk-based capital framework encourages banks to assume exposures that attract a low risk weight, as the capital required to be set aside for these exposures is relatively small. As a result, in absolute terms, bank balance sheets can become highly leveraged and can include assets that would be difficult to liquidate in times of need without incurring large haircuts. Hence, the prudential leverage ratio can serve as an additional measure for constraining banks from becoming excessively leveraged during an upswing, as seems to have happened in recent years. Another benefit of such a ratio is that it helps reduce regulatory arbitrage. The risk-sensitive nature of Basel II can result in the perverse incentive among banks to structure products in order to obtain a high credit rating, so that they qualify for a lower prudential capital requirement. When this incentive is collectively exploited, the system is likely to end up with high concentrations of structured exposures attracting low prudential capital requirements. The prescription of a minimum leverage ratio, among other measures, can dampen such an incentive.

In this light, it is noteworthy that earlier this month the Group of Central Bank Governors and Heads of Supervision (the oversight body of the Basel Committee) reached an agreement towards, among other things, the introduction of a leverage ratio and a liquidity ratio as supplementary measures to the Basel II risk-based framework. To ensure comparability, the details of the leverage ratio will be harmonized internationally, fully adjusting for differences in accounting.

Next, I turn to the role of central banks. The crisis has revealed a general underappreciation of systemic risks in microprudential supervision, and has highlighted the need for a more system-wide macroprudential approach towards supervisory oversight to ensure overall stability in the financial system. By definition, microprudential supervisors focus on individual institutions and cannot effectively assess the broader macroeconomic risks that pose a threat to the financial system as a whole. This is a task best suited to central banks.

The recent moves to reinforce macroprudential oversight internationally are in the right direction. At the EU level, the Council of the European Union (2009) decided in June, based on the recommendations of the de Larosière (2009) report, to set up a European Systemic Risk Board (ESRB) in order to increase the focus on systemic risk in the EU framework for financial supervision. As with the ESFS, draft legislation on the establishment of the ESRB was adopted by the European Commission earlier this month. The main activity of the ESRB will be to identify, monitor, and assess potential threats to financial stability and, where necessary, issue risk warnings and recommendations for action and monitor their implementation. Analytical, statistical, administrative, and logistical support for the ESRB will be provided by the European Central Bank, also drawing on technical advice from national central banks and supervisors. At the international level, the envisaged closer cooperation between the IMF and the FSB is expected to contribute towards better surveillance of macroprudential risks in the international financial system. The ESRB is also expected to liaise effectively with the IMF and the FSB.

In the United States, the U.S. Department of the Treasury (2009a) recommends that the responsibility for macroprudential supervision be assigned to the Federal Reserve. Furthermore, the legislative proposals released by the Treasury last July to address systemic risk give the Fed the authority to regulate and supervise all large interconnected financial firms deemed to be systemically important (U.S. Department of the Treasury, 2009b).

There are important informational synergies between microprudential supervision and systemic risk analysis that make this proposal quite attractive. Central banks can benefit from and rely on extended access to supervisory information and intelligence, especially on systemically relevant intermediaries, in order to appreciate risks and vulnerabilities of the financial system as a whole. In addition, in the area of crisis management and resolution, the financial market turmoil has shown the importance of close interaction between the central banking and supervisory functions, in particular when the provision of emergency liquidity assistance (ELA) becomes necessary. The activation of ELA requires speed and detailed information regarding the conditions of vulnerable financial institutions seeking assistance. In this regard, a supervisor has greater likelihood of possessing institution-specific information, which is vital for a central bank to perform effectively the role of "lender of last resort". Indeed, many central banks have found the presence of financial supervision, especially banking supervision, under their aegis and the information flows within the same organization as essential in enabling them to deal with the current crisis. This has reinforced the arguments in favor of combining the central banking and supervisory functions under one roof.

Bringing microprudential supervision under the umbrella of the central banks may also be the most effective manner for preserving the institutional independence of supervision — an important defense against political pressures and the threat of regulatory capture. Invariably, central banks are among the most independent institutions in democratic societies, as a high degree of central bank independence is required to ensure monetary stability. On the other hand, the concern that adding microprudential supervision may jeopardize a central bank's independence and compromise its ability to pursue its price stability objective is an argument against bringing microprudential supervision under its aegis. This is certainly a serious concern that makes the central banker's job more difficult. However, I believe that the social benefits emanating from the synergies between microprudential and macroprudential supervision outweigh the potential risks.

Another argument in favor of placing microprudential supervision under central banks in countries where this is not already the case is the excellent international cooperation among central banks, as demonstrated during the present crisis. In light of this excellent cooperation, the microprudential supervision of systemically important institutions by the central banks would enhance stability in the international financial system.

For a central bank to be successful as a macroprudential supervisor, it needs to be provided with the appropriate tools. In general, a central bank does not face a trade-off between price stability and financial stability. Rather, most of the time these two goals reinforce each other. Price stability prevents the arbitrary redistribution of wealth and income between borrowers and lenders, which could result from unanticipated price movements and lead to financial stress and potential default. In addition, anchoring inflation expectations results in the stabilization of economic activity and avoidance of debt-deflation spirals. Conversely, financial stability enhances the effectiveness of monetary policy by facilitating the monetary transmission mechanism. However, there may be occasions when monetary policy directed at preserving price stability may not suffice to minimize financial stability risks; an example would be an episode of persistently high credit growth in an environment of price stability. Under such circumstances, the central bank should, in addition to its interest rate instrument, have at its disposal macroprudential levers with which to contain the risk of a potential financial disturbance. These could include the power to vary capital requirements, leverage ratios, loan-to-value ratios, margin requirements, and so forth.

Could the current crisis have been averted if this macroprudential framework had been in place a few years earlier? Such counterfactual thought experiments are very difficult to evaluate with precision, but the following example may illustrate how history might have differed if the Federal Reserve had broader supervisory powers half a decade ago.

The example concerns Fannie Mae and Freddie Mac, the two housing-related government-sponsored enterprises (GSEs) in the United States that, according to Calomiris (2008), played a pivotal part in the crisis. In brief, these two GSEs represented systemically important institutions that could have been under the supervision of the Federal Reserve if it had appropriate regulatory powers, as defined by the Treasury report. These GSEs were allowed to expand their portfolios of assets virtually without limit and with an implicit government guarantee, despite the objections of the Federal Reserve.

As then-Chairman of the Federal Reserve Alan Greenspan stated in his testimony before the U.S. Senate in April 2005:

> We at the Federal Reserve remain concerned about the growth and magnitude of the mortgage portfolios of the GSEs, which concentrate interest rate risk and prepayment risk at these two institutions and makes our financial system dependent on their ability to manage these risks.... To fend off possible future systemic difficulties, which we assess as likely if GSE expansion continues unabated, preventative actions are required sooner rather than later. [Greenspan, 2005, p. 3]

Unfortunately, these warnings went unheeded and the systemic failure that had been a source of concern at the Federal Reserve eventually materialized. In retrospect, if the Federal Reserve had already been the systemic regulator and had the appropriate authority, it could have taken the necessary action and the failure may have been averted. This example also illustrates that, to assure financial stability, it is not sufficient for the central bank to have the responsibility to identify risks and issue warnings; the central bank must also have the authority to enforce corrective action.

In conclusion, the financial crisis has highlighted significant weaknesses in the international financial regulatory and supervisory framework as well as the need to strengthen the resilience and oversight of the financial system. Although we have avoided the worst, difficult challenges still lie ahead. Incorporating the lessons from the crisis, we should strive to build a more robust global financial regulatory and supervisory framework. In this respect, I have focused on the importance of going forward in three areas: moving towards harmonized rules and greater international cooperation, striving to reduce complexity in financial supervision, and enhancing the role of central banks in macroprudential supervision. The worst of the crisis may now be behind us. Nevertheless, we should not allow complacency to stand in the way of making progress towards a more robust global financial order.

References

Basel Committee on Banking Supervision (2009). *Report and Recommendations of the Cross-Border Bank Resolution Group — Consultative Document.* September.

Calomiris, C. (2008). The subprime turmoil: what's old, what's new, and what's next. Paper presented at the Federal Reserve Bank of Kansas City Symposium on "Maintaining Stability in a Changing Financial System", Jackson Hole, Wyoming, August 21–23.

Council of the European Union (2009). Presidency conclusions of the Brussels European Council. European Council, Brussels, June 18–19.

de Larosière, J. (2009). *Report of the High-Level Group on Financial Supervision in the EU.* February 25.

Financial Stability Board (2009). *Overview of Progress in Implementing the London Summit Recommendations for Strengthening Financial Stability.* September 25.

Greenspan, A. (2005). Regulatory reform of the government-sponsored enterprises. Testimony before the Committee on Banking, Housing and Urban Affairs, U.S. Senate, April 6.

U.S. Department of the Treasury (2009a). *Financial Regulatory Reform — A New Foundation: Rebuilding Financial Supervision and Regulation.* June 17.

U.S. Department of the Treasury (2009b). *Bank Holding Company Modernization Act of 2009.* July 22.

Global Financial Reform: Diagnosis and Prognosis — A Network Approach

Andrew L. T. Sheng*
China Banking Regulatory Commission

1. Introduction

The central challenge in dealing with crises in a globalized world is to identify the right questions before we can have the right answers. On whether the rules of finance have changed, the answer must be yes, because the current financial landscape has been irreversibly changed.

Carmen Reinhart and Ken Rogoff (2008) have demonstrated convincingly that financial crises are hardy perennials with common traits but individual peculiarities, so there is no "one size fits all" solution for all crises. That was roughly the conclusion I came to when I reviewed at the World Bank the lessons of banking crises in the 1980s (Sheng, 1996). Crises are events, while reform is a process — one of diagnosis, damage control, loss allocation, and changing the incentives. This paper reviews the process using a network approach.

2. Diagnosis — This Is a Network Crisis

The current financial crisis is global in nature and its diagnosis remains controversial. The distinctive features of this crisis — even more evident than in the Asian financial crisis — are its complexity, interconnectivity, and speed of transmission.

---

* Andrew L. T. Sheng is the Chief Advisor to the China Banking Regulatory Commission. The views expressed in this paper are strictly those of the author and not those of any institution with which he is associated. The author thanks Ms. Wang Ting of Tsinghua University for research assistance in the preparation of the paper.

This is a network crisis (Haldane, 2009) because the world has become networked by globalization, the rise of telecommunication technology, financial deregulation, and financial engineering into a highly complex network of local networks (Sheng, 2005, 2009a, 2009b). We have an architecture of *highly concentrated hubs* (20–25 large complex financial institutions or LCFIs) accounting for over half of the global turnover, particularly in derivatives, concentrated largely in two financial centers, London and New York. These LCFIs are larger than countries, and have become "too big to fail" or "too interconnected to fail". They are *highly interdependent* through extensive real-time trading with each other, hedge funds, and large institutional clients and businesses; and depend critically (as we discovered *ex post*) on AIG for credit insurance, government deposit guarantee and central bank liquidity provision. Hence, once Lehman Brothers failed, a chain reaction occurred throughout the network.

The financial markets are also *highly interactive*, with complex positive and negative feedback mechanisms that are highly procyclical through momentum trading, which is permitted by the accounting and regulatory standards as well as skewed incentives that encourage risk taking. In the lead-up to the present crisis, no one wanted to take away the punch bowl on the way up, but the reverse vicious cycle of lower liquidity, lower asset prices, and insolvency proved very difficult to stop.

The transmission of shocks, once Lehman Brothers failed, was almost *simultaneous*, spreading from financial markets to the real economy through the credit and trade channels. The global real economy is still looking for a bottom, although there are some signs of recovery. Finally, the network is by its very nature *complex*. No one understood the complexity of the financial derivatives, the interconnections, and the interdependencies until it was too late.

2.1 *Why did we not see this?*

I think that the best analysis of the issues is the critique by University of Chicago Professor Richard Posner (2009), who called the U.S. government regulatory reform package "premature", as it "advocates a specific course of treatment for a disease the cause or causes of which have not been determined." He argued that the emphasis on the folly of private-sector actors — investors, consumers, credit rating agencies, and, above all, bankers and defects in the regulatory structure — left out other important causes, such as errors of monetary policy, large budget deficits, deregulation in banking, lax enforcement of existing regulations, and the complacency of and errors by the economics profession.

In hindsight, we had four blind spots. First, we failed to remember the history of all financial crises that began with prosperity, then hubris, and then grief. Second, we ignored the major macro-systemic issues of the unsustainability of the global imbalance, excessively low interest rates, growing asset bubbles, and rising risks of higher leverage. Third, we failed to appreciate the systemic implications of micro-behavior, such as embedded leverage in financial engineering, bad incentive schemes, and poor corporate governance of many institutions.

But, a deeper blind spot was the failure of economic thought. In the last 50 years, our academic disciplines have become so specialized, whilst the government bureaucracies have become so fragmented. As a result, many bright people developed huge blind spots that ignored the really important political economy issues of our time: social inequities, political capture by vested interests, global warming, and complex political economy factors, all of which affect financial stability.

As early as 1982, University of California system scientist and physicist Fritjof Capra (1982) had already identified current crises as "systemic problems, which means that they are closely interconnected and interdependent. They cannot be understood within the fragmented methodology characteristic of our academic disciplines and government agencies." This fragmentation in the financial regulation of global financial institutions is best summed up by Bank of England Governor Mervyn King's dictum that "banking is global in life, but national in death" (Turner, 2009). We have essentially one global financial market, but financial institutions are regulated under national laws. Worse, at the national level, different agencies are in charge of different institutions, and so there are overlaps, gaps, turf fighting, and non-cooperation when attempting to solve complex social issues. We have a serious collective action problem that resembles a global "tragedy of the commons".

3. Damage Control — How Do We Exit from a Massively Distorted System Under ZIRP?

Although I would commend the national authorities and the international community on their speed of action to stop the spread of the financial crisis, I cannot honestly say that I am comfortable with the damage control measures because they create their own set of problems. First, there are those who think that the recovery is back to "business as usual". Second, to protect the financial system from the deflation in the asset bubbles, the public sector has essentially guaranteed all of the deposits, rescued systemically important institutions, injected massive liquidity, and brought interest rates to zero or near-zero under a zero interest rate policy (ZIRP). We have essentially replicated Japan's liquidity trap globally, where a large public debt bubble of roughly twice the size of GDP eventually replaced the deflation in asset bubbles.

There are two problems with ZIRP, which boils down to a fixed interest rate policy, since you cannot reduce interest rates below zero. This implies that the financial and asset markets would adjust either through other asset prices, via greater volatility, or through volatility in quantity adjustments (mostly capital flows).

Since every nation almost simultaneously got into crisis together and reacted alike with a large fiscal stimulus and a very loose monetary policy, we now have a collective action problem of how to exit together. Just as global arbitrage drove everyone into looser and looser monetary policy and lax regulation, we now have a problem where no single country can increase interest rates, tax rates, or regulation without huge capital flows and arbitrage. Somehow, we must work together to exit together at roughly the same pace. This is no easy feat. The second problem with ZIRP is the distortive effect on efficient allocation of resources, as asset prices get inflated with ZIRP and borrowers are subsidized by savers. Whilst ZIRP is understandable in the short run, the Japanese experience shows that long-run ZIRP does not help to reflate the economy.

Recently in New Delhi, Montek Ahluwalia identified that the three most important issues confronting the G-20 Leaders Summit are trade, jobs, and global warming. If we step back a bit, we would appreciate that all three are interrelated but also contradictory. We need to ensure that the trade momentum is not rolled back through protectionism, that jobs are created without protectionism, and that we will be able to achieve agreement on global warming before it is too late.

Allow me to make a highly controversial observation between consumption and global warming. This financial crisis actually exposed the flaws of the current global growth model of excess consumption financed by excess leverage. Excess consumption is ultimately the driver of accelerating global warming, which remains the greatest threat to our ecological survival. To put the order of magnitude into perspective, the total cost of this crisis is in the order of US$2–3 trillion, but the damage to global biodiversity is estimated at somewhere between US$2–5 trillion annually (Sukhdev, 2008; OECD, 2009; Garnaut, 2008). We must fix both.

Our common problem is that the current growth model of consumption today, with higher fiscal spending and social welfare, lower taxation, and frictionless financial markets, has created a global leverage machine that essentially increases consumption based on postponing costs to the future. Leverage is the key to understanding the present Ponzi financial engineering model, based on complexity, moral hazard, and lower and lower interest rates, ending in total bailouts.

4. Loss Allocation — Essentially, Future Generations and Mother Earth Bear the Losses

In plain words, present consumption is achieved through either borrowing from the future or consuming the earth's resources. Neither the consumption rate of our natural resources nor the leverage is sustainable, unless our science and technology can solve both. Consequently, we should address the reform of financial regulation holistically and ecologically, not by the yardstick of what we must do to repair financial markets today, but by what the financial system and the real sector will look like 5–30 years from now.

There are three major trends that are broadly observable. First, there will be considerable de-leveraging of the financial system due to the unwinding of the excesses of the last decade, which will have a considerable impact both on the real sector and on the medium-term profits of the financial system. Second, the unwinding of the excess consumption in different markets will result in the unwinding of the excess production capacity, which will also have a major impact on real-sector profits as well as investments. There is a fundamental supply chain restructuring that is going on globally. Third, global warming concerns and re-engineering towards a better quality-of-life environment will also require huge investments and re-tooling of the current global supply chains, which carry considerable risks to the financial sector. Although it is estimated that carbon trading could easily become a US$2 trillion market (Parsons *et al.*, 2009), this market is still in its infancy and there is not enough understanding of this market in the emerging economies to make as yet a major impact.

We now come to the heart of the architectural issues facing the global financial system. There is sufficient understanding that global imbalance is part and parcel of the global economic structure since, at any one point in time, one part of the world will be running surpluses and another part will be running deficits. However, the current Bretton Woods II system of flexible exchange rates and liberal capital flows together pose a Triffin dilemma for the U.S. as the dominant reserve currency country. The combination of weaknesses in the regional capital markets for emerging countries and the Triffin dilemma means that, if the rest of the world is growing faster than the U.S., the U.S. must run a current account deficit and a looser monetary policy than its own domestic needs. It is this dilemma and the efficiency of emerging market intermediation that must be solved for global financial stability.

Some commentators suggest that the current architectural problems might be solved with a global reserve currency, implying a global central bank plus a global systemic regulator. Putting aside the political economy difficulties of obtaining agreement on having a centralized solution, it is evident that no such institutional structure can be constructed without a global fiscal mechanism to fund global public goods and to compensate disadvantaged regions or sectors which may suffer from global monetary policies that do not coincide with domestic needs.

I have elsewhere indicated that a minimum global turnover tax (to be imposed by all countries alike), together with a standard withholding tax rate, may be the most appropriate way to begin a global fiscal regime (Sheng, 2009c). At US$900 trillion in annual foreign exchange and stock market turnover, a rate of 0.00007% would yield US$60 billion annually — enough to begin to address some of the shortage of funding for global public goods, either for global warming or for resolution of the financial sector. The turnover tax is a complementary tool to capital adequacy ratios in order to slow the financial system down when it begins to overleverage. The reason, to me, is simple: the present "frictionless financial market" model created a windmill that sped up so fast that it shook the structure to bits. Similarly, zero turnover tax allowed infinite financial derivation, which created financial innovation that had little social value.

5. Changing the Incentives — Moral Hazard Is Directly Related to Leverage, so Controlling Overall Leverage Will Keep the System Stable

Conventional financial regulation used to be split between prudential regulators and conduct regulators, which was an artificial way of dividing up the regulation of financial institutions. We now realize that both prudential regulation and conduct regulation are ultimately the same in addressing the behavior of the players and institutions that create financial instability. The regulators also have a role because it is their enforcement or lack of action that shapes market behavior.

In hindsight, much of today's financial-sector problems are principal–agent fiduciary failures because the complexity of the financial products has made the agents less accountable. The more complex the rules, the greater the opportunity for regulatory arbitrage and avoidance behavior. The more complex the financial product, the less the principals (investors, consumers, or regulators) were able to check on the agents (originators, salespersons, or bank managers). The biggest losers in the present crisis were the taxpayers and the shareholders, whereas the management staff retained fairly high salaries and bonuses even while their jobs were largely protected by the government bailouts.

How do we avoid this complexity? My experience suggests that financial-sector behavior is influenced more by a few clear and simple rules, firmly enforced, rather than multiple complex rules, lightly enforced or under-enforced. Hence, whilst I applaud the diligence of the regulatory community in perfecting the existing rules, we should not be surprised that we cannot solve complexity by adding complexity. Just as we cannot solve the problem of excess leverage by more debt, we cannot solve the financial engineering mess by more financial engineering. We must go back to basics and make the overall system more simple, less leveraged, and more transparent and accountable.

By allowing less exemptions and enforcing simpler rules, such as an overall leverage ratio, the regulators can stop the financial community from trying to embed off-balance-sheet leverage by using accounting tricks and through offshore unregulated financial centers. As long as regulation is able to limit the level of leverage, the financial institutions will have their profits capped and bonuses will be limited. Surely financial innovation is not just about higher and higher forms of leverage.

Given the fact that emerging markets still have the largest number of financial institutions which are significantly less sophisticated than the developed market institutions, I would suggest that the focus of financial regulation and reform over the next few years be on effective implementation and enforcement of a set of simpler standards. Complex regulatory rules impose high regulatory costs and are impediments to the capacity of emerging markets to reform themselves to more efficient and robust levels. For example, the International Financial Reporting Standards (IFRS) is already looking at reduced-form reporting requirements for small- and medium-sized enterprises (SMEs). Using this as an analogy, we should aim for simpler forms of Basel, IOSCO, and other standards that prioritize implementation and enforcement for the "bulge" market. In other words, the standard setters, with input from the emerging markets, should aim for a reduced but priority set of standards to help the emerging markets implement their standards faster and more effectively.

Not all of the standards are applicable and useful for emerging markets. For example, the internal ratings-based models rely on data series that are often not available for many emerging markets. The cost of implementation to meet Basel II standards can be very high, since many smaller financial institutions have to hire consultants to train their staff. Similarly, in the implementation of Financial Sector Assessment Programs (FSAPs) as well as compliance with codes and standards, the international financial institutions should avoid enforcing compliance with the "letter" of the latest standards and focus more on the "spirit" of whether emerging market systems are generally robust relative to global systemic risks.

6. Concluding Thoughts

Reform and regulation are institutional processes. We cannot achieve everything overnight, nor are markets ever complete. Development is a continual process of "learning by doing". We lurch in cycles of prosperity and creative destruction.

Given the complex mess that we are in, it is better that we begin the process of putting the important pieces together for a more stable and inclusive global financial architecture. This would imply putting in place a global tax regime for financing global public goods that should be the purview of the Bretton Woods II institutions and development banks. These institutions should have a system of funding not only through equity and debt, but also through taxation. Note that for global property rights to be protected and arbitrated, we would also need a global system of courts.

Complementing the international financial institutions' focus on global public goods, national governments would have the task of concentrating on the implementation and enforcement of global rules and standards at the national level. The pace of implementation and enforcement can be encouraged by putting in place fiscal incentives as well as prioritizing a simpler set of standards that makes the tasks of financial stability easier to achieve.

References

Capra, F. (1982). *The Turning Point*. New York: Simon & Schuster.

Garnaut, R. (2008). *Garnaut Climate Change Review: Interim Report*. Commonwealth of Australia, February.

Haldane, A. G. (2009). Rethinking the financial network. Speech delivered at the Financial Student Association, Amsterdam, April.

OECD (2009). *The Economics of Climate Change Mitigation: Policies and Options for Global Action Beyond 2012*. Paris: OECD.

Parsons, J. E., A. D. Ellerman, and S. Feilhauer (2009). Designing a U.S. market for CO_2. *Journal of Applied Corporate Finance*, 21(1), Winter, 79–86.

Posner, R. A. (2009). The President's blueprint for reforming financial regulation: a critique — part I. July 20. Available at http://www.finreg21.com/lombard-street/the-president%E2%80%99s-blueprint-reforming-financial-regulation-a-critique-part-i/.

Reinhart, C. M. and K. S. Rogoff (2008). This time is different: a panoramic view of eight centuries of financial crises. Manuscript, Harvard University, April 16.

Sheng, A. (ed.) (1996). *Bank Restructuring: Lessons from the 1980s*. Washington, D.C.: World Bank/Oxford University Press.

Sheng, A. (2005). The weakest link: financial markets, contagion and networks. BIS working paper, December.

Sheng, A. (2009a). The first network crisis of the twenty-first century: a regulatory post-mortem. In *Economic and Political Weekly* (ed.), *Global Economic and Financial Crisis*, Hyderabad, India: Orient Blackswan, 81–98.

Sheng, A. (2009b). Financial crisis and global governance: a network analysis. Background paper for the Growth Commission, September.

Sheng, A. (2009c). The political consequences of the economics profession: G20 and the emerging markets. Keynote address at the ICRIER/Bruegel Conference on International Cooperation, New Delhi, September.

Sukhdev, P. (2008). *The Economics of Ecosystems and Biodiversity: Interim Report*. European Commission and German Federal Environment Ministry, May.

Turner, L. A. (2009). *The Turner Review: A Regulatory Response to the Global Banking Crisis*. Financial Services Authority, London, March.

Dealing with Cross-Border Bank Distress: Some Specific Options for Reform

Stijn Claessens*
International Monetary Fund

1. Introduction

The global financial crisis has made clear (again) that current approaches to deal with cross-border banking distress are fraught with many problems and can actually aggravate financial turmoil.[1] In this paper, I briefly analyze the problems dealing with international bank distress. I then describe the current approach, and identify options for improved cross-border crisis management and resolution. The options I discuss include having a world financial regulator, a new charter for internationally active banks, greater harmonization of rules and practices, enhanced coordination, and a decentralized but segmented approach.

Each of these reform options has its own benefits and costs, and the effectiveness of each option depends on actual implementation and enforcement. Ranking is thus difficult. Globally, complex political economy trade-offs will dictate which option may emerge as feasible. Regionally, for some closely integrated financial systems, the scope for achieving solutions closer to first-best may be greater, but so will be the need. Regardless, it will be important to avoid a ring-fencing approach,

* Stijn Claessens is an Assistant Director in the Research Department of the International Monetary Fund (IMF). The views expressed in this paper are those of the author and do not necessarily represent those of the IMF or IMF policy. The author would like to thank the conference participants and especially his discussant, Vincent Reinhart, for useful comments.

[1] For more detail, see Claessens (2009), on which this paper extensively draws.

i.e., a situation in which national, segmented subsidiaries are seen as the solution. This will have high costs for banks and will only risk a bad political economy spiral by reinforcing already nationalistic-oriented approaches in regulation, supervision, burden sharing, and decision making.

Broader reforms of national and international financial systems will need to support any of these options. In the international dimension, I stress the need for better monitoring of global systemic risks and crisis prevention arrangements. More effective monitoring is especially needed for large financial conglomerates and their cross-border exposures and off-balance-sheet activities. While better monitoring and greater cooperation will not reduce all risks, and many implementation challenges exist, it can help address market disruptions as they arise and prevent policy measures that have adverse spillovers.

In terms of outline, this paper first briefly draws lessons from the recent financial crisis by reviewing the sources of cross-border spillovers, the government responses, and the resulting policy issues. This helps identify the issues future reforms will have to address. The next section reviews the current approach; and then presents reform options for addressing large, complex, globally active financial institutions, starting with the first-best solution — a world financial regulator — and ending with the fourth-best solution — national, segmented systems. It discusses the advantages and disadvantages of these and other options in between, stressing though that these are difficult to rank. The last section concludes.

2. The Global Financial Crisis and Cross-Border Banking

The global financial crisis has led to many international spillovers. Some of these arose because of direct links between financial institutions, such as through exposures to U.S. subprime-related claims, collateralized debt obligations (CDOs), and the like. These affected European banks first and then reached other banks. The U.S. problems also triggered turmoil in markets with similar housing booms. A second channel was through spillovers of liquidity shortages, leading to the freezing of credit markets in many currencies. This in part triggered the run on U.K. bank Northern Rock. Combined with stock market declines, the turmoil affected many markets (e.g., U.K. pound sterling, euro, Swiss franc).

A third channel of international spillovers came through solvency concerns. As recapitalization fell short and deficiencies in national resolution frameworks became more apparent, solvency concerns affected systemically important global financial institutions. With the demise of Lehman Brothers and AIG, international spillovers peaked in October 2008, triggering many government interventions. Subsequently, real- and financial-sector links created perverse feedback loops globally in the last quarter of 2008 and the first quarter of 2009. Risks and vulnerabilities remained large in the rest of 2009, albeit much more subdued.

The interventions in the fall of 2008, while necessary, created spillovers themselves as well. The liquidity provision was not always well coordinated, as highlighted by the persistent shortage of dollars. The dollar shortage was eventually resolved with swaps between major central banks, but this took some time. Also, some countries, especially emerging markets, were (initially) left out from the currency swaps, creating turmoil in their financial markets. Because the various governments' guarantees of wholesale funding, retail deposits, and other liabilities differed in terms of coverage, terms, etc., there were adverse movements in capital flows and sharp rises in (differences in) spreads. In some cases (e.g., Ireland), sovereign credit risks quickly replaced banking system risks as guarantees were put in place. While regionally efforts were somewhat coordinated (such as in the EU), globally this happened only in a limited way.

The various restructuring efforts also led to spillovers. The purchases or exchanges of assets at times had a national focus (most often, only local entities were eligible), and rules inevitably varied across countries. Purchases of non-performing assets have been little so far, but the rules do differ and have created distortions. The distortions created were made even greater through the various interventions to support defunct financial institutions. Capital injections and other support to banks and other financial institutions, while necessary, created international spillovers. They tended to favor national financial institutions, as they involved fiscal resources, creating disparities. The few cross-border restructurings that did occur (Dexia, Fortis) still largely followed national lines.

Important from a cross-border perspective, there were some actions that amounted to a ring-fencing of assets (in the U.K., with assets of banks from Iceland; and in Germany, with respect to assets of Lehman Brothers). In addition, differences in legal frameworks were often constraints on supervisors' actions. The asymmetric U.S. domestic depositor preference, for example, made the offsetting of assets against liabilities difficult across borders.

Although still to come, there will be many coordination issues in the process of exiting from the various government interventions. These unwinding measures range from the phasing out of liquidity support, the unwinding of guarantees, and the sale of state-ownership stakes to the disposal of assets acquired. They all risk considerable international distortions, in large part as these are unknown processes in terms of their scale and global reach. Together, these aspects of the recent crisis show how ill-equipped the global system is for dealing with the distress of large financial conglomerates that span multiple markets.

3. Current Approach and Reform Options

I start with further analyzing why the current approach is clearly not a desirable state of affairs. I then review the various approaches proposed over the years. Each one comes with its own advantages and problems, and the ordering of solutions is obviously difficult. I consider the first-best solution to have an international, world financial regulator; however, this is unlikely to be attainable in the near future. The second-best solution, in my mind, is an international bank charter — a new regime. I consider both the increased harmonization of rules and convergence in practices without increased coordination as well as increased coordination with less or no harmonization or convergence as third-best approaches. A model recently discussed is a nationally segmented approach; however, I consider this a worse approach than the current one and classify it as a fourth-best option.

3.1 *Current approach*

In terms of cross-border banking, the current approach is based on the home–host principle, developed by the Basel Committee on Banking Supervision (BCBS). According to this principle, home countries are to supervise the branches and subsidiaries of their banks in foreign countries. Host-country supervisors have responsibilities as well, but their role is largely to provide information.

Many, including the BCBS itself (e.g., BCBS, 2006), have recognized that this principle is not sufficient in light of the rapid internationalization of financial services. A foreign subsidiary of a major international bank may be significant in the market in which it operates, even though it is relatively small for the banking group as a whole. Conversely, a subsidiary that is large for a banking group may not be significant for a host country, say, if it is located in a major financial center. Potential conflicts also exist within banking groups. A local branch or subsidiary manager may disagree with decisions taken at the group level to manage capital in a certain way. Also, legal or governance responsibilities of local management may differ from those at the group level. These differences can adversely affect overall international financial stability, for example, when local managers "grab" assets in times of turmoil to satisfy their specific local obligations.

For those banks with small international operations, where spillovers can be expected to be little (although this criteria can be hard to quantify), the home–host principle might suffice. When foreign-owned entities are large in the host market, however, this model will be fraught with limitations from an overall international financial stability point of view. While improvements are under way (for example, new rules on subsidiaries to correct for divergent interests),[2] they are unlikely to assure that the interests of the shareholders of the parent bank will be fully aligned with those of the host country. From an international financial stability point of view, this approach is then also not satisfactory.

3.2 *First-best option: a world financial regulator*

The first-best option would be to have an international financial regulator, perhaps called a World Financial Authority, that would regulate and supervise all (or at least all large) financial institutions. This was perhaps first proposed by Eatwell and Taylor in 1998.[3] It is the obvious solution to any coordination problem. At the same time, this model is very demanding to

---

[2] For example, Ortiz (2006) and others have called for separate corporate governance and other requirements on local subsidiaries (such as the listing of some shares in the local market to allow for market discipline and to increase information); see also Financial Stability Forum (2009).

[3] The idea was first mentioned in their working paper of 1998, and then published in their book of 2000 (see Eatwell and Taylor, 1998, 2000).

be fully consistent in all dimensions. The international financial regulator would need to be complemented, for example, by "lender of last resort" liquidity facilities, international deposit insurance, and a recapitalization fund — similar to the requirements in a domestic context. This World Financial Authority would also be difficult to govern, as its objectives would be hard to establish. Moreover, from a political economy standpoint, it is unlikely to materialize in the near future. The experiences of the EU and the Economic and Monetary Union (EMU) suggest that — even after achieving very close financial, economic, and political integration — adopting a common, single regulatory and supervisory authority is very difficult.

3.3 *Second-best option: international bank charter*

One approach closer to first-best and perhaps feasible in the medium term is to establish a separate regime for large, internationally active financial institutions, with some elements of voluntarism. Under this "international bank charter" (IBC) model, international active banks would be globally chartered and under the supervision of a single regulator. The European bank charter, which was proposed some time ago (Čihák and Decressin, 2007; see also Decressin *et al.*, 2007), and possibly similar charters could be the equivalent on a regional basis.[4]

Under this model, there would be an international regulatory and supervisory body overseeing (all) international active banks. It could be a separate new institution, or part of one or more existing (international) institutions. It would be staffed with professionals recruited internationally. It would be governed by the nations sponsoring the concept, in accordance with some objective criteria consistent with a mandate of improving international financial stability and efficiency. Moreover, it would need to satisfy the general principles of accountability, independence, transparency, and integrity (Quintyn, 2007).

The set of actions available to this body would have to be the regular tools of any national financial regulator. It would regulate, license, and supervise international active financial institutions, including commercial

[4] Technically, European banks can already establish themselves as a European Company (*Societas Europaea*), but that would not imply a corresponding shift in regulation and supervision from national to supranational authorities (Dermine, 2006).

banks and possibly other financial institutions (such as financial conglomerates, insurance corporations, and brokers). It could, among other efforts, raise capital adequacy requirements for those institutions that contribute to or represent greater systemic risks, or for all institutions in order to deal with the procyclicality of financial markets. The arsenal of remedial actions available would include those normally available to deal with weak banks, such as limits on operations and risk taking, minimum capital requirements, and cease-and-desist orders. Its actions, especially remedial ones, should be as rule-bound as possible.

There are many complementary measures needed for this model to work (again, many of these issues have long been analyzed in the context of the EU; see, for example, Boot (2006), papers in Caprio *et al.* (2006), and Veron (2008)). Liquidity support would have to be provided using common rules. The regulator would need to have access to intervention resources with fiscal back-up. There would, therefore, need to be an "International Deposit Insurance Corporation", funded by insurance premiums paid by the chartered institutions, that should also have some form of callable capital from governments for back-up purposes.

The deposit insurance could be supplemented by a recapitalization fund, which would give the regulator the ability to address weak financial institutions independently of individual countries' support — something which is difficult to organize and secure during times of crisis. The recapitalization fund could collect fees also from the banks themselves (based on their international assets) and/or by more general contributions from the sponsoring countries based on, say, the value added of financial services in the country's GDP, since the ultimate gains relate to the real economy. Like the deposit insurance agency, the recapitalization fund would need to have access to callable capital from its shareholders, i.e., the governments sponsoring the concept. Bailouts and payouts would be centrally administered.

In exchange for being required to participate — or, alternatively, subjecting themselves to this regime[5] — the IBC banks could operate in

[5] One key issue is the degree of voluntarism: should international banks be allowed to choose themselves or should they be forced to be subject to the international regime? Obviously, there can be adverse selection here; weaker banks may not be interested in subjecting themselves to a presumably stronger international regime. Required participation may therefore be the better approach. Then, there need to be clear and common criteria, say, banks above a certain cut-off in terms of international operations.

the sponsoring countries without any further permissions, regulations, or needs for reporting and compliance (except for country-specific requirements, such as macroprudential requirements to mitigate country-specific booms or systemic risks). Because IBC banks would only need to report to one regulator, and branches and subsidiaries would be treated the same for regulatory purposes, they would avoid many compliance and administrative costs. While they would have to pay some insurance premiums, they would do so only to one fund. Furthermore, the possibility of a recapitalization, with burden-sharing rules agreed upon, can be a source of financial strength, especially for a large bank from a small country with limited fiscal resources.

This model could achieve close to the first-best solution for the largest international active banks. It would get around the problem that coordination is hard to agree on *ex ante*, especially with respect to actions aimed at containing and resolving a crisis. In the current crisis, as often in the past, actions regarding large institutions were largely determined *ex post* and aimed only at (near) insolvent institutions rather than being preemptive, and were only done at the national level. A common and well-resourced regulator would assure coordination; and if intervention is necessary, the regulator's powers would be backed by sufficient resources to make it credible.

3.4 *A third-best option: decentralized but converged approach*

One third-best solution could be a decentralized approach, i.e., where actions are not coordinated *ex post* but where regulatory frameworks and practices are made more uniform, even to the point so as to mimic first-best outcomes. This would, at the minimum, involve harmonization and convergence in five areas. One, the set of rules and regulations governing international active banks would have to be fairly uniform across major markets. Second, it would require *ex ante* clarity on the responsibilities for supervision: who will supervise what aspects of international banks? In particular, the coverage of branches and subsidiaries as well as the treatment of offshore financial centers would need to be clarified. Third, there would need to be consistency in "lender of last resort" facilities, liquidity support, deposit insurance, and other forms of the public safety net, i.e., government support and guarantees. Fourth, resolution regimes would have to be consistent, including the modalities for (prompt) corrective action, the treatment of creditors, and the recognition of collateral across legal jurisdictions. Fifth, there would need to be *ex ante* agreed-upon rules on burden sharing and resolution when an international failure requires some form of payout.

Common rules alone will not be enough, however, since differences in practices can arise. The existing mechanisms for assessing actual policy implementation (such as the Financial Sector Assessment Program (FSAP)) can help reduce these differences. Nevertheless, procedures can be further improved, their voluntary nature reassessed, and modalities for raising concerns clarified. At the country level, for example, there could be a "comply or explain" requirement on member authorities. Complementary, improved monitoring of global systemic risk, especially of large financial conglomerates and cross-border exposures of all types of financial institutions, will help.

In principle, this could reduce many of the problems with the current system. Indeed, as some have argued in the context of the EU, common, principles-based means of intervention in weak financial institutions would help overcome coordination issues (Mayes *et al.*, 2007).[6] It will not lead to the first-best solution, however. Similar to the fact that proper regulation and supervision of individual financial institutions does not guarantee systemic stability, common and proper national regulation and supervision does not guarantee international financial stability. There will always be a need for discretionary actions to address weak (or resolve insolvent) financial institutions, particularly when they are large. Thus, coordination issues will remain.

For this model to work, it will therefore be essential that the agreed-upon rules on the sharing of the resolution costs are binding *ex post*. As Freixas (2003) shows, recapitalization facilities will be underproduced in the event of improvised coordination, as in the *ex post* bargaining in the case of failure of a large cross-border bank. Tight *ex ante* rules will help, but *ex post* enforcement is needed as well. One means to achieve this would be through a common recapitalization fund (Goodhart and Schoenmaker, 2006).

---

[6] One complementary proposal is to require all (large) financial institutions to present, on a regular basis, plans to their supervisors for their own orderly wind-down and closure. This could make the system less fail-prone, and help identify and reduce the risks of spillovers.

3.5 *Another third-best option: enhanced coordination, including through colleges*

Another third-best model could be to rely on more coordination of actions, even in the absence of (further) convergence of rules. This is the model largely adopted by the EU for now and laid out in the de Larosière (2009) report. Under the EU model, three new authorities will each oversee their respective (banking, insurance, and capital markets) national regulators and supervisors. The new bodies can mediate in a legally binding way between national supervisors, and adopt binding technical decisions in regard to specific financial institutions. In addition, they can play coordinating roles, especially during financial crises.

Other international financial architecture elements are also moving towards such an enhanced coordination approach. A number of large financial institutions, for example, now have an international supervisory college. While there is still quite some uncertainty on the exact modalities of these colleges, these colleges can help with coordinating actions.

These structures could reduce many coordination issues, even when national rules and practices differ. Nevertheless, limitations remain, potentially leading to risks. Since colleges concern themselves with individual financial institutions only, they will not explicitly consider the stability of the international financial system as a whole. Given the many interlinkages among financial institutions these days, this can leave significant risks of spillovers.

Another related concern is access to information. Presumably the colleges will help with information sharing, but confidentiality arguments and pure power play may still lead to the hoarding of information. For the EU, this need for additional information collection and oversight is reflected in the establishment of the European Systemic Risk Board. It would gather information on macroprudential risks and give early warning of threats to financial stability. At the global level, the Financial Stability Forum (FSF) and the International Monetary Fund (IMF) are called upon to undertake more intense surveillance. For both efforts, though, information sharing and modalities are yet to be defined.

The most important drawback of this model is that none of these agencies have direct intervention powers. More generally, it is recognized that colleges and enhanced surveillance alone are not the sole answer. Unfortunately, other complementary measures may not be forthcoming or sufficient. As such, this approach may create a false sense of security and risk complacency.

3.6 *Fourth-best option: nationally segmented financial institutions*

One model that has received some attention recently is a more restricted version of the current approach (Pomerleano, 2009). Under this model, the operations of international active banks in each jurisdiction would be limited to subsidiaries that can stand alone. Each subsidiary would be separately capitalized according to local norms and would have to satisfy other local requirements, such as liquidity, consumer protection, etc. In the event of financial distress, each subsidiary would be resolved on its own, preferably in a prompt and structured fashion. If firewalls among subsidiaries are adequate (i.e., ring-fencing is complete), possibly assured by a holding company structure, spillovers in case of solvency problems could be limited. This approach could be complemented with other institutional changes, such as requirements for greater use of centralized clearing and settlement in international transactions among banks (and in capital markets).

This approach would help prevent cross-border spillovers. In its extreme form, however, this is a large step backward for international financial integration. It prevents any synergy gains arising from economies of scale and scope for banks operating across borders. The requirement to establish multiple stand-alone units could further increase the cost of cross-border financial services provision. In many ways, therefore, this proposal is a step backwards. It resembles the unit or branch banking model in practice in the U.S. before the 1980s that limited banks from operating outside a narrow geographical area, or the segmented banking markets model that prevailed in much of Europe before the Single Market Program. That model has been found to have large inefficiencies and lead to poor risk sharing (see Strahan and Jayaratne (1997) for the U.S., and Barros *et al.* (2005) for the EU). It has also been shown to be inferior from a social and political economy respect. Moreover, it goes against the general trend towards open financial services markets.

While this model may appear attractive from a stability point of view, it does not fundamentally present a genuine solution to the international coordination issues. Furthermore, since the financial crisis has already led to more financial nationalism, formalizing this by requiring separate subsidiaries could be a serious setback to (regional) financial integration. Importantly, it can trigger a bad political economy cycle by reinforcing the national thinking that is already very strong in regulation, supervision, burden sharing, etc. (see Pauly, 2009). In the longer run, it could therefore undermine the political support for more improvement to the international financial architecture.

4. Conclusions

The need for reforms and greater cooperation and coordination across countries in an increasingly integrated global financial system has become more obvious with the recent financial crisis. There is especially a need for improved mechanisms to deal with cross-border banks and other large financial institutions, which few single countries can deal with on their own. As clearly demonstrated by the failures of Lehman Brothers, Icelandic banks, and other banks, countries cannot deal with large, complex, globally active financial institutions on their own, as these institutions affect many markets and countries. The need for a better approach will increase in the future, since institutions keep getting larger and more complex. A more universal approach will be needed.

Improved cross-border banking resolution, however, is a very complex problem, with many aspects and requiring some fundamental changes. For conceptual clarity, I have presented a number of options on how to deal with cross-border banks. The first-best approach — having a world financial regulator — is unlikely to be attainable in the short run (and, some would say, is not desirable anyhow). Other options — such as increased convergence in rules and policies as well as enhanced coordination in actions — are obviously difficult to rank. Nonetheless, I argue that an international bank charter cum regulator, together with "lender of last resort" facilities, deposit insurance, and recapitalization funds, offers the best approach for the medium term.

References

Barros, P. P., E. Berglöf, P. Fulghieri, J. Gual, C. Mayer, and X. Vives (2005). *Integration of European Banking: The Way Forward.* Monitoring European Deregulation series, No. 3. London and Bilbao, Spain: Centre for Economic Policy Research (CEPR) and Fundación BBVA.

BCBS (2006). Home–host information sharing for effective Basel II implementation. Paper, Basel, Switzerland, June.

Boot, A. W. A. (2006). Supervisory arrangements, LoLR and crisis management in a single European banking market. *Sveriges Riksbank Economic Review*, 2, 15–33.

Caprio, G. Jr., D. D. Evanoff, and G. G. Kaufman (eds.) (2006). *Cross-Border Banking: Regulatory Challenges*. Singapore: World Scientific Publishing.

Čihák, M. and J. Decressin (2007). The case for a European banking charter. IMF Working Paper No. 173, Washington, D.C.

Claessens, S. (2009). International exposure to U.S.-centered credit market turmoil. Paper prepared for the Federal Reserve Bank of Atlanta Conference on "Financial Innovation and Crises", Jekyll Island, Georgia, May 11–13.

de Larosière, J. (2009). *The High-Level Group on Financial Supervision in the EU — Report*. Brussels.

Decressin, J., H. Faruqee, and W. Fonteyne (eds.) (2007). *Integrating Europe's Financial Markets*. Washington, D.C.: International Monetary Fund.

Dermine, J. (2006). European banking integration and the Societas Europaea: from host-country to home-country control. In Caprio, G. Jr., D. D. Evanoff, and G. G. Kaufman (eds.), *Cross-Border Banking: Regulatory Challenges*, Singapore: World Scientific Publishing, 49–63.

Eatwell, J. and L. Taylor (1998). International capital markets and the future of economic policy. Center for Economic Policy Analysis Working Paper Series III, Working Paper No. 9.

Eatwell, J. and L. Taylor (2000). *Global Finance at Risk: The Case for International Regulation*. Cambridge, U.K.: Polity Press.

Financial Stability Forum (2009). FSF principles for cross-border cooperation on crisis management. Basel, Switzerland, April 2.

Freixas, X. (2003). Crisis management in Europe. In Kremers, J., D. Schoenmaker, and P. Wierts (eds.), *Financial Supervision in Europe*, Cheltenham: Edward Elgar, 102–119.

Goodhart, C. and D. Schoenmaker (2006). Burden sharing in a banking crisis in Europe. *Sveriges Riksbank Economic Review*, 2, 34–54.

Mayes, D. G., M. J. Nieto, and L. Wall (2007). Multiple safety net regulators and agency problems in the EU: is prompt corrective action partly the solution? *Journal of Financial Stability*, 71, 1–26.

Ortiz, G. (2006). Cross-border banking and the challenges faced by host country authorities. In Caprio, G. Jr., D. D. Evanoff, and G. G. Kaufman (eds.), *Cross-Border Banking: Regulatory Challenges*, Singapore: World Scientific Publishing, 11–19.

Pauly, L. (2009). The changing political geography of financial crisis management. In Clark, G., A. Dixon, and A. Monk (eds.), *Managing Financial Risks: From Global to Local*, Oxford: Oxford University Press, 27–47.

Pomerleano, M. (2009). A solution to financial instability: ring-fence cross-border financial institutions. August. Available at http://www.voxeu.org/index.php?q=node/3854/.

Quintyn, M. (2007). Governance of financial supervisors and its effects — a stocktaking exercise. The European Money and Finance Forum SUERF Studies series, No. 2007/4.

Strahan, P. and J. Jayaratne (1997). The benefits of branching deregulation. *Economic Policy Review*, 3(4), December, 13–29.

Veron, N. (2008). Europe's banking challenge: regulation without refragmentation. *CESifo Forum*, 9(4), 51–59.

VII. HOW TO MAKE REGULATORS AND GOVERNMENT MORE ACCOUNTABLE: REGULATORY GOVERNANCE AND AGENCY DESIGN

Making Safety-Net Managers Accountable for Safety-Net Subsidies

Edward J. Kane*
Boston College

Accountability is simultaneously an economic and ethical concept as well as a managerial and political issue. The term arises in the context of a principal–agent relationship. We can draw out the concept's meaning from its linguistic roots by exploring the entailments that three embedded words contribute: *account*, *count*, and *ability*. In policy making, the relevant "account" is an official body's self-interested description of its situation and motives and of the effects that particular policies either have had or promise to have on the interests of various political principals. In turn, to "count" up the degree of praise and blame the principal should properly ascribe to the agent's policies, each principal needs considerable "ability".

Accountability is a managerial and political issue because officials report to multiple constituencies and most reports disingenuously claim credit and shun blame. In any enterprise, perfect accountability exists when policymakers have to reveal, explain, and justify their behavior to each of their principals in a plainly truthful manner. Conversely, accountability is imperfect to the extent that policymakers can or do cover up their actions and intentions, or misrepresent the effects that their policies generate.

A country's financial safety net may be visualized as a figurative mesh whose filaments and buttresses tie government officials, financial-institution stakeholders, and taxpayers into a web of mutually reinforcing contracts. Weaknesses in accountability tempt officials who manage national safety nets to shade their policies so as to favor the interests of

---

* Edward J. Kane is a professor of finance at Boston College. For helpful comments on this material, the author is grateful to Richard C. Aspinwall, Robert Dickler, Rex du Pont, James Thomson, and Larry Wall.

the institutions they regulate. Playing favorites is feasible because the terms and effectiveness of individual contracts are opaque. Implicit and explicit understandings are established through largely unobservable give-and-take relationships that take place between short-lived political and regulatory agents and principals who dwell in long-lived economic sectors. Occupants of individual sectors vary in their understanding of the duties that safety-net officials owe them, in the extent to which they can influence safety-net decisions, and in their ability to appreciate the implications of policy decisions promptly enough to protect whatever rights they perceive themselves to enjoy.

Asymmetries in sectoral understandings and enforcement capacities incentivize top safety-net managers to follow policies that, at least at the margin, subsidize powerful and well-informed sectors at the expense of weaker ones. Sectoral influence and perceptiveness are not directly observable; but within and across nations, managers and other stakeholders of large financial institutions have the strongest grasp of their policy interests and enforcement capacities, while households have the weakest. This helps to explain why giant firms' access to safety-net subsidies tends to expand over time.

In the wake of any crisis, proposals for reform proliferate. Blueprints for reform typically begin by characterizing the problem as a market or regulatory failure, and go on to associate particular remedies with selected gaps in regulatees' reporting obligations or in regulators' span of control. This allows advocates to justify the particular adjustments they espouse by showing that, under ideal circumstances, their proposals could bridge or close the gaps they purport to be crucial. However, changes in regulatory arrangements inevitably generate new ways to get around them. Therefore, for a reform to be considered seriously, its sponsors ought to opine about whether and how regulation-induced innovation might defeat their purpose. Proponents should be made to explain how regulators, regulated parties, and competitors are likely to behave in the circumstances being contemplated. This entails focusing on how, if at all, each proposal might improve the incentives of safety-net managers to monitor the subsidies institutions extract and thereby make them more accountable for protecting the long-run interests of ordinary taxpayers.

The paper is organized as follows. Section 1 develops the hypothesis that the current crisis shows that changes in risk-taking technology have outstripped social controls on the job performance of private and public officials responsible for managing country safety nets. It explains that traditionally every country's safety net offers non-transparent subsidies to institutions that find clever ways to increase their leverage and interest rate risk. The availability of these unmeasured and unacknowledged subsidies undermines financial stability by encouraging financial institutions to take on risk in innovative ways, whose safety-net implications do not immediately register on authorities' radar screens. Devising incentives to register and control these implications is the primary goal of this paper.

Section 2 cites five duties of public stewardship that voters might reasonably require safety-net managers to embrace and, as far as possible, expect the Government Accountability Office and inspectors general at each and every supervisory agency to enforce. The purpose of building these duties into agency mission statements and official oaths of office is to strengthen incentives for subsidy control. Section 3 notes that strategies for incentive modification are absent from the blueprints for reform that U.S. officials and the G-2O have been moving forward. Section 4 seeks to persuade readers that feasible accountability and incentive reforms exist and deserve to be afforded a more prominent role in the ongoing policy debate.

1. Role of Safety-Net Subsidies in Crises and Bubbles[1]

An asset-pricing bubble may be defined as an upward price movement that occurs over an extended time period and a wide range of values and then implodes (Kindleberger, 1978). To explain a bubble satisfactorily, one needs to provide a unified account for the contrasting phases of price movement: a lengthy up, followed by a sudden large decline. Bubbles and the crises that usually follow them arise dialectically. The pre-2007 bubble in the prices of securitized claims based on real estate was driven by subsidies. The subsidies came from opportunities to be paid for taking risks in securitized instruments and off-balance-sheet vehicles that could be easily shifted onto the safety net. Capturing these subsidies entailed exploiting defects in the design and administration of national safety nets.

In country after country, politicians handicap safety-net managers by asking them simultaneously to subsidize sectors that politicians favor and to stabilize the financial system as a whole. These are contradictory goals.

[1] This section draws heavily on Kane (2009a).

The need to make trade-offs between these two objectives undermines the quality of financial supervision, and makes financial crises and bubbles inevitable. Subsidies to politically preferred kinds of risk taking lead a country's financial sector to pass through successive three-stage sequences of (1) a pre-crisis bubble in the prices of favored assets, (2) a period of actual crisis, and (3) a post-crisis interval of healthy economic recovery. Although the onset of a crisis makes itself known quickly, no one can say definitively when a healthy recovery degenerates into a bubble. During a bubble, parties invested in sustaining it use accounting trickery to hide their weaknesses and to condemn and lobby energetically against supervisory attempts to label such transitions honestly.

Industry and governmental disinformation intensifies and prolongs the course of bubbles and crises alike. During a bubble, regulated institutions routinely expand their access to implicit safety-net subsidies by devising innovative instruments and structural transformations that increase information asymmetries between the risk takers and the private and governmental watchdogs charged with monitoring and controlling their risk taking. Although no one wants to admit it, regulated institutions game the regulators and the regulators pretend more or less not to notice.

The problem is not just that the existence of a safety net lets financial-institution managers pay less attention to risk. Institutions extract subsidies from national safety nets by expanding, in hard-to-see ways, their leverage and/or the mismatch in the durations of their assets and liabilities. Regulators and supervisors are inevitably saddled with a monitoring technology and particular regulatory tools that are tailored to previous crisis experience. The key step in subsidy extraction is to undercut, ever more perfectly over time, the ability of these technologies to see and control the flow of safety-net subsidies. The more complicated a firm's loss exposures become, the harder it is for safety-net managers to perceive (and the easier it is for the industry to deny) the extent to which the safety net is being forced to absorb the firm's deepest downside risks. Helped by grossly overstated credit ratings and under the cover of what were purported to be purely resource-saving innovations, structured securitizations and other off-balance-sheet vehicles expanded such tail risks in increasingly complex ways.

Issuing securitized claims on a particular collateral pool is a complicated substitute for financing the same assets with deposits. This insight allows us to portray the structured-securitization bubble as a sophisticated extension of the government credit-allocation scheme that subsidized politically favored builders and homeowners during the bubble stage of the savings and loan (S&L) mess. Safety-net subsidies reduce the cost of capital that beneficiary firms confront.

Until the S&L bubble burst in 1989, safety-net subsidies were mainly routed through lending institutions, whose deposit liabilities federal agencies explicitly insured. Some of these benefits were shifted forward to builders and homeowners through interest rate concessions on construction and mortgage loans. Lenders were willing to shade the interest rates they charged and the credit standards they enforced on housing-related loans for two reasons. First, they presumed that Congress would make sure that supervisors treated subsidy-induced risk taking in housing finance activities more tolerantly than it deserved. They also presumed that, in times of banking turmoil, authorities would expand a troubled institution's access to implicit and explicit federal loans and guarantees. In line with the second presumption, when the S&L bubble finally burst in 1989, the obligations of the insolvent S&L deposit insurer — the Federal Savings and Loan Insurance Corporation (FSLIC) — were made good by a massive injection of funds from hapless taxpayers (see Kane, 1989).

The securitization bubble enlisted new players and expanded the risk-taking technology employed in the S&L mess. Poorly capitalized, state-chartered non-bank mortgage brokers stepped in to help deposit institutions originate loans, especially to low-income households targeted by the post-2004 affordable housing program. To make securitized claims appear to be a near-perfect substitute for federally insured deposit financing of mortgage loans, a new layer of agents developed between lenders and safety-net managers. Their job was to either manufacture derivative claims or certify (i.e., exaggerate) their quality. These mediating agents may be described as "financial engineers". They alleged (and credit rating organizations (CROs) rashly or corruptly affirmed) that, by chopping up and reassembling promised cash flows, they could transform mortgage loans to underresourced households into riskless securities. This financial alchemy combined the work of accountants, appraisers, investment banks, derivatives dealers, credit raters, statistical model builders, credit insurers, and financial service providers. The net effect of their work was to overstate collateral values and to understate institutional leverage and other risks.

After the demise of the FSLIC, government-sponsored enterprises (GSEs) — especially Fannie Mae and Freddie Mac — took over from what was left of the S&L industry the lead role in initiating and distributing housing finance subsidies. When this successor scheme began to unravel in 2007–2008, the GSEs were assisted by the Federal Reserve, the Federal Home Loan Bank System, and the U.S. Treasury.

Figure 1 illustrates the incremental dealmaking and oversight entailed in the financial-engineering business model. As shown in the lower right-hand portion of the diagram, securitization introduced a market in which traders priced credit exposures and transferred them synthetically. Even though the safety-net subsidies that defective underwriting could generate synthetically were just as worrisome as those produced in deposit-financed lending, supervisory authorities allowed profit-making CROs to oversee the synthetic market. While the Securities and Exchange Commission (SEC) acquired authority to supervise CRO activities in the Credit Rating Agency Reform Act of 2006, this authority focused on registering individual companies and overseeing their operations.[2] The language of the Act failed to task the SEC with exploring the safety-net consequences that mistakenly exaggerated CRO certifications might generate. Of course, the record suggests that the SEC's staff and

Figure 1. Financial engineering: the modern credit-risk management process uses more outside information and entails extra dealmaking.

[2] Credit Rating Agency Reform Act of 2006, Pub. L. No. 109-291, 120 Stat. 1327 (codified in scattered sections of 15 U.S.C.).

leadership had scant interest or skill in monitoring securities-industry loss exposures in any case.[3]

The gap between the ovals in Figure 1 that represent governmental and credit-rating industry oversight of the safety-net loss exposures generated in risk-transfer transactions signifies a political equilibrium. It underscores a series of deeper gaps in the government's willingness and ability to protect the safety net against regulation-induced innovation.

2. Duties of Public Stewardship[4]

Modern theories of regulation acknowledge that a financial institution has an incentive to disobey, circumvent, or lobby against burdensome rules, and that this incentive increases with the opportunity cost of compliance. This creates tension between regulators and their clientele. The result is that rulemaking and enforcement activities are always in flux.

Rules and the regulatory concerns that underlie them evolve over time. Their evolution is driven by the interplay of economic events with governmental goals and with the waxing and waning of industry pressure to relax burdensome rules or to control disruptive behaviors.

Kane (1981) describes regulation as a dialectical process in which regulation-induced innovation only belatedly engenders regulatory adjustments, while these eventual regulatory adjustments (termed re-regulation) promptly engender new forms of regulatee avoidance. This dialectical theory portrays managers of financial institutions as maximizing stockholder value, and envisions private and governmental regulators and supervisors as watchdog organizations tasked with promoting a set of shifting and conflicting societal goals. Whether public or private in nature, every watchdog organization is also subject to contrary clientele pressures that mutate its objectives and sometimes hamper the implementation of its formal goals. In the context of safety-net management, lobbying pressures typically seek to bend enforcement and rulemaking activities in ways that generate safety-net benefits for client sectors at taxpayer expense.

---

[3] The report filed by the U.S. SEC Office of Investigations (2009) in the Madoff case makes this all too clear.

[4] This section draws on Kane (2009b).

2.1 *Specifying duties that perfectly virtuous safety-net supervisors would embrace*

Commonsense ethics and Kant's second categorical imperative (which forbids treating persons merely as a means to an end) insist that, across every chain of contracts in which principals delegate authority to one or more agents, agents and principals owe one another reciprocal duties of loyalty, competence, and care. Neither principals nor agents should tempt one another to shortchange their duties. In structured securitizations, these obligations have often been honored in their breach.

To clarify the concrete obligations these abstract duties might impose on safety-net managers, I shall introduce the concepts of a perfectly virtuous (PV) supervisor and a perfectly virtuous (PV) trader. A PV trader would always give a "sucker" an even break. In overseeing what it knows to be non-PV traders, a PV supervisor would acknowledge its obligations explicitly and perform them selflessly and conscientiously. To benchmark the performance of real-world supervisors in the securitization process, this paper posits a list of duties that PV supervisors might agree that they owe to the community employing them. I believe that, ultimately, some or all of these duties ought to be incorporated into the oaths of office that future safety-net officials agree to implement. To enforce these duties, the Government Accountability Office and inspectors general[5] at supervisory agencies ought to be required to define corresponding performance standards and audit agency policies for conformance with the standards. Spelling out supervisory duties can help us to identify weaknesses in recent crisis management, and to determine how PV safety-net managers might have handled and better supervised the securitization process during the bubble period.

The fluidity of the financial environment means that regulation must be conceived as a dynamic and proactive process. For this process to correct itself at an optimal speed, obstacles that hinder efficient adaptation must be regularly identified and cleared out of the way. To identify these

[5] At individual federal agencies in the U.S., the Office of Inspector General exists as an independent organizational unit established under the Inspector General Act of 1978 (as amended). An inspector general's mission is to promote the efficiency and effectiveness of agency programs and operations and to protect against fraud, waste, and abuse. Every inspector general is empowered to conduct audits, evaluations, and investigations in support of this mission.

obstacles, it is helpful to draw an analogy between financial supervisors and referees in a sporting contest. In sports, bad calls arise due to both errors of commission and errors of omission. Errors occur for one of four reasons. Referees may have an incomplete or distorted understanding of the rules; they may fail to equip themselves with eyeglasses or other vision aids (such as replay cameras) needed to see the play; they may fail to move themselves into position to see the play; or they may let themselves be influenced either by the reaction of the crowd or by unseen side payments. In theory, to avoid bad calls, PV supervisors should acknowledge the following corresponding duties:

(1) *A duty of vision.* Supervisors should continually adapt their surveillance systems to discover and neutralize regulatee efforts to disguise their rule breaking. To lessen the costs generated by regulation-induced innovations, authorities must continually adapt their surveillance systems to observe the safety-net implications of new, fast-growing financial instruments as well as evolving networks of intracompany and intercompany connectedness. A good start would be to develop metrics that track the value of safety-net subsidies, and to require each agency's inspector general to conduct an annual evaluation of the adequacy of agency supervision of asset classes and technologies whose use has been growing disproportionately.

(2) *A duty of prompt corrective action.* Supervisors should stand ready to propose new rules as they are needed, and to enforce existing laws and rules by disciplining violators effectively as soon as a material transgression is observed. As envisaged in the Federal Deposit Insurance Corporation (FDIC) Improvement Act of 1991,[6] inspectors general must be empowered to make individual supervisors accept responsibility for seeing that loss-making institutions are closed or recapitalized before they can impose large losses onto the safety net.

(3) *A duty of conscientious representation.* Supervisors serve multiple communities. They should be prepared to resolve conflicts among these communities fairly and to put the interests of poorly informed communities ahead of their own. Self-sacrificing behavior is routinely required from military, police, fire control, and nuclear cleanup personnel.

[6] Federal Deposit Insurance Corporation Improvement Act of 1991, Pub. L. No. 102-242, 105 Stat. 2236, 2263 (codified as amended at 12 U.S.C. §§ 1811–1831 (2006)).

(4) *A duty of efficient operation*. Supervisors should strive to produce their insurance, loss detection, loss resolution, and conflict resolution services at minimum cost. To manage the size of safety-net expenditures, this duty entails training personnel in crisis resolution so that they can detect and resolve financial-institution weakness at minimum resource cost.

In principle, the commitment to incentive compatibility embodied in the third duty implies an overarching fifth duty of *accountability*. By definition, if real-world supervisors were perfectly virtuous, they would make themselves politically and financially accountable for the ways in which they exercise their discretion. PV supervisors would fearlessly bond themselves (e.g., by taking some of their salary in the form of a forfeitable claim to deferred compensation) to disclose enough information about their decision making so as to allow principals and interested outsiders to determine whether and how badly supervisors might neglect, abuse, or mishandle their responsibilities in particular circumstances. This requires that authorities explain and document at least the following three points: why they adopted one set of policies rather than another, how they expected the policies they adopted to work, and when and how (if at all) results diverged from their plan.

Democratic accountability exists only to the extent that the contracts taxpayers write with government officials are conditioned on observable information. Observability requires either the immediate or eventual release of the information that policymakers actually review when a controversial decision is made. Pursuing this level of accountability would facilitate meaningful post-mortem analysis, and the desirability of conducting meaningful policy post-mortems forms the logical foundation for both the Freedom of Information Act and the Inspector General Act.

In practice, mission statements do not hold safety-net officials closely accountable for either the efficiency costs or the distributional effects of decisions they make in controlling risk-taking behavior or managing crises. On the contrary, and in country after country, safety-net officials mischaracterize the effects of their policies to deflect blame and enjoy little *ex post* liability for shortfalls in loyalty, competence, or care. In particular, formally independent central banks are allowed to offer inflated and undocumented claims about the size and nature of hypothetical disasters that their decisions served to avoid (i.e., the counterfactual "bullets" they dodged), and to withhold or mischaracterize the information that was available to them when controversial decisions were being made.

Moreover, while markets and institutions have been globalizing, national regulators have simultaneously guarded their regulatory turf and competed to extend it. Supervisory responsibility continues to be assigned locally, connected only by club-like agreements to take account of effects on other countries. In particular, schemes for shifting commercial and investment bank losses to individual taxpayers are still shaped and administered on a nation-by-nation basis.

Gaps in cross-country accountability have survived for any or all of three reasons. First, misaligning responsibility for regulating global firms appears to serve the bureaucratic interests of national regulators by reducing their accountability for undersupervising national-champion firms. Second, it sustains opportunities for rent seeking by these same institutions. It allows important firms to extract relief from their own and other governments when they fall into trouble. Third, it incentivizes national safety-net managers to subsidize the expansion of globalizing firms by adopting prudential regulatory standards and enforcement procedures that promote the international competitiveness of the firms under their aegis.

During the securitization bubble, national regulatory behavior and clientele benefits were increasingly exposed to competition from foreign regulators. In world markets, movements of financial capital and asset values across countries carry into the domestic policy space political, economic, and reputational pressures that individual-country policymakers cannot afford to neglect. It is hard to resist the hypothesis that these pressures disposed authorities in financial-center countries to expand safety-net subsidies by blessing dodgy methods of moving risks off financial institutions' balance sheets and to acquiesce in loophole-ridden agreements for coordinating cross-country supervision (e.g., Basel I and II).

3. Fire! Ready, Aim — Reframing the Issue as Managing Safety-Net Subsidies

The solution that policymakers advance for any policy problem flows inevitably from the way they frame that problem. Misframed problems lead to misaimed solutions.

Financial policymakers in the U.S. and Europe steadfastly refuse to own up to their role in generating or aggravating crises. In particular, official documents almost uniformly attribute the current financial crisis to defective risk management at systemically important private institutions. This leads them to characterize the goal of reform as forcing private managers to do a better job of monitoring and supporting their risk exposures in the future. Officials propose to do this in three ways: (1) by toughening capital requirements; (2) by restricting executive compensation at financial institutions; and (3) by redefining the authority and reach of financial regulators. With minor exceptions, the new authority is to be distributed across the same supervisory agencies that failed to detect the build-up of national and international safety-net loss exposures during the securitization bubble.

In the U.S., the thrust of these strategies is to create a responsibility for monitoring systemwide risk, to develop a supervisory framework for forcing insolvent conglomerate firms into a government-run receivership or conservatorship, and to extend regulatory control into previously unregulated portions of the financial industry. "Too difficult to fail and unwind" (TDFU) institutions are to be identified, but not broken up or downsized. In the event of future distress, the job of forcing haircuts on these institutions' counterparties is to be left to supervisory discretion. Taxpayers are being told that it is enough to subject TDFU firms to additional capital and liquidity requirements, as if the task of designing and administering these requirements was not fraught with incentive conflict. In fact, poorly supervised institutions can eliminate any burden from stepped-up requirements simply by taking on more risk. Allowing TDFU firms to do this in inventive ways serves the interests of politicians, top regulators, and their clientele. Throughout the bubble, the opacity of complex derivative instruments, such as credit default swaps, was downplayed and even encouraged by ill-advised cheerleading voiced by top Fed officials, who should have known better. Preserving the opacity of regulatory forbearances enhances post-government employment opportunities and reduces threats to agency turf. It is no accident that Congress is neither being asked nor is it volunteering to do anything to improve the supervisory incentives that ultimately determine how well risk assessments, insolvency resolution, and other assignments will be performed.

In contrast to the official narrative, our analysis portrays the disastrous meltdown of structured securitization as a layered breakdown of private-market discipline and government supervision. Far from being defective, risk management at systemically important institutions skillfully extracted subsidies from incentive-conflicted watchdogs and unwary taxpayers by arbitraging weaknesses in the way national safety nets have been administered. Expanding regulatory authority over a misanthropic industry without remedying weaknesses in supervisory incentives is not going to curtail institutions' interest in devising new ways to obtain subsidies. It simply invites another round of safety-net subsidies.

The key to getting an efficient result is *not* to force institutions or their insurers to hold more capital year in and year out, but to make sure that (1) authorities and taxpayers can see a TDFU firm's need for additional capital when it arises and (2) TDFU managers can raise more capital as soon as it is needed. In line with this view, Hart and Zingales (2009) propose to measure a firm's incremental need for capital by monitoring movements in the price of credit default swaps that are written on it. Another way to force private recapitalization is to require TDFU firms and other large institutions to issue stock that requires stockholders to attach a contingent guarantee of their firm's debt. Extended-liability stock with this feature was issued by national banks (and many state-chartered ones) prior to the creation of the FDIC (Esty, 1998; Grossman, 2001; Kane and Wilson, 1998).

Extended liability allows a failed firm's receiver to assess each stockholder for an amount equal to the *pro rata* share of the firm's unresolved obligations (Winton, 1993). This contingent liability would intensify private monitoring activity and lessen the degree of government safety-net support the firm would need when and if it falls into financial distress. Stockholders able to monitor the value of the contingent liability could expect to earn an appropriate premium for accepting this exposure. Risk-averse shareholders would be able to strip out the contingent liability synthetically and trade the obligation in a derivatives market. Increases in the price of the synthetic claim would signal officials and taxpayers promptly that safety-net subsidies seem to be growing.

Flannery (2009) has proposed attaching a similarly contingent capital liability to a TDFU firm's debt contracts. In view of regulators' incentive conflicts, it would be best if this liability could be touched off in advance of formal insolvency and activated ideally by a market signal. Assuming that stockholder liability for financial institution losses were extended as part of the contingent recapitalization program, decreases in stock prices could serve as a timely signal. For maximal benefit, it would be useful to divide stockholder and creditor obligations into coupon-like pieces that would turn into cash when and as market triggers (or an institution's net worth or examination rating) decline across a set of laddered thresholds.

The two kinds of contingent capital would work well in tandem and would lessen the need for authorities to regulate executive compensation. Compensation could still be monitored, but only to make sure that the pursuit of safety-net subsidies is not intensified by allowing employment contracts to encourage managers of firms "covered" by the safety net to hold insufficient "capital" to "support" their firms' "risk exposures" (e.g., by offering them golden parachutes). Placing quotes around key terms emphasizes that, in regulation and supervision, the root problem is that these words mean neither more nor less than lobbyists and politicians persuade regulators to let them mean. If blueprinted reforms are truly going to bring safety-net subsidies back under control, top officials have to be made accountable for the care, competence, and loyalty to society with which they formulate their definitions.

Supervisory and market-based metrics are needed to identify and control the opportunity cost of the loss exposure which each institution receives from the safety net. An ideal information system would communicate to taxpayers how well regulators are documenting and controlling the net flow of safety-net benefits to covered institutions.

Discretion over the timing of recognizing losses and institutional insolvency is a longstanding source of abuse. An opportunity-cost reporting system would make supervisory standards for requiring recapitalization, imposing creditor haircuts, and closing institutions less open to abuse than they are today. Backed up by appropriate penalties, the following requirements would enhance regulatory accountability for measuring, pricing, and managing the value of implicit and explicit government guarantees:

- To require costs of safety-net loss exposures to be measured, reserved for, and funded in the federal budget as they accrue;
- To require government officials to eliminate emerging taxpayer exposures to loss in insolvent deposit institutions according to a strict timetable; and
- To require incumbent politicians
    - to set explicit limits on their ability to intervene without penalty in the process of closing or recapitalizing individual institutions;
    - to report all such interventions to legislative committees and judicial bodies for explicit review; and

- to open evidence of favoritism that is uncovered by inspectors general, or that surfaces in committee and judicial reviews, to outside evaluation by watchdog institutions.

4. Accountability Reform

Managing anything begins with defining and measuring it. Finance theory tells us how to define the costs and benefits that safety-net guarantees transmit to firms that are fully covered by a financial safety net. Any firm is fully covered as long as it is TDFU. One goal of reform must be to make it easier for authorities to recapitalize, take control of, or break up insolvent TDFU firms.

Defining bank capital and deposit insurance premiums properly can help agency staff to measure safety-net subsidies. Finance theory defines a firm's "risk capital" as the present-value cost of acquiring complete protection for its creditors and counterparties (Merton and Perold, 1993). This value rises with the potential volatility of the firm's return on its assets and with the value of stockholder-contributed net worth.

Erel *et al.* (2009) establish that the value of a firm's risk capital is the same thing as the firm's default put. With respect to deposit insurers, substantial literature exists on how to model and price a put contract using information on the behavior of an institution's stock price (e.g., Duan *et al.*, 1992; Duan, 1994). Moreover, by selling securities that establish prediction markets for bailouts or transfer safety-net risks in creative ways (Wall, 1988, 1996; Shadow Financial Regulatory Committee, 2009), deposit insurers could improve the precision of these models and of estimates of safety-net benefits that their staff could derive from synthetics and stock-price data. The most straightforward way to start this process would be for the government to issue safety-net puts that pay private parties to participate in specified tranches of all expenditures incurred in taxpayer-financed rescues during specified periods of time, and to bond these investors' evolving loss exposures with futures-like margin accounts.

TDFU firms are seen as too large, too complex, and/or too politically connected to be broken up. The safety-net guarantees these firms extract have been underpriced because the same conditions that make them TDFU also make them too difficult to discipline adequately during bubble and recovery periods. For a completely insured firm, the capitalized value of its subsidy is the difference between the value of its safety-net put and the capitalized value of the annualized costs it pays for coverage. The costs are the sum of explicit insurance premiums and regulatory burdens (i.e., non-pecuniary premiums) that are imposed through supervisory discipline (Buser *et al.*, 1981).

Genuine reform must face up to the incentive breakdowns that generated the crisis and correct them. This entails creating a series of enforceable duties for TDFU firms and their supervisors. The first duty would be to regularly monitor and publicize the flow of safety-net costs and benefits to TDFU firms. The second duty would be for managers and supervisors to keep the estimated value of safety-net support within specified bounds. The idea would be to make high-ranking industry and government officials responsible not only for tracking how innovative financial instruments and procedures affect safety-net benefits, but also for devising ways to reverse these effects. For example, both in government and in industry, compensation of top executives could be docked if an estimated surge in safety-net benefits is not corrected promptly.

To enforce these new obligations requires conscientious oversight.[7] Rather than inventing a new watchdog, the Government Accountability Office and agency inspectors general can be tasked with investigating how well these duties are performed each year and with communicating to the public their analysis of how to improve outcomes going forward. A crucial element of these reviews would be to expose improper attempts by regulated entities and allied politicians to influence officials tasked with overseeing the financial industry.

References

Buser, S. A., A. H. Chen, and E. J. Kane (1981). Federal deposit insurance, regulatory policy, and optimal bank capital. *Journal of Finance*, 36, March, 51–60.

Duan, J.-C. (1994). Maximum likelihood estimation using price data of the derivative contract. *Mathematical Finance*, 4, April, 155–167.

Duan, J.-C., A. F. Moreau, and C. W. Sealey (1992). Fixed-rate deposit insurance and risk-shifting behavior at commercial banks. *Journal of Banking and Finance*, 16, 715–742.

[7] See the chapter by Ross Levine in this book.

Erel, I., S. C. Myers, and J. A. Read, Jr. (2009). Capital allocation. Unpublished working paper, May 26.

Esty, B. C. (1998). The impact of contingent liability on commercial bank risk taking. *Journal of Financial Economics*, 26, February, 189–218.

Flannery, M. J. (2009). Stabilizing large financial institutions with contingent capital certificates. Working paper, University of Florida, September 18.

Grossman, R. S. (2001). Double liability and bank risk taking. *Journal of Money, Credit and Banking*, 33, May, Part I, 143–159.

Hart, O. and L. Zingales (2009). A new capital regulation for large financial institutions. Chicago Booth School of Business Research Paper No. 09-36, October 2.

Kane, E. J. (1981). Accelerating inflation, technological innovation, and the decreasing effectiveness of banking regulation. *Journal of Finance*, 36, May, 355–367.

Kane, E. J. (1989). *The S&L Insurance Mess: How Did It Happen?* Washington, D.C.: Urban Institute Press.

Kane, E. J. (2009a). Incentive roots of the securitization crisis and its early mismanagement. *Yale Journal on Regulation*, 26, Summer, 405–416.

Kane, E. J. (2009b). Unmet duties in managing financial safety nets. Networks Financial Institute Policy Brief No. 2009-PB-06, Indianapolis, September.

Kane, E. J. and B. Wilson (1998). A contracting theory interpretation of the origins of federal deposit insurance. *Journal of Money, Credit and Banking*, 30, August, 573–595.

Kindleberger, C. P. (1978). *Manias, Panics, and Crashes: A History of Financial Crises*, 1st ed. New York: Basic Books, Inc.

Merton, R. and A. Perold (1993). Theory of risk capital in financial firms. *Journal of Applied Corporate Finance*, 6, 16–32.

Shadow Financial Regulatory Committee (2009). Reducing interference with accounting standards and devising securities to price moral hazard. Statement No. 277, Washington, D.C., September 14.

U.S. SEC Office of Investigations (2009). *Investigation of Failure of the SEC to Uncover Bernard Madoff's Ponzi Scheme — Public Version*. Report No. OIG-509, Washington, D.C., August 31.

Wall, L. (1988). A plan for reducing future deposit insurance losses: puttable subordinated debt. *Economic Review — Federal Reserve Bank of Atlanta*, July/August, 2–17.

Wall, L. (1996). Bonding the regulators: a plan for the FDIC to issue capital bonds. Unpublished paper, Federal Reserve Bank of Atlanta.

Winton, A. (1993). Limitation of liability and the ownership structure of the firm. *Journal of Finance*, 48, June, 487–512.

Regulatory Governance and Agency Design: An Old Topic, Made Extra Relevant by the Financial Crisis

Michael Klein*
Johns Hopkins School of Advanced International Studies

Regulatory systems may be thought of as comprising rules, processes, and organizations. Much time is spent in the economics profession on the design of rules. The hope is that rule-based regulation will minimize the need for the exercise of discretion, and thus facilitate the management of regulation and reduce the likelihood of regulatory capture. However, the future is uncertain and people try to pursue their own interests by avoiding or evading rules. As a result, rules or contracts that foresee all circumstances and are adhered to at all times are impossible to write and enforce. Applied to the financial sector, discretion will need to be exercised by regulators and supervisors — the people who interpret, adapt, enforce, and sometimes make the rules.

In light of the recent financial crisis, this paper considers key features of the organizational architecture for financial-sector regulation, which circumscribe the exercise of discretion by regulators and supervisors. For convenience' sake, the term "regulator" shall be used to encompass both financial regulators and supervisors.

The fallout from the crisis has made this agenda more urgent, because it is likely that relatively more discretion will need to be exercised by prudential regulators in financial systems, notwithstanding calls for

---

* Michael Klein is a senior visiting professor at the Johns Hopkins School of Advanced International Studies. He is the former Vice President for Financial and Private Sector Development jointly for the World Bank and the International Finance Corporation. The author would like to acknowledge helpful discussions on the subject matter with Asli Demirgüç-Kunt and Costas Stephanou.

rule-based regulation. This follows if one shares the belief that regulators need to take a macroprudential or systemic view. Here is why:

- First, detecting the build-up of unsustainable imbalances in financial systems that result in boom–bust cycles is the key to macroprudential regulation (Borio, 2007), but it remains more art than science. The last decade has seen a whole literature on how to detect or anticipate unsustainable asset price increases (and how they might matter for monetary policy), yet many believe that it is practically very difficult to do so with any certainty. The current debate is, if anything, even more complex.
- Second, implementing macroprudential regulation is likely not an exercise separate from the conduct of monetary policy. There may be interactions between monetary policy and credit markets in the build-up of imbalances in the financial sector. Furthermore, policy measures may require the coordinated deployment of monetary policy tools (such as policy rates) and regulatory measures (such as capital requirements or loan-to-value ratios). This is a new challenge for regulators with, so far, little guidance on how to deploy multiple instruments.
- Third, the widespread use of guarantees and the current lack of credible exit mechanisms for creditors in financial institutions deemed "too big to fail" shift more burden on those trying to lean against booms, including decisions to determine who is "systemically important".

Currently, various efforts are under way to find regularities underlying these boom–bust cycles so as to derive detection and policy rules. The International Monetary Fund (IMF) concludes its efforts presented in the recent *World Economic Outlook* by emphasizing that "policymakers need room for discretion" (IMF, 2009). Others are more optimistic that reasonably robust rules can be found, minimizing the need for discretion (Borio and Drehmann, 2009). However, while the debate continues, decisions have to be made one way or another and regulatory agency design needs to allow for the potential need for extra required discretion.

Finally, it has always been clear that it is politically hard for regulators to say "the party is over" while things are going well. It is tough to do so with teenagers, before they get too drunk. It is truly hard in the face of strong political pressure to let the good times roll; for example, central banks may feel that interest rates need to be raised. So, if we want macroprudential regulation, we inadvertently make the job of regulators even more difficult, because in the foreseeable future they may not be able to make a fully convincing case that a party is getting out of hand and because their tools to make it peter out are somewhat coarse and unproven. Yet, all those in favor of macroprudential regulation are asking them to confront political pressure from that position of weakness.

It follows that regulators need a very strong position and political independence to embark on the quest for sound macroprudential regulation. At the same time, the uneven performance of regulators in the run-up to the crisis casts doubt on their ability to handle independence well. But, there is no choice. The best we can try to do is circumscribe the discretion of regulators well and build in accountability mechanisms to provide better incentives to exercise discretion with care.

1. How Existing Regulatory Systems Coped with the Financial Crisis

To help design a reasonable regulatory architecture for macroprudential regulation, consider first how different regulatory models fared during the recent crisis.

We know the countries that ran into trouble and experienced problems in the financial sector, such as market turmoil or bank failures. Among them are Iceland, Ireland, the United States, the United Kingdom, Switzerland, Germany, and Ukraine. Other countries avoided trouble in the financial sector. These include Canada, Australia, New Zealand, India, China, Turkey, Croatia, the Czech Republic, Slovakia, Pakistan, Colombia, and most emerging markets outside of Eastern Europe (with exceptions such as Nigeria and Kazakhstan). When comparing these patterns of failure and success with institutional characteristics of regulatory agencies, no clear, high-level correlation is apparent. On the contrary, some conventional wisdom is challenged.

Admittedly, conventional wisdom in this field is embryonic. Some trailblazing work has been done at the IMF and the World Bank. In a paper of the IMF Monetary and Exchange Affairs Department, Quintyn and Taylor (2002) reviewed arrangements for regulatory and supervisory independence and financial stability. They ventured a guess that *ex ante* the best designed systems include those in Australia, Colombia, the U.K., and the U.S. The first two came out well in the recent turmoil; the latter failed miserably.

The debate over the last decade about whether regulation and supervision should be part of the central bank or separate seems to have been of tangential importance for the actual performance of regulatory systems. In the U.K. and Australia, regulation/supervision is separate from the central bank. In the Czech Republic, India, and Ireland, it is a part thereof. In the U.S., the Federal Reserve has a role in supervising important banks. Fragmented state-level regulation of capital markets may have been an issue in one country (e.g., the U.S.), but less so in another (e.g., Canada).

Hence, first-round inspection of the evidence does not show clear patterns of effective regulatory models. Yet, on the positive side, recent events show that financial systems can be fortified and rendered more stable. Many countries that previously experienced deep crises have so far made it through "the big one" with limited damage to financial institutions and markets. This includes most emerging markets, with notable cases like Turkey, a country with a troubled past in the crisis vicinity of Eastern Europe. Canada shows that modern systems can be managed prudently. Spain and Colombia show that one can try to lean against bubbles (via provisioning or monetary policy). Croatia experimented successfully with its version of macroprudential regulation, including limits on credit growth.

One common trait of many of these successful cases may be that they have been burned in the not-too-distant past and have thus developed a more cautious attitude towards financial-sector management. "Once bitten, twice shy" seems to work and at least shows that whole countries can learn to cope with financial distress. At the same time, it could also be that financial imbalances have not yet had sufficient time to develop afresh.

There are clearly no simple miracle solutions, and the school of hard knocks still matters. Our knowledge about the link between regulatory system design and desirable outcomes remains limited. This calls for a two-pronged approach to:

- clarify our attitude towards "best practice" based on common sense and limited evidence; and
- advance knowledge by undertaking more detailed and complex studies to tease out further insights about the relation between institutional design and outcomes.

2. The Primacy of Market Structure

Work at the World Bank allows us to step back from the current crisis and review at least some initial cross-country evidence on patterns of regulatory design (Barth *et al.*, 2006), drawing on information from over 150 countries. One way to read the evidence goes as follows.

More checks and balances in political systems are associated with more narrowly defined mandates and powers of regulators, and also with more independence. In other words, systems that circumscribe the power of the ruler(s) through checks and balances and rules unsurprisingly develop clearer delegation models. Overall, history suggests that rule-based systems perform better than those relying on "big men" rule. Poorer countries have step-by-step gotten the point, and are moving at various paces towards more rule-based systems.

As countries clarify the structure of delegation of economic functions, they also tend to give greater scope to market forces where these can be harnessed. Clearer rules, including property rights and reliance on self-regulating forces of markets where feasible, are features of successful systems. Institutional incarnations may vary a lot, but the broad point holds. In this context, it may be useful to recall that Article 17 of the Universal Declaration of Human Rights upholds the right to private property. Private property was, and remains, fundamentally a protection of the individual against capricious expropriation by the ruling elite(s).

Obviously, real markets are non-Walrasian and generally require "regulation" in the broad sense — i.e., a system of rules, processes, and organizations that upholds the institutional foundations of markets. For the financial sector, we might usefully distinguish between four areas: (1) the legal, contractual, and governance arrangements; (2) the information infrastructure, including accounting and auditing systems, credit bureaus, and rating agencies; (3) the trading and settlement system; and (4) prudential regulation. The first three areas might be called financial market infrastructure, and pose regulatory issues (in the broad sense) that are found in many other sectors of an economy and "simply" constitute the institutional arrangements required for markets to work. The prudential area is more "special", and is typically what people have in mind when discussing "regulation" in the financial sector.

Barth *et al.* (2006) may be read to say that more restrictive, clear delegation of prudential regulation combined with reliance on market forces works best. It gives regulators a chance to perform, which in better-designed, richer countries they seem able to do (although clearly not always). Countries that do not allow even simple, market-based price formation tend to be where regulators are quite dependent on political winds.

The less market forces can be relied upon, the greater the challenge for regulators. Avoiding excessive guarantees, establishing effective resolution regimes for financial institutions deemed "too big to fail", reducing subsidies, and fully pricing remaining government support to financial institutions are all actions that should help improve the performance of prudential regulators.

In countries where the capacity and, above all, the political will to pursue sound policies are lacking, there is an argument to use cruder, intrusive forms of intervention to give prudential regulators a fighting chance to perform. This could involve placing size limits on banks to reduce the "too big to fail" syndrome, just as telecommunications or electricity policymakers see market structure regulation as the key to gaining more efficient systems and to discharging their function well. Also, strong forms of transparency might help; this could include publishing the names of major defaulters, as tried in Pakistan at some point and recently in Nigeria. After all, a key source of patronage in many countries is bank loans extended to powerful people who have no intention of paying back.

Of course, for the very same reason that prudential regulation is hard, such drastic reforms are difficult and require special political opportunity, often coming out of a crisis. When discussing such reforms, we also need to remember that at times regulators may rightly fear that they are physically in danger. Reform, or the exercise of "normal" regulatory functions, requires a great deal of personal courage.

3. Rules of Thumb for Financial Regulatory Agency Design

The challenges for improving regulatory systems often appear overwhelming. Yet, miraculously the world has moved ahead over many years. The experience of providing central banks with greater independence shows that progress is possible in several countries within just a decade or two. Although it is not clear what ideal reform looks like, we need some rules of thumb to orient reform efforts while we wait for greater insight from research.

What we are looking for is a sensible delegation structure combining the use of market forces and rules that circumscribe regulatory discretion. The major role for discretion is in the area of prudential regulation. Taking this as a starting point, the following basic approach to financial regulatory design would appear sensible (and similar to the view taken in Fischer (2009)):

- The area of financial market infrastructure (legal and contractual infrastructure, information systems, and trading and settlement systems) needs less discretion. *Ex ante* rules can be set more easily. Regulators require less rule-making power and less independence.
- One particular consequence is that the "twin peaks" model of regulation would seem appropriate, as it separates more rule-based issues (e.g., business conduct, investor and consumer protection) from more discretionary ones (prudential regulation). Hence, business conduct regulation should be dealt with by someone other than the prudential regulator.
- Monetary policy and prudential regulation should be run together to benefit from easier information flow and to provide greater ease in coordinating monetary policy with regulatory intervention (e.g., adjustments to capital requirements). This means that having central banks with a combined mandate to control inflation and assure financial stability would be the default setting.

The core issue, then, is how to provide the right combination of autonomy and accountability for the prudential regulator. The basics of how to design independent regulatory agencies have been well described in a variety of settings (OECD, 2009; Smith,1997a, 1997b, 1997c). Central banks with a mandate for prudential regulation should benefit from the following standard trappings of sound design for independent regulatory agencies:

- Clear mandate;
- An income source that need not be appropriated by the fiscal authorities;
- Some freedom to determine expenditure budgets;
- Checks and balances on the appointment of top officials involving both executive and legislative branches;
- Appointment of officials for lengthy terms well exceeding the terms of elected governments, with overlapping terms for committee members where such bodies are appropriate;

- Attractive employment conditions; and
- Protection of employees from lawsuits/liability, except maybe for cases of gross negligence.

4. Special Incentives for Regulators

The crisis has unfortunately taught us that reasonably well-designed regulatory authorities can also be "asleep at the wheel". So, the search is on for special incentives that make it more likely that regulators will do their job and not fall prey to capture. Any such incentive design effort naturally has to be aware that regulatory agency design is a variant of the "who guards the guardians" problem, which may preclude high-powered incentive schemes, because there are unlikely to be simple and robust metrics for regulators' performance to which one can link rewards.

Some possible suggestions are as follows:

- Improve the analysis and anticipation of boom–bust cycles.
  - A lot of burden of analysis under current proposals falls on prudential agencies, which also enforce regulations or intervene in markets as lenders of last resort. Analysts who are independent from those who implement regulation may be less conflicted in the way they assess, for example, the build-up of imbalances; at the same time, those intervening in markets need to be on top of the information.
  - Theoretically, one could go for full disclosure of all information available to regulators and let the market analyze macroprudential issues. However, confidentiality concerns by competitors and policymakers make this potentially problematic.
  - It may thus be sensible to have a few competing institutes or commissions prepare regular reports on the state of financial stability, including the macroprudential regulator. Multiple views might stimulate debate and make it more likely that inconvenient analysis is not suppressed.
- Provide incentives for regulators to act well.
  - Today, developed regulatory systems subject agencies to special reviews by a variety of auditors. Yet, rarely (if ever) is there a public, regular, substantive, and comprehensive review of how the regulatory system affects financial markets and stability. A dedicated

agency could be charged with regular, periodic monitoring of the performance of prudential regulators, leading to periodic public debate (e.g., the sentinel proposal by Ross Levine in this volume). Ideally, one would combine the introduction of such a review with simplification of other audits to reduce the spiraling yet ultimately ineffective multitude of audits. We might say that regulators should be exposed to "sunshine", but we should also avoid "sunburn".

- One day, we may find reliable metrics that predict booms and busts and that guide policy intervention, like the Taylor rule for monetary policy. We can then use such metrics to trigger a presumption for regulatory intervention (a modified form of Prompt Corrective Action), for example, when some key relationships get "out of bounds" (e.g., excessive credit growth, excessive debt to income). Also, we might then become adventurous and link the compensation of key regulators to their performance, such as that of the New Zealand central bank governor who is paid based on the achievement of an inflation target. A recent paper by Borio and Drehmann (2009) provides some hope that halfway useful rules can be found; but for now, discretion will have to reign if one wants to lean against booms and busts.

5. International Institutions

The United States has a bewildering set of regulatory arrangements; the globe, even more so. Global action is obviously even harder than regulatory reform in the United States. This is made particularly difficult as the world is moving into a period of decades without a leading power that can cajole and enforce.

Hence, there will be no global monetary authority, no global regulator, and no global fiscal authority for some time to come. Talks of a "Bretton Woods II" were always good for sound bites at best. Consider the example of New Zealand, where banks are typically Australian-owned. There, regulatory authorities require that foreign-owned banks do not outsource critical operational functions to other countries. This is to give the regulator the power such that banks can be intervened and made to "open again on Monday" in a crisis. Even the European Union has a hard time moving to a Union-wide regulator. It is plain impossible to imagine that a global regulator will, any time soon, be able to intervene in Moscow, New York, and Shanghai alike.

The current step-by-step progress is the only promising way for now to deal with the cross-border issues thrown up by financial globalization. The emerging key actors are, on the one hand, the standard-setting system hosted in part in and around the Bank for International Settlements (BIS), including the Financial Stability Board (FSB); on the other hand, there is the IMF, with help from the World Bank, for surveillance and crisis intervention. While some broad division of labor is clear, the framing of the FSB mandate raises issues of overlap with the IMF; for instance, surveillance vs. peer review and the organizational state of the FSB currently raises questions about ability to perform (Fischer, 2009).

Within the IMF (and the World Bank), as mentioned before for national authorities, there is a potential tension between those who provide financial resources to countries and those who analyze. Those who want to lend may ignore warning signs in good times; in bad times, those who have lent may be reluctant to admit lack of progress. Also, during good times it is sometimes hard to maintain a budget for those who analyze weaknesses in financial systems without leading to loans. For these reasons, some clearer institutional separation with appropriate clear budget authority for the analysis part may be of use. At the "extreme", one could argue that the FSB should indeed have a dedicated analysis part while relying on the IMF and others primarily to provide liquidity support.

While there are fledgling global institutions (some quite old already but fledgling nevertheless), the concert of nations will remain the key to global cooperation. It worked well enough during the crisis for liquidity provision via central banks and via somewhat less coordinated fiscal policies. But, the lasting relevance of groupings like the G-20 still remains to be established.

Within this global patchwork, national authorities will shape their financial systems. It remains an open question whether this "system" is enough to preserve the good side of financial globalization. Alternatively, the proliferation of national differences may lead to regulatory arbitrage by markets, which in turn will prompt greater national controls in a spiral leading to a more segmented world financial market.

6. What to Do to Get a Better Handle on the Issues

While the world moves on, some steps could usefully be taken to enhance our understanding of regulatory system design.

Case studies should be performed to develop better, fine-grained intuitions about which institutional features matter in which contexts. One option is to create a workstream under the FSB. The work would require that agencies in varying countries are willing to expose their dirty laundry. If this cannot be done under the auspices of the FSB, it would augur badly for its ability to inspire trust.

At the same time, comparative data and studies need to be improved. This could build on the cross-country regulatory systems database developed in the World Bank. At a minimum, the IMF/World Bank should continuously develop that database *inter alia* with the help of the regular Financial Sector Assessment Program (FSAP) of countries and draw more detailed lessons, for example, by building on work by the OECD (2009).

Finally, someone — possibly the World Bank — could undertake a program to study the political economy of finance, including the influence financiers have on policymaking. After all, an understanding of the interplay between finance and politics is at the core of the design of effective regulatory agencies. The model could be studies on the politics of trade reform conducted at the World Bank in the 1980s.

References

Barth, J. R., G. Caprio, Jr., and R. Levine (2006). *Rethinking Bank Regulation*. Cambridge, U.K.: Cambridge University Press.

Borio, C. (2007). Change and constancy in the financial system: implications for financial distress and policy. BIS Working Paper No. 237, October.

Borio, C. and M. Drehmann (2009). Towards an operational framework for financial stability: "fuzzy" measurement and its consequences. BIS Working Paper No. 284, June.

Fischer, S. (2009). Preparing for future crises. Paper presented at the 33rd Annual Symposium of the Federal Reserve Bank of Kansas City, Jackson Hole, Wyoming, August.

IMF (2009). Lessons for monetary policy from asset price fluctuations. In *World Economic Outlook, October 2009*, Washington, D.C.: IMF, 93–120.

OECD (2009). A cross-sectoral regulatory governance perspective — regulatory quality management tools and strategies for financial sector regulation. Paper presented to the Committee on Financial Markets, April.

Quintyn, M. and M. W. Taylor (2002). Regulatory and supervisory independence and financial stability. IMF Working Paper WP/02/46.

Smith, W. (1997a). Utility regulators — the independence debate. Public Policy for the Private Sector Note No. 127, World Bank, October.

Smith, W. (1997b). Utility regulators — roles and responsibilities. Public Policy for the Private Sector Note No. 128, World Bank, October.

Smith, W. (1997c). Utility regulators — decisionmaking structures, resources, and start-up strategy. Public Policy for the Private Sector Note No. 129, World Bank, October.

The Sentinel: Improving the Governance of Financial Policies

Ross Levine*
Brown University and National Bureau of Economic Research

"A dependence on the people is, no doubt, the primary control on the government; but experience has taught mankind the necessity of auxiliary precautions."

— James Madison (1788)

1. Introduction

According to the precepts of a representative democracy, the people elect representatives who both enact financial regulations and select financial regulators, who in turn interpret and apply the regulations. If regulators perform poorly, the elected representatives will replace them. If elected representatives enact harmful policies or select unsuitable regulators, the public will elect new ones. According to these principles, oversight by the people motivates elected officials and regulators to act on behalf of the public, not on behalf of narrow (albeit powerful) special interests.

Experience, however, plainly shows the practical limitations of achieving these democratic ideals, especially with regard to the governance of financial regulation. First and foremost, it is exceptionally difficult for the public to obtain, process, and evaluate information on the enactment, implementation, and effects of financial regulations. Second, financial institutions

* Ross Levine is the James and Merryl Tisch Professor of Economics and Director of the Rhodes Center for International Economics and Finance at Brown University, as well as a research associate at the National Bureau of Economic Research. He thanks James Barth, Maria Carkovic, Gerard Caprio, Stephen Haber, Ed Kane, Lindsay Mollineaux, and Yona Rubinstein for materially improving his understanding of the governance of financial regulation.

may directly pressure and lobby elected officials and regulators, breaking the line of influence running from the public through elected representatives to the execution of financial policies. In particular, the financial sector is the largest contributor to political campaigns, and many senior financial regulators use the revolving door by moving from the financial sector into public office and then returning to private financial institutions. Third, the Federal Reserve — a major financial regulatory institution — is largely independent of the government and hence partially removed from public oversight. While there are good reasons for having highly skilled individuals with private-sector expertise regulate the financial sector and for creating an independent central bank, there are similarly good reasons for supplementing the public's ability to accurately evaluate and effectively shape the design and implementation of financial-sector policies.

Although James Madison (1788) viewed people as the primary sentinel over the government, he recognized that history demonstrates the need for "auxiliary precautions" due to the realities of human nature. Since humans are not angels, they sometimes use the coercive power of their official positions to achieve private objectives that do not necessarily coincide with the goals of the public. Thus, Madison argued that "ambition must be made to counteract ambition", so that contending institutions scrutinize and compete with each other (Montesquieu, 1748, reprinted 2002). These tensions and rivalries not only limit the concentration and abuse of power; they also enhance the proper design and implementation of policies.

There has been too little public debate about designing auxiliary methods to improve the governance of financial regulation. We rely almost exclusively on the public's ability to evaluate the efficacy of complex financial regulations and then to compel their elected representatives to induce regulators to act in the public's best interests. While this must remain the primary method for governing financial regulation, experience — including the current crisis — demonstrates the desirability of creating complementary mechanisms for enhancing the governance of financial regulation, which includes the design, interpretation, and implementation of financial regulations in a timely manner.

2. Governance Failures Contributed to the Crisis

The negligent implementation of financial-sector policies by financial regulators and their political overseers contributed to the collapse of the financial system. Yes, there were regulatory gaps. Yes, some financial regulations were poorly designed. Yes, the insatiable greed of financiers played a role. But the crisis — and, in particular, most certainly its severity — was not an inexorable event. Prudent, reasonable observers could have recognized (and did recognize) that perverse incentives, partially created by official policies, had undermined sound financial intermediation. Yet, financial regulators and politicians failed grossly in the basic execution of their responsibilities. The financial regulatory governance system as currently structured failed to act in the public interest not only because regulators lacked the proper tools, but also because they lacked the proper incentives.

For brevity, consider two examples of governance failure: (1) the regulation of credit default swaps (CDS) and bank regulatory capital, and (2) the creation and operation of Securities and Exchange Commission (SEC)-approved credit rating agencies. There are many more examples that would illustrate how financial regulators, with frequent help from their political overseers, did not act in the public interest. These include housing finance policies associated with Fannie Mae, Freddie Mac, the Federal Housing Administration (FHA), and the Federal Reserve (Wallison and Calomiris, 2009); recent evidence from the Federal Deposit Insurance Corporation (FDIC) Inspector General's material loss reports and the Federal Reserve Inspector General's investigations that bank regulators were frequently fooled by the short-term profits of banks and avoided confronting banks with troubling risk profiles; the SEC's blundering in dealing with and examining Bernard Madoff; and many more. I do not argue that the two examples used here are the most important regulatory failures. Rather, I use them to motivate the need for a substantive rethinking of the governance of financial regulation.

2.1 *Credit default swaps and bank regulatory capital*

Credit default swaps (CDS) were invented to provide banks with a mechanism to reduce their credit risk exposure and to free up regulatory capital for other investments. A CDS is essentially a bilateral insurance contract written on the performance of a security or a bundle of securities. For example, purchaser A buys a CDS from issuer B on security C. If security C has a predefined "credit-related event", such as missing an interest payment, receiving a credit downgrade, or filing for bankruptcy, then issuer B pays purchaser A. However, CDS were carefully crafted so that they are not formally treated as insurance contracts, which would expose them to much greater regulation; rather, they were designed as financial derivatives so that they could be transacted in less regulated, over-the-counter markets. By 2007, the CDS market had a notional value of about US$62 trillion (Barth *et al.*, 2009).

Some of the largest banks relied heavily on CDS to hedge themselves against losses on securities and to reduce regulatory capital. Regulators treated securities guaranteed by a seller of CDS as having the same risk level as the seller of the CDS. For example, a bank purchasing full CDS protection from AIG on collateralized debt obligations (CDOs) linked to subprime loans would have those CDOs treated as AAA securities for capital regulatory purposes because AIG had received an AAA rating from a Nationally Recognized Statistical Rating Organization (NRSRO), i.e., from a government-approved credit rating agency. Thus, banks purchased CDS so that they could free up capital reserves to invest in more lucrative assets.

Much has also been written about the supposed inability of regulators to even monitor CDS due to the Commodity Futures Modernization Act of 2000. Through 2008, virtually all CDS transactions were done over the counter, so there was no centralized clearing house or exchange to collect basic information about the CDS market. With the passage of the 2000 Modernization Act, the SEC was granted authority over CDS. The SEC argued that the Act impeded them from collecting information about the CDS market and from requiring disclosures regarding the credit default positions of financial institutions.

Yet, once the crisis hit, the Federal Reserve Bank of New York successfully called for market participants to submit a cleared facility solution for CDS contracts before the end of 2008. Four major contenders are competing to become leaders in clearing CDS. The rapid response to the Federal Reserve's call for clearing houses and exchanges for CDS occurred without the repeal of the Commodity Futures Modernization Act, suggesting that the constraints felt by the SEC in terms of collecting information on the CDS market had more to do with the will to act rather than its legal ability.

More importantly, bank regulators, such as the Federal Reserve, were not compelled to allow banks to avoid setting aside reserves to cover potential losses when banks purchased CDS: this was a choice. For instance, see Interpretive Letter No. 988 of April 2004, which was jointly issued by the Board of Governors of the Federal Reserve System and the

Office of the Comptroller of the Currency. It was no secret to the Federal Reserve and other regulators that several large banks were using CDS to reduce regulatory capital, and it was no secret that AIG was a large seller of CDS to financial institutions around the world. The regulatory apparatus chose to allow this.

Regulators could have made a different choice based on the following assessment: (1) the Federal Reserve does not have a sound method for assessing the true counterparty risk associated with those selling CDS to banks, and the Federal Reserve is unsure whether the credit rating agencies have the incentives and ability to assess the risk of financial institutions selling CDS to banks; (2) the largest banks are heavily using these CDS to reduce capital requirements; (3) the Federal Reserve's responsibility is to maintain the safety and soundness of banks, which relies on banks having capital commensurate with their risk; and (4) therefore, the Federal Reserve will prohibit banks from reducing regulatory capital by purchasing CDS until it can accurately assess the counterparty risk of those selling CDS to the banks. This very simple, prudent assessment would have materially changed one factor fueling the increase in bank risk taking. This choice would have hurt the short-run profits of banks, and banks would have ferociously lobbied against such a decision. Nevertheless, bank regulators had the discretionary power to limit the ability of banks to use credit derivatives to reduce their capital cushions.

The Federal Reserve and other bank regulators made the choice to allow banks to reduce capital through the use of CDS, even though they knew of the growing problems in the CDS market, the growing counterparty risk facing banks, and the lax mortgage standards underlying the deteriorating state of the U.S. financial system. For instance, Tett (2009, pp. 157–163) recounts how Timothy Geithner, then-President of the Federal Reserve Bank of New York, became exceedingly concerned in 2004 about the lack of information on CDS and the growing counterparty risk facing banks. In an exhaustive study, Barth *et al.* (2009, pp. 184–193) demonstrate through the use of internal documents that the Federal Reserve was aware of the myriad of problems surrounding mortgage financing for many years before the bubble burst: "[E]ven if the top officials from these regulatory agencies did not appreciate or wish to act earlier on the information they had, their subordinates apparently fully understood and appreciated the growing magnitude of the problem" (Barth *et al.*, 2009, p. 184).

2.2 *Credit rating agencies*

The major incentive problems that plague credit rating agencies have been well understood for over two decades and carefully documented by a range of scholars, including Partnoy (1999). Yet, over these decades, credit rating agencies grew to play an increasingly pivotal role in the global financial system, spurred by the support (if not blessing) of financial regulators. This official support included both the active sponsorship of credit rating agencies by the SEC as well as the passive acquiescence by financial regulators as the quality of ratings deteriorated and rating agency incentives became dangerously distorted.

In the 1970s, credit rating agencies experienced two huge interrelated changes. First, the SEC created the Nationally Recognized Statistical Rating Organization (NRSRO) designation, which the SEC granted to the largest credit rating agencies. The SEC then relied on these SEC-approved agencies to calculate the credit risk of numerous entities, including the broker-dealers regulated by the SEC. The SEC set capital regulations based on the risk assessments of the NRSROs.

The creation of and reliance on NRSROs triggered a cascade of regulatory decisions that dramatically increased the demand for the services provided by these SEC-approved agencies. The SEC, bank regulators, insurance regulators, other federal/state/municipal agencies, regulatory agencies in other countries, foundations, and numerous private entities all started using NRSRO ratings to establish investing rules and set capital regulations on virtually all financial institutions. For example, the SEC and bank regulators used the ratings of NRSROs to evaluate the risk of financial institutions and establish their capital requirements. Federal agencies used the risk designations of NRSROs to define the types of securities various organizations, including government-sponsored enterprises (GSEs) like Fannie Mae and Freddie Mac, could purchase and how much capital needed to be held in reserve against particular assets. The investment opportunities, the capital requirements, and hence the profits of insurance companies, mutual funds, pension funds, and a dizzying array of other participants in financial markets were materially shaped by how NRSROs rated securities.

Indeed, Partnoy (1999) argues that NRSROs sell regulatory licenses. If an issuer wants the major financial institutions — commercial banks, broker-dealers, insurance companies, pension funds, etc. — to have the regulatory latitude to purchase its securities, the issuer must obtain a particular rating from an NRSRO. As long as the financial regulatory authorities defined asset allocation restrictions and regulatory capital using NRSRO ratings, there was an enormous demand for NRSRO services. This demand was not always sensitive to the actual quality of the rating agencies.

Second, in the 1970s, credit rating agencies started selling their ratings to the issuers of securities despite the clear conflicts of interest. Issuers also have an interest in paying rating agencies more for higher ratings, since those ratings influence the price that issuers can obtain for a security.

While recognizing the conflicts of interest, credit rating agencies have argued that reputational capital reduces the pernicious effects of these conflicts. If a rating agency does not provide sound, objective assessments, it will lose its reputation and investors will no longer use ratings from that agency in making asset allocation decisions. This will the reduce the demand for all securities rated by that agency, and so all issuers using that rating agency will face lower prices for their securities. In other words, reputational capital is vital for the long-run profitability of credit rating agencies and will therefore contain any short-run conflicts of interest associated with "selling" a superior rating on any particular security. From this perspective, reputational capital will reduce the short-run temptations created by conflicts of interest if the following two, related conditions hold: (1) decision makers at rating agencies have a long-run profit horizon; and (2) demand for securities responds appropriately to poor rating agency performance, so that decision makers at rating agencies are punished if they "sell" bloated ratings on even a few securities.

These conditions did not hold, however, suggesting that reputational concerns provided exceedingly weak constraints on the conflicts of interest distorting rating agency behavior. First, especially with the explosion in the rating of structured products and the ability of rating agencies to sell ancillary consulting services, rating agencies could book massive profits in the short run and worry about reputational losses later (if at all). Besides purchasing ratings, issuers of securities would also pay the rating agency for pre-rating evaluations, corporate consultations, and guidance on how to package securities. Thus, financial innovations — the boom in the issuance of structured products and the increased provision of consulting services by the NRSROs to issuers — intensified the conflicts of interest facing rating agencies, but the regulatory community did not adapt. Distressingly, the intensification of conflicts of interest through the selling of consulting services by rating agencies closely resembles the amplification of conflicts of interest when accounting firms increased their sales of consulting services to the firms they were auditing; this facilitated the corporate scandals that emerged less than a decade ago, motivating the Sarbanes–Oxley Act of 2002. Yet, regulators still did not respond as rating agencies pursued these increasingly profitable lines of business.

Moreover, official regulations actually weakened the degree to which reputational concerns would constrain rating agencies; that is, regulators effectively weakened the feedback from poor rating performance to a drop in NRSRO revenues. Many purchasers of securities were forced by regulation to purchase only securities rated at a particular level by an NRSRO. This regulatory requirement held regardless of NRSRO performance, moderating the degree to which poor rating performance reduced the demand for NRSRO ratings and hence reducing the impact of ratings quality on an agency's bottom line. The feedback from rating agency performance to their bottom line has been further weakened by the inability of purchasers of ratings to sue rating agencies in general and the executives of these agencies in particular. Rating agencies claim that their ratings are simply opinions, which are protected by the Fifth Amendment right of free speech. The agencies and executives claim that they bear no responsibility for the quality of those ratings. Thus, rating agencies face little market discipline and no regulatory oversight, yet virtually all major issuers of securities in the world must purchase their ratings and virtually all major purchasers of securities in the world face regulatory constraints on what they can purchase based on these ratings. It is good to be an NRSRO.

Given the regulatory-induced incentives and regulatory-created protections enjoyed by NRSROs, their behavior and profitability are unsurprising. Lowenstein's (2008) excellent description of the rating of a mortgage-backed security by Moody's demonstrates the speed with which complex products had to be rated, the poor assumptions on which these ratings were based, and the profits generated by rating structured products. Other information indicates that if the rating agencies issued a lower rating than Countrywide (a major purchaser of NRSRO ratings) wanted, a few phone calls would get this changed (Morgenson, 2008). The profit margins enjoyed by NRSROs were extraordinary. For example, the operating margin at Moody's between 2000 and 2007 averaged 53%; this compares to operating margins of 36% and 30% at the exceptionally profitable Microsoft and Google, respectively, or 17% at Exxon. It is true that the performance of the rating agencies played a central role in the crisis. But, it is also true that the financial regulators established the privileged position of rating agencies and protected them from the discipline of the market.

3. Dynamic Financial Innovation and Sluggish Financial Regulation

Another failure of financial regulatory governance structure involves the fatal inconsistency between a dynamic financial sector and a sluggish regulatory system. Financial innovations, such as securitization, CDOs, and CDS, could have had primarily positive effects on the lives of most citizens. However, the inability or unwillingness of the apparatus overseeing financial regulation to adapt to changing conditions allowed these financial innovations to become malignant tools of financial destruction. A more publicly responsible — and a more responsive and accountable — regulatory system could have captured the benefits, while avoiding the pain, associated with these new financial tools.

Financial innovation is crucial, perhaps indispensable, for sustained economic growth. As discussed in Michalopoulos *et al.* (2009), financial innovations have been essential for permitting improvements in economic activity for several millennia. These include the design of new debt contracts 6,000 years ago that boosted trade, specialization, and hence innovation; the creation of investment banks, new accounting systems, and novel financial instruments in the 19th century to lower the barriers to ease the financing of railroads; and the development and modification of venture capital firms to fund the development of new information technologies and innovative biotechnology initiatives. Financial innovation has been a critical component of fostering entrepreneurship, invention, and improvements in living standards.

While perhaps natural in the current climate, I believe it would be counterproductive to caricature and dismiss the historical evidence on financial innovation as either an idealized view of financial innovation or a banal truism. The evidence does not imply that financial innovation is unambiguously positive. Financial innovations are frequently implemented simply to avoid regulations, and they played a role in triggering our current suffering. At the same time, the evidence implies more than the trivial axiom that financial innovation is not always bad. Existing research suggests that financial innovation is an indispensable ingredient in fostering economic growth and expanding economic opportunities, and this should be incorporated into our rethinking of the governance of financial regulations.

These observations advertise two desirable characteristics of a system for governing financial regulations: (1) the financial regulatory regime should not focus exclusively on stability, since financial development and innovation matter for the well-being of the population; and (2) the regulatory regime must adapt to financial innovation, or else well-reasoned, well-structured regulations will become obsolete and potentially detrimental to economic prosperity.

4. Need to Reform the Governance of Financial Regulation

The conclusion that governance, and not simply specific regulations, contributed to the crisis has major implications for reforming financial regulation. The Obama administration outlined a comprehensive package of reforms to reduce regulatory gaps, develop better crisis management tools, and consolidate the regulation of all systemically important institutions in the Federal Reserve. But, if technical glitches and regulatory gaps played only a partial role in fostering the crisis, then the administration's package of reforms represents only a partial and thus incomplete step in establishing a stable financial system that promotes economic growth and expands economic opportunities. This is not an argument against Obama's proposed reforms. It is an argument for "auxiliary precautions" (Madison, 1788) to improve the governance of financial regulation.

5. The Sentinel

I propose the creation of a sentinel — an auxiliary institution — for improving the design, reform, and implementation of financial regulations in a more dynamic manner, including regulations associated with the corporate governance of financial institutions, could materially improve the governance of financial regulations. To be clear, I am addressing the problem of regulatory governance and avoiding other key questions, such as (1) which are the right regulations for achieving desirable outcomes, such as stability, growth, and innovation; (2) what are the right trade-offs among these potentially competing outcomes; and (3) how should uncertainty concerning the actual effects of particular regulations influence policy decisions? I address some of these questions in Barth *et al.* (2006). Instead, this paper proposes a mechanism for improving regulatory governance: the system for selecting, interpreting, and implementing regulations.

The only power of the Financial Regulatory Commission (FRC) that I am proposing would be to acquire any information that it deems necessary for evaluating the state of financial regulation over time, including the rules associated with the corporate governance of financial institutions. Any information collected by the FRC would be made publicly available, potentially with some delay. Transparency is necessary; thus, the law establishing the FRC must clearly and unambiguously assert that the FRC should be granted immediate and unencumbered access to any information it deems appropriate from any and all regulatory authorities and financial institutions. FRC demands for information should trump the desires of regulatory agencies for discretion, secrecy, and confidentiality. Besides allowing the FRC to assess the state of financial regulation, transparency will enhance market oversight of financial institutions and regulatory bodies. While many have expressed concerns that transparency will destabilize markets, there is more evidence that concealing information in the name of confidentiality hinders the efficiency of financial intermediation, the effectiveness of financial regulation, and the stability of financial systems. Experience suggests erring on the side of transparency. This "sunshine" regulatory approach has a long and promising history in the United States, as discussed in McCraw's (1984) impressive book. This approach is also fully consistent with the checks and balances deeply ingrained in the fabric of U.S. political institutions. In other words, the basic purpose and power of the FRC are quite conventional, not radical.

The only responsibility of the FRC would be to deliver an annual report to Congress and the President, assessing the current and long-run impact of financial regulatory and supervisory rules and practices on the public. By having no official power over either the regulatory agencies or financial markets and institutions, the FRC would be less constrained in its assessments than an entity with operational responsibilities. While regulators might avoid taking various actions against financial institutions it regulates since that might imply a failure of regulation, the FRC would face fewer hindrances. While one regulator might avoid criticizing another regulator's actions to avoid cross-regulatory conflicts, the FRC would be less reticent. While existing regulatory agencies have internal auditing departments, the FRC would play a different role. Whereas these auditing departments perform an important role in assuring that the particular regulatory agencies adhere to their particular rules, the FRC would have much broader responsibilities for assessing the impact of the overall constellation of regulatory and supervisory practices on the financial system. No other independent entity has this role; and the absence of such an institution was clearly evident in the design, implementation, and evolution of financial policies during the last decade.

The major design challenge is to create an FRC in which the professional ambitions and personal goals of its staff align with its mission of boosting the degree to which financial regulations reflect the public interest. As argued by James Madison (1788), the goal is to set ambition against ambition, so that the private interests of those working in the FRC align with its mission.

Here are a few suggestions toward this end. The most senior members of the FRC would be appointed by the President and confirmed by the Senate for staggered and appropriate long terms. As with the Board of Governors of the Federal Reserve System, the goal is to limit the short-term influence of politics on the evaluations of the FRC. The senior members of the FRC would also be prohibited from receiving compensation from the financial services industry, even after completing their tenure at the FRC. Since exactly those individuals with sufficient expertise to achieve the goals of the FRC would also have lucrative opportunities in the private sector, this could involve such an enormous personal sacrifice that it would severely limit the pool of qualified people available to the FRC. Thus, staffing the FRC with talented, well-motivated individuals would require a different compensation schedule than currently contemplated in public-sector jobs. While problematic, a more lucrative compensation plan is necessary for limiting conflicts of interest while attracting excellent people to the FRC. At the same time, the FRC would be a prominent entity. Those working for the FRC could advance a wide array of professional ambitions and attain considerable prestige and influence after leaving the FRC by accurately assessing financial regulations. The opportunity to improve financial-sector policies and achieve these career aspirations would work to attract talented individuals to the FRC.

5.1 *Benefits of the sentinel*

As a sentinel over financial regulations, the FRC would improve the entire apparatus for writing, enacting, adapting, and implementing financial regulations. As an extra group of informed, prying eyes, the FRC would reduce the ability of regulators to obfuscate regulatory actions and would instead make regulators more accountable for the societal repercussions of their actions. As an additional group of experts reviewing and reporting on financial regulations, the FRC would reduce the probability and costliness of regulatory mistakes and supervisory failures. By boosting transparency, the FRC would increase the number of individuals and entities capable of monitoring the design, implementation, and effects of financial regulations. As a prominent institution, the FRC's reports to Congress would help reduce the influence of special interests on the public's representatives. By continuously reassessing how regulatory and supervisory practices affect the incentives faced by the financial system, the FRC would reduce the chances that financial policies become obsolete or even dangerous. As an entity whose sole objective is to evaluate the state of financial regulation from the perspective of the public, the FRC would help inform the public and thereby augment public influence over financial regulations.

6. Really? Another Institution?

A natural complaint about the FRC proposal is perhaps best expressed as an exasperated question: given the existing myriad of regulatory agencies, quasi-regulatory bodies, and other oversight entities, do we really need another one?

The crucial answer is that no other existing entity currently has the incentives, power, or capabilities to perform the FRC's role as a public sentinel over the full constellation of financial-sector policies. Besides the natural difficulties of having the Federal Reserve, the SEC, and other agencies conduct self-evaluations, the internal inspector general departments of these agencies do not have the broad mandate to assess how the complex matrix of financial policies across many regulatory bodies shapes the incentives of financial-market participants. Moreover, the FRC needs (1) the power to demand information from private institutions and regulatory bodies; (2) a staff with expertise in banking, securities markets, corporate finance, regulation, the law, and financial economics that has both an ongoing commitment to evaluating financial policies and the professional stature to confront powerful private institutions, regulatory bodies, and Congress itself; and (3) an explicit Congressional mandate to evaluate how the full spectrum of financial policies affects the incentives of financial-market participants in particular and the economy in general. With these requirements, however, an FRC-type sentinel would fit comfortably within the general designs of the Government Accountability Office, which would therefore eliminate the need for a completely new institution.

The FRC proposal will not eliminate financial and regulatory malfunctions. But, the FRC fits comfortably within, and should help improve upon, the successful U.S. institutional template of checks and balances. In this case, rather than checking power with power as advocated by Madison (1788), the potent influences of transparency and independent assessments will boost the likelihood that the design and execution of financial regulations reflect the public interest. The goal is to improve a system that has not been functioning well for far too long using methods that are consistent with the cultural and institutional norms of our country.

References

Barth, J. R., G. Caprio, Jr., and R. Levine (2006). *Rethinking Bank Regulation: Till Angels Govern*. New York: Cambridge University Press.

Barth, J. R., T. Li, W. Lu, T. Phumiwasana, and G. Yago (2009). *The Rise and Fall of the U.S. Mortgage and Credit Markets.* Hoboken, NJ: John Wiley & Sons, Inc.

Lowenstein, R. (2008). Triple-A failure. *The New York Times*, April 27.

Madison, J. (1788). The Federalist No. 51: The structure of the government must furnish the proper checks and balances between the different departments. *Independent Journal*, February 6.

McCraw, T. K. (1984). *Prophets of Regulation.* Cambridge, MA: Harvard University Press.

Michalopoulos, S., L. Laeven, and R. Levine (2009). Financial innovation and endogenous growth. National Bureau of Economic Research Working Paper No. 15356.

Montesquieu, C. de (1748, reprinted 2002). *The Spirit of the Laws.* New York: Prometheus Books.

Morgenson, G. (2008). Debt watchdogs: tamed or caught napping? *The New York Times*, December 7.

Partnoy, F. (1999). The Siskel and Ebert of financial markets: two thumbs down for the credit rating agencies. *Washington University Law Quarterly*, 77, 619–712.

Tett, G. (2009). *Fool's Gold.* New York: Free Press.

Wallison, P. J. and C. W. Calomiris (2009). The last trillion-dollar commitment: the destruction of Fannie Mae and Freddie Mac. *Journal of Structured Finance*, Spring, 71–80.

Holding Regulators and Government More Accountable: Comments

R. Christopher Whalen*
Institutional Risk Analytics

Each of the panelists — Ross Levine, Ed Kane, and Michael Klein — is attempting to answer the question, "Why does regulation not work or at least not seem to work as well as we are led to hope and believe?" The panel is focused on governance, but I fear that probably flatters most regulatory agencies. Each panelist puts forward some suggestions as to how the outcome of regulation might more closely approximate the stated goals in the laws which enable it.

New layers of regulatory oversight, but perhaps not necessarily checks and balances, are suggested in the form of a "sentinel" by Levine. He nicely uses the example of the Fed and its failure to effectively regulate or even understand complex derivatives such as credit default swaps, especially when it comes to offsetting regulatory capital requirements. However, this criticism assumes that anybody in the markets truly understands the risk characteristics of securities that do not trade on open, public markets and that can see daily shifts in price volatility measured in triple digits.

For example, during the past week or so when this paper was finally written, the CBOE Volatility Index (VIX) increased by 25% after my friend Mike Mayo reminded everyone about Citigroup's deferred tax assets. It is fair to say that most banks probably did not trim their risk exposures to compensate for this change in perceived risk, nor should they. The VIX, after all, is a new era derivative in search of a cash basis, so one should not get overly worked up about moves in the VIX that are described in hours rather than weeks.

---

* R. Christopher Whalen is Managing Director and Co-Founder of Institutional Risk Analytics (IRA), a Los Angeles-based provider of risk management tools and consulting services for auditors, regulators, and financial professionals.

Levine is right when he focuses on governance as a core issue, much like the work of Kane regards incentives and how markets tend to ooze around static regulatory boundaries. However, I do not buy the Levine argument for creating another "sentinel", much as I like the traditional American metaphor. We have a sentinel known as Congress and, regrettably, it is less than perfect. But, in my view, hanging yet another monument in Washington will not change the efficacy of regulatory agencies.

Congress was meant to be ridiculous and to do ridiculous things, such as allow banks to create pseudo markets in over-the-counter (OTC) derivatives to enhance their profitability. Congress and the industry thoroughly discouraged any regulatory efforts to prevent or even moderate OTC markets and, indeed, are fighting reform legislation as these words are being written. The degree of political sway by banks over regulators and Congress is as great today as in the 1920s, whereby it eventually created the circumstances for the Great Crash of 1929.

The election of Warren Harding and the resulting "return to normalcy" of the 1920s is a very underappreciated analogy for the U.S. under George W. Bush, and now Barack Obama. During the Harding, Coolidge, and Hoover years, let us recall, successive Federal Reserve Boards were populated by familiars of the big New York banks and offered more and more credit to an overheated market. Only when the economy essentially collapsed in 1929 were reformers able to muster sufficient political support to offset the power of the large banks — and only for a very few years.

Kane offers some interesting thoughts on ways to better align regulatory performance and public good, a theme he has developed even further since the conference. But, the question I always ask is whether such concerns are (or should be) primary in our thoughts. More often than not, regulation creates a new problem that did not previously exist even as the regulators are focused on the initial objective. For example, veteran securities attorney Fred Feldkamp (2009) writes that in the spring of 1998, over the objections of many market commentators, the Securities and Exchange Commission (SEC) decided that changes to Rule 2a-7 (under the Investment Company Act of 1940) were necessary to prevent a repeat of the problem which arose when the Fed dramatically increased short-term rates at the start of 1994. The 1994 problem proved temporary and was resolved by the Fed. The 1998 changes to Rule 2a-7, however, based on comments by the banking industry, had the effect of creating a market monopoly for the "bank conduits" that the Fed had used to liquify markets after the 1987 stock market crash.

By all means, I think that the key points of Kane regarding virtue and effectiveness are well taken. I recall Ambassador Richard McCormack arguing years ago that the key issue facing the executive branch was that the intent of Congress and the orders of the President to make that intent real were often not carried out by the agencies responsible. But if you recall that the intent of the founders of our nation was to make the national Congress ineffectual and thus less dangerous to freedom, then the "friction" of an often useless, at times captured, regulatory framework might be seen as a good outcome. In the same vein, the nation's founders might like the idea of competition among regulators and arbitrage of the same as freedom of choice.

Kane (2009) himself wrote in a draft paper that will be published by the Networks Financial Institute at Indiana State University in an upcoming policy brief and that was reprinted in my newsletter after the conference:

> In the U.S., the *de jure* barriers between the banking, securities, and insurance industries that the GLBA [Gramm–Leach–Bliley Act] finally eliminated had by 1999 become loophole-riddled remnants of their original selves. They provided no more protection for contemporary citizens than the scattered fragments of ancient city walls that tourists admire in ancient European cities today. In Europe, city fathers stopped maintaining these walls for good reason. Technological innovations in weaponry and ordnance prevented the benefits of repairing them from covering the costs. In a similar manner, blasts from the ever-improving artillery and munitions of regulation-induced innovation destroyed the effectiveness of Glass–Steagall and Bank Holding Company Act barriers to cross-industry operation. Fresh blasts will destroy them again if Congress decides to resurrect them.

Kane and I are in agreement that regulation is a dynamic, quantum problem. It is not a risk that can or should be managed via static regulation, but instead a flexible, learning regime that seeks to understand the markets and not impede them. We seek not a Maginot Line nor a Great Wall of China, but rather something more akin to a deep zone defense in professional football, only with five men down on the line of scrimmage blitzing every play. Levine's "sentinel" model is not inconsistent with this approach; however, I think he is arguing in favor of a platonic guardian to oversee the bungling regulators, whereas I think we need to make the regulators more effective. I prefer to make the regulators more relevant and less intrusive, so there may be a difference in approach.

Klein seems to agree with me in terms of both focusing on market structure as a determining factor in the overall success of any marketplace and also identifying the key problem in the current crisis, namely reduced transparency and accountability via OTC markets and other canards. Yet, since the development of OTC derivatives was actively encouraged by Congress, the Fed, and other regulators in the G7 summit as a means of boosting the apparent profitability of large banks, one wonders what hope there is for any regulatory approach to be successful, at least insofar as the majority of people in the industrial nations would define "public good".[1]

In that sense, at least, nothing has changed in the past century when it comes to the ability of the "banksters" to define and mold the direction of public policy. Just as the reaction by Congress, the SEC, and the Financial Accounting Standards Board (FASB) to the Enron and WorldCom scandals was to focus on corporate governance and ignore off-balance-sheet credit exposures, the financial regulators and Congress seem incapable of shaking off the servile yoke imposed by the likes of JPMorgan Chase and other large dealer banks. For example, Klein states in his chapter:

> The less market forces can be relied upon, the greater the challenge for regulators. Avoiding excessive guarantees, establishing effective resolution regimes for financial institutions deemed "too big to fail", reducing subsidies, and fully pricing remaining government support to financial institutions are all actions that should help improve the performance of prudential regulators.

Indeed it would. However, when Congress directs the regulators to actively write regulations that enable developments such as OTC derivatives and, furthermore, embrace such unsafe and unsound market structures as being not only acceptable but "innovative", then there is no surprise when a calamity is the result. How can anyone look at the history of the past decade in Washington and the EU and not conclude that the largest banks are calling the shots? But at least nothing has really changed

---

[1] The most recent Economic Capital study of the U.S. banking system prepared by my firm suggests that risk-adjusted returns in the U.S. banking industry are continued to fall through 2009.

in the century since the Panic of 1907. As Ron Chernow noted, "By 1924, the House of Morgan was so influential in American politics that conspiracy buffs could not tell which presidential candidate was more beholden to the bank. . . . The bank's peerless renown in the Roaring Twenties was such that the Democratic candidate was the chief Morgan lawyer, John W. Davis" (2001, p. 254).

Klein goes on to suggest, "Monetary policy and prudential regulation should be run together to benefit from easier information flow and to provide greater ease in coordinating monetary policy with regulatory intervention (e.g., adjustments to capital requirements)." But my question is this: how does one conduct prudential regulation when monetary policy is encouraging greater and greater speculation?

At the root of all the financial instability we have witnessed in recent years is the tendency of the U.S. to tax too little and borrow too much, covering the difference with deficits that are enabled by the emission of a compliant central bank. The great sea of fiat paper dollars is the engine of global financial instability and related speculative fervor, not failed regulation by itself. Blaming financial regulators in the industrial nations for the fact that investors must navigate a largely speculative market is like blaming the police in Venice for the slow but steady subsidence of that ancient city into the Adriatic Sea.

Thus, when Klein recommends that the ideal configuration for effective market governance is "central banks with a combined mandate to control inflation and assure financial stability" as the "default setting", I find myself in strong disagreement, although in functional terms his view is quite efficient and reasonable. It is amazing to me how many members of the regulatory community throw themselves into the arms of efficiency, never realizing that this is directly contrary to the system of checks and balances used by the founders of the U.S. and in many other nations to provide for effective governance — whether of a nation, a regulated industry such as banking, or a corporation. Effective governance requires friction and is therefore not efficient in terms of time, but hopefully in terms of risk-adjusted return on capital (RAROC).

Klein states, "The core issue, then, is how to provide the right combination of autonomy and accountability for the prudential regulator." To this end, he lists some entirely sensible, practical steps to take to make a regulator work well. But to me, Klein is far too trusting and perhaps even a little naive to think that any of the regulatory structures will ever be able to surmount the pressure of politics. In his classic book, *The Mirrors of*

Wall Street, Clinton Gilbert (1933) described the scene as Congress passed the Federal Reserve Act of 1913 and the subsequent two decades:

> It is now almost twenty years since J.P. Morgan and Company, its associates and its satellites attempted to induce Congress to create a central bank of issue instead of the Federal Reserve System. They were determined that control of the national purse should remain in New York. The theory underlying the proposed system that the several sections of the country should control their own finances was preposterous. To them it was anathema. Ten short years later the same group, represented by the same agent who had led their lost cause in Washington, took charge of the Federal Reserve System. For practical purposes the system was transformed into a central bank, and was manipulated to the very ends that its authors had sought to guard against. [pp. 9–10]

Regulatory capture is something that can only be dealt with at the margins because, ultimately, all agencies of government come under the sway of money politics. Over the past two centuries, the U.S. has conducted one of the more remarkable regulatory experiments and has still ended up in 2009 facing one of the most hideous and thoroughly ridiculous financial crises of modern times. There are no "black swans", only failures to perform effective risk management. So when we complain about the failure of regulation and the tendency of regulators to be advocates of (and to be captured by) the industries which they are charged to police, it may be useful to consider that this is a normal situation.

In the nations of the EU, where regulation is supposedly more effective, we have little or no new capital formation or competition in banking. As I am fond of reminding audiences, prior to the moratorium on *de novo* bank charters, U.S. states such as Texas routinely saw the creation of more new banks than in all of Western Europe during a given period of time. In the U.S. banking sector, we arguably had too much capital come into the housing sector and of the wrong kind, fueled by all sorts of tax and regulatory incentives put in place by Congress.

Given a choice between the chaos and political corruption of the U.S. and the statist bureaucracy of the EU, my choice is still the former because it seems to leave the greatest degree of freedom and opportunity for our people, albeit at a great cost in terms of blessed "efficiency". Supposing a perfect regulatory framework is like dreaming about a full-employment economy or a perfect equilibrium in terms of economic policy. These are nice things to argue about over dinner, but they bear little resemblance to the actual conditions in an economy created by human action.

References

Chernow, R. (2001). *The House of Morgan*. New York: Grove Press.

Feldkamp, F. (2009). The miracle of Rule 3a-7, riskless arbitrage and other artifacts of the crisis. *The Institutional Risk Analyst*, October 16.

Gilbert, C. (1933). *The Mirrors of Wall Street*. New York: Putnam & Sons.

Kane, E. (2009). Systemic risk is all about innovation and incentives. *The Institutional Risk Analyst*, November 2.

VIII. POLICY PANEL: WHERE DO WE GO FROM HERE?

Status Quo? I Hardly Think So

Wayne A. Abernathy*
American Bankers Association

Critics of the critics of some of the more radical proposals to change financial regulation claim that the naysayers just want to preserve the status quo. However, that is not what I have seen in the banking industry. I have attended several recent meetings with bankers in various U.S. states. I have asked them, "Who in the room wants the status quo?" I have found few takers. In fact, you will need good hunting dogs to find bankers who favor the status quo. The last thing that bankers want and need is continuation of the status quo, because it is killing us, banks and customers alike.

Two major reforms are needed, one right away and the other as soon as possible. We need to end, right away, the doctrine of "too big to fail". As soon as possible, we need to bring the consumer protection standards of non-banking firms up to the same level in practice as the consumer protection program in which banks operate.

1. End "Too Big to Fail"

A good starting place in addressing the "too big to fail" doctrine is to reject all of the "never again" talk that is so loosely thrown about in public discourse. It reminds me of the dangerous talk in the wake of World War I that what turned out to be a rehearsal for World War II was to be "the war to end all wars". Such kind of loose talk increases systemic risk

* Wayne A. Abernathy is Executive Vice President for Financial Institutions Policy and Regulatory Affairs at the American Bankers Association (ABA), and was formerly Assistant Secretary for Financial Institutions at the Treasury. The views expressed are not necessarily those of the ABA.

by inflating the illusion that we can achieve a system that ends systemic risk, and it increases the public pressure to claim that whatever system is developed has succeeded in creating a new regulatory utopia. It lures people into letting down their guard, convincing people who should not be convinced that our system has solved all of the problems and that risks are contained, or at least that someone else will worry about the risks. Investor worry is good discipline.

We need to learn the lessons of the identifiable mistakes and address them. Equally, we need to have the wisdom to recognize that there will be new challenges, that not all systemic risks will be recognized and resolved in advance. We must resist the temptation to waste time, effort, and resources on building a regulatory Maginot Line. For that reason, our regulatory program needs to be a resilient one. It needs to be a program where adjustment and response to new developments are facilitated.

With that important preliminary point made, I must stress that the "too big to fail" doctrine has to be addressed right away, as investment decisions are being made now on the assumption that it exists. This assumption means that investments made today will be distorted and risks will be underpriced — conditions which will continue until the "too big to fail" doctrine is ended and understood to have been ended.

How do we do that? While the details are the stuff of legislation and regulatory action, in its effective outlines the system should include as its essential ingredient a publicly credible program for unwinding, in an orderly way, *all* financial firms that are failing. Any exception becomes a firm that is seen as "too big to fail" and contributes to the public perception that there are other firms that will not be allowed to fail. So, there can be no exceptions. The banking sector has such a program; and but for the unwise meddling of the Paulson Treasury Department last fall, no failing bank would have been propped up — not to say that any were. Of course, that is the problem: by propping up some institutions and forcing several clearly healthy banks to take the Secretary's shilling, the markets lost any way of knowing for sure which banks were healthy and which were not, so investors abandoned the banking sector *en masse*. Hence, the financial crisis became a financial panic.

What was chiefly missing as 2009 went on was a credible and recognized program, with rules set out and understood in advance, for unwinding systemically significant non-bank financial firms. The markets did not know how the government would respond to a failure of one of these firms. Subsequent government support for Bear Stearns, AIG, and

Fannie Mae and Freddie Mac made "too big to fail" a demonstrably real doctrine (albeit an unpredictable one).

What we need in order to end "too big to fail" is a program that reaches any and all such firms that fail, and that resolves them in a predictable and orderly process that is no less predictable and orderly than the bankruptcy laws. We need an interagency program that draws upon the expertise of the relevant financial agencies, and a resolution authority using the principles of fairness and transparency from the bankruptcy process that can wind down systemically significant failing firms in a way that minimizes systemic risks. For example, systemically significant functions of such firms can be sold and transferred in an orderly way to healthy firms. But, the failing firm — for all the orderliness of the process — must be allowed to fail.

I stress again that the model must be the bankruptcy code, not the Federal Deposit Insurance Act (FDIA). The FDIA was designed to protect insured depositors. This issue does not exist outside of the banking world, and so the FDIA is the wrong model. The bankruptcy code, with its focus on fairness and transparency as well as its resulting investor discipline, is a better model.

1.1 *Do no harm, or at least do no more harm*

While developing and implementing a program to address systemic risk and the resolution of systemically significant firms, policymakers need to avoid doing more harm. In the early 1990s, examination excesses contributed to a credit crunch. Today, there are strong signs that examination practices in the field are repeating that experience. It is hard to make new loans when bank examiners are forcing write-downs and reserves on existing performing loans. Lenders are being taught that it is safer to sit on their funds and buy Treasuries.

Bankers understand this examination cycle, even while they lament it. They understand that we are in a period where all examination calls go against the bank. More troubling are the regulatory proposals that will extend the credit crunch beyond the current economic downturn. Chief among these are the variety of new ways to slice, dice, and rearrange capital standards, all of which mean at bottom more capital to be held by banks. The regulatory authorities seem to be planning to kill banks softly with more capital demands. There seems to be little public recognition by policymakers that more capital is contractionary — capital is a ratio, not an amount; thus, as the return on capital is diminished and capital is made more expensive, banks will increasingly be forced to improve capital ratios by reducing assets.

The banking industry recognizes that risk-based capital models have not advanced to the point where they can reliably predict and flawlessly measure risk. We recognize that the leverage ratio plays an important role in covering model risk and risks that are unforeseen or unpredictable. However, more capital cannot be the regulatory cure-all. My former colleague from the Treasury Department, Peter Fisher, recently wrote an essay in a very interesting book in which he warns that the emphasis on capital can distract from the importance of quality supervision. There is not enough capital for a loan that goes bad:

> After a quarter century of developing ever-more complex risk-based capital rules, it turns out that if you lend money to someone who cannot pay you back, it does not matter whether you hold six, eight, or ten percent capital against that loan because you will end up with losses and be undercapitalized in any event. ... In the absence of greater underwriting discipline, higher capital requirements will make our banking system less efficient but will not make it more stable. [Fisher, 2009, pp. 34–35]

Recognize the reduced return on capital that comes from higher capital ratios. Recognize the negative impact on the availability of capital from a reduced return on capital. Recognize the deflationary impact of making capital harder to get. Yes, capital is king, but do not make it a tyrant.

2. Protect Consumers, Don't Control Them

As I mentioned, we need as soon as possible to bring the consumer protection standards of non-bank financial service providers up to the standards that prevail in the world of bank supervision. Unfortunately, the Obama administration has instead proposed to build a new Washington bureaucracy: the Consumer Financial Protection Agency (CFPA). This radical and risky new scheme, if adopted, would control consumers as much (or more) as it would regulate banks. It would stifle lending, particularly consumer lending. It would also harm businesses that rely upon consumer lending, including retail, entertainment, and travel businesses, as well as small businesses that get much of their working capital from consumer credit sources. To borrow a metaphor from a friend of mine, creating the CFPA would be like planting a kudzu vine in a rose garden. The CFPA is structured like a kudzu: without any checks, it prospers and spreads everywhere, but the roses are smothered.

A chief flaw in the radical CFPA proposal is that it would artificially tear consumer protection away from safety and soundness supervision. This would be harmful to the program of bank supervision and would be destabilizing to the banking system. Regulations of the same products offered by the same institutions would come from separate agencies with separate institutional interests, creating regulatory conflicts that do not exist today. Each supervisory function would be administered by regulators made partially blind by statute, looking at only a part of the whole regulatory picture.

Few financial services do not involve both consumer protection and safety and soundness issues. Therefore, the integrity of those supervisory concerns should be reflected in the supervisory program. Separating them would weaken both elements of supervision, and the confusion would cause banks to retrench in order to reduce the exposure to regulatory risk.

Rather than responding to chronic weaknesses in consumer protection that arise in the non-banking world by embarking on another round of federal institution building, efforts should focus on using the regulatory agencies and tools at hand and strengthening them as necessary. This will bring better consumer protection sooner compared to spending the next several years creating a new bureaucracy that will cripple bank supervision and weaken existing consumer protection.

3. Deliver Us from the Status Quo

Let me conclude with a story from the famous Bennett Cerf (1945). Longtime editor at Random House, Cerf had a lifelong hobby of collecting humorous stories. I find one from his collection to be metaphorical for the current condition of the banking industry:

> A man gave his son a sound box on the ears in the day coach of a New Haven train one morning, and an outraged lady who sat behind him pointed her umbrella at him and said, “If you don’t stop abusing that boy, I am going to make trouble for you.”

> The man gave a hollow, mirthless laugh. "Lady," he said, "my wife just ran away with the ice man. The bank foreclosed my mortgage yesterday. We are on the wrong train. My son just told me he swallowed the tickets. And you're going to make trouble for me?" [Cerf, 1945, pp. 39–40]

No, we do not want any more of the status quo. What the banking industry does want and need, what we all need right away, is to end the current "too big to fail" doctrine made all too real in recent months. To do that, we must have a recognized program to resolve and wind down any failing financial firm. What the banking industry does want and need, what we all need as soon as possible, are effectively enforced and uniform consumer protection standards that bring non-bank consumer performance up to the standards applied to the banking industry. To do that, we must have a program that focuses on the real problems, where standards are chronically low. What none of us needs is a new consumer control bureaucracy that — with what Charles Dickens called "rapacious benevolence" — would destroy the consumer financial system that has progressively provided more and better financial products to more people, at lower costs, than anywhere else on earth.

References

Cerf, B. (1945). *Laughing Stock.* New York: Grosset & Dunlap.

Fisher, P. R. (2009). The market view: incentives matter. In Ciorciari, J. D. and J. B. Taylor (eds.), *The Road Ahead for the Fed*, Stanford, CA: Hoover Institution Press, 33–48.

Where Do We Go from Here?

Anil K Kashyap*
University of Chicago

1. Introduction

It is a treat to be able to participate in this capstone session of this conference. I am grateful to the organizers for including me.

The title of the conference asks, "Have the rules of finance changed?" I say no; most of what happened can be understood using standard analytical frameworks. However, this does not mean that regulation has kept up with innovations in how we think about finance, so there are many reforms that are needed.

To organize my call for reform, I will proceed in three steps. First, I want to identify a few of the places where I think regulation has lagged. Next, I announce four principles to guide us to fill in the gaps in the regulatory toolkit. Finally, I will close with some specific suggestions. Most of the specifics come from the Squam Lake Group that has developed. But, I do not want to hold the Squam Lake Group or any of the other organizations with which I am affiliated accountable for what I am about to say.

---

* Anil K Kashyap is the Edward Eagle Brown Professor of Economics and Finance at the University of Chicago's Booth School of Business. Research support was provided by the Initiative on Global Markets. These remarks were prepared for the 12th annual International Banking Conference, Federal Reserve Bank of Chicago and World Bank, September 25, 2009. Many of the ideas presented here draw on the work of the Squam Lake Working Group on Financial Regulation. The author thanks Darrell Duffie, Mark Mitchell, Douglas Diamond, Raghuram Rajan, and Jeremy Stein for helpful conversations. These remarks reflect only the author's personal views and all errors are his own.

2. Back to Basics

One of the peculiarities of this crisis is the path by which we arrived at it. The crisis came after roughly 25 years of relative macroeconomic stability. The bulk of research within central banks had shifted to studying inflation determination. The workhorse models used by central bankers mostly ignored the financial system. This is especially ironic in the U.S., since the Chairman of the Board of Governors of the Federal Reserve System was among the most prominent advocates of paying more attention to the role of financial factors in monetary transmission.

But Chairman Bernanke held a minority view, and most macro models reflected the view that the Modigliani–Miller view of capital structure was approximately correct. By that, I mean that the liability side of a firm's balance sheet was irrelevant. There was no need to figure out financing arrangements for firms (and, by implication, banks) because financing constraints were unimportant. More precisely, the structure of liabilities would not change anything about the cash flows generated by an enterprise or its value. I think the crisis has taught us that this approximation is woefully inadequate.[1]

In deciding what we missed, it is helpful to recall the three assumptions that must be maintained for the Modigliani–Miller capital-structure irrelevance proposition to prevail. Berk and DeMarzo (2007) describe them as follows:

(1) Investors and firms can trade the same set of securities at competitive market prices equal to the present value of their future cash flows;
(2) There are no taxes, transaction costs, or issuance costs associated with securities trading; and
(3) A firm's financing decisions do not change the cash flows generated by its investments, nor do they reveal new information about them.

Many of the unexpected and confusing aspects of the crisis came from underestimating the transaction costs associated with bankruptcy, and from not appreciating how financing decisions do change cash flows.

---

[1] Given the central role of financial factors in the Great Depression, the "lost decade" in Japan, and the financial crisis of the last two years, I predict a paradigm shift such that the financial system will be included in standard macro models in the future.

Because of the short time, I will focus on leverage and the role it played in the crisis. I make this choice because I believe the failure to understand the forces that contributed to a build-up of leverage in the financial system — and costs of unwinding the leverage — was probably the biggest mistake we (academics, policymakers, practitioners, and the media) made.

3. Frictions Begat Leverage

There are several ways in which the failure of the Modigliani–Miller assumptions contributed to leverage. First, leading theories of banking give a special role to the value of funding banks with short-term obligations. The most recent work in this area, by my colleagues Douglas Diamond and Raghuram Rajan,[2] explains why having demandable debt serves as a disciplinary device for banks that allows them to undertake more lending than if they were financed differently. Put differently, banks have a good reason for having plenty of short-term debt in their capital structure.

Second, banks specialize in activities that are difficult for outside parties to monitor. Unlike an operating company, a bank can transform the risks it faces very quickly. Investors that take an equity position in a bank, therefore, are exposed to much more managerial discretion with how the funds might be used than would be the case for a typical operating company whose risks are relatively well understood. The possibility of management not acting purely in the interest of shareholders is another departure from the Modigliani–Miller assumptions that seems particularly salient for financial institutions. This force also pushes banks to have more debt and less equity.

Once we understand that banks have good reasons for high leverage, several additional implications follow immediately. First, if capital regulation simply seeks to push banks to hold more capital, they will likely try to avoid the regulation. The amount of equity in their capital structure is not a matter of indifference. Many of the complicated off-balance-sheet entities that were created over the last few years were a natural response to the regulations, which had much lower capital charges for off-balance-sheet assets than for assets held on the balance sheet.

---

[2] See Douglas W. Diamond and Raghuram G. Rajan (2000) for a summary of this thinking.

Second, with high leverage, a loss that might be small relative to a bank's total assets or loans can still be large relative to the bank's equity. The trigger for the recent financial crisis was losses on low-quality mortgages. Many believed that the impact of these losses would be limited because the total eventual losses would be in hundreds of billions — the kind of loss that routinely occurs for the collection of investors who own U.S. publicly traded firms. Had the losses been spread across a disperse set of investors, the impact probably would have been contained. But, with substantial holdings residing on the balance sheets of highly levered financial institutions, the impact was much larger (Greenlaw *et al.*, 2008).

Once the banks realized that their exposure put much of their capital at risk, they began trying to bring the risk of their assets in line with their remaining equity. In principle, they could have responded by holding onto their assets and simply raising equity. But raising equity was costly, especially when uncertainty of the assets' value was high. So, the banks began reducing assets. We learned during this crisis that de-leveraging through the shedding of assets was not costless.

These costs stem from the fact that bank credit appears to be special. The Modigliani–Miller assumptions imply that, when a bank decides to de-lever and not to roll over a loan, the borrower simply obtains the funds through another source. Especially after the failure of Lehman Brothers, however, bank credit declined precipitously and economic activity slowed sharply. Apparently, it was not easy for most borrowers who lost bank credit to make it up immediately from other sources (Ivashina and Scharfstein, 2010).

The Lehman Brothers failure (and the associated chaos in financial markets) has also suggested that bankruptcy for a large, complex organization is expensive. For some of the other megabanks engulfed in the crisis, a bankruptcy under existing rules appears to be infeasible. For instance, for Citigroup the complicated legal structure of its international subsidiaries would make it impossible to seize the entire institution and be able to secure control of all its (and its customers') assets. Moreover, the agreements governing its derivatives contracts would greatly raise the cost of declaring the institution bankrupt; all contracts of a failed firm must allow its counterparty to recover the market value of a counterparty's position. This means that winning and losing trades would be settled at disadvantaged prices. Finally, because customers of financial institutions can run at the mere hint of trouble, it may not be possible for a large organization with many subsidiaries that have many interlocking liabilities to salvage any value in potentially viable subsidiaries. Thus, recovering potential value in the non-bank parts of a holding company to support a bank subsidiary may be difficult.

In addition to any direct losses in the Lehman Brothers failure, another consequence was the collapse of the market for convertible debt (Mitchell and Pulvino, 2009). When Lehman declared bankruptcy, convertible bonds represented a great deal of the collateral that its counterparties received. Any hedges that Lehman had that reduced the risk of these securities, however, were not transferred to the counterparties. This left the counterparties exposed to considerable risk and many chose to immediately sell the bonds. Over the next weeks, trading volume surged and prices crashed. This provides perhaps the best example of a fire sale (defined loosely as a collapse of prices below fundamental value due to the inability to absorb a surge in supply).

4. Some Guiding Principles for Regulatory Reform

Based on these observations, we can identify several problems with current regulations that could be addressed in reforms. Let me focus on four issues:

(1) The standard Chapter 11-style bankruptcy rules for handling a failing firm do not work well for banks. Thus, some special rules to guide the bankruptcy process are needed.
(2) Anticipating that a failure will be expensive, it is prudent to adjust regulations to reduce those costs (conditional on a failure) or to make failure less likely. Banks that have large amounts of short-term debt are more fragile. Banks with lots of illiquid assets will be more expensive to unwind on short notice. Banks that have more counterparties and are more interconnected in the financial system will be more expensive to resolve. Regulation can take account of all of these observations.
(3) De-leveraging is costly, but more so for society if a bank responds to a shock by shrinking its balance sheet. Proposals that lead banks to rebuild equity rather than sell assets should be preferred.
(4) The de-leveraging during a bust in part reflects market requirements for lower leverage. A free market financial system is procyclical in that more capital will likely be required during bad times than during good times. Thus, even absent regulation, banks would be less able to lend in recessions than in booms.

5. Some Specific Suggestions

These observations, in turn, yield a set of specific suggestions for reform that naturally complement each other. All that I will describe seek to reduce the likelihood or costs of de-leveraging and/or reduce the likelihood or costs of bank failure.

The first proposal is to amend capital regulation to reflect the externalities mentioned earlier. Capital standards should vary based on the proportion of short-term debt, the illiquidity of assets, and bank size. Yet, even if these changes are implemented, during a downturn the ability to continue to attract funding may require the bank to have higher capital than during normal times (French *et al.*, 2010).

This market constraint implies that there will be limits to using time-varying capital requirements to battle de-leveraging. High regulatory capital requirements during good times might constrain a bank from increasing leverage, but cutting capital requirements during a recession might not lead to additional lending. In order for this to be feasible, the regulatory capital requirement during good times would have to be higher than the market requirements during bad times.

Kashyap and Stein (2009) offer a proposal that might be modified to address this issue. They suggest that the central bank issue "capital forbearance certificates", which could be counted towards regulatory capital. These certificates would be supplied to the market and traded amongst banks. By supplying a large quantity of these certificates, a regulatory capital requirement could be set very high (say, 20%). Each bank would be prohibited from substituting too many of the certificates for actual equity. The market would not worry about the presence of the certificates and the artificially high regulatory requirement in normal times because the banking system would be massively overcapitalized relative to what debt holders would require to provide financing. As trouble develops and market capital requirements creep up, the value of the certificates would rise. The price of these certificates would reveal to regulators that the shadow value of capital is rising. At that point, the regulators could decide to lower regulatory requirements or have an objective market price to guide other decisions.

These permits could complement other policies to limit the adverse effects of de-leveraging. One element could be some debt that would be converted into equity in certain circumstances. Flannery (2005) proposed that a conversion occur for any bank experiencing distress. Kashyap *et al.* (2008) suggest that conversion occur only when the aggregate bank system is in trouble (as measured by industry loan losses). French *et al.* (2010) propose conversion when two conditions are satisfied: first, there must be an industry-wide capital shortage (as declared by a systemic regulator); second, an individual bank must be in trouble. While there are some important differences in how these triggers would work, any of these securities would help combat de-leveraging.

A third proposal is to amend the regulations to reduce the costs of distressed institutions. Ideally, a new, special set of bankruptcy rules would be proposed that would work for all major financial institutions. These changes would need to deal with the problems related to the connections between subsidiaries and bank holding companies. The new rules should also deal with the complications that arise because of the master swap agreements for derivatives. Ideally, the changes would eventually handle the cross-border problems too. But since any international harmonization of bankruptcy rules will take time, it would be preferable to have a flexible set of rules that work as well as possible given existing international constraints.

In addition to reforming the bankruptcy code, the regulators could force banks to spend more time contemplating how a resolution might proceed if it were to become necessary. These living wills would include a full description of a bank's ownership and organizational structure (including interlinkages), its assets, liabilities, contractual obligations, and the jurisdictions covering all of the above. They would also describe the cross-guarantees tied to different securities, a list of major counterparties, and a process for determining where the firm's collateral is pledged. The bank should be required to sketch a few major distress scenarios and the likely resolution processes under each scenario. Finally, the bank would be asked to provide a list of potential parties who could take over the institution's contractual obligations at low cost.

The living will would include an estimate of how long it would take to take control of the institution and begin the process of closing it. Banks that require more time could be required to hold more capital. The extra resolution time presumably would mean that taxpayers face more risk if the bank were to fail; charging the bank in advance for this possibility is therefore appropriate. The capital charge would also give the bank's management an incentive to reduce its complexity. Currently, there is little in the regulatory system that pushes back against complexity.

6. Conclusions

I have tried to make three basic points that we can discuss further during the question-and-answer period. First, it is appropriate to rethink our approach to regulation from first principles. Second, in my attempt to do so, the problems associated with de-leveraging and high resolution costs stand out as not being handled well by existing rules. Any reforms should tackle these problems head on. Finally, there are now many good, specific suggestions for how to get started on these reforms.

References

Berk, J. and P. DeMarzo (2007). *Corporate Finance*. Boston: Pearson/ Addison-Wesley.

Diamond, D. W. and R. G. Rajan (2000). A theory of bank capital. *Journal of Finance*, 55(6), 2431–2465.

Flannery, M. (2005). No pain, no gain? Effecting market discipline via reverse convertible debentures. In Scott, H. S. (ed.), *Capital Adequacy Beyond Basel: Banking Securities and Insurance*, Oxford: Oxford University Press, Ch. 5.

French, K. R. *et al.* (2010). *The Squam Lake Report: Fixing the Financial System*. Princeton: Princeton University Press.

Greenlaw, D., J. Hatzius, A. K. Kashyap, and H. S. Shin (2008). *Leveraged Losses: Lessons from the Mortgage Market Meltdown*. U.S. Monetary Policy Forum Report No. 2. Rosenberg Institute, Brandeis International Business School and Initiative on Global Markets, University of Chicago Graduate School of Business.

Ivashina, V. and D. Scharfstein (2010). Bank lending during the financial crisis of 2008. *Journal of Financial Economics*, 97, 319–338.

Kashyap, A. K., R. G. Rajan, and J. C. Stein (2008). Rethinking capital regulation. In *Maintaining Stability in a Changing Financial System*, Kansas City: Federal Reserve Bank of Kansas City, 431–471.

Kashyap, A. K. and J. C. Stein (2009). A cap(ital) and trade proposal for banking. Work in progress.

Mitchell, M. and T. Pulvino (2009). Slow and fast moving capital: the arbitrage crash of 2008. Unpublished mimeo.

Suggested Financial Structure for Developing Countries

Justin Yifu Lin*
World Bank

This conference has, in the last two days, hosted a very good discussion about the need to improve the incentive system in the financial sector so as to make the incentives of a financial institution's managers compatible with those of its investors; in this way, financial institutions will be self-disciplined. In addition, many commentators have pointed to the need for strengthening regulations in order to make financial institutions more accountable. While economists may not agree with each other, both adequate incentives and better regulations are desirable.

However, as I am from the World Bank, I would like to ask, "Is the current direction in financial markets in advanced economies the right direction to go for a developing country?" It may not be the right direction. My remarks derive from my paper, "Toward a theory of optimal financial structure," where I argued that there is an optimal financial structure that is compatible with each stage of a country's development process (see Lin *et al.*, 2009). In particular, we know that the financial structure in developed countries is dominated by large banks and equity markets. There, credit and equity markets are subject to usual information asymmetries and moral hazard problems that require adequate regulations and mechanisms to make managers' and investors' incentives compatible. We also know that the complexity of the new financial products has made the prudential relationship between assets in balance sheets and equity more complicated, perhaps too complicated to regulate. In addition, we delved in the recent past into prudential deregulation together with the emergence of financial techniques so complex that bank management was not able to

* Justin Yifu Lin is Senior Vice President and Chief Economist of the World Bank.

fully understand the risk implications: modern financial markets embodied all kinds of market failures. But even if we can improve institutions, incentives, and regulations to effectively avoid moral hazard problems in the large bank/equity market-dominated financial system in developed countries, is this financial system the right model for a developing country?

We know that, in a typical developing country, very large portions of production activities (i.e., employment) are provided by either small agricultural households or small- and medium-sized enterprises in the manufacturing and service sectors. Moreover, we know that under the current large bank/equity market-dominated financial system, small agricultural households, small manufacturing firms, and small service firms get only very limited access to financial services despite their needs. This failure is a reality in almost all developing countries, even though small- and medium-sized enterprises and agricultural households are important to achieve the country's sustainable and inclusive growth objectives. This is because the sectors they operate in are typically consistent with the country's comparative advantage, which is the foundation for competitive advantage. The government does not need to give those sectors too much protection or subsidies. Since they are consistent with the country's comparative advantage, their products and services can compete domestically and internationally. At the same time, these small enterprises can contribute to economic inclusiveness because they provide jobs, and it is mainly when you provide jobs to people that they receive the benefits of development. Hence, it is critical to build an institutional framework that helps these small firms to access financial services, achieve their goals, and sustain employment and growth.

However, under our current mindset, our tendency as regards financial development is to encourage developing countries to build financial institutions that are similar to those in developed countries, i.e., to favor large banks and/or equity markets. Now, given the above-mentioned shortcomings of this model, we might have a chance with the financial crisis to revisit this approach and to clearly spell out the desirable objective(s) and financial structure for an inclusive growth pattern in developing countries.

We know that, in high-income developed countries, large banks and/or equity markets are the major financing vehicles. Those financial arrangements are appropriate in developed countries because the majority of production activities there are undertaken by large corporations, whose technologies are located on the global technology frontier. They require large amounts of capital for operations, and need to invest in risky R&D for technology and product innovations. In such a framework, you need large banks to provide the required capital and/or equity markets to be able to spread and offset risks.

Now, if you look at the history of high-income countries, you find that, in the early stages of their development process, most firms were small- and medium-sized and financial institutions in these economies were small local banks. Some of those small local banks gradually grew or consolidated into big banks, and then eventually equity markets emerged because production activities became gradually dominated by large enterprises and the risk nature of their production activities changed. Those changes in the financial system were consistent with the evolving reality of the real economy. Moreover, in developed countries today, small firms still have small- and medium-sized local banks to serve them. However, if you look at developing countries today, their financial structure is different: you hardly see small local banks. This is a very important challenge for developing countries today.

The proposal advocating the need to develop small and local banks in developing countries might be criticized. It is true that today there is more competition in local financial markets with the entry of foreign banks, as well as new technological changes that affect risk assessment. Surely it can be acknowledged that technological change and competition may help to improve access to financial services, and that this should force large banks with modern financial instruments to service enterprises smaller than they would otherwise do. Therefore, with more competition and new technology, large banks may be able to serve more medium-sized enterprises. However, consider the following: when we rank firms in terms of size in developing countries, we obtain a pyramid. The big firms on top are only a small number; and then going gradually down in size, the number of firms increases to constitute the base of the pyramid. The problem is that financial services start from the top, covering all large firms, after which supply gradually fades. The medium-sized firms and smaller agricultural firms at the bottom of the pyramid hardly get any financial service, even when we observe competition between banks for new market share with more sophisticated technologies.

Hence, how do we answer the question of "where do we go from here" from the viewpoint of developing countries? My answer is that, first and foremost, we need to realize that developing countries need to change their financial structure from the present one, which is currently dominated by large banks and equity markets. A first suggestion is that developing countries need to favor the emergence and/or entry of local small- and medium-sized banks, which should form the core of their financial system. A second suggestion for developing countries is that they also need to solve the issue of incentive compatibility and make their financial institutions' behavior accountable. However, the incentive and accountability problems faced by small- and medium-sized banks are different from those faced by big banks. Small- and medium-sized local banks tend to be operated by their owners using family-business models, whereas large banks have professional management staff. In both cases, there are principal–agent problems, but the nature of the problem is different and so the regulatory framework should also be different. Unfortunately, no matter in Basel II or in Basel I, such differences are not taken into account. Therefore, financial regulations need to be specifically designed and adapted to this suggested structure of financial institutions in developing countries. In addition, we need to allow financial institutions in developing countries to evolve as their economy gradually evolves. By having a financial structure that is closer to the development stage of a country's productive structure, it is possible not only to avoid financial crises in developing countries but also to achieve the goal of sustainable and more inclusive growth.

Thank you.

Reference

Lin, J. Y., X. Sun, and J. Jiang (2009). Toward a theory of optimal financial structure. World Bank Policy Research Working Paper No. 5038.

Comments on "Where Do We Go from Here?"

Deborah J. Lucas*
MIT Sloan School of Management

"You never want a serious crisis to go to waste. And what I mean by that is an opportunity to do things you think you could not do before."

– Rahm Emanuel, February 2009

I would like to touch briefly on two issues in answer to the question posed for this session: first, the integration of housing finance into the financial and regulatory mainstream; and second, the need to modernize budgetary and regulatory accounting. I have chosen these topics for several reasons. They are important, they get less attention than is deserved, and I have thought quite a bit about them from both an academic and policy perspective.

For those of us who have long worried about Fannie Mae and Freddie Mac — in particular, their spectacular political and market power, their lack of transparency, and the costs and risks to taxpayers associated with their implicit guarantee — the crisis has opened up the tantalizing possibility of rationalizing the structure and regulation of housing finance. Yet, although it is widely agreed that the housing bubble precipitated the financial crisis and that Fannie and Freddie posed a serious systemic risk as "too big to fail" institutions, there is still no official, articulated vision for how housing finance will be structured and regulated in the future. When these issues are mentioned at all, it is usually outside of the broader context of any regulatory restructuring of banking and financial markets. The omission can be seen, for instance, in a series of Treasury proposals for restructuring the financial system — both under the previous

* Deborah J. Lucas is a professor of finance at MIT's Sloan School of Management and a research associate at the National Bureau of Economic Research.

administration and under this one — that are largely silent on the regulation of housing finance (U.S. Department of the Treasury, 2009). Avoidance is also evident in the current state of the Federal Housing Finance Agency (FHFA). The FHFA has been left with the peculiar task of regulating Fannie and Freddie, which are now effectively federal entities themselves; and regulating the Federal Home Loan Banks, institutions that serve as wholesale liquidity providers to financial institutions (Ashcraft *et al.*, 2009) but that have only an indirect effect on housing finance.[1]

There are, of course, many proposals for housing finance reform that have been put forward by researchers working in academia, government agencies, think tanks, and advocacy groups. However, the ghosts of Fannie Mae and Freddie Mac, together with the legacy of regulatory segregation, seem to constrain the set of possibilities that are seriously under consideration. The proposals often presume a continuation of the pre-crisis model of a small number of dedicated conforming mortgage securitizers, guarantors, and regulators (e.g., Government Accountability Office, 2009; Mortgage Bankers Association, 2009). Policy options are taken to be the extent of government backing for mortgage-backed securities (MBS), with options ranging from total privatization to full federal guarantees.

A priority I would suggest going forward, then, is a fundamental rethinking of the structure and regulation of housing finance (in both the primary and secondary mortgage markets), including consideration of to what extent it can be integrated into the financial and regulatory mainstream. To quote recent comments by James Lockhart that were made in reaction to a Government Accountability Office (GAO) options paper, we "should consider what the secondary market should look like before considering specific institutions." He goes on to suggest that "one such possibility would be a market characterized by many privately owned issuers of MBS with the government providing insurance against catastrophic losses, either directly or in partnership with private companies" (Lockhart, 2009).

Certainly, there are industrial organization and political economy reasons to favor solutions like the one sketched by Lockhart, which reduce market concentration and make explicit the extent of government backing. If that were to occur, a case can be made — although the Fed has argued against it in the past and Lockhart certainly did not suggest it in his comments — for reassigning the oversight responsibilities of the FHFA to

[1] The FHFA is also without a permanent director. James Lockhart, who was appointed by President Bush to direct the FHFA at its inception, recently resigned.

a regulator with broader safety and soundness responsibilities, perhaps avoiding some of the vulnerability to political interference of a dedicated housing regulator.

Turning to my second suggestion for what urgently needs to come next, it is to modernize budgetary and regulatory accounting. I realize that this is not on everyone's top 10 fix-it list; and although it would be a stretch to claim that ill-conceived accounting rules are largely to blame for the financial crisis, I believe they have significantly exacerbated it. Going forward, failure to correct the structural flaws in government accounting will make it more difficult for the federal government to understand, and to extricate itself from, the extensive credit market obligations it has recently assumed. Regulatory reforms will also be less effective than they otherwise might be.

I want to elaborate on these assertions by way of several specific examples. First, accounting rules determine the budget cost of federal financial obligations. If budget rules cause the cost of a policy to be understated, there will be a tendency to over-rely on that policy. An obvious example was the implicit guarantee of Fannie Mae, Freddie Mac, and the Federal Home Loan Banks, which allowed housing policy to be executed through these entities at zero budget cost but with a substantial hidden cost to taxpayers. In fact, this is often emphasized as contributing to the lack of political will to control their growth.

Although not as dramatic as for implicit guarantees, the rules of budget accounting cause the cost of all federal credit assistance to be systematically understated in the budget relative to the market value of those commitments (Lucas and Phaup, 2008). By law, loans and loan guarantees are valued without any adjustment for a market risk premium; in other words, they are discounted at too low an interest rate. The discrepancies between budget cost and economic value can be large. For instance, in the case of student loans, recent estimates suggest that the inclusion of a risk premium increases the subsidy rate by more than 20 cents per dollar of loans originated (Lucas and Moore, 2010).

Interestingly, recognition that complying with the normal budget rules for credit would result in a severe understatement of the economic cost of the Troubled Asset Relief Program (TARP) led to an exemption in that legislation, which allowed it to be accounted for using risk-adjusted discount rates. Similarly, the Congressional Budget Office (CBO) reports on the cost of Fannie Mae and Freddie Mac by adjusting for the cost of risk. Had it not done so, the eventual transfer of the activities of Fannie and

Freddie back to the private sector would likely appear to come at a significant cost to the government, making a difficult separation even more problematic. Still, this accounting bias remains in place for most credit activities, including the much-expanded guarantee obligations of the Federal Housing Administration (FHA) going forward.

A second, distinct, reason to be concerned with accounting conventions is that regulations are communicated in terms of accounting numbers, and compliance is measured against them. Hedge accounting can be particularly problematic in this regard. Anecdotal evidence suggests that when the two are at odds, financial institutions choose to hedge regulatory risk, not economic risk. This results in greater risk and expenses for institutions and taxpayers than if accounting conventions were more closely aligned with economic principles.

A final example arises from the acrimonious debate over mark-to-market or fair value accounting rules. Before the crisis, Financial Accounting Standards Board (FASB) rules and international accounting authorities were marching steadily towards a greater embrace of fair value concepts, and recent reports suggest that this trend will likely resume. These developments are welcomed by many economists, including myself. Market prices are generally the best available measure of economic value, they are forward-looking and aggregate private information, and they are reasonably hard to manipulate in active securities markets.

The crisis brought about a plunge in market values, a disappearance of market prices for many securities, and angry calls from bankers to abandon ruinous fair value rules. Like many of my academic peers, my initial reaction was dismissive: if bankers had accepted the high valuations on the upside, why the uproar on the downside? Upon further reflection, and in a recent Carnegie–Rochester paper written with John Heaton and Robert McDonald (Heaton *et al.*, 2010), we suggest that placing blame on fair value accounting is misplaced, but that real costs are incurred when these accounting rules interact with regulatory capital requirements. It is the static nature of regulatory capital requirements, which have not responded to the greater earnings volatility that accompanies fair value accounting, that may deserve the blame. Over time, capital requirements are periodically revised by bank regulators, as is the FASB's definition of capital, but the two types of regulatory actions are not coordinated. A sensible solution to the problems caused by the interaction of more volatile, market-based capital measures and a static capital requirement would be for regulators to periodically redefine the capital requirements in order to neutralize unwanted side effects of changes in financial accounting standards, and to allow them to continue to evolve in a direction that provides better information to markets and regulators.

References

Ashcraft, A., M. Bech, and S. Frame (2009). The Federal Home Loan Bank System: the lender of next-to-last resort? Manuscript, Federal Reserve Bank of Atlanta.

Government Accountability Office (2009). *Fannie Mae and Freddie Mac: Analysis of Options for Revising the Housing Enterprises' Long-Term Structures.* GAO Report to Congressional Committees, GAO-09-782.

Heaton, J., D. Lucas, and R. McDonald (2010). Is mark-to-market accounting destabilizing? Analysis and implications for policy. *Journal of Monetary Economics*, 57, 64–75.

Lockhart, J. (2009). Comment letter on: Government Accountability Office (2009), *Fannie Mae and Freddie Mac: Analysis of Options for Revising the Housing Enterprises' Long-Term Structures*, GAO Report to Congressional Committees, GAO-09-782.

Lucas, D. and D. Moore (2010). Guaranteed vs. direct lending: the case of student loans. In Lucas, D. (ed.), *Measuring and Managing Federal Financial Risk*, Chicago: University of Chicago Press, 163–205.

Lucas, D. and M. Phaup (2008). Reforming credit reform. *Public Budgeting and Finance*, 28, 90–110.

Mortgage Bankers Association (2009). MBA's recommendations for the future government role in the core secondary mortgage market. MBA Council on Ensuring Mortgage Liquidity.

U.S. Department of the Treasury (2009). *Financial Regulatory Reform: A New Foundation.* Available at http://www.financialstability.gov/docs/regs/FinalReport_web.pdf/.

Where to from Here? Have the Rules of Finance Changed?

John Silvia*
Wells Fargo & Co.

I wish to thank Professor Kaufman for the opportunity to speak at this conference and for the chance to catch up with some longtime friends.

In line with this conference's theme, I will highlight some of the ways in which the rules have changed. But even more so and with great disappointment, I will highlight how much the underlying economic and political forces have not changed.

First, in contrast to the views expressed by a previous speaker, I see no reason why stress tests and risk simulations cannot account for the boom/bust cycles of the economy and the financial system. Moreover, both economic and financial cycles can be (and are) integrated in a Bayesian vector autoregression model which, in fact, we do work with at Wells Fargo. This approach to stress testing is far superior to the common approach of merely changing one input, often the federal funds rate or the unemployment rate, and then producing a scenario that represents a "valuable" test to a financial institution. Such one-variable tests are unrealistic, as we know very well that the real world will often experience several economic series changes moving at the same time. For example, a lower/higher federal funds rate is accompanied by changes in the inflation, growth, and exchange rates as well.

Second, one factor in the economy that has not changed is the underlying social/political bias in public policy towards housing that has been part of our society for most of the post-WWII era. America's overinvestment in housing has been a chronic complaint, with this overinvestment being assisted by federal and state tax laws, bank regulatory policy, and credit/interest rate subsidies. This has not changed in

* John Silvia is Chief Economist at Wells Fargo & Co.

recent years; in fact, the trend has continued this year with the increase in Federal Housing Administration (FHA) loans offered in recent months at below market rates or with very low down payment requirements, even as delinquency rates rise on these same FHA loans.

Third, we have witnessed a change in the short run, but without resolution in the long run, of the Fed's role as policeman in the credit markets. Increased liquidity at the short end of the yield curve has brought down Libor and TED spreads, but are these short rates too low given that current yields are below those of the often-criticized pre-Lehman Brothers period? What about long-term rates? Currently, the Fed has indicated that it will reduce its support for Treasuries by the end of October and will gradually withdraw support for mortgage-backed and asset-backed securities by March of next year. Will the Fed's involvement in these markets really diminish in the face of relatively high unemployment and a likely upward move for interest rates in general?

Fourth, the zero interest rate policy at the Fed has already signaled a change in global financing, as the U.S. is increasingly finding itself as the source of borrowing in a global carry trade with lending and investing abroad. Moreover, this zero interest rate policy returns policy to the pre-1951 Treasury–Fed Accord period and brings into question whether such a policy is consistent with an independent central bank. At this time in the business cycle, Federal Reserve intervention has created a set of below-market interest rates in many financial instruments. These rates are likely to move up as the Federal Reserve exits. Therefore, it is very difficult to know if financial markets have indeed better accounted for risk in setting interest rates.

Fifth, the massive intervention and support for the housing market has brought into question whether public policy has really moved away from the overallocation of capital to housing. Almost 10 years ago, Wayne Abernathy, Linda Lord, and I wrote a new legislation replacing the Humphrey–Hawkins language with new language on monetary policy and there was no special place for housing or consumer credit as a goal. Yet, the focus of policy today appears to place too strong an orientation to supporting these markets.

Sixth, as outlined by Charles Calomiris in his paper, there appears to be little change in the policy environment that gave rise to the subprime crisis. As stated in that paper, "The predictable risk-taking mistakes of financial managers were not the result of random mass insanity; rather, they reflected a policy environment that strongly encouraged financial managers to underestimate risk in the subprime mortgage market."[1] Calomiris cites the lending subsidies and policies that promoted risky mortgages, and yet such policies continue today.

Seventh, as outlined by Professor Goodhart, greater regulation of banking in America will generate several side effects. These include a movement of bank capital offshore, an increase in shadow banking, and a move of trading operations in commodities and foreign exchange abroad. Limits on compensation for energy traders in New York, for example, will provide incentives to move such trading operations abroad.

Eighth, American experience does support the view that regulation crowds out good due diligence by the consumer, as Professor Goodhart also mentioned in his presentation. Recent increases in the maximum coverage of deposit insurance have discouraged consumer vigilance, and run counter to the lessons of the savings and loan credit crunch as well as a long history of economic research. In addition, advocates of market discipline had historically called upon the use of subordinated bank debt as a discipline on risk taking, but that approach, too, has been forgotten. Instead, we have witnessed increasingly complex consumer regulations and the proliferation of complex, fine-print disclosure documents on credit cards and mortgages that are seldom read by consumers. We can recall our own experience in recent years, as we frequently just discard the many privacy disclosure statements we receive without reading them.

Ninth, one comment at this conference reflected, at least to me, a significant change in attitude about the incentives associated with regulation. The commentator asserted that regulatory competition produces the worst result. In contrast, the belief had been that regulatory competition would avoid the worst tendencies of governments to over-regulate. These same attitudes are reflected in many countries today with respect to the tax harmonization debate.

Tenth, another change in attitude that has crept into our economics profession is the willingness to use "force" to get a result. This came up earlier in the discussion on international bank charters, where banks that did not wish to have such a charter would be forced to accept such a charter and its attendant rules. For a profession that prides itself on choice, such force suggests to me that the problem lies in the design of the charter and not in the willingness of banks not to join. Unfortunately, there has

---

[1] See the Calomiris chapter in this book.

also been too much discussion about "force" by many of the political leadership in the past year.

Eleventh, Vince Reinhart raised an important point stated by others as well. That is, the length and character of the protracted aftermath of a financial crisis reflect two separate forces: first, those forces associated with the crisis itself; and second, forces due to the policy response to that crisis. In this regard, it is too early to know the strength and shape (L, U, W) of the economic recovery until the exit and regulatory policies of the federal government are defined.

Twelfth, Allan Meltzer commented that the underlying changes in society's incentives and voting patterns have increased the challenge to democracy and independence of the Federal Reserve. The philosophy of "no taxation without representation" has been replaced with "representation without taxation". Thus, there is a huge bias to federal spending and, thereby, political pressures to use the central bank to finance that spending.

Finally, the challenge we face in our society is not "too big to fail", but the inability politically to close the "too big to fail". These institutions/companies have already failed. We just do not have the decency to bury them. Instead, such institutions persist to reallocate resources in our society in order to allocate capital to politically favored constituencies. This has not changed in response to the crisis, and therefore suggests more future crises in the same places.

Conference Agenda

Twelfth Annual International Banking Conference

Thursday, September 24, 2009

Registration **8:45 AM**

Welcoming Remarks **9:30 AM**

The World Bank
Justin Yifu Lin, Chief Economist and Senior Vice President

Federal Reserve Bank of Chicago
Charles L. Evans, President and Chief Executive Officer

The International Financial Crisis: Asset Price Exuberance and Macroprudential Regulation **9:45 AM**

Speaker
Charles L. Evans, President and Chief Executive Officer, Federal Reserve Bank of Chicago

Session I: What Broke? The Root Causes of the Crisis **10:00 AM**

Moderator
Douglas D. Evanoff, Federal Reserve Bank of Chicago

Speakers
Martin Neil Baily, Brookings Institution and
Douglas J. Elliott, Brookings Institution
Charles W. Calomiris, Columbia University
Michael Mussa, Peterson Institute for International Economics

Discussant and Commentator
Edwin M. Truman, Peterson Institute for International Economics

Luncheon and Keynote Address — 12:00 PM

Moderator
Charles L. Evans, President and Chief Executive Officer,
Federal Reserve Bank of Chicago

Keynote Speaker
Christina Romer, Chair, President's Council of Economic Advisers

Session II: Containing a Systemic Crisis: Is There Really No Playbook? — 2:00 PM

Moderator
Asli Demirgüç-Kunt, The World Bank

Speakers
Masahiro Kawai, Asian Development Bank Institute and
Michael Pomerleano, World Bank
Vincent R. Reinhart, American Enterprise Institute
Robert K. Steel, Wells Fargo

Discussant and Commentator
Robert Kahn, The World Bank

Break — 3:45 PM

Session III: Dealing with the Crisis: The Role of the State — 4:00 PM

Moderator
Richard Rosen, Federal Reserve Bank of Chicago

Speakers
Andrew G. Haldane, Bank of England and
Piergiorgio Alessandri, Bank of England
Francesco Papadia, European Central Bank
Phillip L. Swagel, Georgetown University

Discussant and Commentator
Peter J. Wallison, American Enterprise Institute

Reception 5:45 PM

Dinner and Keynote Address 6:45 PM

Introduction
Daniel Sullivan, Senior Vice President and Director of Research,
Federal Reserve Bank of Chicago

Keynote Speaker
José Viñals, Financial Counselor and Director of Monetary and Capital Markets,
International Monetary Fund

Friday, September 25, 2009

Registration and Continental Breakfast 7:30 AM

Session IV: What to Do About Bubbles: Monetary Policy and Macroprudential Regulation 8:15 AM

Moderator
Gadi Barlevy, Federal Reserve Bank of Chicago

Speakers
Claudio Borio, Bank for International Settlements
Charles A. E. Goodhart, London School of Economics
Allan H. Meltzer, Carnegie Mellon University

Discussant and Commentator
Marvin Goodfriend, Carnegie Mellon University

Break **10:00 AM**

Session V: Dealing with Crises in a Globalized World: Challenges and Solutions **10:15 AM**

Moderator
Richard Porter, Federal Reserve Bank of Chicago

Speakers
Athanasios Orphanides, Central Bank of Cyprus
Andrew L. T. Sheng, China Banking Regulatory Commission
Stijn Claessens, International Monetary Fund

Discussant and Commentator
Carmen M. Reinhart, University of Maryland

Luncheon and Keynote Address **12:15 PM**

Moderator
Charles L. Evans, President and Chief Executive Officer, Federal Reserve Bank of Chicago

Keynote Speaker
Kevin M. Warsh, Governor, Board of Governors of the Federal Reserve System

Session VI: How to Make Regulators and Government More Accountable: Regulatory Governance and Agency Design **2:15 PM**

Moderator
Hesna Genay, Federal Reserve Bank of Chicago

Speakers
Edward J. Kane, Boston College
Michael Klein, formerly The World Bank
Ross Levine, Brown University

Discussant and Commentator
R. Christopher Whalen, Institutional Risk Analytics

Break **4:00 PM**

Session VII: Policy Panel: Where Do We Go from Here? **4:15 PM**

Moderator
George G. Kaufman, Loyola University Chicago and Federal Reserve Bank of Chicago

Panelists
Wayne A. Abernathy, American Bankers Association
Anil K. Kashyap, University of Chicago
Justin Yifu Lin, The World Bank
Deborah J. Lucas, Massachusetts Institute of Technology
John Silvia, Wells Fargo Securities

Reception **6:00 PM**

Dinner and Keynote Address **6:45 PM**

Moderator
Douglas D. Evanoff, Senior Financial Economist and Vice President, Federal Reserve Bank of Chicago

Keynote Speaker
Philipp M. Hildebrand, Chairman (appointed) of the Governing Board, Swiss National Bank

Conference Coordinators

- Douglas Evanoff, Federal Reserve Bank of Chicago
- Asli Demirgüç-Kunt, The World Bank
- George Kaufman, Loyola University Chicago and Federal Reserve Bank of Chicago

Index

www.ingramcontent.com/pod-product-compliance
Ingram Content Group UK Ltd.
Pitfield, Milton Keynes, MK11 3LW, UK
UKHW020402150926
8624IPUK00004B/308

9 789814 322089